BOOKS BY WILLIAM H. GASS

FICTION
OMENSETTER'S LUCK
IN THE HEART OF THE HEART OF THE COUNTRY
WILLIE MASTERS' LONESOME WIFE

NONFICTION
FICTION AND THE FIGURES OF LIFE
ON BEING BLUE
THE WORLD WITHIN THE WORD
HABITATIONS OF THE WORD

HABITATIONS
of the
WORD

Essays

William H. Gass

SIMON AND SCHUSTER · NEW YORK

Designed by Irving Perkins Associates
Manufactured in the United States of America
10   9   8   7   6   5   4   3   2   1
Library of Congress Cataloging in Publication Data
Gass, William H., 1924–
    Habitations of the word.

    Includes bibliographical references.
    I. Title.
PS3557.A845H3   1984   814′.54   84-22917
ISBN: 0-671-52726-6

*The essays collected here have appeared previously in the following publications, although
frequently in quite a different form:*

"Emerson and the Essay": *Yale Review,* Vol. 71, No. 3 (Spring 1982), pp. 321–62. Copyright © 1982 by Yale University. Used by permission.

"The Neglect of Ford Madox Ford's *Fifth Queen*": A shortened version appeared in *The
New Republic,* March 28, 1981, pp. 26–32. Copyright © 1981 by William Gass. A longer
version appeared in *The Presence of Ford Madox Ford,* edited by Sondra Stang. Copyright © 1980 by University of Pennsylvania Press. Reprinted by permission of University of
Pennsylvania Press, Philadelphia, Pa.

"Representation and the War for Reality": *Salmagundi,* No. 55 (Winter 1982), pp. 61–
102. A publication of Skidmore College. Copyright © 1982 by William Gass.

"The Soul Inside the Sentence": *Salmagundi,* No. 56 (Spring 1982) pp. 65–86. A publication of Skidmore College. Copyright © 1982 by William Gass.

"Tropes of the Text": First presented at a conference on Postmodern Fiction at the University of Nice in April 1982. First published in the volume, *Representation and Performance in Postmodern Fiction,* edited by Maurice Couturier, as an issue of *Delta,* 1983.

" 'And' ": First presented to the 10th Alabama Symposium on English and American
Literature, October 15, 1983. A shortened version was originally published in *Harper's
Magazine,* Vol. 268, No. 1605 (February 1984), pp. 54–61. Copyright © 1984 by William
Gass.

"Culture, Self, and Style": First presented to a symposium on "The Study of Culture"
held at Syracuse University in October 1979. Originally published in *Syracuse Scholar,*
Vol. 2, No. 1 (Spring 1981) pp. 52–68. Copyright © 1981 by William Gass.

"On Talking to Oneself": A commencement address at Washington University in St.
Louis, May 1979. Originally published in *Washington University Magazine,* Vol. 49, No. 2
(Spring 1979). A fuller version was published in *Harper's Magazine,* Vol. 268, No. 1608
(May 1984) pp. 71–74, as "The Unspeakable State of Soliloquy." Copyright © 1979, 1984
by William Gass.

"On Reading to Oneself": A commencement address at George Washington University,
May 1982, and at Kenyon College, May 1983. Originally published as "Of Speed Readers
and Lip-Movers" in *The New York Times Book Review,* Vol. 133, No. 46001 (April 1,
1984). Copyright © 1984 by William Gass.

"The Origin of Extermination in the Imagination": First presented to the 7th Bertram
Morris Colloquium in Social Philosophy as "Annihilation: From Genocide to Omnicide"
at the University of Colorado at Boulder on March 11, 1983. First published in *Antaeus*
(The Ecco Press), No. 53 (Autumn 1984), pp. 26–40. Copyright © 1984 by William Gass.

"The Habitations of the Word": An essay contributed to the third Faculty Seminar at
Washington University on Plato, Spring 1983. First published in the *Kenyon Review,* Vol.
VI, No. 4 (October 1984). Copyright © 1984 by William Gass.

"The Death of the Author": An essay contributed to the third Faculty Seminar at Washington University on Roland Barthes, Spring 1984. First published in *Salmagundi,* No. 65
(Fall 1984). Copyright © 1984 by William Gass.

FOR MARY, OF COURSE,
AND IN MEMORY OF RICHARD RUDNER,
COLLEAGUE AND FRIEND

Contents

EMERSON AND THE ESSAY

1

Our oblivion has been seen to . . . and unless we write as though the ear were our only page; unless upon the open slopes of some reader's understanding we send our thoughts to pasture like sheep let out to graze; unless we can jingle where we feed, sound ourselves and make our presence heard; unless . . .

So you hear me read me see me begin.

I begin . . . don't both of us begin? Yet as your eye sweeps over these lines—not like a wind, because not a limb bends or a letter trembles, but rather more simply—as you read do you find me here in your lap like a robe? And even if this were an oration, and we were figures in front of one another, columns perhaps, holding up the same thought, it still would not be the first time I had uttered these sentences (though I might seem to be making them up in the moment of speaking like fresh pies), for I was in another, distant, private, country-covered place when I initially constructed them, and then I whispered them above the rattle of my typing (expert and uncaring as the keys); I tried to hear them through the indifferent whirring of their manufacture as if my ear were yours, and held no such noise. My mind was book-bound and mist-mixed. Then no snow had intervened. God knows what or where I am now— now as you read. Montaigne, Lamb, Emerson, are dead. Our oblivion has been seen to . . .

And what is the occasion for my writing, or your reading, other than some suggestion from a friend, a few fine books sent in the mail, an invitation to speak, an idle riffle through a few sheets of a stale review, the name Emerson, an essay, an open hour. No one can number the small signs which may revive this distant figure, a figure behind us, safely in our past (can't I confidently assume it for us both?); not even a warm hole in the air remains of all those solemn flames he lit: "Love," for instance, "The Lord's Supper," "Self-Reliance." Doesn't he dimly seem, sometimes, an Ayn Rand beforehand? and of that former earnest heat now nothing but disposed ash. Yet the shadows he casts are the shadows of an honest shade; his work remains fertile, volumes explaining him continue to appear—the progeny of his present, not his past.

Emerson is himself a man of occasions, of course, and he has considered his, and wondered whether these halls he fills like a thermos will keep his high hopes hot. He has once again gone to the lectern: that parlor pulpit and the modest phallus of the teacher. "I read the other day some verses," he will say, perhaps, or ask, "Where do we find ourselves?" (strange question!), and he knows he is up to something different and possibly enduring—a pose his immortality may assume. He is giving definition to his Being. He is waiting for himself to sail from behind a cloud.

"A lecture is a new literature," he writes. "It is an organ of sublime power, a panharmonicon for variety of note." If necessary—to exercise this organ—he will travel. Anywhere. To St. Louis. The West Coast. He is Emerson, is he not? the lapsed saint, the great energy of life itself; and he will speak when he is tired; when he is ill, frightened, nervous; he must represent the spirit even overweight, stand for unweakened resolution, unfailing courage, though faint. His public presence is the presence of his language; and the language of "Fate" or "Self-Reliance" will be formed and reformed often, just as he heard it first above the sound of his own heart, each time as though the occasion were just freshly occurring: "I read the other days some verses . . . The eye is the first circle . . ."

But life is not all eloquence and adulation: life is wiping the baby's bum; it is a bad case of croup; it is quarrels with one's spouse; it is disappointment, distraction, indignities by the dozen; it is the death of friends, wife, son, and brothers, carried off like fluff in the wind; it is alien evenings, cold stairwells, frosty sheets, lack of love; for what does the great spirit need that touches the body but the touch of the body, as oratory needs silence, and revolution peace? We are nourished by our absences and opposites; contraries quench our thirst.

Yet nature turns a dumb face toward us like a cow. When we read its wonders, we wonder whether we haven't written them ourselves. We are in ferment, but our greatness grows light like a bubble of froth. We sense that existence itself lacks substance; that it is serious in the wrong sense; that its heaviness is that of wet air. The sublime . . . ah, the sublime is far off, though we call for its coming. Yes. Life falls short— is never what it should be. Rhymes will not rescue it. Days end, and

begin again, automatically. Only the clock connects them. Sullen sunshine is followed by pitiless frost, and the consequence is that we are a
tick or two nearer oblivion, and the alarm for our unwaking. Emerson
never tires of telling us this. "Illusion, Temperament, Succession, Surface,
Surprise, Reality, Subjectiveness—these are the threads on the loom of
time, these are the lords of life."

'Life'! . . . short, grand, graceless word. We partake of it, yet spread
before us all like the proverbial feast, once its fruits and sweets are eaten,
its vintages are drunk, the remaining bones tossed to the dogs, that same
feast—life!—is carried away in a spotless cloth, as whole and unmarked
as though we had never licked or torn or toothed it. What do we piss of
it later but air? Our breath is just such a vacation.

Distantly we hear our children feeding on what we left and didn't
leave . . . the bonbon we'd bitten not quite across, the turkey neck we
had refused. Wait. Is that a song . . . ? Can it be that we have vanished,
and our sons are singing . . . ?

Emerson wants us to feel our thought more literally than we phrase
it. He puts face after face on the obvious to renew our recognition. How
he hammers his sentences into our innocent psalm-holding hands! "That
is always best which gives me to myself." He will not trouble to say once
what he cannot say twice. "It is said that the world is in a state of bankruptcy . . ." At first he adopts a threatening tone, as if something could
be done about this state of the world and ourselves. "Beware when the
great God lets loose a thinker on this planet." And he is full of self-
admonishment. "Nothing is at last sacred but the integrity of your own
mind." Because his own problems, his own resolves, are never far away.
"Why should we fret and drudge? Our meat will taste tomorrow as it did
yesterday, and we may at last have had enough of it."

Though read aloud and delivered repeatedly this way, the lectures become essays as if the sound of them were sunshine burning the page. At
first they are addressed to crowds—in Boston or Hanover—but they
always aim at the single ear, the solitary listener: the silence of the word
syllabating in the silence of the reader's world—in the silence of the private house, in the hall of the whole body. "To fill the hour,—that is
happiness; to fill the hour . . ." So when Emerson gathers his talks up
in books, these books are much like albums full of photographs of his
former thoughts—not always well lit, unfortunately, though often grace-
fully, soberly, sometimes even stiffly, posed. "We live among surfaces,
and the true art of life is to skate well on them." Bitter wisdom, unhappy
skill, beleaguered phrase.

The full ear, full heart and hall, is fast empty; the tireless are now weary; what we thought was profundity is made of smeary surfaces like a stack of dirty plates; the noble spirit who spoke is soon horny, hungry, in need of another hall and still more redemption. The pronouns which steer Emerson's thought through the essays painfully display the problem. There is that outer, objective, commanding "you," on the one hand (stern, consoling, accusatory), the gruff, redoubtable "I," on the other, and they frequently come together in a "we"; but a "we" of what kind? Does it designate the unity of a common nature, this "we"? an illusory compound, a projection, a complicity? Does it resemble a handshake, a simple mixture, a seething mob, a complaisant copulation?

Thus we (we "we"s) say him to ourselves, press him to our inmost ear, though he seems more a stone than pillow. We are "we," "I," "you," "they," "me," moment by moment, as the pronouns pass. Still, even if we said him frequently, would that be often enough (what will it take?) to hold him like frozen smoke in the cold immortal air? Yes, unless . . . unless we can sound ourselves, reach our depths, draw them up, and make our passions heard . . .

So I begin . . . I begin again . . . but you have put the pages down; you have drifted off in the oratory. The accident which brought you here is over. The crowds have cleared; existence calls. Diminished by curtains of sky, the sun fades where it once fell in colors through the glass; and my voice wearies of noising itself abroad like old news; courage in a dark wood fails. What will follow such a doleful "unless" like a promise, a threat?

This: the space which my speech occupied during its slender moment of aspiration will empty itself again, and unless this "unless" like a ransom note is met—I shall be for good. The snip of Atropos is sudden. Quick. Complete. The way the cleaning woman quits. There will be silence, an appallingly simplified silence: a walk without its footfall. There will be no more conversation, self stuffed into self like a chair; no desultory musing, no inner irrigation or any substance to the soul. If no one pronounces us . . . If no one finds for us a voice . . . Says: "In this refulgent summer, it has been a luxury to draw the breath of life." Well—to go wordless is to go without a soul to shit with. It is but to go.

What will any word be, then, in that simple silence, the silence of the utterly unuttered? The sum of its effects won't fat the stomach of a zero, since life essentially is what we think throughout a day; what we have said to ourselves; what we have readied ourselves to say to others: that "man is only half himself, for instance, the other half is his expression," or that "every man should be so much an artist that he could report in

conversation what had befallen him," a wish we may share among ourselves with little cost to comfort; but are these sweet notions alms now
pennied out; are they a warm cup at the shelter? Where is our solace
when we're told that "sleep lingers all our lifetime about our eyes, as
night hovers all day in the boughs of the fir-trees"? Here we receive no
idea, but a feeling seen.

"Our moods do not believe in each other," Emerson writes in a different condition, and we watch his language give terse expression to his
contradictions: why is he vigorous one day, impotent another? "I am God
in nature; I am a weed by the wall." Yet hearing it put precisely this way
(placing an abstract and distant 'God' by a near and general 'nature,'
the hard and simple 'wall' next to the low mean 'weed'—and thus making
these discordancies into music) lets us know that Emerson, our determined teacher, did not want his thoughts to rattle in his readers' ears like
coins in a tin cup. "The poet sees the stars because he makes them." But
" 'Tis the good reader that makes the good book."

Emerson's ambitions were enormous, and endangered his desires. "He
burst into conclusions at a spark of evidence," Henry Seidel Canby said,
accurate about Emerson's urgency, Emerson's need to be immense. He
was the Horatio Alger of our youthful hopes. He would Do & Dare. He
would Strive & Succeed, and drag us, unwilling as we often were, into
virtuous accomplishment. He spent himself freely, but he counted his
change. However lassitude might overcome his ego, Emerson's id was un-
aging: he would swallow the world, though little of the world could swim
against the flow of all those pious, hortatory, and calamitous words which
streamed forth in his voice. He sometimes seemed a grimacing spout to a
drenched roof. He did fancy the idea, though: that passing through him
(as if he were the categories of our consciousness) flesh would become
symbol; matter would be refined like ethyl and emerge as volatile, ignit-
able mind.

It was an anxious exercise, nevertheless, undeniably desperate, because it risked absurdity. It risked derision. Every metaphor proves
treacherous if only partly meant, and Emerson was made of oppositions
and quarrelsome contrasts like a character in *Alice*. In the least likely
places (that is: everywhere), his language schemed against his innocence.

It is perhaps a disagreeable comparison, but the food we eat divides
itself naturally into stool and spirit; fat falls from the trimming edge to
be pushed to the side of the plate; so what is the good of these splendid
phenomena we are to become One with (which we're to ingest)—the
"chill, grand, instantaneous night," for instance—if all one receives is

the meaning, the bloodless significance? What is the good to you of my loving glance, my mouth moist with entreaty, if you never meet the lip; if we never embrace the body of the sign, and nature is metabolized without remainder?

But Emerson was always of several minds like a committee. He writes this in his journal:

> May 11, 1838
>
> Last night the moon rose behind four distinct pine-tree tops in the distant woods and the night at ten was so bright that I walked abroad. But the sublime light of night is unsatisfying, provoking; it astonishes but explains not. Its charm floats, dances, disappears, comes and goes, but palls in five minutes after you have left the house. Come out of your warm, angular house, resounding with few voices, into the chill, grand, instantaneous night, with such a Presence as a full moon in the clouds, and you are struck with poetic wonder. In the instant you leave far behind all human relations, wife, mother and child, and live only with the savages—water, air, light, carbon, lime and granite. I think of Kuhleborn. I become a moist, cold element. "Nature grows over me." Frogs pipe; waters far off tinkle; dry leaves hiss; grass bends and rustles, and I have died out of the human world and come to feel a strange, cold, aqueous, terraqueous, aerial, ethereal sympathy and existence. I sow the sun and moon for seeds.

For Emerson this is just another ordinary evening in Concord, but he hates the ordinary. It is eating up his life, and we see him strain in this passage to elevate the occasion, make it matter. The house is "resounding with few voices" (strange phrase), and the din drives him abroad. To the eye the scene is sublime, but to his mind it is boring. The sympathy he says he feels eventually, he feels at home in his study, facing the bright page with its lines of sober signs as conductible as a choir, each syllable more human than any hut; and in the ring of these words, 'aqueous,' 'terraqueous,' 'ethereal,' and 'aerial,' the sound of both the metal which makes the coin and its value as money are intimately mingled, with the sign and its sense not separate and confused as they are in the unsatisfying albeit sublime light of night, where nature grows gravely over him; and I can believe, as he sets them down ('carbon,' 'lime,' and 'granite'), and hears them singing within the chamber of his inner self, that he is one with *them,* and not the primitive elements he so carefully lists, or even the cool unstartled stars.

A night later, walking beneath a "pleasant, cloud-strewn, dim-starred sky," Emerson is considering "topics for the young men at Dartmouth," for he has his customary business to attend. Something further must be said. Something eloquent and honorable. Something which will move even its author's slow heart to a faster motion.

> But only then is the orator successful when he is himself agitated & is as much a hearer as any of the assembly. In that office you may & shall (please God!) yet see the electricity part from the clouds & shine from one part of heaven to another.

So we must put our words together in a way to tempt the tongue, and entice it to pass from one round sound to another—platform to pulpit, stage to stage—until, beneath the reader's steady breath, we're reenacted like a play; because to live is to speak and to be spoken, just as Emerson is once again alive in me when I realize his words. He preaches: I read. I read to become the preachment. Then "I" preach, and so "I" listen, finding an Emerson in myself just as he did—an ear, an audience, an oracle—and so a future in the protracted shiver I am caught by when I say:

> If you would know the power of character, see how much you would impoverish the world, if you could take clean out of history the life of Milton, of Shakespeare, of Plato,—these three, and cause them not to be. See you not, instantly, how much less the power of man would be? I console myself in the poverty of my present thoughts, in the paucity of great men, in the malignity and dullness of nations, by falling back on these sublime recollections, and seeing what the prolific soul could beget on actual nature;—seeing that Plato was, and Shakespeare, and Milton,—three irrefragable facts. Then I dare; I also will essay to be.

Emerson's mind and his imagination, the height of his royal aims, his loyalties, his hopes, the democratic cadence of his heart, are here. You or I read, and he is resurrected in that recitation. It matters very little that Emerson is mistaken, for what would the world lose in the loss of these three it has not already lost; what has Shakespeare meant to most men, who have not even read his name? We would mine other texts for our quotations (those of us who still quote); we would ham it up in other plays; appoint another teacher to tell us why we should forsake our bodies and forlorn the world; we would justify God's ways with Pope, and the industrious would make do glossing Aristotle and Dante and Cervantes, until we had sent them packing too, replacing everyone with Proust; but we are already a bit of dust in the wind—we friends of the Forms, lovers of the *logos;* we cannot leave a smudge on the air; we cannot pollute. Among a billion, what are a million? and for what million, dispersed like the Jews among malign dull nations, can Emerson, himself, have any meaning? And what Asian sages have shaken a hundred thousand hearts with a single sentence, and we know neither the sentence nor the sage? Do not suppose we have fallen on evil times because Shakespeare now has so little significance, Gibran more and Milton less. We cannot fall without having first attained a height. And height we have not.

You would not need to remove Plato from the world, of course, only his dialogues, as our book burnings have removed so many of the plays of Sophocles. We know little of Shakespeare's character, which seems to have been mild and agreeable enough, though we might want to wipe out Wagner's, and pretend that grand and windy music had been written by a nobler man; the lack of late Keats does not pain us past the sentences which suggest it, nor do we much miss Mozart's gray airs; but as Emerson's mind moves from what is true (that the world would be impoverished—for a few) to what is unlikely (that man would feel a loss of power as if a racing engine quit), we can *hear* how it happened; how the present was put beneath the past, power placed next to poverty in this thought of his, paucity measured against what is prolific—arrangements which argue the poet; and we can also understand what Emerson really means, because human accomplishments frequently transcend the humans who accomplish them; in fact, in time, the dross body drops away, the peevish tongue is still, greed is gone because the gut is, vanities collapse with the lungs, the long competition with the Great concludes, the very arcs of energy and impotence, of which Emerson so often complains, finally slow and cease like a swing with an empty seat, and our author is at last that: the lonely words of his work. And Emerson tries to take heart, and to become, himself, such an irrefragable fact. He will essay to be.

2

Essaying to be, Joel Porte writes in his fine book on Emerson,

> is the fundamental conceit of this greatest of American essayists. He too dares, endeavors, tries, attempts, essays . . . to

create himself in the very process, in the very act, of setting words on paper or uttering them aloud. In order to exist, he must speak, for the speech validates itself—brings into being that which is envisioned or hoped for and gives Emerson a solid platform on which to stand.[1]

Emerson had a sacred fear of the superfluous. He wished to become a Hero as his own heroes had (just as Plato, with his works, or Napoleon, through action, had become uniquely universal, or the way Shakespeare and Swedenborg were, he thought, spokesmen for the human spirit, as Goethe and Montaigne had been). He wished to be, more democratically than the elevating word 'great' suggested, a *representative man* (an honor, now, Porte's book confers upon him). To be one in a sum of simple ones, although that sum amounted to a million, was completely not to count. And not to count was unthinkable . . . it was purely not to be. By means of this mathematics, 1 was equivalent to no one, and all was lost though never wagered.

As Professor Porte argues, Emerson was obsessed by the problem of the Fall. In this new clime—America—with Calvin presumably put back aboard ship and sent home to the Swiss, what one was most free from was sin; one could not blame Eve again, or any ancient crime; yet that meant that the responsibility for failure fell on us like an enemy from ambush; and if death was with us despite our sinless state, in the stalk and leaf, the blood, the flesh, real as the last rattle of the breath, then the general injustice was that for an imaginary malfeasance in a legendary age, we were to be hung tomorrow from a loop of quite unimaginary rope. Our death, too, in this case, was to be a slow prolonged closing—the squeezing to a frightened whistle of our wind. We drop from the umbilical of our birth like one condemned. The image is dismayingly familiar. And this is the illicit learning which dispels us from paradise.

"After thirty," Emerson wrote in his journal, "a man wakes up sad every morning excepting perhaps five or six until the day of his death." And he woke in Concord, in Boston, Buffalo, or Chicago, to face a new crowd, new opportunities, new uncertainties, old-fashioned fanaticism and fresh irreverence. In ancient Europe (as it seemed), and the God-ruled world from which Emerson was in the process of setting free his soul, what could be vain or pointless in the Divine Performance? However, the continent he now approached like a pilgrim seemed to be nothing but wilderness and waste, or was until Swedenborg rewrote Nature

---

1. Joel Porte, *Representative Man, Ralph Waldo Emerson in His Time* (New York: Oxford University Press, 1979), p. 153.

as a novel. Prodigal, abundant, vast: great grim words, and Emerson's fears were justified. These shores were longer and more indented than the lines on any palm. The country teemed with savages. Cold deep lakes lay in its glacial scratches. It offered endless vistas full of trees and creepers; beasts of all kinds were as at home here as birds in the air. Even the clouds bore the look of the land they passed over. Night came down like the shutter of a shop, and one more day was added to history, one more thistle shed to the breeze.

Nature, indeed, is prodigal to the point of embarrassment, filling the air, the deepest reaches of the sea, the whole earth, with seed. Both men and nature select by means of increase and cancel. We take many snaps and hope for a good shot. We grow thousands of flowers in order to encounter the perfect rose. Burton and Bunyan go on and on in search of virtue and a fine line. The rice we toss at the bride of course resembles the teeming hurray of sperm the groom will soon send after it. We replace the precision of the bow with the spray of the machine gun. We rain down bombs and hope something will die. The very word 'nature' becomes protean, accepting every meaning like a vase's indifferently yawning mouth. A possibility seems barely conceived and it is realized somewhere, in some tub or plot or community; for what wave has not been ordered out of the sea by now, and the beach felt its special fall; what thought, what untidy passion, what inane or selfless desire, what quirk, what constancy, has not been bitterly or beautifully expressed by this time in the long random life of the world? and Emerson's comfort could have come from that, and sometimes did so ("Man feels the blood of thousands in his body and his heart pumps the sap of all this forest of vegetation through his arteries . . ."); but the method is also wasteful and reckless and chancy and insecure, like America itself, once the Great Experiment and now just a child's play ("it runs to leaves, to suckers, to tendrils, to miscellany"); and what personal satisfaction can be derived from being a genius when that only means you were a lucky pull on the slots, a brief shower of change? so in one mood Emerson is ready to set himself against Nature, making himself up like a poem (all artifice and calculation), while in another he would grow tall with the implacable instinct of the oak; yet "our moods do not believe in each other," our moods merely watercolor the world; they will wash out.

For instance . . . it is raining everywhere within me now—in and around me now—and I can look out of a wet window at the mulberry's yellow leaves and wish my barren backyard tree were an emperor's willow; I can thereupon let fall every autumnal thought: whistle up the west wind; wish we could pot our souls like plants and remove them from the coming winter of our age to a warm protected interior life (fresh thought indeed; but freshness is only unfamiliarity); or I can celebrate the discards, in effect, and damn the hand; speak of the mulberry as if it were a tree of myth holding a hard god gnarled in its wrinkled wood; I can claim this apparently weeping world has actually reached that exultant moment when joy cries out like grief itself, and comes; and in that benevolent revision be correct; because just as philosophy turns into literature by being tied to a temperament, a tone, a style, a time of life, a rhetoric, a scaffold of categories, a schedule of rhymes; and we speak, in proper names, of Kant and Plato and Schopenhauer, of Nietzsche and Hobbes, not merely of utility, of the positive or existential, pragmatic or transcendental (terms which, like language itself, are no one's property and in sloppy general use); so for Emerson, the literary man, feelings were philosophies become atmosphere and weather (surely there are nights when we feel our eyes, like Berkeley's sleepless god, keep the world awake); a metaphysics was a metaphor made from a mood; it modeled the world for a moment, not only as it might be, but as it was in its best hour, its darkest or its last, in one kind of circumstance, in one exhausted posture, in one strong mind.

Summer, 1841

The metamorphosis of Nature shows itself in nothing more than this, that there is no word in our language that cannot become typical to us of Nature by giving it emphasis. The world is a Dancer; it is a Rosary; it is a Torrent; it is a Boat; a Mist; a Spider's Snare; it is what you will; and the metaphor will hold, and it will give the imagination keen pleasure. Swifter than light the world converts itself into that thing you name, and all things find their right place under this new and capricious classification . . . Call it a blossom, a rod, a wreath of parsley, a tamarisk-crown, a cock, a sparrow, the ear instantly hears and the spirit leaps to the trope . . .

I call it a connivance, an uncombed mount of Venus, a bear pit, a turkey farm, a kettle of spit . . .

It is raining. In my heart and on the town. "How variously our passions react upon our thoughts and reasoning faculties, and change our ideas to their very opposites!" Emerson's master, Montaigne, exclaims. I call it paradise. And then the sun comes through the clouds like a melon through a wet sack. The mechanics of the mind must not be allowed to show; yet where else, if not here, may they reveal themselves, for the hero of the essay is its author in the act of thinking things out, feeling and finding a way; it is the mind in the marvels and miseries of its makings, in the *work* of the imagination, the search for form. Should we be, like Bacon, all smooth conclusion and marble floor? I am drenched beyond my skin, my bones rust like pipes, and soon the world will be wet with me and my mood. The distractions of daily life gnat and gnibble at me. Cowardice and craving defile my leafiest ideas like dogs. You turn away to listen: was that a car door? or the reluctant slide of a bureau drawer? Suddenly I sneeze upon the page and hurl an angry "god bless" after the stains.

Look upon the tempest like a pig, with perfect equanimity, Pyrrho advised his frightened, sea-thrown companions, and Montaigne, who cites him in "Apology for Raimond Sebond," reminds us of the men who interpret all things, such as the lines on their palms, ocean foam, the behavior of birds and direction of the wind, as threats and promises to them.

> Compare the life of a man enslaved to such fancies with that of a labourer following his own natural appetites, who measures things only as they actually affect his senses, without either learning or foreboding, who is never ill except when he is ill; whilst the other often has the stone in his soul before he has it in his bladder.

Our concerns collect like pigeons, and anxious men and women, such as you and I and Emerson, interpret the world in order to make a home of it, even if our image of ourselves is of Prometheus bound to a rock where an eagle feeds serenely on our liver, as Hobbes writes, devouring in the day as much as we manage to repair during the night; because our agonies are at least grand and romantic; because replenishment is equal to decay and balances the books; because then, at least, we know who and what and where we are. The world is a rain of light! Why not? Plotinus had a similar thought. "What is life," Emerson wrote, "but the angle of vision."

> Dream delivers us to dream, and there is no end to illusion. Life is a train of moods like a string of beads, and as we pass through them they prove to be many-colored lenses which paint the world their own hue, and each shows only what lies in its focus. From the mountain you see the mountain. We animate what we can, and we see only what we animate. Nature and books belong to the eyes that see them. It depends

on the mood of the man whether he shall see the sunset or the
fine poem . . . Temperament is the iron wire on which the
beads are strung.

But if anyone would make a mood into a metaphor, and a metaphor
into a metaphysics; if all the world's a library, or a prison, a cathedral or
a stage; if the curtain rises with the first word and falls finally to God's
catcalls and applause; if the fact our parents fucked to get us damns us
all; if the soul is like smoke in a bottle or ghost in a machine; if the flesh
is a flail or a whore on call; *if*—and we are serious (the body *is* a coffin),
if—and we believe (the graves *will* open); then one must also be prepared to see how a mood solidifies like grease to coldly coat the pan; how
feeling, in some systems, has the finality of the wound, not the evanes-
cence of the anger which caused it; how *Angst* becomes one of the ultimate elements, memory a monument, consciousness a skeleton compressed in stone, passion a movement like molasses among the inertias of
matter, and consequently how that instigating mood is no longer a momentary thing but the tantrum of eternity; for now the philosopher, the
theologian, takes over from the poet like the Hyde in Jekyll, and wearily
works his world out, describing the mechanisms of its perception, its hierarchies of value, the limits of our knowing and unknowing within that
image, since he is at once the owner and surveyor and policeman of the
dream.

I am inclined to think that it is just this lack of loyalty in Emerson,
this moodiness of mind, the unfanatical hold he had on his hopes and
ideals, despite the urgency of their expression, which appeals to us today
(an essay like "Self-Reliance" is important only as history now, while
essays like "Experience" or "Fate" are more than ever alive). Perhaps
I should not employ the speaker's "we" so readily, and confess it only
for myself, but it is Emerson's ability to "circle" his subject; it is the
saving grace of his skepticism, that I admire; and his genuine enthusiasm
for the thought he will in a moment see the other, shabby, self-serving
side of.

"The universal impulse to believe," as Emerson both manifested and
expressed it, was as positive in his time as it is negative in ours, because
beliefs are our pestilence. Skepticism, these days, is the only intelligence.
The vow of a fool—never to be led astray or again made a fool of—is
our commonest resolution. Doubt, disbelief, detachment, irony, scorn,
measure our disappointment, since mankind has proved even a poorer
god than those which did not exist. Faith has always fallen on men like
a lash, yet it has also driven them, occasionally, into an admirable

selflessness. Cranks overran Concord, and Emerson was a witness to their witlessness; indeed, as Van Wyck Brooks writes, he felt obliged, in defense of toleration, to tolerate and defend them:

> The vegetarians came, for whom the world was to be redeemed by bran and pumpkins; and those who would not eat rice because it was raised by slaves; and those who would not wear leather because it was stolen from animals; and those who rejected vegetables the roots of which grew downward (and food that fire had polluted). And they sat at Emerson's table and criticized or abstained. ("Tea? *I?* Butter? *I?*") They made his Thanksgiving turkey an occasion for a sermon; they lectured him over his mutton on the horrors of the shambles.[2]

But pots of poison are served at the last supper now; the crank may control an army; ideas carry bombs in their briefcases; every sector of society, every sexual preference, every whim, has its own banner, banner holder, hubbub and hoopla; every nation, race, and trade, hobby and sporting club has its own sword-rattling simplicities; there's a lie on the tip of every tongue like a bubble of spit; while the urge to permit some grand marshal of opinion to advance one's cause or determine one's fate has never been stronger, and no mind is safe which has let that yearning in its door.

Emerson, however, did not escape the beliefs of his forebears with the simple relief of the pardoned prisoner, but as one who leaves an ancestral home, with pride and gladness and regret felt together, and with the great need to replace them with others equally grand and elevating, since it was essential to have large views and strong opinions about ultimates, else you would be incomplete, low, and lack seriousness.

The crucial problem, for Emerson, Henry Nash Smith has suggested, was a choice of vocation, and the philosopher's task would naturally seem attractive to one who felt so close to Swedenborg and Plato, so freshly cut off from a preaching parent and the church. "My belief in the use of a course on philosophy is," Emerson told his classes at Harvard, "that the student shall learn to appreciate the miracle of the mind; shall learn its subtle but immense power, or shall begin to learn it . . ."

---

2. Van Wyck Brooks, *The Life of Emerson* (New York: Literary Guild, 1932), p. 127. Brooks does well by this odd lot: "Dunkers, Muggletonians, Agrarians, Abolitionists, Groaners, Come-outers . . . The Phrenologists came too, and the Mesmerists, and the Homeopathists, and the Swedenborgians. And the Rat-hole Spiritualists whose gospel came by taps in the wall and thumps in the table-drawer . . ."

and he went on to express confidence in philosophy as the only source of truth. "When he has known the oracle he will need no priest." Characteristically, though, Emerson's confidence came from the rival he had set it against, not from philosophy itself, for he rarely thought of things in calm isolation, but in angry and anxious juxtaposition: next to God it is nothing to be a weed, yet put that weed by a wall and it is suddenly seen to be greedily alive, voracious and grasping; eventually that life will overclimb the stone; weeds will bring the wall down. To call philosophy oracular is to pay a compliment in counterfeit. The oracle's superiority to the priest is dubious indeed: both pronounce and neither reasons; often one is merely a coarse tone in the other's speech.

The essay induces skepticism. It is not altogether the fault of Montaigne. The essay is simply a watchful form. Hazlitt's thought is not shaken out like pepper on the page, nor does Lamb compose in blurts. Halfway between sermon and story, the essay interests itself in the narration of ideas—in their *unfolding*—and the conflict between philosophies or other points of view becomes a drama in its hands; systems are seen as plots and concepts as characters. Consider the description of idealists and materialists, brilliantly laid out, which Emerson furnishes us at the beginning of "The Transcendentalist."

> The idealist, in speaking of events, sees them as spirits. He does not deny the sensuous facts: by no means; but he will not see that alone. He does not deny the presence of this table, this chair, and the walls of this room, but he looks at these things as the reverse side of the tapestry, as the *other end,* each being a sequel or completion of a spiritual fact which nearly concerns him . . .
>
> The materialist, secure in the certainty of sensation, mocks at fine-spun theories, at star-gazers, and dreamers, and believes that his life is solid, that he at least takes nothing for granted, but knows where he stands, and what he does . . .

Here Emerson puts a nose to a notion, describes the personality of a proposition, outlines the habits of an ideology. The pair are reduced to sets of quirks, but at the same time humanly enlarged.

The essayist speaks one mind truly, but that is far from speaking the truth; and this lack of fanaticism, this geniality in the thinker, this sense of the social proprieties involved (the essay can be polemical but never pushy) are evidence of how fully aware the author is of the proper etiquette for meeting minds. Good manners are not merely reflections of a more refined and leisured life; they signify, here, equality and openness, a security which comes to a mind which has been released from dogmatism. If there is too much earnestness, too great a need to persuade, a want of correct convictions in the reader is implied, and therefore an *absence of community.*

> November 12 [?], 1841
> I own that to a witness worse than myself and less intelligent, I should not willingly put a window into my breast, but to a witness more intelligent and virtuous than I, or to one precisely as intelligent and well intentioned, I have no objection to uncover my heart . . .

Thought must be true to its conclusions, as personal as thought is always believed to be, so that the essayist frequently begins by setting these conditions forth quite honestly, as Hazlitt does to open "On Living to One's-Self."

> I never was in a better place or humour than I am at present for writing on this subject. I have a partridge getting ready for my supper, my fire is blazing on the hearth, the air is mild for the season of the year, I have had but a slight fit of indigestion to-day (the only thing that makes me abhor myself), I have three hours good before me, and therefore I will attempt it. It is as well to do it at once as to have it to do for a week to come.

It is perfectly imaginable, and no contradiction, no dishonesty, that on another occasion, the slight fit of indigestion having become a thumping ache, the results of Hazlitt's reflections might be otherwise.

The suggestion to the reader that the essay is a converse between friends can be made into an actual invitation, as when Walter Benjamin begins:

> I am unpacking my library. Yes, I am. The books are not yet on the shelves, not yet touched by the mild boredom of order. I cannot march up and down their ranks to pass them in review before a friendly audience. You need not fear any of that. Instead, I must ask you to join me in the disorder of crates that have been wrenched open, the air saturated with the dust of wood, the floor covered with torn paper, to join me among piles of volumes that are seeing daylight again after

two years of darkness, so that you may be ready to share with me a bit of the mood—it is certainly not an elegiac mood but, rather, one of anticipation—which these books arouse in a genuine collector. For such a man is speaking to you, and on closer scrutiny he proves to be speaking only about himself.

And so he is—as essayists always are. But first one must be, as Emerson saw he must be, a self worthy to be spoken of, and a self capable of real speech.

A certain scientific or philosophical rigor is therefore foreign to the essay; ill-suited, as when a brash young student challenges even one's most phatic observations on the weather with demands for clarity, precision, and proof. Consequently, jargon in an essay is like a worm in fruit; one wants to bite around the offending hunk or spit it out. The apparatus of the scholar is generally kept hid; frequently quotations are not even identified (we *both* know who said *that,* and anyway its origin doesn't matter). The essayist is an amateur, a Virginia Woolf who has merely done a little reading up; he is not out for profit (even when paid), or promotion (even if it occurs); but is interested solely in the essay's special *art.* Meditation is the essence of it; it measures meanings; makes maps; exfoliates. The essay is unhurried (although Bacon's aren't); it browses among books; it enjoys an idea like a fine wine; it thumbs through things. It turns round and round upon its topic, exposing this aspect and then that; proposing possibilities, reciting opinions, disposing of prejudice and even of the simple truth itself—as too undeveloped, not yet of an interesting age.

The essay is obviously the opposite of that awful object, "the article," which, like items picked up in shops during one's lunch hour, represents itself as the latest cleverness, a novel consequence of thought, skill, labor, and free enterprise; but never as an activity—the process, the working, the wondering. As an article, it should be striking of course, original of course, important naturally, yet without possessing either grace or charm or elegance, since these qualities will interfere with the impression of seriousness which it wishes to maintain; rather its polish is like that of the scrubbed step; but it must appear complete and straightforward and footnoted and useful and certain and is very likely a veritable Michelin of misdirection; for the article pretends that everything is clear, that its argument is unassailable, that there are no soggy patches, no illicit inferences, no illegitimate connections; it furnishes seals of approval and underwriters' guarantees; its manners are starched, stuffy, it would wear a dress suit to a barbecue, silk pajamas to the shower; it knows, with respect to every subject and point of view it is ever likely to entertain, what words to use, what form to follow, what authorities to respect; it is the careful product of a professional, and therefore it is written as only writing can be written, even if, at various times, versions have been given a dry dull voice at a conference, because, spoken aloud, it still sounds like writing written down, writing born for its immediate burial in a Journal. It is a relatively recent invention, this result of scholarly diligence, and its appearance is proof of the presence, nearby, of the Professor, the way one might, perceiving a certain sort of speckled egg, infer that its mother was a certain sort of speckled bird. It is, after all, like the essay, modest, avoiding the vices and commitments of the lengthy volume. Articles are to be worn; they make up one's dossier the way uniforms make up a wardrobe, and it is not known—nor is it clear about uniforms either—whether the article has ever contained anything of lasting value.

Like the article, the essay is born of books, as Benjamin's essay, "Unpacking My Library," points out about itself; and for every essay inspired by an event, emotion, bit of landscape, work of plastic art, there are a hundred (such as Montaigne's famous "On Some Lines of Virgil") which frankly admit it—to having an affair; because it is the words of others which most often bring the essay into being. "I myself am neither a king nor a shepherd," Hazlitt writes apropos a speech from Henry VI he's cited, "books have been my fleecy charge, and my thoughts have been my subjects." Hence the essayist is in a feminine mood at first, receptive to and fertilized by texts, hungry to quote, eager to reproduce; and often, before the essay itself is well underway in the reader's eye, its father will be briefly introduced, a little like the way a woman introduces her fiancé to her friends, confident and proud of the good impression he will make. Thus Lukács begins "Longing and Form" with a quote from *La vita nuova,* and Roland Barthes, to outdo all, opens *The Pleasures of the Text* with one in the Latin of Thomas Hobbes. It is the habit of Emerson to add these mottoes later, and to compose them himself, which is not surprising, for we do find Emerson moved by his own hand more than most.

Born of books, nourished by books, a book for its body, another for its head and hair, its syllable-filled spirit, the essay is more often than not a confluence of such little blocks and strips of text. Let me tell you, it says, what I have just read, looked up, or remembered of my reading. Horace, Virgil, Ovid, Cicero, Lucretius meet on a page of Montaigne. Emerson allows Othello and Emilia words, but in a moment asks of Jacobi, an obscure reformer and now no more than a note, a bigger speech. A strange thing occurs. Hazlitt does not quote Shakespeare but Henry VI, whose voice is then lined up to sing in concert with the rest:

the living and the dead, the real and the fictitious, each has a part and a place. Virginia Woolf writes of Addison by writing of Macaulay writing of Addison, of whom Pope and Johnson and Thackeray have also written. On and On. In this way the essay confirms the continuity, the contemporaneity, the reality of writing. The words of Flaubert (in a letter), those of Madame Bovary (in her novel), the opinions of Gide (in his *Journal*), of Roger Fry, of Gertrude Stein, of Rilke, of Baudelaire (one can almost imagine the essay's subject and slant from this racy cast of characters), they form a new milieu—the context of citation. And what is citation but an attempt to use a phrase, a line, a paragraph, like a word, and lend it further uses, another identity, apart from the home-town it hails from?

It was inevitable that a compilation should be made of them. In my edition (the second) of the *Oxford Dictionary of Quotations,* there are 104 from Emerson, one of which is "I hate quotations," while another states that "Next to the originator of a good sentence is the first quoter of it." (Have I just now quoted Emerson, or have I quoted the *Oxford Dictionary of Quotations?*) Occasions call for quotations, qualify them, sanctify them somewhat as the Bible was—that book from which the habit stems and still draws sustenance, since the essay is, after all, a sort of secular sermon, inducing skepticism, and written by the snake.

And how they dispose themselves, these voices: inside the writer's sentences like an unbroken thread; in an isolated block upon the page, a lawn of white space around them like a house in a clearing; or in a note dropped out of the text like a piece of loose change from the author's pocket. Sometimes they stand alone like inscriptions on gates or conclude like epitaphs on tombs; they filter through a text like light through leaves or are enclosed like a hand in loving hands. Emerson's own essay "Quotation and Originality" permits me to make another point: that the essayist's subjects—in a sense always the same: other books, loneliness, love and friendship, human frailty—constantly provide a fresh challenge to thought, for if I were to write on quotation now, I should have to take into account a whole history since, not only Herman Meyer's *The Poetics of Quotation in the European Novel,* for example, but certainly Beckett's *How It Is,* which is mainly a buried quotation:

> how it was I quote before Pim with Pim after Pim how it is
> three parts I say it as I hear it

The essay convokes a community of writers, then. It uses any and each and all of them like instruments in an orchestra. It both composes and conducts. Texts are plundered precisely because they are sacred, but the method, we are essay-bound to observe, is quite different from that of the Scholastics, who quoted authorities in order to acquire their imprimaturs, or from that of the scholar, who quoted in order to provide himself with a set of subjects, problems, object lessons, and other people's errors, convenient examples, confirming facts, and laboratory data. However, in the essay, most often passages are repeated out of pleasure and for praise; because the great essayist is not merely a sour quince making a face at the ideas of others, but a big belly-bumper and exclaimer aloud; the sort who is always saying, "Listen to this! Look there! Feel this touchstone! Hear that!" "By necessity, by proclivity,—and by delight, we all quote," Emerson says. You can be assured you are reading an excellent essay when you find yourself relishing the quotations as much as the text that contains them, as one welcomes the chips of chocolate in those overcelebrated cookies. The apt quotation is one of the essayist's greatest gifts, and, like the good gift, congratulates the giver. T. S. Eliot could alter our critical perceptions simply by pointing to the right place in a text. And here is Virginia Woolf, writing about an Elizabethan play, smoothing out the satin on which she'll set her gem.

> At the outset in reading an Elizabethan play we are overcome by the extraordinary discrepancy between the Elizabethan view of reality and our own. The reality to which we have grown accustomed, is, speaking roughly, based on the life and death of some knight called Smith, who succeeded his father in the family business of pitwood importers, timber merchants and coal exporters, was well known in political, temperance, and church circles, did much for the poor of Liverpool, and died last Wednesday of pneumonia while on a visit to his son at Muswell Hill. That is the world we know. That is the reality which our poets and novelists have to expound and illuminate. Then we open the first Elizabethan play that comes to hand and read how
>
> > I once did see
> > In my young travels through Armenia
> > An angry unicorn in his full career
> > Charge with too swift a foot a jeweller
> > That watch'd him for the treasure of his brow
> > And ere he could get shelter of a tree
> > Nail him with his rich antlers to the earth.
>
> Where is Smith, we ask, where is Liverpool? And the groves of Elizabethan drama echo "Where?"

We should note in passing her casual choice of the "first . . . that comes to hand." We'd be naïve indeed to believe that. But she is right about the manner and the tone.

We would be less than honest if we said that all was always sweetness—the page a piece of warm toast—because sometimes the quote is put there to be bitten, chewed, gnawed, spat out. Great essays have been written on vulgar errors, and Montaigne, for one, does delight in them. He is listing the various places philosophers, divers sages and divines have suggested as the likely and proper domicile for the soul—an intrinsically amusing game—when he reaches Cicero:

> The Stoics, around and within the heart;
> Erasistratus, adjoining the membrane of the epicranium;
> Empedocles, in the blood; as also
> Moses, which is the reason why he forbade the eating of the
>   blood of beasts, with which their soul is united.
> Galen believed that every part of the body has its soul.
> Strato placed it between the two eyebrows.
> *What aspect the soul bears, or where it dwells, must not be*
>   *even inquired into,* says Cicero. I gladly allow this man to
>   use his own words; for why should I mar the language of
>   eloquence? Besides that there is small gain in stealing the
>   substance of his ideas; they are neither very frequent, nor
>   very deep, and sufficiently well known.

There is, nevertheless, a profound good humor in the way Montaigne puts most of these pages of human absurdity before us, and he is never overtaken by the unworthy feeling that these other thoughts and ingenuities and turns of phrase or sudden shifts of mood may cast a dismaying shade upon his, but rather delights in being out of the sun, because he knows that admiration is a mirror and returns a fair image. Whom would Hemingway's adolescent envy allow to take a good turn in his text?

Have we digressed, however? I hope so. For we must. What is a stroll without a stop, a calculated dawdle, coffee in a café we've surprised, some delicious detour down a doorway-crowded street, the indulgence of several small delays?

Yet these qualities of the essay suggest, sometimes even to the authors of essays themselves, that there is an absence of seriousness, of severity, of rigor in the writer, a fundamental failure of commitment, a basic lack of preparation even, and a withdrawal from life; because to live in books is not to live, it's often believed; since books are smooth and flat throughout, can inflict but paper cuts, and offer joys as superficially felt as ink on a thumb; then to steal from books like silver taken from a dinner table; to brood as if you were another Hamlet (though your mother's faithful and your father alive); to pass from one thought, fact, object, or attitude to another like food passed at a picnic; to set down sentences of high design on low and common matters; to worry about words when life lies dying for want of warmth, energy, and blood: all this is frivolous and enervating; it is evidence of an ambition set at "Low." Where are the essay's epic aims? its novelistic scope? its grandiose schemes and ardent explanations? Ah, no, the essay is for the amateur, all right, for the narcissist, the dilettante, for tepid souls who profess a kindly skepticism only to avoid the duties of faith, or the strenuous disciplines which define the search for truth.

Essays do not create—neither new worlds nor new philosophies. They are always written *about;* they are always either Of or On. On Reading. On Patience. Of Friendship. On the Knocking at the Gate in *Macbeth.* On and On. Out of old and often ancient texts the essayist makes another to throw like a shawl across the knees of a third. This is an activity for men? The admiration of the world is directed toward Dante or Tolstoy or Balzac or Proust, not toward Cowley or Lamb, let alone Breton or Hunt.

See if many of them aren't effeminate and sickly, full of resentment and weakness, procrastinators, passive as hens, nervous, unwed; and see if they haven't turned to the lecture and the essay because they failed in the larger roles, the finer forms, and could not get a real preacher's wind up, or populate a page with people, with passionate poetry, or with a philosophy of such profound penetration that the very body of our world—God's doll, God's Marilyn Monroe—is disclosed; then uncomfortably and inadequately redressed. After all, what do they get by on, these blue-belles of our letters; how do they succeed? They only survive on style. So if Emerson said he would "essay to be," he could not have expected to be much.

3

It is the poets, Emerson tells us, who are the liberating powers, but they do not write in the same way as the rest of us; somehow their signs sing differently, to an inward audience, as if the syllables themselves were separate singers, and the word were one tenor or soprano voice, and the line one choir. Such immaterial music is movement in its greatest purity. The mimesis that matters, for Emerson, is the one that follows the continuous transformations of nature, and thus, like Whitman, is again like nature: energetic, changeable, plentiful, and various. "The quality of the imagination is to flow, and not to freeze." It is the failure of every mysticism (and most philosophy, I'm prepared to suggest, on Emerson's behalf) to fix upon a single symbol and codify it, making of itself *"at last nothing but an excess of the organ of language."*

Not only did Emerson command us all to greatness, he demanded greatness of himself; and John Jay Chapman's remark that "Emerson seems really to have believed that if any man would only resolutely be himself, he would turn out to be as great as Shakespeare" is only somewhat overlarge. Since philosophy and theology failed as vocations, the burden of the discovery of Emerson's genius lay upon his poetry, and his poetry, as he realized with repeated anguish, was a failure: it was prose squeezed into rhymes and meters like an ungainly bumpkin into a dainty suit. Everywhere in the poems we encounter the effort to write as one inspired. We hear the expressive grunt of a marshaled strength, but we do not see the lifted bars, only the glisten of sweat on a surface of stone. We sense the desperation of his desire; but wishes have no wings but wished ones, no Pegasus to mount and then to rise with; ambition beggars us even of our bones.

In terms which seem to be always accurate, David Porter's excellent book, *Emerson and Literary Change,*[3] recounts Emerson's failures as a poet in precise and grim detail, exposing the weakness of verse after verse with almost painful completeness; nevertheless this cruel critical encounter with the poetry is necessary, not only because the poems have received much misplaced praise, and not simply because Porter can, in such a context, demonstrate effectively Emerson's own disappointment with his work, and even the accurate depths of that discontent; but especially because the strength of Emerson's essays rests, in a way, on the weakness of everything else. One hates to say they exist out of compensation, yet clearly, if Emerson was to be, he *would* have to "essay it."

When Matthew Arnold concluded that Emerson was not one of the great poets, he was still being generous, and John Morley was more nearly right when he wrote that "taken as a whole, Emerson's poetry is of that kind which springs, not from excitement of passion or feeling, but from an intellectual demand for intense and sublimated expression." Referring to an unfinished poem which Emerson initially called "The Discontented Poet, a Masque," Porter says (in something that is not quite

3. David Porter, *Emerson and Literary Change* (Cambridge, Mass.: Harvard University Press, 1978).

a sentence), "The formal impoverishment of the poetry, its rigid monumentality, the stolidity of the language, the predictable gestures that failed of passion—the elements I have been at pains to point out—Emerson's recognition of these failures is latent everywhere in this plaintive poem . . ." and then he goes on to quote Emerson in weak verse complaining of his other weak verses:

> Discrowned and timid, thoughtless, worn,
> The child of genius sits forlorn . . .
> A cripple of God, half true, half formed,
> And by great sparks Promethean warmed.

Emerson needed room in which to achieve his effects. The words he had previously written were the source of his greatest excitement, and when they were weak, he was weakened by them. He lacked opulence, his line was already lean enough, and the local formalities of verse hobbled his thought, for he would have to swing it shut upon some rhyme before it had scarcely begun to open out; nor could he write innumerable placid stanzas like Lord Byron: instead he lost voice at the moment his entire being was calling for a closer connection between self and language.

What Emerson wanted from poetry—masses of detail to drive a moral home; strong, swift strokes as if the writer were propelling a scull, yet a slow engorgement of the line which would lead to a kind of spasm of passion in the finally completed thought, with then a gentle ebb at the end to mark the close; and consequently an effect upon the reader like similar culminations in nature—none of this could be accomplished except in prose.

The constructive posture of the self-defining self, the freedom which the crude new nation offered it, the implicit promise of democracy to exalt mankind, to praise as well as work the earth; and, above all, the gift to that emerging individual of limitless opportunity—breathing space—space for rebeginning—space to the edge of every coast—space to infinity: each required the resettlement of language on the page, an equalitarian diction, a pioneering line, the big book, the great theme; each asked for energy and optimism; each egged American authors on to annex, plunder, quote and cite, to wahoo and yawp; and none of these conditions could be realized without the lush entanglements of complete speech: the voyages of discovery, exploration, and conquest, which made it possible, the personal tone, the pied variety of voice, the ebb and flow, the strut, the brag and ballyhoo of talk; for it would take the flabbergasting virtuosities, the visionary range, the gumptious reach, the raw muscularities, the baroque vibrations, yet the flat, irregular Patersons, of prose; and nearly all the best American poets do write prose: Melville and Faulkner and James, Robinson, Thoreau, Eliot, and Frost. I mean that they remained in the service of the sentence. I mean that they sought "the poem of the idea in the poem of the words." Even Whitman, to create his extraordinary, quintessentially American poetry, had to invent a prose which would explode into verse on contact with the page. Notice what happens when we hold one such poem in the good firm grip of the paragraph:

> When I heard the learn'd astronomer, when the proofs, the figures, were ranged in columns before me, when I was shown the charts and diagrams, to add, divide, and measure them, when I sitting heard the astronomer where he lectured with much applause in the lecture-room, how soon unaccountable I became tired and sick, till rising and gliding out I wander'd off by myself, in the mystical moist night-air, and from time to time, look'd up in perfect silence at the stars.

This is not perfect, although the conclusion is clever and the rhetorical form is managed well enough, but here is Edwin Arlington Robinson in the practice of it:

> I doubt if ten men in all Tilbury Town had ever shaken hands with Captain Craig, or called him by his name, or looked at him so curiously, or so concernedly, as they had looked at ashes; but a few—say five or six of us—had found somehow the spark in him, and we had fanned it there, choked under, like a jest in Holy Writ, by Tilbury prudence.

This sentence has a beautiful pace, and the two similes are spectacular, but is there only an inscriptional difference between poetry and prose in this instance?

This New World prose is prose which resembles talk of one kind or other: the tall tale, the loud spiel, or the sermon's moral prod; often it has the gentle swing of slow and sober reflection, the laudatory march of patriotic speech, or the unspoken assumptions of private conversation; and it is deeply marked—in theme, in pattern, rhythm, and diction—by the thumper's Bible; but there is always a point of origin, a human voice, a source in the psyche's animal squeak; and it aims at enlargement; it is always after ethical force and eloquence, like Emerson, its earliest master.

It was not America, of course, but the vision of America, the hackneyed dream, which was so spacious, so liberating, and so challenging to the writer. There was also the America the writer woke to (the towns of New England, quiet Concord, withdrawn Walden), the fields and forests as a fact; and the fact was that we were still colonists in many ways; we lived largely in little villages, our pants covered a rural seat; we worked on isolated farms; we went west in wagons which held two or three people, a straw mattress, and a dog; so that the great spaces, the small population, the wilderness, the Indians, the grizzly bears and wildcats, all combined to close us in, and a thin book could seem to open on a vast world; we were really at home in our head . . . that was our household . . . we were in violent love with the word; but this loneliness also meant we were hungry for company, for conversation, for what little could be mimic'd of the great urban (and European) ways. Had even Athens offered the orator a grander opportunity?

Emerson himself did not sprout from his native soil like the local corn, for he was full of Old World inclinations; he was the Old World gone to seed. He wanted to respect the past, yet seem wildly free, untamed and well mannered like clover in a field. He would be both above and of the people, his open, plain-folks, Yankee look a reflection from the finest glass. Our emblem and our entertainer, Emerson wished to see through common things to their uncommon core; to be all pith, yet not lack a shaping rind. His lectures, his essays, his orations, were consequently composed of planned surprise and calculated happenstance. These contradictions tore at him and shaped his style: what better banner than a flag in tatters?

It is David Porter's claim—and one I think he sustains—that "Emerson's prose *is* his power"; that his theory of poetry is really the theory of his prose; and that his view is original and radical. "He reattached language to process rather than to conclusion, to the action of the mind wonderfully finding the words adequate to its experience."

Emerson made the essay into the narrative disclosure of a thought. It became an act of thinking, but not of such thinking as had actually occurred. Real thought is gawky and ungracious; it goes in scraps, gaps, and patches, in sidles and byways, hems and haws; it is both brutal and careless, unpredictable and messy. Instead, Emerson's essays present us with an ideal process, an *ought;* yet it is, again, not one of rational confirmation; it is not the logician's order we encounter; it is the orator's: an order of revelation and response, the intertwined exfoliation of fact, feeling, and idea. In this sense, exposition becomes the narrative, and the form that of a fiction.

The unity of each essay is a unity achieved by the speaker for his audience as well as for himself, a kind of reassociation of his sensibility and theirs; so from its initiating center the mind moves out in widening rings the way it does in Emerson's first great essay, "Circles," where the sentences surround their subject, and metaphors of form control the flow of feeling.

> The life of man is a self-evolving circle, which, from a ring imperceptibly small, rushes on all sides outwards to new and larger circles, and that without end. The extent to which this generation of circles, wheel without wheel, will go, depends on the force or truth of the individual soul.

Yet the energy of the essay, like the energy of life, is always in danger of dissipation. Pages lie in unsorted heaps, full of notions which have not been extended to their complete reach. Somewhere in those piles, inferences may lie quiet now like a powerful figure hidden in clay, but where are the shaping hands, the steady intent, the attention? Where is the ardent ambition? Friends have fallen ill; one's own ailments are acting up; a relative has been disgraced; children disappoint; the sexual itch faintly remains like an old bite; yawns break apart on the face; one's oblivion has been seen like an image in an empty mirror: these distractions are the real disease.

> For it is the inert effort of each thought, having formed itself into a circular wave of circumstance . . . to heap itself on that ridge and to solidify and hem in the life.

Emerson's image beautifully resembles his dilemma, for two ideas are competing in it, and neither is the one he wants to embrace. There is, first, the conception of a course of thought (and the lecture, itself, which expresses or contains it) as spreading out in ripples like those which follow the plop of a pebble in a pool; and, second, the picture of an analogous life (and all accomplishment) growing gradually in yearlike rings to reach a crusty edge and the eventual bark of some trunk. Each variation suggests limits, and these are exactly what Emerson will stubbornly go on to deny.

> But if the soul is quick and strong it bursts over that boundary on all sides and expands another orbit on the great deep,

which also runs up into a high wave, with attempt again to
stop and to bind. But the heart refuses to be imprisoned; in
its first and narrowest pulses it already tends outward with a
vast force and to immense and innumerable expansions.

This denial, strictly speaking, makes no sense. It is quixotic. It is futile.
But Emerson is not arguing for a constitutive principle here. He is recommending a directive one, an *as if;* and to act within a figure of thought
rather than upon some thought itself is at least half of his transcenden-
talism. To fly in the face of a fact ("We grizzle every day. I see no need
of it.") is not to strike a solid wall, but to feel the fact yield, if only a
bit; we can become younger by growing old the right way; limits can be
overstepped, as Rilke says, so long as we respect the bounds; but only if
we reject *"rest, conservatism, appropriation, inertia"* as a way of life;
only if we embrace the future with the body of the present: "Why should
we import rags and relics into the new hour?"

In short, to live some fictions, rather than others, improves our
chances; enriches, elevates, and regulates life; allows us "to work a pitch
above" our last height; and this Emerson proceeds to do in the turns his
prose takes—clearsighted as a circling hawk. The essay begins with the
ego perceived in the punning image of an eye ("The eye is the first
circle . . ."), with the round horizon line it shapes the second; soon we
encounter the "cipher," then we meet the sense, natural to space, that
about every circle a larger circle can be drawn; that time, too, is endless
in the ease of its addition. The energy of all things flows out in waves;
round moons and planets move in rounder orbits; by the steps of ladders,
by degrees, successive choirs are reached; by several stages, then, the
thrones of angels. The circle is not only endless without and infinite
within, it returns continuously to itself, and every opposite is seen to
meet and blend. "The virtues of society are vices of the saint," he says.
"One man's justice is another's injustice . . ." This doesn't mean merely
relativity; it means reciprocity. Every point upon a curve is to the right,
left, and center of others. All are different. All are alike. A curve cannot
be concave without being convex; every balm is someone's hurt. Point of
view, perspective, position, line of sight—angle is everything. "Life is a
series of surprises," he says, but we can no longer be surprised by the absence of any disciplined philosophy. He dislikes distinctions. Clarity dis-
mays him, makes him suspicious. He dotes on degrees but damns kinds.
He is dangerously devoted to the continuum. He does not want to finely,
plainly *think;* scrub things clean, draw cutting lines, laboriously link. He
wants to writhe.

Now, while thinking, as any essayist is, he is alive. The power of the process fills him with light. It is like that. Montaigne attests to it.

> Meditation is a powerful and ample exercise for a man who is able to search his mind and employ it vigorously. I would rather fashion my mind than furnish it. There is no exercise that is either more feeble or more strenuous, according to the nature of the mind, than that of entertaining one's thoughts. The greatest make it their profession, *for whom to live is to think* (Cicero).

(Cicero is temporarily OK to quote. But wait. The weather is changeable.)

Emerson's verbal maneuvers concluded, his listeners are sent away with their hearts a little higher in their chests, in a Dionysian mood, intoxicated by their own powers and possibilities, not by bottled artificialities, drugs, the falsehoods of gambling and war, or still further fraudulent rites.

Yet the freshly inflated soul begins immediately to leak. What porous tissues we are made of! We have scarcely gotten home, our feet wet and chilly from the snow, or our chest asweat from the deep summer heat like a heavy coat we can't remove, when our children's sneezes greet us, skinned knees bleed after waiting all day to do so. There is the bellyache and the burned-out basement bulb, the stalled car and the incontinent cat. The windows frost, the toilets sweat, the body of our spouse is one cold shoulder, and the darkness of our bedroom is soon full of the fallen shadows of our failures. Now the quiet night light whispers to us: you are unloved—unlovely—you are old. These white sheets rehearse the corpse they will cover. None of our times change. We are the same age as our essayist. Wrinkles squeeze our eyes shut, and we slide into sleep like a sailor from beneath his national flag. Tomorrow our tumescence must be resumed. Tomorrow, Emerson realizes, he must again be a genius.

Joel Porte's graceful study, by interlacing life and language, lets us see clearly many important things about Emerson, among them what a victim of entropy he was. In the most tactful way he discloses some of the strongest of Emerson's impulses, and shows us how they mix and mingle: money and sexuality, for instance, energy and the essay. My motto, my central phrase, is taken from him, and he not only seizes on the expression himself, he makes exactly the right use of it. Porte is an impressively observant reader. His understanding can slip beneath the surface of a style without scratching its features or destroying the structure of its soil. He picks up Emerson's puns, whether they are easy ones like "The eye is the first circle," or crucial ones like "I also will essay to be," or some of the more subtle which lighten Emerson's sentences with their smile, such as "In spite of all the rueful abortions that squeak and gibber in the street . . ." and carries them to our attention. He does not allow the rhythm of "I also will essay" to escape him either. He notes the allusions to Hamlet's famous soliloquy in our emblematic passage; indeed, he notes the Shakespearean resonances which occur throughout those early pieces; and points out how important they are in suggesting something of Emerson's relationship to his father:

> The result seems to be, as with the paradigmatic Hamlet, a crippling habit of self-consciousness and self-questioning that threatens to paralyze the will.

The audience for these essays is not a single or a simple congregation, nor are the motives for writing—as if speaking each one—open and easy; although many have their germ in the journals, where an "I" is implicit. When we talk to ourselves, as we do in journals and diaries, we do not normally make speeches; nevertheless Emerson often addresses himself as if he were a crowd:

> May 28, 1839
> There is no history. There is only biography. The attempt to perpetuate, to fix a thought or principle, fails continually. You can only live for yourself; your action is good only whilst it is alive,—whilst it is in you. The awkward imitation of it by your child or your disciple is not a repetition of it, is not the same thing, but another thing. The new individual must work out the whole problem of science, letters and theology for himself; can owe his fathers nothing. There is no history; only biography.

Here he is already halfway to the hall. And what the hall holds. Emersons.

Who owe their fathers nothing . . . that's the destination . . . and a monetary word is used to express the moral and cultural debt he feels, and would like to cancel. *To owe our father nothing* . . . it is the impossible idea of this nation, still a child of Europe.

Two of Emerson's voices are those of the secular preacher. He wishes to speak his own mind, and thus convey his own ideas: that envy is ignorance, for instance, as he says in "Self-Reliance"; that imitation is suicide, and nonconformity a duty. Yet he also wishes to provide, as preachers do, some consolation. A little more than a week before Emerson wrote the passage quoted above (in which he is forming some of the thoughts which will comprise that famous Declaration of Everyman's Independence), Emerson puts this powerful paragraph in his journal:

> May 19, 1839
> At church today I felt how unequal is this match of words against things. Cease, O thou unauthorized talker, to prate of consolation, and resignation, and spiritual joys, in neat and balanced sentences. For I know these men who sit below, and on the hearing of these words look up. Hush, quickly: for care and calamity are things to them. There is Mr. Tolman, the shoemaker, whose daughter is gone mad, and he is looking through his spectacles to hear what you can offer for his case. Here is my friend, whose scholars are all leaving him, and he knows not what to turn his hand to, next. Here is my wife, who has come to church in hope of being soothed and strengthened after being wounded by the sharp tongue of a slut in her house. Here is the stage-driver who has jaundice, and cannot get well. Here is B. who failed last week, and he is looking up. O speak things, then, or hold thy tongue.

The desire to digress is strong now, after this manifestation of Emerson's genius and good will. For the relation between the parish priest, who has the confidence of the confessional, and his congregation; the teacher, who knows a few names because she has regularly called the roll, and her raucous kids; the congressman, who is filled in on regional issues by the local pols, to his so-called constituents; the lecturer to large crowds, in distant cities sometimes—places he can't locate on a map but flies to like a thrown stone—the huckster treating a drowsy, idle, TV eye to an earache of hype; and the author to a reader, finally, the complete Anybody who has the price or the loan or the theft of your book: that difference, at every step, is prodigious, total, yet scarcely anything at all. I can write Teacher/Priest, Article/Essay, and only a slant intervenes. I can step down from the podium and take my seat. I can write, and then read what I have written. I can cease loving in order to be loved.

The essayist pretends to be wise. No scholar, no philosopher, has to pretend that. The philosopher can be mean, narrow, vindictive, suspicious, vain, small. It needn't show. *"Die Welt ist alles, was der Fall ist,"* he writes. His traffic is with Reality, not with the real; with The Case, not cases; not with anyone's hopes and fears and household tragedies. What is Substance, he asks of a man whose daughter has been abducted. Yet is the Will free, he wonders while watching the smoke rise from the ovens. O should he speak things, then, and descend toward Emerson, toward Rilke, toward the province of the poet, toward the particularities of deprivation, loss, pain? The philosopher speaks of Good, of Evil, of Duty and Desire, of Ideas, but of other people's hungers only on days off, on feast days, during festivals, when his thoughts are on things, those things which call out to Emerson, where he hovers like a kite between Mr. Tolman's unfortunate daughter and "the plight of Mankind." If the novelist and the poet probe the particular, and the philosopher deals with the Grand Design, what is left? The preacher is wise too, and carries comfort in his Bible the way the physician carries his bag, but the preacher's wisdom is the wisdom of the Church, and for him "the case" is always cautionary. Speak solidities, Emerson advises himself. But to whom? with what right? The essay has less of a place to be, and less an ear, an eye of its own to address, than a message painted on the side of a truck.

Emerson reports (the poet writes) that

> It is time to be old,
> To take in sail:—
> The god of bounds,
> Who sets to seas a shore,
> Came to me in his fatal rounds,
> And said: No more!

A book of poems has no electric eye which will open its covers automatically when a literate reader passes by. It is not a flytrap. Although it is presumably addressed to everyone, whether young or old, in every situation of life, it is not like an advertising sign: BUY MATTRESS BREAD! which is in a permanent state of being blurted. The command LOVE GOD! pasted on a bumper, or posted on a barn like CHEW MAIL POUCH!, awaits the accident of our passing, and then, like the beggar, threatens or entreats us. Still, we can shake our heads and go on. The bumper dwindles down another drive. In short, the sign does not cause or continue its occasion. The poet's reader, on the other hand, reaches for the poet, so to speak, and creates their encounter. Yet it would not be correct to say that Emerson's little defeatist verse was ready to adapt itself to any situation; rather it is addressed to none. His poem is, like all good poetry, quite occasionless; it is not a piece of mood music, or a set of lines to make love by.

However, when Emerson begins, so conversationally, "I read the other day some verses . . ." or more formally, "I greet you on the recommencement of our literary year," he is not beginning a talk or an address, although such a deliverance may lie in its past; he is opening an essay: something meant to be experienced, not simply heard; something meant to be understood and savored, not believed and followed; something meant to be enjoyed, admired, but not obeyed. The essay must wait its readers the way the poem does, yet it is active in establishing the conditions of its reception. The essay imagines a situation in which it would make sense to say what it will say. This is not always easy for the reader to grasp, and may take a while. "Whoever looks at the insect world, at flies, aphides, gnats, and innumerable parasites, and even at the infant mammals, must have remarked the extreme content they take in suction, which constitutes the main business of their life." Where are we, we may wonder. In the essay on "Quotation and Originality," of course, but our arena, more importantly, is the book, where we shall feed like a fly ourselves on this sweet text made up of texts.

Now—who dares call this diverting spell we've had a digression? Only those who drive one road through town and consequently miss the landscape, the local belles, the odd shops, the bandstand, and the park.

We have so far found five voices, five intentions, in our essayist: (1) the desire to talk to himself, to say "buck up, be better, stand forth, do not change your course for a little windy criticism," while (2) at the same time hoping these admonitions will offer others encouragement and solace too. Since he must speak against his hearers' weaknesses as well as his own, (3) it is essential that he become "representative," and address himself to all those men and women who may later live and chance to read him (pronounce him, I prefer to say), and confer upon him the poet's glory: the immortality of the tongue.

Like any good lecturer, however, Emerson's exchange is ultimately with his subject (4), and with those admired predecessors who have also spoken or written about it. His theme soon speaks in its own voice, and on its own terms, whether the theme is fate, Plato, Montaigne, memory, or the conduct of life. Emerson, himself, is of no importance in these moments, just as his audience, now, can do no more than "overhear" a truly transcendental conversation.

Yet can Emerson really believe what he says in these essays: that "With consistency a great soul has simply nothing to do," for instance, or "I think nothing is of any value in books excepting the transcendental and extraordinary"; since we see him regularly exaggerate his case? He becomes hyperbolic the way others grow hysterical. Overstatement creates the Oversoul, and Emerson's tight lapidary style contributes to it, for it is a style intolerant of qualification, reservation, convolution. Nothing is less Jamesian than the hard precise bites of his mind. Although his meaning may enlarge itself in reverberating rings, his sentences themselves do not circle through a center; they do not gently wander, seep, or shower, but cover their territory by rushing from side to side, rebounding as though from rubber bumpers, hurrying out to edges, sounding alarms; so that a paragraph of them is like the knicknacknocking passage of the pinball, with its braggy totals and loud yet intermittent message, its electric enlightenment, desperate to do its business but on a downward slope and shortly out of play.

Emerson is speaking to a deeper self than he can recognize (5), and he must shout as if it were far away, and he were on a French phone. The uncertain hand slaps down its weak cards hard. So he shouts at this self which would not owe its father anything; which feels guilty about the inheritance it has from Emerson's first wife, the leisure it has therefore enjoyed, the chances this has enabled it to take; he shouts at the self which fears it cannot be the man its other ego calls for. It would reassure him mightily if the commands he issues for his own conduct could be categorical as well for the world. Then he could hide his failure, like the fig leaf furnished by the Fall, behind a universal condition. He shouts. He shakes his fist. But he is a weed by a wall . . .

> Society everywhere is in conspiracy against the manhood of its members. Society is a joint-stock company, in which the members agree, for the better securing of his bread to each shareholder, to surrender the liberty and culture of the eater.

Money, food, and manhood are here, in Hobbesian terms, uncomfortably connected. There is a curve in the communication. Emerson is certainly not telling his listeners that his virility is threatened, but he is telling somebody.

When Emerson lectures in Lowell or Boston or somewhere else nearby, his wife, some relatives, a few friends, will often be in the audience. He will on those occasions stand to speak in the close clutter of his life, and Emerson's sixth voice is reserved for home and household. Sometimes it breaks out angrily to say, "Take heed, this is how I feel."

> Live no longer to the expectation of these deceived and deceiving people with whom we converse. Say to them, "O father, O mother, O wife, O brother, O friend, I have lived

with you after appearances hitherto. Henceforward I am the truth's . . . I shall endeavor to nourish my parents, to support my family, to be the chaste husband of one wife,—but these relations I must fill after a new and unprecedented way. I appeal from your customs. I must be myself. . . . If you are noble, I will love you, if you are not, I will not hurt you and myself by hypocritical attentions. If you are true, but not in the same truth with me, cleave to your companions; I will seek my own . . .

The immortals are the ultimate elite, and one watches the artist in Emerson finally satisfy his need to escape our common cancellation by appealing to the only forces which could draw him safely away: the angels of order and energy. The qualities he could not give his poetry were inherent in the passionate persistence of his public themes, and in the structure of his discourse about them—a structure which was remarkably original in its spatial radiation and free rearrangements of meaning, although his bitten-off sentences surprised only through their frequency, and his rapid, epigrammatic presentation of ideas was contradicted by a somewhat halting delivery.

His final voice (7) is thus the voice of Form. It is a voice which has no sound of its own, but lives in, and directs, the others. It is not the wind, but the weathervane. It is not the force of the wind, but the rhythm of its gusts and lulls, its steady stream. It appears not in the message, but in its unfolding, as if the greatest pleasure in any gift lay in how the package was unwrapped, the beloved body unclothed, the psyche gradually discovered.

> I remember when I was a boy walking along the river, how the colours and shapes of shells used to enchant me. I would collect handfuls of them and put them in my pockets. When I got home I could find nothing of what I had collected: nothing but wretched snails' shells. From this I learnt that composition and context are more important than the beauty of individual forms. On the shore they lay *in solidarity* with the sky and the sea.

Form is the habitat of thought, the survival of style. How we have collected these pieces of him here, where they lose their luminous elasticity and seem hard dim things!

So to his immediate audience, Emerson offers moral education and spiritual consolation; to his manifest self, he brings encouragement that is much needed, and to his private self, he promises continued conceal-ment; to his subject matter, Emerson guarantees the responsive shifts of his thought like any good dancing partner, as well as the whirling steps of the waltz of form; while to his family and friends he utters sidelong warnings, admonishments, and threats.

Though his sentences fall like single stones, the general pattern on the pond is interlaced and strong. We can cry out, in complaint: what a babble of tongues! what a scrabble of aims! what a Carroll of contradic-tions—this politics of push and pull—what an uncommon crowd of ears! but time after time, especially in essays like "Experience," "Montaigne," and "Fate," Emerson succeeds in putting down just the right, plurally significant note. He reaches all the ears and hence the hearts he hopes to, and among his listeners are the gods.

The customary objection to Emerson's style is that he tends to shuffle his sentences like cards, and in his late, less energetic years, he did so almost casually; but for the most part Emerson lets his exposition drift because he wants a more complex, more rhetorical, more poetic, effect; because, paradoxically, he wants to exercise a more exact control.

To survive on style is not simple, as De Quincey explains:

> Rhetoric, according to its quality, stands in many degrees of relation to the permanencies of truth; and all rhetoric, like all flesh, is partly unreal, and the glory of both is fleeting. Even the mighty rhetoric of Sir Thomas Browne, or Jeremy Taylor, to whom only it has been granted to open the trumpet-stop on that great organ of passion, oftentimes leaves behind it the sense of sadness which belongs to beautiful apparitions start-ing out of the darkness upon the morbid eye, only to be re-claimed by darkness in the instant of their birth, or which be-longs to pageantries in the clouds. But, if all rhetoric is a mode of pyrotechny, and all pyrotechnics are by necessity fugitive, yet even in these frail pomps there are many degrees of frailty. Some fireworks require an hour's duration for the expansion of their glory; others, as if formed from fulminating powder, expire in the very act of birth. Precisely on that scale of dura-tion and of power stand the glitterings of rhetoric that are not worked into the texture, but washed on from the outside.

It is not true that Truth is permanent. That is a piety. Falsehoods both outnumber and outlast. We should reread our Montaigne and carry care-fully with us what he says. De Quincey knows the truth, though, even if he is not telling it, and puts his energies where he must. His style is so much at one, here, with his image, that it countervenes it, as if the fire-works had turned the sky dark. The comparison "as if formed from fulminating powder," we must observe, was not formed from fulminating powder.

As a public speaker, a rhetorician, Emerson was in plentiful company. There was John Grissom, who lectured on chemistry, and who tried to illustrate every point with an experiment—preferably one which went POUF!; there was Ormsby Michel, marvelous at making the sky clear and the heaven otiose, often applauded in mid-sentence, and possibly the learned astronomer of Whitman's poem; there was the tough, iras-cible Fanny Wright, who took the stump for abortion and the fallibility of the Bible, who stood against slavery and in favor of easy divorce (on one occasion, they tore down the platform from under her); there was John Lord, whose Beacon Lights of History were all great men: King Alfred, Muhammad, Saint Bernard; there were phrenologists like George Combe, abolitionists like Wendell Phillips, who would speak for free if he could speak against slavery and that ape Abraham Lincoln; Bayard Taylor customarily came in Arab costume and brandished a scimitar; it would be a problem to prevent Edward Everett from giving his address on the character of George Washington (some said he delivered it 135 times, or did it simply seem so?); Oliver Wendell Holmes would inevita-bly be witty; many, of course, were interminable; one could learn about electromagnetism from Dr. Boynton, and John B. Gough would warn of the evils of drink; for the right fee, Henry Ward Beecher might be willing to preach against avarice; then there were many under-Emersons as well, like Star King and E. P. Whipple, shades more comfortable to their crowds than the sun they took their shadow from.[4]

Audiences did not, on the whole, require eloquence or other oratorical skills from their speakers, although they often got them. From Gough they wanted vivid testimony about what alcohol could do; from John Lord, "who read his notes in a frayed, unmusical voice interrupted with a periodic Thoracic sneeze," they wanted popular history—easy and up-lifting information; but Emerson was not interested in informing or entertaining his hearers, nor was he concerned to reform them, when that most often meant confirming prejudices and providing shocks and titillation. Joel Porte is especially good at defining Emerson's deepest attitudes here—both to his material and to his audience. Scholars have

---

4. A nice account of these and other speakers on the circuit can be found in Carl Bode's *The American Lyceum: Town Meeting of the Mind* (Carbondale, Ill.: Southern Illinois University Press, 1968).

exhibited a curious reticence about Emerson in this regard, ignoring his imagery even when quoting his words. The following two passages from Emerson's journals bracket the problem precisely:

Feb. 4, 1841

If I judge from my own experience I should unsay all my fine things, I fear, concerning the manual labor of literary men. They ought to be released from every species of public and private responsibility. To them the grasshopper is a burden. I guard my moods as anxiously as a miser his money; for company, business, my own household chores, untune and disqualify me for writing. I think then the writer ought not to be married; ought not to have a family. I think the Roman Church with its celibate clergy and its monastic cells was right. If he must marry, perhaps he should be regarded happiest who has a shrew for a wife, a sharp-tongued notable dame who can and will assume the total economy of the house, and, having some sense that her philosopher is best in his study, suffers him not to intermeddle with her thrift.

Dec. 1841

All writing is by the grace of God. People do not have good writing, they are so pleased with bad. In these sentences that you show me, I can find no beauty, for I see death in every clause and every word . . . The best sepulchres, the vastest catacombs, Thebes and Cairo Pyramids are sepulchres to me. I like gardens and nurseries. Give me initiative, spermatic, prophesying, man-making words.

The action he has in mind is reciprocal. Because his words make men of men, they also make a man of Emerson, whose emotional ups and downs are sexual in a straightforward sense, it seems to me. This back-and-forth flow of the blood may be the principal psychological element in any dialectical personality. The domestic round has enfeebled his sexual life. Babies and bereavement are the dismal consequences of his romantic passions, and the ensuing daily routines, the morning-to-night disappointments, of which I have made a *leitmotif,* the drudgeries he cannot find the strength of spirit to transcend, the petty trivialities which are the very furniture of family life, distract him from his work, bedevil his mind, weaken his optimism, undermine the moral superiority of his preacherlike position, endanger the honesty of everything.

For instance: the ardents of Brook Farm have forgathered to complete their wonderland plans, and Emerson feels nothing of their fire.

And not once could I be inflamed, but sat aloof and thoughtless; my voice faltered and fell. It was not the cave of per-
secution which is the palace of spiritual power, but only a
room in the Astor House hired for the Transcendentalists. I
do not wish to remove from my present prison to a prison a
little larger. I wish to break all prisons. I have not yet conquered my own house. It irks me and repents me. Shall I raise
the siege of this hencoop, and march baffled away to a pretended siege of Babylon? It seems to me that so to do were
to dodge the problem I am set to solve, and to hide my im-
potency in the thick of a crowd.

Emerson's essays are aggressive. They nettle their readers. His audiences were rarely pleased with what he said, though they had to admire
him, his sincerity, his vigorous speech. Emerson's ambivalent attitude is
perfectly expressed in the following dream which Joel Porte quotes and
comments on quite correctly:

A droll dream last night, whereat I ghastly laughed. A congregation assembled, like some of our late Conventions, to debate the Institution of Marriage; & grave & alarming objec-
tions stated on all hands to the usage; when one speaker at
last rose & began to reply to the arguments, but suddenly
extended his hand & turned on the audience the spout of an
engine which was copiously supplied from within the wall with
water & whisking it vigorously about, up, down, right, & left,
he drove all the company in crowds hither & thither & out of
the house. Whilst I stood watching astonished & amused at
the malice & vigor of the orator, I saw the spout lengthened
by a supply of hose behind, & the man suddenly brought it
round a corner & drenched me as I gazed. I woke up relieved
to find myself quite dry, and well convinced that the Institution of Marriage was safe for tonight.

Porte asks, "Would it carry us beyond the bounds of simple description to call this a 'wet' dream?" It is, in fact, wet in more than one way.
Much later, Porte follows this revelation of Emerson's unconscious and
ambiguously hateful and amorous relation to his audience with another
passage, this one a fantasy written when Emerson was only nineteen. It
concerns a kind of great water organ formed from the roots and trunks
of Siphar (i.e., siphon) trees, which Emerson imagines growing along
the banks of a river on some Pacific island. The rise and fall of water
through the tubes makes musical sounds of such beauty that the natives

erect a great temple to enclose hundreds of these trees and complete the dim resonations of their notes. Six thousand gather to listen on the fatal day, and the instrument begins to emit a music which makes them mad—laughter and sorrow combine in a single embrace.

> Owing to the unusual swell of the River and to some unaccountable irregularity in the ducts the pipes began to discharge their contents within the chapel. In a short time the evil became but too apparent, for the water rose in spouts from the top of the larger ducts and fell upon the multitude within. Meantime the Music swelled louder and louder, and every note was more ravishing than the last. The inconvenience of the falling water which drenched them, was entirely forgotten until finally the whole host of pipes discharged every one a volume of water upon the charmed congregation . . . Many hundreds were immediately drowned . . . Thenceforward there was no more use of the Siphar trees in the Pacific Islands.

The lecture is also an organ of great power (a panharmonicon, indeed), and Emerson's speech, he felt, should be a fertilizing seed. It was to have an energy which would engender energy in every listener. It was to be an example of a liberated mind which would free other minds to follow its example. In fact, what Emerson intended to do when he spoke was wipe away his audience like chalksmoke from a blackboard, and replace it with his essay, heard in their hearts like an adopted beat.

> September, 1849
> Today, carpets; yesterday, the aunts; the day before, the funeral of poor S.; and every day, the remembrance in the library of the rope of work which I must spin;—in this way life is dragged down and confuted. We try to listen to the hymn of gods, and must needs hear this perpetual *cock-a-doodle-doo,* and *ke-tar-kut* right under the library windows. They, the gods, ought to respect a life, you say, whose objects are their own. But steadily they throw mud and eggs at us, roll us in the dirt, and jump on us.

Time took his nights first. Soon there were only days. The youthful fever of his blood breaks, and he is restored to another illness. The dents on the bed are old and dismal signals. Porte argues it admirably, and one imagines a world of winter setting in. There is a pale cold sunlight everywhere, in all the uninvaded corners, under covers, in back of books.

Snow slowly clings to the summer air like dust. Emerson has a gaze which cannot close. He complains. Between the rows of listening ears he speaks to his wife, his friends—his soul worn thin from the pacing of his passion all these years. He complains; yet as Emerson ages, he does not become an old man mad—full of lust and rage, of memories of what he might have had. Harpies do not come to hold his hand, and he does not take to drink like Dylan Thomas, or put on intemperate attitudes the way Yeats did his beggar's clothing, or collect curses to keep cleanly oiled and ready like old guns; no, he begins to husband his strength ("husband" is the wretched word), recommend restraint, suggest that it is better to save than spend.

But it is not.

To be—don't we know by now?—is to burst with energy and enterprise like a hive of bees. It is to draw from just that daily drudgery, which you contend has betrayed your genius, all its sap and substance—siphon *it* dry—and seed new sentences with life. Begin again. Oblivion is miles away and only moments off. Begin.

But his only recourse was to write, to fade when he had to—die—and then to rise once more inside us when we say, "In this refulgent summer, it has been a luxury to draw the breath of life . . ."

THE NEGLECT OF
FORD MADOX FORD'S
FIFTH QUEEN

At the conclusion of the 600 pages which comprise *The Fifth Queen,*
Katharine Howard is given a great long speech which she delivers to the
King. She has confessed to the King's Council what is probably not true:
her adultery; and in this moment Henry refuses to believe it. "You shall
not die," he exclaims.

> "Aye," she said, "I must die, for you are not such a one as
> can stay in the wind. Thus I tell you it will fall about that for
> many days you will waver, but one day you will cry out—Let
> her die this day! On the morrow of that day you will repent
> you, but, being dead, I shall be no more to be recalled to life.
> Why, man, with this confession of mine, heard by grooms and
> mayors of cities and the like, how shall you dare to save me?
> You know you shall not."

It is a speech, for there are Speeches in this novel. And it is given, because there are Gifts. There is Passion, Knavery, Foolishness, Nobility—
Greatness—as in the old plays. She concludes, for there are also Conclusions. The King is staggered by the dispassionate clarity of her words.
We know, from the theater's conventions, how he will recoil. And this is
very nearly the last we shall see of our heroine (and Heroine she is):

> She went slowly down over the great stone flags of the great
> hall. It was very gloomy now, and her figure in black velvet
> was like a small shadow that fell softly and like draperies
> from the roof. Up there it was all dark already, for the light
> came downwards from the windows. She went slowly, walk-
> ing as she had been schooled to walk.

Yes. The style is stagy, melodramatic, artificial, even quaint; themes are packed into paragraphs like fish in tins; individuals are addressed as though they were crowds; terms are dragged from their graves and put once more in the line of fire like ghosts given rifles; qualifying phrases are repeated like Homeric epithets; scenes are set the slow deliberate way posts are sunk in concrete; there is such a high tone taken you really might believe you were at court . . . but are these merely history's playing cards—these characters? Do they stand precariously propped in their designs like figures in *Alice?* History, that great fictioner, surely did not create the honest, stubborn, beautiful, and saintly Katharine Howard, so richly realized she might have had some other life outside imagination, yet so near perfection we could not wish for her a lesser world to drag a dress in. The pouf of an unbeliever could not make its way against the pure gale of her talk, for indeed she is a soul made out of passionate speech. We have already heard her monosyllabic eloquence ("Thus I tell you it will fall about . . ."), and heard the steady march of her music ('stay' 'day' 'day,' 'fall' and 'recall,' 'about' 'out,' and 'not' 'not').

As for Thomas Cromwell, Lord Privy Seal, a man both duplicitous and dedicated, murderous and admirable, and one who well knows he has outlived three queens and a thousand plots—is he simply another slick and deftly painted surface? does the shaded tablelight slide like frightened water from his smoothly insinuated shape?

And Nick Throckmorton, whose golden beard is the devil's mane, or Magister Udal, wrapped in his furs like a ferret—are they only as thin as pasteboard, too, flat as any knave, although of the suit of diamonds?

Then there's Lady Mary, as cold to the King as ice is to itself—is she of no account, to be sloughed off in a losing trick? Perhaps Thomas Culpepper, the Hotspur of this piece, has taken too much of his nature from his name; but consider, instead, his royal grace, the fat, beleaguered King, who, because he is the King, must use everyone in the service of the crown, and whom everyone, because he is the King, would use in the smaller service of themselves—does he not weigh upon his horse as heavily as his armor, and heavier on history? is he not even wider than his portraits? does he not clot every entrance like a wound?

Will the value of these characters simply vary with the course of play, then, though their stiffly posed and tinted images remain vividly the same? There will be a small critical fuss about this. Why, in a world of change, don't these people alter something other than their loyalties? And we might answer by asking how the stream of time might run but between unyielding banks, or how we might measure its motion except in the eddies it makes about rocks. Or do we prefer illusions, and like to fancy people grow new characters like their beards and bellies, whereas, in fact (if facts matter), by the time the bosom has budded and the first blood run, even the sweetest maid is beyond shaping. Again we might answer by saying that conditions change apace because people won't vary theirs a jot, though Lady Mary grows a little warmer, I remember—later—in a warmer room.

The Fifth Queen resembles the maze at Hampton Court. Meanings multiply like echoes along and down the corridors its sentences suggest. When a torch flares, they return like luminous reflections from concealed corners, cul-de-sacs, and distant doors. In fact, the work is so intensely visual, so alternately light and dark, you might think the words were being laid on the page like Holbein's paint.

> Whilst the maids sewed in silence the Queen sat still upon a stool. Light-skinned, not very stout, with a smooth oval face, she had laid her folded hands on the gold and pearl embroidery of her lap and gazed away into the distance, thinking. She sat so still that not even the lawn tips of her wide hood with its invisible, minute sewings of white, quivered. Her gown was of cloth of gold, but since her being in England she had learned to wear a train, and in its folds on the ground slept a small Italian greyhound. About her neck she had a partlet set with green jewels and with pearls. Her maids sewed; the spinning wheels ate away the braided flax from the spindles, and the sunlight poured down through the high windows. She was a very fair woman then, and many that had seen her there sit had marvelled of the King's disfavour for her; but she was accounted wondrous still, sitting thus by the hour with the little hound in the folds of her dress. Only her eyes with their half-closed lids gave to her lost gaze the appearance of a humour and irony that she never was heard to voice.

The style of this novel cannot be escaped, and readers who prefer their literature to be invisibly literary should shun it.[1] There are no merely workmanlike words here, anxious to get the job done so they can suds themselves up at some pub on the way back to the dictionary. Even the

---

1. In *The March of Literature* (New York: Dial Press, 1938), Ford says of Scott, a competitor, "His literary merits are almost undiscoverable" (p. 711), and again, that "perhaps the main characteristic of writers like Jane Austen and Trollope is their complete non-literariness" (p. 789).

common people—Badge, the printer, or Margot Poins—aren't ordinary, nor is their language, nor any of the spaces they inhabit: cottages, inns, attics, ingles.

The Fifth Queen constructs the secret theater of history. There are labyrinthine hallways here, bewildering forests of passages and pillars through which the darkness whispers as though through parted teeth. There are secret and spiral stairs, low dupes, cat's-paws, double agents, devious aims, false alarms, unreported catastrophes. Characters are caught in their own schemes like ants in honey. They move no more, then, than the patient queen. Wide Venetian velvet surcoats, ceremonially embroidered, jeweled, furred, do more than hide a corpulence like Henry's. There are cold wet walls, weeds pushing up through pavements like unmentionable desires, chills which can't be overcome. Chimneys smoke. Innuendoes slip past like drafts impossible to trace. Yet there is much lip service, courtly talk, and rumors as difficult to slap aside as gnats. A barge carries Cromwell quietly down the Thames, but there is noise and turmoil in the street. And lies . . . lies both petty and prodigious: those which are baldfaced, arrogant, and inept, and those subtle, careful, clever lies which lie so near the truth they might be lovers taking warmth from one another's intermingling limbs. In a world where trust is as provisional as loyalty, and loyalty as provisional as its profit, there are more than many spies. Faith stiffens character while it warps the mind, and treason (justified by citations from the Good Book, and by arguments pilfered from the philosophers, and by examples extracted from divines) enters and exits in every contentious breath. Speech is dangerous—speech of any kind. Your most innocuous opinions may be used to indict you, and the written word is like an incriminating print. There are purloined letters, falsified documents, peepholes, sleeping potions, bribes. There is blackmail, whoring, theft, torture, threats, and countless other machinations. And there are also bearded, moist-mouthed villains straight from the great age of Webster, Tourneur, John Ford, and Machiavelli.

The Fifth Queen, then, is like Eisenstein's *Ivan*: slow, intense, pictorial, and operatic. Plot is both its subject and its method. Execution is its upshot and its art. *The Fifth Queen* is like Verdi's *Otello*: made of miscalculation, mismaneuver, and mistake. Motive is a metaphor with its meaning sheathed like a dagger. It is one of Shakespeare's doubtful mystery plays. Even though it includes clowns who berate one another, they make no successful jokes, and *The Fifth Queen* remains relentlessly tragic. It must be read with the whole mouth—lips, tongue, teeth—like a long slow bite of wine. For prose, it is the recovery of poetry itself.

This last effect is clearly Ford's intent. He has not been brought up in a gray-thread, black-bread, Protestant world. The studied emblems, the romantic leanings, the medievalisms of the Rossettis, Hunts, and Ford Madox Browns—their sentimentalisms, their garish overcoloring, too—were part of his inheritance. He had no desire to write like Defoe just because he was writing prose. The novelist did not have to assume a severe, undecorated, screwed-down style, as if weakness were a show of strength, as if only the simple were sincere, or the plain ennobling; it was not necessary to adopt a false modesty for your talent as if it were a mark of virtue to write as though you hadn't any. Besides, he fancied himself an English gent:

> To put it roughly, we might say that the great periods and cadences of the seventeenth century had, by the eighteenth, deteriorated into a sort of mechanical rhythm and that by the nineteenth century, in the avoidance of the sort of pomposity and the dry rhythm of the eighteenth century, the language became so timid and indefinite that it was impossible to use it for making any definite statement.[2]

The struggle which *The Fifth Queen* represents—between the Old Faith and the New Learning—occurs at the stage of style and literary theory, as well as within the local practice of the genre, and not merely at the level of political, religious ideology or historical event. And the loss to later English life which Katharine Howard's fall signifies to Ford is regained by the writing itself. Rather than butt helplessly against the conventions of that coal-stove Realism which stands for the triumph of the Puritan business spirit,[3] *The Fifth Queen* seeks a language which springs from the traditions of land and can be cultivated like another crop; so that Ford's return to the historical romance, despite its dubious popularity and retinue of pleasing scribblers, is intended to recover and release the word.[4]

---

2. *The March of Literature*, p. 512. Unfortunately, this charge itself is very poorly put. The cadence of *The March of Literature* is frequently slack and uneven, as are the qualities of its judgments.

3. At least in Ford's mind it does.

4. Not all were scribblers quite, and not quite all were pleasing, but there was Scott, Hugo, Dumas *fils* and Dumas *père*, Stevenson, Bulwer-Lytton, Cooper, Hewlett, Haggard, Verne, Doyle, Quiller-Couch, Ainsworth, and Munro, among others. There is a good account of Ford's relation to his forerunners in H. Robert Huntley, *The Alien Protagonist of Ford Madox Ford* (Chapel Hill: University of North Carolina Press, 1970). Huntley calls appropriate attention to the historians who influenced Ford, although he misses Clarendon for some reason, and also discusses, usefully, Ford's physiognomic types.

To call a novel historical is nearly always to accuse it of something. Even among unreal objects, where fictions are said to belong, the "historical" has a special place; for if any history, by the necessity of its nature, is already full of unreliable representations, then its further reflection in fiction has to be wavering and dim indeed. The curious conjunction which makes up the name (historical facts in their causal connections as against the manifold misdirections of invention and dream) indicates that its very creation is suspect, as if a shadow were to be wrapped in further shadows until the smoking semblance of some enemy's cigar were ominously shaped, or a daggered figure in a cloak suggested, or the hiss of a hidden snake.

In historical fiction a superficial sense of antique reality can be easily achieved, but what is obtained is frequently felt to be facile and cheap, like the glib alterations—the blatant vulgarity—of masquerades. It is an amusement—an escape—and melodrama is its mainspring. Thus its tick is loud just because the time it pretends to tock for is far away. Unlike history, what the fiction recounts is rarely sordid or simply stupid, nor is it often tragic, because its heroes and heroines pass through the most terrible events unscathed, like driftwood down a rapids.

Where the historian looks for laws and regularities, patterns and steps and stages, the novelist admires what merely decorates the dance. He prefers the exotic, colorful, and unique. He measures quirks and curiosities like a tailor, but cuts no cloth to the true weight and temporal figure of things. He shuns the normal, the plain. It has no zap. He dotes on gossip, slander, hearsay, anecdote, lies. He wants to recreate the past, not understand it as a historian should. The contents of constitutions and the import of decrees are tedious to get through; congresses are too boring to attend; committee reports too dry to report upon. Figures fill his heart with horror. He turns his back on bills of lading, tables of organization, and balances of trade. He wants amusing conversation—clever, witty, perceptive—and conversation is as out of place in history as a count of our morning cups of coffee.

So the novelist floats happily about on the edges and in the eddies of events and rarely moves in the mainstream. He habitually goes beyond the evidence, oversteps the bounds of probability, and invents occasions, speeches, feelings, thoughts, and scenes, which no doubt never were nor could have been, simply to enliven his narrative and entertain, rather than instruct, his readers. If it would further the drama to have minister and field marshal meet—no matter that their lives at no time touched—he need only scribble a few more paragraphs and the impossible deed is done.

The novelist's point of view tends to become passionate and heedless at the exact point the careful historian should become cold and cautious. Human decisions always seem supreme to him, and he does not suffer his characters to be vast natural forces like climate and disease, or even complex, indifferent social orders, or ponderous and mysteriously moving bureaucracies. He is customarily precise and fussy about trifles, but vague about the central and most effective matters, liking battles basically because there is much movement, excitement, noise, and blood, since it is the courage and fate of the hero that counts, not the cost or consequences of victory.

When Romance mates with History to fertilize fairy tales with the seed of the real world, they beget Myth. We are given young Abe Lincoln on the one hand, reading by log-light, and Robin Hood on the other, splitting infinity with an arrow as neatly as one of Abe's rails. The form of the swashbuckler, the border tale, the costume romance, seems essentially unserious, and in our day it has become just another popular genre, no more significant than the thriller or the sit-com, the western or the soap. Ford Madox Ford contributed to the neglect of his great Tudor trilogy by remarking, in his book on Conrad, that "an historical novel even at best is nothing more than a *tour de force,* a fake more or less genuine in inspiration and workmanship, but none the less a fake."[5] If all of these heavily prejudicial and, indeed, greatly misleading words ('none the less,' 'even at best,' 'nothing more,' *'tour de force,'* 'fake') suit Ford's real feelings, then his ghost cannot complain when even critics rather well disposed to him paste the word 'pastiche' across *The Fifth Queen* like a warning on a box to go easy.

Ford led an unwise life, as Walter Allen has observed.[6] An unwise life indeed. For one thing, he wrote simply too much sheer "stuff," and his best books got submerged in the accumulated glib. He badly mismanaged his divorce, and in the incredible confusion forfeited the sympathy of writers like Galsworthy and Wells, whom he should never have allowed to enjoy a moment of superiority at his expense, while also losing the friendship of stiff-necks like Henry James, who recoiled from impropriety as though it were snot on a custard. Ford's "Germanness" had always troubled him (he wanted to be French—what decent writer does not?), but his change of name didn't help him, and later, because he was unfortunately gassed during the war, so that afterward he always heaved

---

5. In *Joseph Conrad: A Personal Remembrance* (Boston: Little Brown, 1924), p. 186. Ford is saying, rather fatuously, that before forty he had done little more than exercises.
6. In *The English Novel* (New York: Dutton, 1954), p. 396.

and huffed, his original name returned to his lungs to taunt him. His habit of altering the facts to make the truth more truthful than it had been on the "real" rather than the "related" occasion, didn't help either, nor did his tendency, quite kind in itself, to condescend (according to Pound, after God, even to Pound).

Ford's collaboration with Conrad, of which he was proud, nevertheless hurt his reputation, because Conrad was older, had had the flattering good sense to choose to write in English rather than in Polish or French, and was clearly an exotic genius; consequently Ford's account of their relationship seemed to many just so many self-serving lies, dependent as it was on the assumption that the two writers were equals, and that, when it came to the English language, Ford naturally knew a good deal more.

Ford was a sort of Don Juan with ideas, too, and it was difficult for him to sustain his interest in a project once it was obvious he had conquered it; thus he was inclined to finish up quickly in order to run after another—possibly prettier—notion.[7] He often needed a gimmick to get him going (the train wreck which propels his hero into the fourteenth century, for example, in *Ladies Whose Bright Eyes*),[8] but these mechanicalities invariably betrayed him, and their thin elaborations defied even splendid writing.

Ford was a success with women, always a bad sign, since they are certain to see that you fail somewhere else to prove your dedication. It is furthermore unsettling to other men if you look, as Wyndham Lewis wrote, like "a flabby lemon and pink giant who hung his mouth open as though he were an animal at the Zoo inviting buns."[9] Ford was a success as an editor, too, so people knew where his skills really lay, and could put him in his editorial place. There he earned the gratitude of many excellent authors of every school, style, and age, who promptly repaid him with malicious slanders, vulgar innuendo, and other Hemingways. Gradually Ford became known as one of those who circle the great as buzzards do, a loquacious "hang-about," padding his reputation by dropping names, telling tales, and remaining bravely aboard foundering magazines until they disappeared beneath their virtues and their debts. Oh yes. He

---

7. Ford says that Conrad often grew weary, and "would occasionally try to rush a position. . . . That is why the ends of his books have sometimes the air of being rather slight compared with the immense fabrics to which they are the appendages." He, on the other hand, worked more nearly "to contract." *Joseph Conrad*, p. 185. The fact is that Ford's fictional "schemes" were frequently silly.

8. By now, surely, some critic or reviewer has called it a "Twain wreck."

9. Quoted by Arthur Mizener in *The Saddest Story: A Biography of Ford Madox Ford* (New York: World, 1971), pp. 239–240.

wrote. A man mad about writing, he said. Wrote. Easily. Much. Fairy tales, biographies, travel, commentaries, criticism, memoirs and other states of mind, novels, poems. He had plays fail. One was his dramatization of *The Fifth Queen.* But how was one to keep such a dizzy flock of authors in view? Well, he had his small popular successes, his critical acclaim, but he was always broke. He retired to the country. He played, for a while, the gentleman farmer, embraced simplicity like another mistress, put on airs. He went on and on about Provence. Was a snob. Some claimed he was a conniver, a bounder. He got by on small change. He bragged by disparaging himself. He hated scenes and then arranged his life like a ragged procession of them. He needed connections, though his family was widely known, and he had been raised to be the genius he was. He had also sat on Turgenev's knee, he said, or was it Tennyson's? Liszt's? Of Swinburne he had once caught a glimplse. He had an early romantic attachment to the Middle Ages. He liked Christina Rossetti. The poetry, I think. His form grew shapeless, his face puffy; he was always fairer than was a good idea. He had a wheeze. He formed strange ménages. He became minor.

Ford's greatest crime, however, was his migration to America. Not only did he come to the United States, he allowed us to discover him. Malcolm Lowry is another victim of our praise. *The Good Soldier* had to be stuffed down English craws like a pill poked down a cat's throat. Only Graham Greene (a man of amiable perceptions, and a Catholic capable of understanding Ford's obsessions) befriended his work.[10] Certainly the writers whom Ford so faithfully celebrated did not bang many pans in his behalf.[11]

Still, when Ford said that his historical novels were fakes, or when, in a badly bungled and widely misunderstood dedicatory foreword to *The Good Soldier,* he said that until that book he had not really extended himself and described his previous works as being "in the nature of pas-

---

10. This is not entirely true, of course. What was lacking was a *sustained* support. Rebecca West understood the greatness of *The Good Soldier,* yet when she wrote, "It is impossible for anyone, with any kind of sense about writing to miss some sort of distant apprehension of the magnificence of his work," she was mistaken, for it was not impossible. When I talked to graduate students at the University of Leeds in 1966, they professed never to have heard of Ford. Perhaps it was because he was not in "The Great Tradition." Auden's defection was not easily forgiven either. From his critics Ford has suffered more than most. Only a few of them even bother to spell his heroine's name—Katharine—correctly.

11. According to David Harvey, "it was the confusing multiplicity of his literary personae coupled with the failure of his friends among the great to speak out in his behalf that most impeded Ford's critical recognition" (*"Pro Patria Mori:* The Neglect of Ford's Novels in England," *Modern Fiction Studies* 9: 1 (Spring 1963), p. 15). I have taken the West quotation from p. 14 of Harvey's article.

tiches, of pieces of rather precious writing, or of *tours de force*,"[12] then the critics took it into their woody hearts to believe him; they believed him as they had never believed him before; they believed as war departments believe in their weapons of war; and that word—'pastiche'—was cut on a stamp like EXPEDITE or AIRMAIL, DO NOT BEND, and brought down on Ford again and again with a kind of coward's eagerness, and a now legendary stupidity.

Ford's modernist esthetic is derived from Flaubert, and it is based upon a formalism which is rarely popular with critics, while it fails even to come to the notice of the ordinary reader. It is a position which, if taken, requires some unpleasant reassessments of the Anglo-Irish-American literary tradition, and none of these alterations is likely to be tolerable to a history shaped largely by chauvinism and defended to schoolboys by bachelors and marms.

> It is to be remembered that a passage of good prose is a work of art absolute in itself and with no more dependence on its contents than is a fugue of Bach, a minuet of Mozart, or the writings for the piano of Debussy.[13]

The exceptional range of Ford's own writing allowed him to see the obvious (that fiction is written in prose) with a scarcely commonplace consciousness of the consequences: one being that the novelist must first of all be a master of the medium, and not merely a toothsome doughnut soaked in life.

> English, as we have said, is rather short in the item of great novels. It would, then, be almost a minor literature were it not for the prose writers whom we have been citing.[14] They, it will be observed, are none of them novelists. And, indeed, it was not until comparatively lately that the English novelist paid any attention whatever to his prose.[15]

The failure of the famous ruminative styles of Donne and Milton, Browne and Taylor to set the standard, and the consequent disappearance of rhetoric's art and rhythmic richness from English prose, beginning roughly and symbolically with the death of Swift in 1745 (as Ford

---

12. It was, after all, a love letter to Stella Bowen, and he wanted to offer her his best.
13. *The March of Literature*, p. 512.
14. Ford has been writing about Sir Thomas Browne, Clarendon, Pepys, Walton, and White, and will go on to cite Graham, Doughty, Hudson, Borrow, Beckford, and Thoreau.
15. *The March of Literature*, p. 520. He makes an exception of Dickens.

marks it), is perfectly coincident with the progressive adoption of anti-
Ciceronian models on the one hand, and the mounting influence of science, its societies, and its stylistic aims on the other. But the loss of that
solemn periodic movement, that gay interior mime, which is the end and
final music of the mind, is simultaneous, too, with the vast heady successes of colonialism, the increasingly thick and callused grip of Protestant ideals on the heart like a misplaced cold in the head, and the infec-
tious spread of a crude monetary utilitarianism which would allow Art
to flourish only if it were called Moral Education, and education to continue only so long as it could be shown to be suitable to the starchy new
rulers of an empire.

Thus the decline of the ornate style commences at the conclusion of
the late Renaissance. As the world's geography enlarges and men see
strange new lands on which to fatten, its pretensions shrink. The spread
of learning overlaps it, and the old grand manner is everywhere beset.
Perhaps it is merely a "manner"—of bows and scrapes and cuffs and
laces—unmanly and impotent. So the self-assurance of this style weakens
at a time when nation states are being set up like megaliths, crowds
count, and crude is king. Commerce, manufacture—the sheer multiplicity of *things*—overwhelms its own opposing wealth of *words*. It is sick-
ened slowly, done in by distribution, by vulgar masses and their love of
sensation, by mindless duplication. The magazine serial becomes the
madame. Lending libraries boss the block, and books are built like row
houses, chapter connected to chapter, volume following volume, with a
dreary sameness. The paragraph is replaced by the sentence; the sentence
is shortened like a dress; the dress is moreover designed to be as plain
as a Mennonite's nightgown; and that majestic, endlessly elaborating language, subtle and continuously discriminating, that joyful, private, yet
publicly appointed prose, that mouthmade music, once headlong, resonant, and roaring, is reduced to a mousy squeak by the rising noise of
the novel. That, at least, is Fordie's myth, and it is a myth he will live to
write by.

It is not, of course, merely a myth. Robert Adolph's assessment of
these matters is much more careful, scholarly, and discriminating than
that of Ford, who polemically lumps whole legions of differences together as you might melt old soldiers down to make fresh ones from the
same lead. Still, Adolph's ultimate point is precisely the same:

> That we commonly regard Defoe, Richardson, and Field-
> ing as the first important "real" or "modern" novelists is an
> admission that we, too, have lost the Elizabethan taste for the

"qualitatively unique." We prefer to regard all action in fiction as part of a causal series. Like Burnet, we see things as "useful" only if there is an "argument" and a "pattern" both chronological and spatial. Here is another union of Truth and Utility. In the Platonically inclined Renaissance, truth was independent of time and space, a reflection of some timeless and spaceless Ideal. With the triumph of the new nominalism, there are no more such Ideals.[16]

Ford knew, and knew he knew, and what's more (unfortunately combining the correctness of his conceit with an unmannerly candor), *said* he knew more about the strategies of the traditional novel than anyone writing in English. *The Fifth Queen* is a textbook of technique, a catalogue of resources, an art of the English fugue. The struggle it depicts is both historical and literary. But Ford is not an innovator in the same sense that Joyce is, or Gertrude Stein, or Faulkner, or even Virginia Woolf. He is essentially a nineteenth-century novelist—the last of his line—with twentieth-century theories and a sixteenth-century taste on his tongue. His themes concern the conflict between periods, the dependence of principles (alas!) on times, our changing attitudes toward vice and virtue. Katharine Howard's sweet waist is grasped by the *Geist*. There is no future forward, yet there is no going back. Where rib confronts rib, Ford has none of the hope the lung has for its next breath. He has Hardy heavy on his one hand, Joyce will soon weigh down the other, Lawrence is standing on his chest. Ford will soon hail with regret that "finely sculptured surface of sheer words," as Wyndham Lewis wrote, which will protect the novel's center from the world, and constitute the main concern of much of the work to come.

So if, as Conrad declared, *The Fifth Queen* is the swan song of the historical romance, then *The Good Soldier* brings the Jamesian tradition to a close, just as *Parade's End* concludes the lifetime of its kind. There are other modes of English fiction for which Ford did not perform the last rites—the picaresque, for instance, the Wodehouse, the Waugh; but what serious artist would want to imitate, now, the beautiful bloat of late James? desire to create that particular world of hesitation and concern again, or become obsessed once more with the unsaid, the distantly implied, the cleverly concealed design, as if the carpet weren't there to

16. *The Rise of Modern Prose Style* (Cambridge, Mass.: M.I.T. Press, 1968), p. 267. We should not imagine that Ford's enemies had been overthrown by Cardinal Newman's Oxford victories at the time he wrote *The Fifth Queen*. If one thinks only of the enlightened, liberal, no-nonsense obtuseness of Wells, it will not be necessary to go on to Arnold Bennett and Galsworthy.

receive a tread or please the eye, but to entrap the mind? who would willingly attempt still another time those elegant weekend garden parties which were always so richly walked, sedately tea'd, astir with clever conversation and subtle avowals, so abloom with intricate plans and genteel betrayals, that everyone was soon in vexation, doubt, and moral uncertainty as though lost behind a high meandering hedge? who would wish to impale themselves upon that impossible appointment? especially since Ford Madox Ford inherited the whole wealth of fictional capacities which Henry James spent a career amassing for the once impoverished novel of marriage and manners he had initially taken up and brilliantly brought out, the way those avuncular European villains of his take up some well-to-do, young, innocent American to sadden her into scintillation; consequently, *The Good Soldier,* with such funds at hand, could realize the genre's accumulated powers beyond any penny of further purchase.

The Tudor trilogy is a muscle show, all right, a strut, a flex of force, but it is not a simple deceptive flourish like General Beauregard's marching the same small squad round and round his camp to simulate the nick-of-time arrival of a rescuing army. Its surface is more accessible than that of *Pale Fire;* it plays no games with its readers and is never facetious like *Lolita.* There is no parody like that which sends the humorless reader away from *At Swim-Two-Birds.* It is not as exotic and apparently "worked up" out of history as *Salammbô,* nor is it as narrowly focused as *The Awkward Age,* although equally and severely scenic. It is tragic, but not as fanatically gloomy as the writing of Samuel Beckett. Unlike John Barth's *Letters,* it wears its learning lightly, and even lets its Latin sound like Oscar Wilde. The linguistic difficulties are minor, and its length does not exceed that of *Ulysses* or many of the novels of Thomas Mann, or George Eliot's *Romola,* for that matter. It is a virtuoso performance—the first of Ford's great shows—and closes out the historical novel like an emptied account. Later he will try for a similar triumph over the realistic novel by inventing Christopher Tietjens, a truly good "good soldier." In an arrogant display of literary genius, Ford Madox Ford brought the nineteenth-century novel, in each of its principal areas of excellence, to its final and most complete expression. For this he has not been forgiven.

The Fifth Queen's ambitions, if we have understood them correctly, require it to be quintessentially historical. Yet there remains a real uneasiness, and Ford feels it. Like dust, there is so much accumulated death in history, whereas the novel has always been dedicated to life— life of every variety—often, indeed, to crowds, to the multiplicity of kinds, to cities, to human vitality itself.

Of course, a novel may be called historical simply because it is set in the past, with real times and places serving as exotic color—props and scenery—for the invented action; or it may be historical because, whatever the story it tells, its language is of another age; or it may be considered so because its characters are actual historical figures, even if they sit on stools in hell and calmly read out conversations, or are otherwise lifted from their period and milieu like dolls from decorated rooms. A novel may be *about* history—have history as its theme—or it may be epical in the old way by purporting to be a true account of times beyond our ordinary knowing and claiming to tell us of the Trojan War or about how Rome was founded, or what happened to certain knights on some crusade. Naturally enough, a fiction could be historical in several of these ways at once, just as a dish may be a disaster because it has been overcooked, as well as badly sauced and crudely seasoned.

Any novel set in the present will shortly become historical. We need only wait. It is not the subject so much that matters as it is the author's attitudes and resources, for the principal difference between the historical novel and any other kind lies in the former's reliance upon texts, rather than upon the author's direct experience of events. Joyce knew the shops that lined the Dublin streets; he had looked in their windows and entered them, chatted, bought; but Ford knows Greenwich or the London of Henry VIII's time only through documents, paintings, and prints. Historical novels are thus almost purely linguistic, because they are derived from the author's knowledge of books, although these books may be understood entirely in terms of contemporary life—whatever that mishmash may be at any particular moment.[17]

The belief that an author ought to write from experience—from experience, indeed, of a deeply personal, challenging, even agonizing kind—rather than contrive its effects at second hand: from books about the bullfight, for instance, whorehouse, Great War, Great Wall, social scene, or local wine, because otherwise the work will smell of the lamp, seem forced, lack life—is a ninny's notion; but it is firmly established, and as hard to discourage as a fungus. Conrad's career is such a distinguished and romantic example of the principle: live, then write, that who could fail to feel the impulse to follow it? and Henry James's desire that the novelist render an impression of life comes from such an august source, such perfect practice, who would want to refuse it? and so it is

---

17. Other writers' worlds are essentially imaginary, even though that imagination may be stimulated by experience the way John Hawkes's was, in writing *The Cannibal*, by his duties as an ambulance driver in World War II, or by the texts of the pornographic tradition when composing *Virginie*.

not surprising that Ford suffered from the itch of the idea, even to the point of denying his first masterpiece, and playing Judas to his muse; although he knew that Flaubert, to invoke another model, very carefully "noted up" his novels from books and papers, drew on his diaries, more than on the days they represented, to put a written Egypt down over a real one. We write about what moves us—that's true—and that is why poems are daily addressed to Dutch interiors and antique statuary as well as handsome men and lovely women, and composed both in rowdy taverns and in solitary towers. Anyway, if you want to write about great deeds and grand events, you will have to read or hear about them first, for whom do you know who is great enough? and what have you gone through yourself that has such height? Ford understood perfectly well, too, that among the most important and powerful experiences for all serious authors would have to be figured those intensely significant sentences which pierced them as Saint Sebastian was, as well as those the wretched writer put down in despair . . . might it not have been that day when the sun delayed its dawn and winter spread over the page like a pall? . . . yes, set down in dismay indeed; and then was grateful and amazed, half a lifetime later, as it might turn out, to read what had been once written there and find such large and living lines the soul was reshaped by their weight and a multitude of follies forgiven.

Reshaped, rescued, rewarded . . . because, although one's life may be most heavily oppressed, and sorrow, docility, suspicion, hang like divers' weights about it, the spirit is elevated easily even by mere bibelots of beauty, exquisite ivories and glistening enamels, too, or other pretty *objets d'art*—presumably emblems of an overlacquered life. It can be carried off just as readily by a portrait, a paragraph, an image which takes it unaware, as you once might have been beset by a sudden ring of changes on a Sunday walk, so your soul sang the phrase, itself a bell; or remember how, in rivers of red and yellow light, you struggled like a salmon toward Christ's image streaming from the tall cathedral windows, or how you were briefly made brave by brass bands bombulating in a summer park, or how you shrank inside a grave and holy silence when, Othello dead, Emilia down, and Iago struck, the curtain slowly closed on the sight of Desdemona's desecrated bed.

"God!" the King cries. "You have not played false with Culpepper?" "Most times you shall not believe it," Katharine answers, "for you know me. But I have made confession before your Council. So it may be true." She leaves the room, and then, upon the faithless shadows of his life, the King casts down his hat. It is an awesome moment.

These occasions of modest and mild-mannered sublimity have their rights. They are not less than life, but life sharpened sweetly—given purpose, value, substance, point—and so are more than mere experience, as a ballet is more than simple dance.

Nevertheless, if Ford Madox Ford had known Katharine Howard as a schoolgirl, rather than as a figure in a set of texts, he would not have referred to her novel as a pastiche.

When Madame Bovary sets forth on her adulterous course, she is not already dead; however, when Katharine Howard arrives at the King's court; on a mule, as is appropriate to her religious role; in the midst of a riot, which signifies the quarrels in the realm; with the hot-tempered Thomas Culpepper, whose love shall be her ruin; and buffeted, injured by the crowd, weary with the journey, says: "I would find my uncle in this palace"; the head that speaks has been buried beside that of Anne Boleyn's for several centuries.

Because Katharine Howard is a character in history, she is never able to move toward her own death in the same free way an invented character does. Katharine, indeed, has her fate, and we know what that fate is, not because we have read reviews, or the book, before; but for reasons which lie outside it, in past space, former time, other works. The notion that the author must revivify history is not an empty or an idle one. Katharine Howard must be brought back from the grave before Henry can cast his eyes upon her, love her, make her queen, and toss his hat down like a soft blow upon her hopes. Ford's account is openly inaccurate in many ways, but the path he has chosen narrows as she strides it, because if he keeps, as a historian should, to the facts, he loses the heroism of his heroine, the villains fail of real villainy and become petty and mean, Henry's majesty is gone, and no clear straight line can be drawn through the story's cloud of lies; whereas, if he departs from the truth, as the novelist must, immediately a more satisfying development or dénouement is seen, but then the reader rightly wonders why he chose to write about history anyway.[18]

The important historical novel must remove history from history the way Colette removed her mother from her life to resettle Sido again in *La Maison de Claudine*. Ford's success at liberating Katharine Howard from *her* texts for service in *his* seems effortless and nearly instantaneous.

"Where be we?"
They had entered a desolate region of clipped yews, frozen fountains, and high, trimmed hedges. He dragged the mule

---

18. Francis Hackett calls Katharine "a juvenile delinquent" in his *Henry the Eighth* (Garden City, N.Y.: Garden City Publishing Co., 1933), p. 352.

after him. Suddenly there opened up a very broad path, tiled for a width of many feet. On the left it ran to a high tower's gaping arch. On the right it sloped nobly into a grey stretch of water.

"The river is even there," he muttered. "We shall find the stairs."

"I would find my uncle in this palace," she said. But he muttered, "Nay, nay," and began to beat the mule with his fist. It swerved, and she became sick and dizzy with the sudden jar on her hurt arm. She swayed in her saddle and, in a sudden flaw of wind, her old and torn furs ruffled jaggedly all over her body.

The perception is exact, the final phrasing perfect, and there the real woman is—as we first encounter her—in the ruffled features of a few words. Her reality will remain relentless, she will not fade.

The history that is taken from history takes on the status of myth. Anyone who wishes may place Katharine Howard in a fiction, and fill her mouth with words, just as Gide may write of Oedipus as rightfully, if not as well, as Sophocles; but no one may reasonably remove Madame Bovary from her book, and only her author might essay another version.[19]

The figures which move so magnificently through *The Fifth Queen* are quite properly more luminous than life, because they are no longer mere men and women in the world. Men intend, and act, but rarely mean, while characters signify, and their vows and desperate ventures are simply little curvatures in the creation of the larger sign.

It is morning when Katharine Howard arrives at Greenwich in her raddled furs, upon her old mule, in the middle of a riot, but Thomas Cromwell, Lord Privy Seal, has slid down the river the night before through pages which are pure evocation. Udal has come too, foolish young Poins, the King preceding. We have seen the spy, Throckmorton, lean near Privy Seal's ear and fear form like frost on the Chancellor's beard. Lies flicker in time to the torchlight on the dark water. Careers bob up and down like boats. Ford is peopling his scene, setting his situation in motion. The rumor is already about that the King has turned sick at his sight of Anne of Cleves, and Cromwell, whose hopes hang about the neck of this Protestant Queen like a locket, is given to us, in a typical passage, arriving at his quarters:

---

19. It is likely that Beckett regards many of his novels as a reworking of the "same story."—"my life last state last version ill-said ill-heard ill-recaptured/ill-murmured in the mud brief movements of the lower face/ losses everywhere" is the fifth verse of *How It Is*.

> He entered his door. In the ante-room two men in his livery removed his outer furs deftly so as not to hinder his walk. Before the fire of his large room a fair boy knelt to pull off his jeweled gloves, and Hanson, one of his secretaries, unclasped from his girdle the corded bag that held the Privy Seal. He laid it on a high stand between two tall candles of wax upon the long table.

Cromwell enters, not his room but his door, which we must presume is held open for him. His entrance is as swift and terse as this simple, yet remarkable, first sentence. Cromwell's position, his power, his tenacious grip on things, is presented through a rapid series of possessives, each the same: it is *his* door; the men are in *his* livery; they remove *his* outer furs, deftly, for they do not wish to hinder *his* walk. The room is *his,* the jeweled gloves, the girdle, and the secretary too.

'In,' 'out,' 'before,' 'off,' 'between,' 'upon': spatial prepositions predominate, and the actions are those which specifically rearrange things in space: 'enter,' 'remove,' 'pull off,' 'unclasp,' 'held,' 'lay between'/ 'upon.' Many of the adjectives are spatial, too ('ante-,' 'outer,' 'large,' 'high,' 'tall,' 'long'), and often held against their nouns by an unstressed syllable: 'ánte-róom,' 'óuter fúrs,' 'jéweled glóves,' 'córded bág.' We see the action of removing the furs just as we might see it on the stage.

> The boy went with the gloves and Hanson disappeared silently behind the dark tapestry in the further corner. Cromwell was meditating above a fragment of flaming wood that the fire had spat out far into the tiled fore-hearth. He pressed it with his foot gently toward the blaze of wood in the chimney.

Again we begin with an ambiguity. As blouse with skirt, the boy does go well with the gloves. We understand the point of this paragraph when we remember that a beefeater, guarding the ardently Catholic Lady Mary's door, had spat upon the ground as Privy Seal passed. By this time everything has been put in its place: clothes have been removed, the Seal is resting between its two candles, the page and the secretary have retired, and the fragment of wood gently returned to the fire with a foot which knows how easily it may be scorched, even though its gesture is also a sign for the ruthless exercise of power.

Nor do we find any fear in Ford of the letter *f*'s faintly whiscular puff. Then:

His plump hands were behind his back, his long upper lip ceaselessly caressed its fellow, moving as one line of a snake's coil glides above another. The January wind crept round the shadowy room behind the tapestry, and as it quivered stags seemed to leap over bushes, hounds to spring in pursuit, and a crowned Diana to move her arms, taking an arrow from a quiver behind her shoulder. The tall candles guarded the bag of the Privy Seal, they fluttered and made the gilded heads on the rafters have sudden grins on their faces that represented kings with flowered crowns, queens with their hair combed back on to pillows, and pages with scolloped hats. Cromwell stepped to an aumbry, where there were a glass of wine, a manchet of bread, and a little salt. He began to eat, dipping pieces of bread into the golden salt-cellar. The face of a queen looked down just above his head with her eyes wide open as if she were amazed, thrusting her head from a cloud.

This passage, because of the way Ford is able to embody in it the many themes and oppositions of the book, is exemplary; but it is not an isolated instance; rather it is a perfectly fair sample of the style and quality of the work as a whole. The *mise en scène* is the Tudor tongue. The language depicts a situation which functions at once as action, characterization, atmosphere, emotion, and symbol; there are no idle gestures here, arms do not flail, legs kick, to make the puppets look alive. We see in the text what Cromwell sees in the fire, and the world of the work rises up around us from the first page.

As pictorial as *The Fifth Queen* is, and as frequently static, it is not stitched the way Rilke's Cluny unicorn is, or his carefully posed outcasts, walls, his ghosts and nervous dogs, because the mind of Malte brings all things to a standstill, whereas Ford's castle corridors contain thieves, murderers, maidens, metaphors in motion.

Cromwell's snakelike lips are repeatedly invoked, as is the roundness of his face, an un-Homeric use of epithet which Gertrude Stein found effective in writing *Three Lives,* a work, like *The Notebooks of Malte Laurids Brigge,* strictly contemporary with *The Fifth Queen.* Cromwell's lips slide as his mind slides—in coils of continuous cold calculation. We have felt his power, seen his self-control. The wind, like a rumor, lends the illusion of motion to the chaste Diana and her hounds, while fluttering candles do the same for the carvings of kings and queens. Appropriately, Cromwell approaches an aumbry, a cabinet for keeping things. It is a meat safe, sometimes, but alternately, it is a chest, in churches, for sacred utensils. He stands, in short, in a system of relations, the perfect politician, since his meal is spare, yet the flour of his bread is expensively fine; the salt is such a simple substance, yet it lies cupped in gold; facts are in front of him, myths behind, though both waver; above, kings crowned with flowers seem to grin, while around this pious Protestant, Papist trappings suggest the blasphemous character of his frugal snack: a secular ritual carried out with Christian symbols against a background of pagan gods and severed heads.

The writing is as ritualized and formal and rich as the scene. Ford repeats the word 'quiver'; he rhymes 'round,' 'hound,' and 'crowned'; he follows a phrase like "where there were . . ." with 'manchet,' one of his favorite antiques; he rolls around in his vowels, throws out lines of alliteration, risks outrageous puns (hiding a 'hind' in 'behind' to go with the stags and hounds); and has, generally, a great good time.

Finally:

> "Why, I have outlived three queens," he said to himself, and his round face resignedly despised his world and his times. He had forgotten what anxiety felt like because the world was so peopled with blunderers and timid fools full of hatred.

"His round face resignedly despised his world . . ." It is roundly said; and one senses that Cromwell possesses the world's roundness as thoroughly as his full face possesses its phases.

The trilogy is composed of a series of great confrontations: moments which represent Katharine Howard's passage to the block. One of these is Katharine's visit to Anne of Cleves, whom we have already seen sitting in her painted gallery at Richmond. I have tried to suggest that the narrator's general point of view is one with the language of the time, but Ford does more than give the writer leave to play the sedulous ape to Burton and Sir Thomas Browne. He gives his invented historical creatures a tongue of sometimes Shakespearean splendor. The mouth is full again, as it should be, as it once was, and words rest on a breath which would otherwise be idle, since characters need to speak but not to breathe.

Katharine addresses the Queen in German, which surprises her; it is the form of Anne's replies, however, that counts with us:

> "I learned to read books in German when I was a child," Katharine said; "and since you came I have spoken an hour a day with a German astronomer that I might give you pleasure if so be it chanced."

"So it is well," the Queen said. "Not many have so done."

"God has endowed me with an ease of tongues," Katharine answered; "many others would have ventured it for your Grace's pleasure. But your tongue is a hard tongue."

"I have needed to learn hard sentences in yours," the Queen said, "and have had many masters many hours of the day."

Anne of Cleves has not learned her German from books because she cannot read. She has in consequence, Ford tells us, a memory she can rely on, and reply with.

"You seek my queenship"; and in her still voice there was neither passion, nor pity, nor question, nor resignation . . . "You have more courage than I . . ."

Suddenly she made a single gesture with her hands, as if she swept something from her lap: some invisible dust—and that was all.

The Queen knows that in England they slay queens. She also knows—well remembers—what she wants in her swept-out lap. And through that knowledge, we know Anne of Cleves, her cautions, and her comforts.

"I am neither of your country nor for it; neither of your faith nor against it. But, being here, here I do sojourn. I came not here of mine own will. Men have handled me as they would, as if I had been a doll. But, if I may have as much of the sun as shines, and as much of comfort as the realm affords its better sort, being a princess, and to be treated with some reverence, I care not if ye take King, crown, and commonalty, so ye leave me the ruling of my house and the freedom to wash my face how I will. I had as soon see England linked again with the Papists as the Schmalkaldners; I had as lief see the King married to you as another. I had as lief all men do what they will so they leave me to go my ways and feed me well."[20]

The neglect of this novel, the critical obtuseness which the Tudor trilogy has had to endure, the indifference of readers to an accomplished art, and a major talent, the failure of scholarship to disclose the real clay feet of the real Ford, even the esteem in which *The Good Soldier* is held, as if that book were being used to hide the others, but, above all, the

---

20. I have somewhat abridged these passages from Chapter 6, Part Two, of *Privy Seal,* the second volume of the trilogy.

unwillingness of writers to respond to a master, constitute a continuing scandal which hushing up will only prolong; yet one does wonder what is to be done. Certainly no adequate history of the recent English novel can be composed that does not recognize the door through which that novel passed to become modern.

In a typical piece of polemic, Wyndham Lewis outlined what he called the taxi-driver test for fiction. One is simply to imagine inviting a cab driver into the house and asking him to open some literary work at random. (One dare not attempt to vivify this situation in any way.) Then *"at whatever page he happened to open it,* it should be, in its texture, something more than, and something different from, the usual thing that such an operation would reveal." He goes on to reproduce, in facsimile, the opening pages of *Point Counter Point* and *The Ivory Tower* with predictably decisive results. The fact is that the opening page of *The Fifth Queen* would drive many of the first pages of Ford's own novels to cover. In Ford's version of this game,[21] one picks the first substantial paragraph to be found on page 90. Let us do so, and take Ford's chances for him. We find ourselves in the middle of one of *The Fifth Queen*'s greatest set pieces: the revels given by the Lord Privy Seal in honor of Anne of Cleves. Men dressed as Roman gladiators are using a mannikin in mock combat with a lion. Lewis is satisfied simply to point his pen at his specimen page of Henry James, and so, at Ford, shall we. Even through a veil of contextual ignorance, a little quality can be seen.

> The ladies pressed the tables with their hands, making as if to rise in terror. But the mannikin toppling forward fell before the lion with a hollow sound of brass. The lean beast, springing at its throat, tore it to reach the highly smelling flesh that was concealed within the tunic, and the Romans fled, casting away their shields and swords. One of them had a red forked beard and wide-open blue eyes. He brought into Katharine's mind the remembrance of her cousin. She wondered where he could be, and imagined him with that short sword, cutting his way to her side.
>
> "That sight is allegorically to show," Viridus was commenting beside her, "how the high valour of Britain shall defend

---

21. Wyndham Lewis, *Men without Art* (London: Cassell, 1934), p. 295. Ford carries out this test on Sir Thomas Browne in *The March of Literature*, p. 513, with the success you would expect. For fun, I have played Ford against Ford. *The Rash Act,* for instance, published in 1933, is a poor-quality counterfeit. One taste will not tell you how a whole dinner may be designed, but if the cook is incompetent, it scarcely matters what the order of his dreadful dishes is or how elegantly they are served.

from all foes this noble Queen."
The lion having reached its meat lay down upon it.

Confronting this passage point-blank, as we have done, we'd not know that Katharine's cousin is Thomas Culpepper, with whom she arrived at court, and because of whose love she shall be condemned. The allegorical defense of the Queen is ironic in several directions at once. The man, Master Viridus, who explains its meaning to Katharine, is in the pay of the hated Protestant, Privy Seal. He has changed his name from Greene, and is a worshipful student of the Italian tongue (i.e., Machiavelli). The Romans are the Pope's persons, of course; but it will sadly turn out to be Katharine Howard herself who is the "sweet" meat hidden in the tunic of the mannikin. The final lines are therefore especially poignant, and furnish us with a summary of the fifth queen's fate:

> The lion . . . having reached its meat . . . lay down upon it.

REPRESENTATION AND THE WAR
FOR REALITY

1

MATTER   Suppose, with a relaxed mind, we examine any ordinary object: this or that lamp or chair, piece of sweet cake, melt of custard; or imagine we consider some sensation: odor of onion, glisten of shellac, low mutter of thunder; or that we follow the ruminating length of the digestive tract, travel the highway from Nîmes to Nantes, study the calamitous course of a seduction; in short, that we take a lightly general account of things and our varied experiences of them—survey, as they say, the whole—will it not seem entirely natural that our speech as we proceed should seem to be about all that; should seem to serve all that; should be shaped, even if from nothing more substantial than a system of fixed sounds, into a hollow in which we try to hold our world like water in leaking hands? since, indeed, our world is this or that wet towel or wanton glance; it is the stupid stone we stumble over, the dark star we wonder at, the brute bulk of Being; yes, the catalogue of this and that includes the Lambeth Walk, a sentimental feeling, shred of cabbage, piece of bruised fruit; it is life lit by a neon lining; for what are the words 'sweet cake' worth compared to the layered torte our teeth are gently sublimating? and the glisten of shellac—what wood would want the word as its protection? and why should we, like Whitman, be enchanted by an aimless list? a hollow litany of names?

clothesline

dashboard

bloodstain

twitch

If consciousness itself seems strangely vaporous and evanescent—as near to nothing as we care to come, like the crumbling edge of a steep cliff—it is nevertheless clearly referential; it is as insistently intentional, as much made, like the zero, by its blank as by its circle, the way a land's end is equally an onset . . . a rise, a float . . . of earth; and we can, comforted by this realization, return for another helping of that dessert, and smile at our friends whose minds are momentarily in their mouths where ours is, secure in our communal assumptions; that we share with them a moist cube of cake and a number of not dissimilar crumbs; that calories will not capriciously cling to one of us rather than to another; that, in one sense, we lick our fingers with the same tongues.

A name, as we know, is not so securely attached as all that. The color of a leaf/a term for a tree: there is an ontology of difference. Colors do not come in Yugoslavian. Fall will not find the forest barren of characters inscribed there in Japanese. A name can be any minor meow a cat can manage, any donkey bray or honk in a hankie. 'Kamikaze,' we cry, running for cover; 'Geronimo,' we shout, falling through the floor of the plane. Just as well: 'Philadelphia!' Why not: 'mashie niblick'? How we squeak and clack and whistle! Starlings are no more vociferous. 'Turnpike,' the judge decides, and the defendant's wife bursts into tears: ruthless sentence, callous word.

So even if we are not sure how the thunder's rumble registers in us; even if, between the fruit and our feel of its flavor, a gulf a tall god could not ride a cycle across has opened, it is, in truth, a gulf, a gap—this Cartesian cut—a wound in Reality which is precisely defined by its sides and separation, its type of spilled blood; but neither the name nor its arrangements, the propriety of its prepositions, the sweet taste *of* the cake, for instance, has the faintest resemblance, or any other reasonable relation, to the light coat of chocolate on my tongue[1]; and, again, even if the expression 'light coat of chocolate' fell away out of the world altogether, the sweet taste would linger, just as the glistening lips of my dinner companion, smiling and full, exist outside the sentence which describes them (unless, of course, I'm composing a fiction; then, if the words go, all is gone—away in the erasure without leaving an ash—unless there remains a small roll of rubber on the paper where they were like a slight smear of sugar on the chin). How can we weigh or reach around the world with these merely verbal measures; and may not every beautifully substantial thing recoil at the scentless breath of the Word as from the kiss of Nothingness itself?

---

1. I have discussed the formal and semantic emptiness of such expressions as "the X of the Y," in "The Ontology of the Sentence, or How to Make a World of Words," in *The World Within the Word* (Alfred Knopf: New York, 1978), pp. 308–338.

Jean-Paul Sartre's early novel, *Nausea,* concerns itself, in part, with this problem. The narrator's revulsion, felt as outside himself—as a feeling *for* the feeling in things, as a feeling that has been passed to him *from* things, like the transfer of dampness from glass to hand—is a consequence of what was at first a dim apprehension of real existence, and finally becomes a revelation of what it is for anything, simply and completely, *to be;* hence, of course, the perception (we cannot call it "an understanding") of what his own existence can be reduced to. To look on Being bare, we must strip it of signs. Our knowledge of it, clothed in concepts like figures at a masquerade, is only of this or that smelly black witch or fairy princess, harlequin and clown. Naked—naturally, we know them better. As we enter reality, we are entered, and we understand it, then, in a way beyond knowing—absolutely—as Bergson claimed:

> If there exists any means of possessing a reality absolutely instead of knowing it relatively, of placing oneself within it instead of looking at it from outside points of view, of having the intuition instead of making the analysis: in short, of seizing it without any expression, translation, or symbolic representations—metaphysics is that means. *Metaphysics, then, is the science which claims to dispense with symbols.*[2]

When all the signs are removed, all significant relationships shall cease, since the mystical experience (like the esthetic one) is one unmediated by concepts; but without such relation and meaning, this pure presence, this total *there-ness,* is only that. It is, in the case of the novel, *Nausea,* the knotted black mass of a chestnut's root rising out of the earth beneath the narrator's park bench like a serpent from the sea; a root Roquentin becomes—not in its role as a root, for it has lost that identity—but by sharing the sense of its sheer existence. Paradoxically, then, his experience is of *rootlessness:* the sublime sort of which Rilke wrote in the *First Elegy,* when the dead are suddenly able to perceive everything fluttering loosely in space like a sleeve.[3]

---

2. Henri Bergson, *An Introduction to Metaphysics* (New York: Liberal Arts Press, 1949), p. 24. Sexual imagery seems to cling to these ideas with the insistence of cheap perfume.

3. Rilke writes of an experience very similar to Roquentin's in his little essay "Erlebnis": "Walking up and down with a book, as was his custom, he had happened to recline into the more or less shoulder-high fork of a shrub-like tree, and in this position immediately felt himself so agreeably supported and so amply reposed, that he remained as he was . . . It was as though almost imperceptible vibrations were passed into him from the interior of the tree . . ." Quoted in *The Duino Elegies,* trans. by J. B. Leishman and Stephen Spender (New York: Norton, 1939), p. 124. The character of the experience, for Rilke, is plainly benevolent, but this is not entirely the case for Roquentin.

Dizzied by the spin of things out of all relation, the narrator—Roquentin—through the cancellation of any sense of himself like a cashed check, by a total loss of footing, by an almost tropical proliferation of life, as though he were suddenly caught in a cloud of midges while taking a calm autumn walk; the narrator—Roquentin—by the sliding away of everything, like snow from a warming roof, toward who knows what it will be . . . soon again won't be—never quite wasn't—isn't . . . becoming neither more nor less so, but simply is-zing: eating, sleeping, shitting, fortuitously finding a gold coin in the garbage or unhappiness in honey, lying still and cold as stone or rapturously fucking, being a bench or, just as likely, an upturned dead donkey's bloated belly; the narrator—Roquentin—noticing the indifference of thing to thing and thing to self and self to selves like streetless rows of the one same shuttered house di Chirico'd in the silver glaze of a turning mirror; the narrator—Roquentin—impressed by the complete pointlessness of letting go, of persisting, getting on, in Bouville to begin with—mudville—in the primeval slime which Beckett will later render so well in *How It Is;* the narrator—Roquentin—convinced of the absolute adventitiousness of every event, the speciousness of every value, the absurdity of the genital spasm, sperm like a billion midges, love an acid rain; the narrator—Roquentin—with such turns taken, feels a nausea which sickens the sidewalk, the shoes, the clothes, the soul, the cells, till the eyes vomit their perceptions, and the mind lies down in swill to thank an empty heaven, author of all—like Roquentin—a dotard, knockabout, another nil among nillions: narrator.

Many Greek philosophers apparently felt that existence was a property which they, as human beings, had, but which the gods, for example, as clan and family fictions, did not. Hamlet has irresolution, but not is-ness. Later, it became fashionable to describe existence as a relation between things, and not a thing or property itself; it was a condition, much like drunkenness or having the croup. If Hamlet dies, he does not cease to breathe, because his breathing in the first place was only say-so. His death means merely that Hamlet has no more lines (unless, of course, he returns as a ghost). As a character, there are certain existential relations he lacks, among them a kind of material causality. Hamlet cannot give Ophelia the flu or the pox, although the actor who plays *him* may give his cold to the actress who plays *her.* In *Nausea,* however, the narrator experiences existence as an ultimate substance, much as Heraclitus considered fire, or Anaximenes air. It is the primal stuff, the true $\phi\upsilon\sigma\iota\sigma$, and this simple, daring, yet primitive solution has much to be said for it—as attitude, at least as poetry.

If we dissolved appearance, and thus plurality, by force, Thales seems to have suggested: if we squeezed the orange, melted the ice, condensed the steam, we would find they were made of water, as everything is—our bodies are mainly rivers, swamps, and slush; and this discovery suggests that the power of producing particularity must lie in actions of water itself, as it drifts off as air, or congeals as a solid of some sort; just as, in later thought, the *élan vital* was seen to explode in the direction of every possibility. Existence is infinitely, randomly, pointlessly changeable; yet, although it does change constantly, we insist on seeing the same face in our mirror or across the breakfast table, our eyes sew up all the holes in our clothes; habits like a healthy heartbeat are never heard; we live in the comfortable communities of cliché.

Still, if we see Sartre's solution as pre-Socratic, we must also see to what degree existence (in *Nausea*) is identified with the objective side of the Cartesian slice: with prime matter and flat fact. The other side might be represented by Valéry's M. Teste, who puts on shows in the theater of the head. Consciousness must naturally feel this external reality to be its enemy, for the movement of consciousness reflects the movement of matter only by dissolving its substantiality, and depriving it of the very *there-ness* which had distinguished it. Yet what marks off this bench, the man who sits upon it, the root beneath, from the slots which help to drain the seat, the rise of the bench above the earth, the arm's-reach-away the root is, if it's not the fact that space is never *in the way* (in the novel's repeated and italicized phrase)? As Descartes had defined it, the only difference between matter and the void was matter's relative uninvadability. So you exist if you can be said to be *in the way*. However, the root, the bench—lodged in the experience of Roquentin, Anny, or the Self-taught Man—will become will-o'-the-wisps: multiplicities corrupted by self-concern, insensitivity, convention; and never, like a roller skate or kid's trike or slow truck, *in the way*.

We are balanced, as on Beckett's bicycle, between one fall and another: between the madness of those disembodied creatures of his, kept alive only through an obsessional flow of words; and the insanity of the desensitized, those lowered below the level of the living as the narrator is in *Nausea*. Both approach silence as a limit: in one, it is the silence of the shattered and scattered stone; in the other, it is the silence of the exhausted, embittered soul. Beckett's characters lose almost all ability to act; they merely, if barely, speak. Sartre's protagonist finds himself in a reality so indeterminate he believes himself terrifyingly free, although how his will can direct his actions without the assurances of some determinate causality is inexplicable.

The voices in Beckett, which we overhear, suffer from a language which lacks nearly all denotation, whereas Roquentin's mystically uncovered world is nothing but; because essence, if we dare to introduce that unwanted notion, belongs to language, where definition dwells, and not to things. Words mingle in more ways than thrown rice; they interconnect the interconnections they basically are; and with a number of them rightly placed, I can make the moon jump over the cow and the fiddle play the cat. Things, however, do not modify one another; they do not intersect (not in a realm without relations); they can only displace something *from their way,* and if the sledge shatters the stone, it is, as Hume averred, only another habit which may be altered itself as readily, for it is not the blow but happenstance which sends those fragments on their separate ways.

Surreal metamorphosis is the rule, and in a passage which cannot help but remind us of Rilke's *The Notebooks of Malte Laurids Brigge* (as *Nausea*'s entire text does: in theme, attitudes, imagery, ideas, even upshot) Roquentin wonders "what if something were to happen?" What if chance *were* king, and a red rag were to change into a side of rotten meat, a pimple split like an opening eye in a painting by Magritte; or what if one's clothing came alive, or one's tongue turned into a centipede? New names will have to be invented for a spider's jaw, or, as Borges has imagined, for transparent tigers and towers of blood.

It is precisely in such passages, as effective as they are, that Sartre's literary and philosophical problems, in a novel like *Nausea,* are most evident and unavoidable. As we watch the red rag blow across the street, what are we watching? And as it approaches us, meat now, spurting blood, where is the change taking place? It is taking place the only place it could take place—on the patient page, in among the steadfast words, the metaphors of mind and imagination.[4] No one wants to seem dense about poetry, but we must not believe poetry at the expense of the world. There is not the slightest chance that a red rag, however windblown, will reach us as bleeding meat. The cards I am dealt may be Q K 10 A 2 one time, 3 J 9 8 8 another—who knows?—but the Jack of Hearts will never be other than pasteboard, the Queen cannot give me a lewd kiss, threes become trees by losing a letter, not their nature. Roquentin can be as

---

4. Compare Sartre's passage with any number from Lautréamont, for instance: "O, that inane philosopher who burst into peals of laughter when he saw a donkey eating a fig! I am inventing nothing: ancient books have related in the greatest detail this voluntary and shameful spoliation of human nobility . . . Very well then, I witnessed something even funnier: I saw a fig tree eating a donkey! Such miracles are easily performed on the page." *Les Chants de Maldoror* (New York: New Directions, 1966), pp. 168–169.

full of error as bile, deep in his metaphysical miseries, but Sartre cannot chance being so mistaken about chance, unless he thinks it also has no nature; because there is no likelihood that whiteness will become musical, as Aristotle insisted, for even randomness wanders along logical lines, so that what's white may impulsively become green, perhaps—that is possible—or what's musical may fall firmly silent—that's possible—or the red rag may flutter unaccountably thither rather than inexplicably hither—that's possible—Mr. and Mrs. Wholesome American may beget loathsome freaks—that's possible—what is possible is possible—trying to fill a straight and receiving the Joker by the dealer's mistake—that is possible.[5]

Roquentin can have his imaginary nightmare. Let us not stand *in the way* of literature. But we must remember that it is just that. It is fiction. A fiction at furious odds with its own form, its own style, and even its own dénouement. When Sartre was young, he tells us, he believed that words were the quintessence of things, and so they are—for the writer of quintessences. "The written word . . . worried me," he reports.

> At times, weary of mild massacres for children, I would let myself daydream; I would discover, in a state of anguish, ghastly possibilities, a monstrous universe that was only the underside of my omnipotence; I would say to myself: anything can happen! and that meant: I can imagine anything. Tremulously, always on the point of tearing up the page, I would relate supernatural atrocities. If my mother happened to read over my shoulder, she would utter a cry of glory and alarm: "What an imagination!"[6]

The accidental glimpse, we can be sure, was not accidental; and there is a certain glory, as well, in causing alarm. Sartre was practicing his role as Roquentin.[7] He goes on to say that he did not invent his horrors, but found them in his memory, and then he gives an account of several "supernatural" events of the sort which exhilarate children and sustain the superstitious. Pure chance is embraced by the New Faith because it

---

5. This is the point of Aristotle's theory of privation. It is interesting to compare Roquentin's "possibilities" with Malte's. The latter wonders whether he has seen or said anything important; whether he has ever lived elsewhere than on the surface of life, that the whole history of the world has been misunderstood, and so on. In short, he worries about real possibilities.

6. Jean-Paul Sartre, *The Words* (New York: Braziller, 1964), pp. 148–149.

7. Throughout *The Words* he describes his childhood rehearsals, without, I think, being completely aware of them as preparations. At one point, he says, "I decided to lose the power of speech and to live in music" (p. 125), an exchange which is critical in *Nausea*.

can do what an absent god cannot: perform miracles and confound science. Why not turn water into wine? Why not imagine a dead man restored to sight, only his eyes alive in his rotting head?

But let us back over our issue a bit. It will not cry out or protest.

We begin with a desire to describe, to render, to capture even a bit of the world. We wish to stand *in the way* of time. We wish to gain a little information about things. We wish to understand the make-up and the connection of events. But first we must make things stand still. We must lift things from their world of things and find a place for them in the realm of thought. We must represent. I take my example from an extraordinary and beautiful book by Danilo Kiš.

> Late in the morning on summer days, my mother would come into the room softly, carrying that tray of hers. The tray was beginning to lose its thin nickelized glaze. Along the edges where its level surface bent upward slightly to form a raised rim, traces of its former splendor were still present in flaky patches of nickel that looked like tin foil pressed out under the fingernails. The narrow, flat rim ended in an oval trough that bent downward and was banged in and misshapen. Tiny decorative protuberances—a whole chain of little metallic grapes—had been impressed on the upper edge of the rim. Anyone holding the tray (usually my mother) was bound to feel at least three or four of these semicylindrical protuberances, like Braille letters, under the flesh of the thumb. Right there, around those grapes, ringlike layers of grease had collected, barely visible, like shadows cast by little cupolas. These small rings, the color of dirt under fingernails, were remnants of coffee grounds, cod-liver oil, honey, sherbet. Thin crescents on the smooth, shiny surface of the tray showed where glasses had just been removed.[8]

This tray is not handed to us on a tray, all its elements in order, coexistent, communal, clean of commentary. Rather the tray is broken apart and strung out, the glaze preceding its surface, the flaky patches on the raised rim as much in front of its frieze of metal grapes as the soup is in advance of the fish. Our reading runs in loops of understanding as we gather a phrase together and then carry it on through the sentence like a package under our arm. The complexity, character, the length, the chronology of every quality's occurrence is carefully regulated by the

---

8. Danilo Kiš, *Garden, Ashes* (New York: Harcourt Brace, 1975). The book opens with this passage. The translation is by William J. Hannaher.

writer. It is true that in "real life," as we continue so foolishly to call it, our experience of the tray would have many serial characteristics. We turn the tray over in our hands, for instance: first front, then back. We look here, then there. We try this, then that. Taste the sherbet; run our finger along the tray's rim; look through the curtains, through the window's haze at the lawn escaping toward the trees. How ideal language is for that. Meet Gertrude. Meet Ophelia. Meet Maud. Put on the left shoe, drop the right. But the tray is not entirely present, even in this recital of bits and pieces. I remember there was a maker's mark on the back of the real one, crudely indented, as if stepped on. The boy for whom honey and cod-liver oil are being brought cares only for its bearing surface, where a teaspoon might rest along with the jars. We have all the tray we need, for it is a tray we hold in our heads, and not in our hands. We think not only *to* the nickelized tray, but *through* the details of its development. The odd sound of the word 'nickelized' stands in for the nickelization itself. We watch a thought in the process of composing itself. No "real-life" tray does that. It does so, futhermore, largely in terms of visual details. The tray is touched but once. It is not a *thing* we're thinking, with its molecules and secret laws, but a *perception,* a perception *remembered.*[9]

Of course (and the passage was chosen in part for this reason), *this* tray is only a version of the Slavic one; only *this one* has been nickelized; only *it* orders its construction carried out in English; only *it* will be "perceived" by most American readers.

It is just a tray, a mere tray, we can hear our Sartrean narrator say, a trifle of no worth but for the sad or simple little memories it harbors. True. But the paragraph has superseded the tray, devoured it, if it ever was (indeed, if it ever dared to be); we need it no longer now that we have this unfolding thing of words in front of us; this path the mind will follow in search of a feeling; this thought-out object upon which will always lie the remnants of coffee grounds, the cod-liver oil, the honey, the sherbet, in precisely that marching order, and there will be, in addition, the author's attention to it—close, precise, loving—a shine which can rest upon even lead without changing its lack of gleam.

We reach the surreal world which *Nausea* envisions in two, not quite

---

9. The recursive character of reading is almost impossible to represent. The first sentence of our specimen "reads" something like this: Late in the morning, late in the morning on summer days, my mother, late in the morning on summer days, would come into the room softly, late in the morning on summer days, my mother would be carrying that tray of hers, late in the morning on summer days, when my mother would come into the room, softly, with that tray.

coherent, stages. In the first, we feel the root for what it is apart from our categories and classifications (created by a bourgeois science and society in any case, and hence corrupt beyond mere metaphysics); in the second, we pass beyond that to the experience of undifferentiated existence itself: i.e., from what it is for the root to be (as root, presumably) to what it is for anything to be (as any *thing*). However, when we deprive the world of words, do we deprive it of anything at all, unless we have only taken away what rationalists have said was there like spooks in a haunted house? Having denied a logical structure to reality, are we compelled to conclude that it is actually a heap of nonrational rubble? Our reasoning seems to be that if we remove universals *from thought,* we shall immediately *see singular things.*

So each time the mother came in with the tray—she, the tray, the carry, contents, motive, sticky spoon, soft light and summer ambiance— would be unique, and really unlike every other time, thing, space and movement. In a sense, if *Nausea* had its way, the habitual past tense, in which this paragraph is written, as well as all its general terms, its logical connectives, would vanish into vicious particularity—vicious because it is a particularity without classes, without repetition, without universals. Borges' madman, Funes, is in touch with reality, but Kiš has simply falsified it, implying the existence of a humble singularity which he describes in arrogant generalities.

Actually (and I have been present there, on my scientific mission, clock in hand, thermometer in case, a beeper at my belt, an obedient camera staring like an owl's eye pasted on a box, pad of wet black paper on my shivering knee), yes, actually Roquentin is right: differences are epidemic. The first time the mother-figure in our small example came in the room, she was wearing high heels and a paper hat, swaying a little from last night's champagne; the second time she was downcast and held the tray as low as her waist, as low as her spirits; the third time all the bottles and the spoon had slid to one side as if they were on a capsizing ship; the fourth time the honey had crystallized, the sun came through the curtained windows like a knife; the fifth time . . . ah, the fifth time she fairly flew, clothing in charming disarray, a light flush had risen from between her breasts . . . but enough—this inspection is as superfluous as our added lace. Nevertheless, she did come each time, and she was carrying a tray each time, and, in fact, everything alleged in the paragraph was exactly there, unaltered, thanks to the virtuous generality of language—virtuous because it leaves the particularity I have just generally described quite undisturbed, quite untouched.

We can, moreover, determine just where the monstrous mutations of chance may occur—within the metaphors—as the nickel becomes tin-foil, the metal grapes ripen, and little cupolas crowd the room with their insistent shadows. We can say of *Nausea* what Montaigne said of natural science: In words are its questions asked, in words are they answered.

One final fact or two about this paragraph and the tray it presumes to create. Our object—unlike the chestnut tree whose root has tripped us up—our tray is acutely aware of itself. It does not, in our account, pretend to any grander existence than the Forms have—wee modest thought that it is. It is not *out there* beneath a bird-shat bench being stepped on, being mystically merged with a foreign corporation. Nothing is being represented. A thought, instead, is being *constructed*—a memory. Nor is the language out of which it is built any different from the thought itself. There is, at this point, no fatal separation. Although nothing but universals are employed, although every word is in common parlance—even 'cupola' and 'protuberance' must be used many times daily—and although there is nothing unusual or outrageous about its syntax or its rhetorical patterns; it is, notwithstanding, a quite singular paragraph—this Englished Kiš—as are the parts and whole of *Nausea*. As a passage of felt thought, this bit is perfectly adequate, even beautiful. As a description of things, it is misleading and false—only, however, *if it is believed to be a mimetic representation; only, that is, if its nature is misunderstood.*

It is a matter of immense difficulty (and I am thankful I do not need to go into it very deeply here), but it *does seem* that words, by themselves, can't tell us what and how things are; that only the things in question can do that; it *does seem* that syntax is surprisingly indeterminate, that objects and actions settle on their own effects and relations. Things give rise to thought, thoughts do not give rise to things, except secondarily, as plans for action.

I said our paragraph was aware of itself. Words must be aware of one another when they are put into play, otherwise each one would lie down on the page indifferently, as satisfied simply to be there as the things of pure existence are. The word 'absurdity' is coming to life under my pen, Roquentin writes, and, indeed, that is how it happens, for words have only a second-rate reality so long as the book's covers remain closed over their heads. *Out there,* the word is only ink and paper or a tremor in the atmosphere, unaware of its existence, unaware of its freedom, just as the root is, asleep in its being like a bed. Only *in here* is the word alive, in reflection, for language is the vehicle of the upper self.

If language is like consciousness in always urging objects on us, it is also always an emissary of the mind.

Roquentin's journey into the root reveals to him the freedom conferred on things by chance. And it is sickening, in the deepest sense, to lose the world, the self, the soul, the sight and feel of flesh, one's circumstance. But to remain in the root like a ghost in the grave is to refuse the freedom one has found there. Now we see that existence is simply indeterminate, not free; that freedom requires consciousness, requires choice, requires (and here the paradox becomes extreme) just that language, that baggage of bad ideas, that really bum belief that the word 'woman,' say, wraps her round like a robe, and babies and boudoirs her in the comfortably heated houses of the bourgeoisie; requires, that is, a return to a world where words are little more than social criminals in the pay of the *saludes,* the police of chief.

Sartre grew up among rationalists (as one in France must) the way Nietzsche grew up among women, and his dislike of their designs is deep, as is the strength of their hold on him. If you believe, as rationalists do, that the structure of language reveals the structure of thought, and that the structure of thought is in harmony with the structure of the world (as it must be, if the world is to be an object of thinking); then, of course, to remove that language, as Roquentin does, would uncorset everything; but it does so only if the rationalists are right, and if, in addition, *thought is as essential to things as language is essential to the thought of things.* The sort of freedom Sartre's hero finds is terribly iffy: he may have removed my belt and left me still in handcuffs. Suppose I sweep out language like a dirty room (as I earlier suggested), and all the furniture of the universe remains in place?

Furthermore we found (we claimed) that the indeterminacy which is discovered is a kind it is possible to particularize only in language, in the existential productivity of metaphors, where we may imagine any outrageous image to have a literal referent. Anything that can be thought has Being, Parmenides said. Unicorns are possible, and the left-handed head.

There is only one reason for believing in this kind of unconditioned, universal, category-crossing tychism—since experience confounds it everywhere—and the reason is that language can be so arranged and manipulated. Watch me lift 'lattice' out of a sentence about flowers and put it down so the sun lies like a lattice across Barbara's husky breasts. There, the . . . But we cannot linger to admire her nipples, justly famous: how they seem like the buds of flowers, and so forth. These glories are moving on, anyway, into a livelier context. In short, the freedom Sartre finds for Roquentin is made only of words, like the words of the rationalists he despises. But it is true that a writer—an artist—must be a rationalist within the work—just *because* it is not the world. And Roquentin is allowed to perceive that. The forms of fiction and the aims of art support Idealism, whatever the sentences of any novel assert. Such worlds are worlds of thought, where a kind of Platonism reigns, and the very fact that it describes so well what occurs there is good reason to believe that fictional, too, is its account of things. *Nausea* is a young man's book, even if it seems to be Sartre's most enduring, purely literary achievement. It was also written before the war and the fall of France. In it Sartre takes the esthete's way out, but he will not do so again.

Behind the physicality of the word are banalities; but behind those, in the music of their motion, there is something which escapes the blunt inertness of existence, and the *blague* of the bourgeois. Although the narrator knows how we deceive ourselves by turning our futile and foolish lives into stories; how we shape a trivial event into an amusing anecdote, an incident into an adventure; how we hunt for perfect moments, like the perfect fuck, which can occur only in daydreams; although he knows how we trim life like an artificial tree to celebrate a merchandiser's version of an ancient canard, and then dress up and mask our faces for another, and get drunk for yet another, and for a fourth commit this asininity, and for a fifth, that . . . he nevertheless thinks that if the *right words* were put in the *right order* for once, he might be permitted to claim for his work and himself some of the reality of the little four-note phrase he has heard on the saxophone—as unlikely an instrument of spiritual elevation as one might imagine. And the tearful tune is "Some of These Days." Do not smile. Such songs sound better in French and in France. It is a bit of suffering, this song; it has a suffering rhythm, although it is not yet a signature, like Vinteuil's "little phrase."

> It does not exist. It is even an annoyance; if I were to get up and rip this record from the table which holds it, if I were to break it in two, I wouldn't reach *it*. It is beyond—always beyond something, a voice, a violin note. Through layers and layers of existence, it veils itself, thin and firm, and when you want to seize it, you find only existants, you butt against existants devoid of sense. It is behind them: I don't even hear it, I hear sounds, vibrations in the air which unveil it. It does not exist because it has nothing superfluous. It *is*.

Not to exist, but *to be, to be* is now the aim. So Mallarmé might have said. However, Sartre will emerge from this dismal Valéry. His later novels will not wonder whether their language, their form, will betray him.

Still seeking freedom, the imagery will be of roads. They will embrace "realism," the esthetic of the middle class, like a mistress one has mistakenly married—no longer with enthusiastic lust, but out of a guilty sense of duty. The notebook's exploratory, open form will be abandoned, and the language will try to be as direct and useful as a roofing nail. There will be suits, coats, ties. Many people. Important themes. There will be a lot of dialogue. Trains. Different cities. Much dust. And long lengths of slow discussion. Though the real rain of the word is still falling—back in that earlier, more impassioned book—back in Bouville.

2

MIND   From the first the novel has been a fact-infested form, almost as if it had been made from their adhesion—this small bit clinging to that like bees in a swarm—and if the facts weren't heaths and hedges, street names and silken gowns, cows in a wet meadow following a storm, they were transports and follies, love affairs lingered over more lovingly than the lovers ever did their own ardent flesh. Unhurried, calm, as if the world would await its rape like a whore, the novel has looted one Nature to compose another—in Richardson, Proust, Gide, Musil, Mann. As faithfully now as when it initially appeared, the novel has been dedicated to the trifling, trivial, minor, and minute, to the first and second footstep, the half-smile, the sneeze, the skintight trouser, powdered bosom, little oddity of speech or dress. It has been and remains a realm where the passing of a thought is celebrated like a change of crowns; where a whim receives the solicitude due a desperate resolve.

Yet it is not simply particulars—passions, people, daring deeds—which the novel seeks so greedily; but all the properties of these, their clumsiest qualities—accidents of every kind like a wet bed—the blush of an embarrassment now grown cold; no, it's not merely the tree and its scaling bark which writing wishes to immortalize, but the clatter of cottonwoods in a wind, the silver maple's glistening leaf like a happy whistle. It even wants to render in words the cake's moist taste, the crazed surface of the serving plate, a look which candlelight has blown across the dinner table: the longing of that look divided into onset, tyranny, despoilment, overthrow, release, as a doctor might understand the course of a disease, or a lease might be drawn by a diligent attorney.

The telescope brought wonders into the world which weren't even dreams—neither of India nor the dread edge of the ocean—before the voyaging lens laid claim to them; and the imagination of the microscope did the same; yet what does fiction do for Cervantes, in enlarging life and bringing it as close as the nose, that these gadgets didn't do for Galileo and his friends?—in a prison, one way or another, of matter or mind, each of them. We must never forget how important prison has been to the art of fiction, for it is always from within walls, literal like Malory's and Dostoevsky's arrest, or, like Lowry's, dreamed; whether of cork and self-imposed like Proust's, like Lawrence's, of flesh, or because, as in the case of Borges and Joyce, the writer is going blind; whether the world outside is defined, like Balzac's, from the middle of a shade-drawn, coffee-stimulated night as still and solid as a cloud; whether in sexual retirement or alcoholic haze, Céline's embittered hate; it is always from the point of view of the confined, the shut-in, that the work is performed; and the scenes of public life we see when we look through the pen appear only at the ink end where there seems to be a light, because the cell of the self stares back at us from the other.

I introduce these examples and their images (scope, sky, the rhythm in a barred Spanish window); I write Galileo's weighty name, because I believe it's in his day (in Descartes', Kepler's, Harvey's hour) that we must begin our attempt to understand fiction's special relation to things; a relation which Sartre's narrator in *Nausea* drew his doubts from, as if the world of objects were a blackboard which, when wiped, would register an undifferentiated darkness, a threatening lack of distinction like an overdemocratic club, a dizzying absence everywhere of both uniqueness and resemblance.

In England Francis Bacon was collecting facts like coins—any kind, from any place—you never knew when an ugly penny might be found stamped with a rare mint mark or distant date. Meticulous observation, the natural history of anything, an open notebook, careful records were the rule; and it was expected that then, out of the mass, would emerge a sudden saliency; the sea would proclaim its contents, as in a noisy mob of men it is felt that those of quality will quietly stand out. The scientist, with exactly the impulses of a novelist, should dissolve disfiguring accumulations; clear away the moss, grime, verdigris, and pigeon shit from the shoulders of things; so that, with all her masks and make-up removed, modest Nature can disclose her virtuous secrets. Innocent of bias, preconception, even hypothesis, a clear eye will perceive an equally honest and undefiled reality. The spirit of such an empiricism is a splendid one, its energies admirable, but it has always been disconcertingly naïve.

Not so across the Channel, on the mind's side. There Descartes was deploring the disorders of his favorite subject—mathematics. Mathematicians not only treated geometry, arithmetic, and algebra as fields without common borders, problems were dealt with one by one and separately—*pragmatically*—as if they were stones encountered in a garden, simply to be removed each time as seemed best. There was no general method; little unity or correlation between this "fact" and that; small sense that a solution might exemplify some broader principle; although matters were shifting significantly toward the better end: for instance, letters were now being used to stand for indeterminate quantities, and mathematical notation had been importantly improved by the introduction of signs like $>$, $<$, $\times$, and $- :: -$, for ideas like "greater or lesser than," operations like times, and for relations like proportionality.

Still, while the lines of battle were being drawn between fact and form, matter and mind, sense and reason (a war for reality which would be fought in the novel as furiously as anywhere), the possibilities of peace were being sought for, and possibly found, in the work of Descartes and Galileo; although in philosophy, perverse as it is, arbitration produces anger, and peacemaking means war.

On the one hand there were the observer's facts like so many spilled beans, the multiplying masses and an increasing democracy of data, while on the other there was the clearly more rigorous realm of geometry, with its relatively crisp ideas, its careful proofs, its orderly procedures—the aristocracy of figure. The problem was, in effect, to unite the two: to introduce mathematics into the confusions of observation, and the loud rich tumult of the world into the thoughtful reticence of angle, plane, and cube.[10] Apart, one was blind, the other empty, as Kant later unsymmetrically remarked.

If we simplify, for a moment, what was, in fact, a rather complex history, part of Galileo's accomplishment can be understood as the successful representation of motion in terms of geometry.[11] First, the time during which any movement took place was seen as a horizontal line. This line was divided into equal units in such a way that the length of the line was like a running sum of ones. Then velocity was conceived as another, vertical coordinate. The formula for the area of a rectangle, and the formula by which we compute the distance traveled along a line by something moving at a uniform speed are, of course, thanks to these designs, seen to be the same. *Of course.* We are so accustomed to this miracle it seems, now, never to have been one.

---

10. I have discussed this problem before, in "Groping for Trouts," in *The World Within the Word,* pp. 262–279.
11. Strictly speaking, this is kinematics. Mechanics would include a study of forces and causes, or what is called dynamics, as well. Nor should we really imagine that Galileo managed all of this by himself. It may have culminated in Galileo, but it did not begin or end in him. With Newton, mathematical description *became* explanation.

It is necessary to notice, at this point, a number of things: first, that our problem was simplified by considering only uniform, straight-line change, already an abstraction; second, that we made a number of rules of representation: for instance, that time and velocity were lines seen as sums—the moving object was a point, and its path a straight line [············•→]; that not only were our observations stripped of local interest and excitement (the body in question is actually a carriage containing the Princess Cassamassima en route to a rendezvous with her Sicilian lover, the despicable Count Luciano), so the object and its motion became *just and only* that; but the process of addition also had to leave its abstract center for the suburbs, to become concrete and contain itself in the line's little visualization [++++++++ ⫢]. Galileo, in short, had gone a long way toward establishing mechanics as the geometry of matter in motion.

Continuing to foreshorten, we can next consider Descartes' contribution, which was to elevate geometry into algebra by finding a way to represent any point upon a line as a pair of numbers (as a, b or x, y), a procedure already implicit in our earlier schema.[12] Mathematics, having descended for a time like Hermes into Hades, has now returned to its proper place in the Light, dragging the science of mechanics with it by the so-called scruff. One abstract system (algebra) has enveloped another (geometry), to find with a certain surprise, as perhaps the whale did when it swallowed Jonah, another science in its stomach.

Pebbles were once numbers [•   ••   ∴   ∷] before they were *imagined to be* numbers, for then they were no longer numbers; just as the child may begin by thinking: this building block is a building block; and with them build a little wooden heap; only later to realize that these are the stones of forts, the glass panels of skyscrapers, the concrete sections of a highway, the squat shape of a Russian tank, the first step of a stair. Both are forms of pretending.

The day of Descartes' discovery (November 10, 1619) may have been the day on which we determined, fundamentally, one way in which science worked: by a series of correlations in which the particular, changing, concrete world of things is advanced into a realm of increasingly clarified, complicated, and independently productive calculations. In

---

12. Tannery considered Descartes to have geometrized algebra, rather than the other way round, but in fact it is the "higher" system which always works its will upon the "lower" one. Nevertheless, to mark the mutuality of the movement between them is important, as my later suggestions about metaphor will, I hope, show. See S. V. Keeling, *Descartes,* 2nd ed. (London: Oxford University Press, 1968), pp. 11ff.

this rarefied arena (the world as well as it can be *figured out*), the external and accidental relations between things, if that is what they are,
are systematically replaced by internal, analytic, necessary, and universal
ones (or by statistical connections—whatever the scheme requires); and
all actions of organization and unification, which Kant attributed to the
Categories of the Understanding, take place, as it were, *outside the thinking self,* in the explicit construction of the scientific model. We must remember, too, that similar correlations were being made in the arts, and
that geometry had been introduced into painting (again in terms of our
organization of things in space) with what were to be revolutionary
results.

The objects which the new science requires are only surrogates for
things: they are dots, points, lines, extensions, coupled numbers, alge-
braic equations; they are "things" as a system of thought will revise and
devise them, and, in that sense, they are idealized poles of our scientific
intentions.[13] Any satisfactory theory has its own momentum, and will
carry its objects on as it must, transforming them, conferring upon them
a reality within their own realm which first rivals, then replaces, the
original—now a paltry object of merely ordinary perception—by a kind
of *coup de vrai.* Thought goes best when its object is also a thought.
Equal in the willpower of its wishes to any of our most urgent desires,
thought thinks beings into being. Of the scientist, Bachelard shrewdly
wrote: He must force nature to go as far as the mind goes.[14]

The first sort of mistake we might make would be to attribute to
nature properties which properly belong only to the medium of its description; hence the error of imputing necessary connection to causality
on the grounds that the hypothetical syllogism seems a perfect model
for it, so that affirming the antecedent is like producing a cause; or the
erroneous notion Descartes himself was led to, that there is a place of
pure extension somewhere—a kind of machine without ordinary gross
materiality: perfect, ineluctable, precise, silent, a mechanical image of
the mathematical mind. Nor should we confuse a rule of representation
with a law of nature, as we would if we thought light traveled in straight
lines simply because we had decided to draw it that way in our newly
lit up Euclid, since such a resolution allows us to calculate successfully
the height of towers from their shadows, to predict paths of reflection

---

13. For an interesting application of the notion of ideal objects, where a constructed
thing might be the concrete and intermediate expression of a struggle between several
intentional poles (the practical, the structural, the generic, the formal, etc.), see Christian Norberg-Schultz, *Intentions in Architecture* (Cambridge, Mass.: MIT Press, 1965).
14. Gaston Bachelard, *The Philosophy of No* (New York: Orion Press, 1968), p. 30.

and recreate objects from their images, to make the head of a horse out of dark air or a swan sail slowly across a wall like a white lake.[15]

We need to notice, too, that some of our conceptual apparatus falls away out of sight, like the middle term in an argument, never to appear in the conclusion of the proof, although facilitating it, just as the *x*- and *y*-axes do, as we pass from the planet we have made into a point, and then move through the plain geometry of its path to the complex algebra of its orbit.[16]

If things have no significance except as thoughts, how is it that our thoughts have significance? Our thoughts are often thoughts of things, of course, but when we think about a thing, we do so by thinking about our thoughts. I may dream of Jeanie, but it is always the Jeanie of my dream I dream of, and so it is with thinking, which can only have another thought as its central concern. One might object that I can perfectly well think about my toothache, or my date, or the road ahead, since these can be immediate perceptions, not merely memories or expectations; but I would like, very gingerly, to suggest that what I think about are my implicit descriptions, which is another way of saying that our knowledge is only of universals. In any case, these considerations return us to philosophy, whose method has always sought logical not calculational equivalence, and whose products have been conceptual fictions, for the most part, not elegant nets of number; they have been thoughts, that is, with much meaning, but only to the mind.

Most of the characters created by philosophers during their long novelizing history have come from their meditations on the nature of words: the Forms, for one, and the One, for another—Universals and Particulars, of course—all Essence; or from their meddling with the structure of the sentence, which has yielded Substance and Accident, the Mutt and Jeff of our paper cosmos; or from their love affair with logic, which has illegitimately engendered Necessary Existence, Cause, God, Certainty, and the ubiquitous *A Priori*. They have derived rather less from mathematics. Although philosophers have frequently and piously invoked it, rarely has geometry been gainfully employed. Still, we can trace the monads to their mathematical origins, and we can try to shoo

---

15. Stephen Toulmin, *The Philosophy of Science* (London: Hutchinson's University Library, 1953).

16. There is a possibility that entire theories may be lost in this way, for once a theory has established a firm correlation between two phenomena, a direct "causelike" connection can replace it. The problem is formulated nicely as "The Theoretician's Dilemma" by Carl Hempel, *Minnesota Studies in the Philosophy of Science,* Vol. II, edited by Herbert Feigl, Michael Scriven, and Grover Maxwell (Minneapolis, Minn.: Minnesota University Press, 1958), pp. 37ff.

infinity, like a hobo at our picnic, back to the doubtful class it came from. Nor is it hard to see how the distinction between Primary and Secondary Qualities helped to free physics from the common sense of Aristotle. Determinism, with its villainous archenemy, Free Will (or is it the other way round?), sprang like Cain and Abel from the union of premises in the syllogism, that is, via the idea of necessity and its collusion with cause; just as part of the notion of Perfection (for instance, in "The cause must be as perfect or more perfect than its effect") was derived from the concept of logical extension or the denotative range of terms ("You cannot say more in your conclusion than you have said in your premises").

We have been allowed to look on with considerable esthetic pleasure while Socrates conceived the soul, so that his favorite subject, ethics, would have a self to concern itself with; and is it not a moving story of how the seeded soul makes its perilous way through many bodies, and the vulgar married lives they lead together, to a final vision of the Forms and a reunion with its star? Indeed, we need that soul, for otherwise there would be nothing to soil or save. Think, then, of the creatures of convenience theology has called into being, and the tales it has told of them, as it has explained to us in dazzling sky-borne allegory the vast tragedy of all existence. Yet for sheer drama, what can rival the ravenous Will which Schopenhauer has invented like a Golem for the globe? Or what could exceed, for intrigue and excitement, the paradoxes of Zeno— the result of just the kind of confusion I've been discussing (in Zeno's case, that of mathematics with motion)—arguments which deny the evidence of our senses, and freeze us in the middle of our most nervous leap, even if we're frogs? And surely no one now seriously considers the *élan vital* apart from Bergson's novels about it.

There are all kinds of characters and characters of all kinds. Flaubert's creation, Madame Bovary, is a member of the petty Bourgeois, the sociologists' invention; and the actions of the Bourgeois exemplify exactly the mood of the *Zeitgeist,* the historians' concoction; while this last is an episode in that continuing and always stirring serial—the Search for the Absolute—which philosophers have scripted. One difference between the fictions of the novelist and those of historians and philosophers is that it is not only permissible, in the latter case, to take up these patterns, plots, and characters, to continue their adventures and to enlarge upon their baffling elucidations, it is expected—it is hoped—this will be a consequence. It is not an entirely wholesome game, however. Sartre's novel *Nausea* has taught us that you cannot escape or deny Essence, in order to affirm the brutal, babylike "Da" of particular existence, without playing patty-cake with the concepts of your captors.

Now is perhaps the moment to say straight out what I've been intimating: that there are two fundamental methods for describing the
world. These, with no originality but considerable prejudice, may be
called the Concrete and the Abstract, the Terminal and the Relational,
the Real and the Ideal, or, as I prefer, the Thick and the Thin (there
will be other names); and for each of these, again, there are two basic
strategies. If we divide the Thin like a hair to reach the thinnest, most
rarefied Thin of all, we obtain the Scientific, which writes the world
down in numbers like a dry-goods clerk (such is its reputation); which
pictures motion in terms of stationary figures—the triangle of accelera-
tion, the steady area of the square—and which must manage to represent things as if they were integrals or sums—forces parading in their
parallelograms, light like a line from which one hangs wash; and then
there is the Philosophical, that less thick thin, also all bones (such is its
reputation), which employs the language of logic; and through definitions, distinctions, and deductions endeavors to think its way through
the world like a small mole after grubs. Both may be called abstract
because the systems they use in constructing their models are perfectly
pure and unempirical, or so we imagine them. Each leaves *things* out of
its theory of things. And even if its own conclusion is, as Hegel reached
it, that nothing is trivial, accidental, or of little worth, that everything
counts, the account itself is at an elevation and a distance our astronauts
might cry "Wow!" from, when they look upon a whole so far away it
has forbidden itself parts.

This temper is reductionist. Thins diet, jog, keep regular hours. Thins
firmly believe that explanations should be simpler and quite other than
the things explained. But they are easily converted into "true believers"
because it is the theory they love, the principle, the law that has the
power. And their explanations are soon as complex as those of any Thick
because they cannot forbear to create a doctrine to account for their
dogma. Thus the theories of the Thins tend to be Tall.

Analogous to their opposite numbers, Philosophy and Science, the pair
which occupy the Concrete, somewhat like dead feet in such shoes, are,
naturally enough, more like arts than sciences, more concerned with the
skills of writing than calculating, with amassing facts rather than dis-
covering laws, preoccupied with time more essentially than space, satisfied with pattern instead of principle. The first is history, astride chronology like a huntsman, but more interested in the terrain it rides over
than in the quarry itself, if there is one. And finally, there is fiction, of all
unlikely things: the large, lazy, slop-about novel, whose representations
of the world no more *resemble* it than the models of science and philosophy do, and whose weapons are the cast-off equipment of the sophist—

the esthetic grammar of the language, of course, and then the schemes, tropes, figures and fancy forms of rhetoric and oratory, table talk and kitchen gossip.

If the chief aims of science appear to be description, prediction, and control; then the principal goals of philosophy are understanding, explanation, and moral direction; while history is after an adequate description, too, but always at the level of immediate human life, of whose sorrowful vicissitudes and glorious achievements it hopes to retain a record, and where its predictions also live, if it is able to make any; on the other hand, the object of the art of fiction is esthetic order, reconciliation, celebration, pleasure, for fiction creates worlds for us to live in that are designed to satisfy our deepest feelings, not our intelligence. Oh, not that intelligence should be insulted; reason must be reckoned with as well, but only as it gives a sense of structure and stability and completeness to the huge moods, like clouds of stellar dust, the novelist is coalescing in the great space of the page.

Aristotle saw the relation between genus and species in typically Thin terms. Concepts were arenas: the pin went in its cushion, the cushion in its box, the box in a bag, the bag in a closet, the closet in the house, the house on its street, its block, neighborhood, section, city, and so on, in the customary way the Thins think of thinking—in spatial metaphors, mainly of occupancy and containment. Thus Being, the most general class, surrounding everything like the horizon, is itself almost without meaning, since it has had to share itself equally with everything. Plato's Forms were supposed to be thick. The Form of the Good contained all the Forms, not as a pen contains sheep, but as a soup circulates its flavors, or stage lights mix their hues. Every Form is a compaction of terms. Although Forms, they are like things filled with things. It is this thickness the historian and novelist seek: redolence, richness, intensity, focus. The essences they are after are cores of concentration.

The thickheaded know that any adequate explanation must "contain" the explained; they are uncomfortable with simplification; what is left out worries them; they want width. If I am a Thick, then you can't understand how I feel until you feel as I feel; so Thicks tend to be Dionysian and to rub out distinctions and move toward the undifferentiated. Feelings flow better over bounds which have been withdrawn.

We know there are people who prefer Proust to Peano, Gibbon to Gödel; there are Jack Sprats who will eat no fat, and despise history as a waste of already wasted time. But the war for reality is not to be won or lost in the quarrels between historians and scientists or fictionists and philosophers, because each discipline has its thick and its thin side, its solid terms, and their invisible relations. There must be data; there must be observations; there must be facts, incidents, events, the Thick side says, while the Thin reminds us that there also must be order, structure, form; otherwise, and without math, there is no science; without logical analysis and argument, no philosophy; without arrangement and connection, no history; and without rhetoric, without pattern, without coherence, there is only the ordinary novel.

The war for reality is therefore a struggle between data and design, and if the data win there is a tendency to see nothing in the world but brute dumb fact and indifferent chance; and then, ironically, there appears the thinnish impulse to introduce the laws of probability into this rubbish heap, and to publish, shortly, a careful catalogue of trash. If design wins the data are deformed, the system runs ahead of the load it was carrying, and there is a multiplication of artificial entities and metaphysical myths. Thins really wonder whether facts aren't entirely the creations of abstract schemes, like the golf courses, lakes, and tree-lined streets of desert real estate developers; and Thicks tend to think that concepts carve continuities into discrete chunks, that laws are lies of some system of society, some secret legislature illegally elected.

But what meets what in the thick world of the novelist? Where is the war, when we perceive no system of design to begin with—no logic, no method, no geometry? In fiction, the war of which I speak is fought within the word, and is fought within the word wherever the word is. Faust, who is in one sense the Word at its most tempted and beset, admits to Wagner that

> Two souls, like hearts, beat in my breast
> each struggling to outbeat its brother.
> The one is flesh embracing flesh,
> feeding, copulating without rest,
> while the forceful yearning of the other,
> is to replace this dust with the breath of ancient stars.[17]

A word begins as a small sound fastened to a thing—a thought—like a balloon tied to the worried finger of a child; it is a nearly nothing noise, almost immediately gone; and then it is uttered in the company of others, among maturities of meaning, in a crowd of uniforms and gowns, possibly it appears first of all between a pair of beauties, both of whom have lovely hillious chests and lissome limbs, whereas our fledgling term has

---

17. Goethe's *Faust,* Part One, Section Two. My translation.

only two thin veins to bleed from, two dark flat eyes and half a boneless shoulder: alas! what can this wretched Cinderella do to modify such miracles of completeness and complexity as 'chest' and 'lovely' are? I set down several others earlier: 'lattice,' 'clothesline,' 'dashboard,' 'bloodstain,' 'twitch.' It perhaps survives unnoticed like the player of the triangle in the symphony. But words are formed as often and as ceaselessly as sunshine—evolve through millions of expressions—so as time passes, 'hillious,' for instance, takes on the character of its contexts; its station is defined; its substitutes and similars are recognized (it is similar to 'bilious' in one sense, like and unlike 'hilly,' while 'lumpy' is way off the mark); in any case, its contribution is anticipated (it is a bit clownish, perhaps, eternally *nouveau*); eventually the additions to the sum of meanings it has become are no longer large and crude as great straw bales forked from a loft, but light and slim and subtle as the single straw. Yet this being which began with a frail umbilical to its referent—a mother who will not remain to sustain it but comes into view on occasion the way a busy parent sees its children—this being that began so slimly soon has grown a core, a center, and although it is only a crossing of contexts, a corner, a relation between relations, it is a city of sorts, and has its own life in it, its own character, it has a nature—a 'hilliousness' like San Francisco's; so that now our word, a vacant universal when its meanings were not yet its own, but assigned it like busywork for the otherwise unemployed, is a complete, complex, and quite singular creature, conscious of its rights, its past, its rich roundabouts of reference and suggestion, definition, its variety and ambiguity of use, its layered ironies and opposing inclinations, its elegance, status, social tone, its fully formed though frazzled and untidy self; and it is in this refulgent condition that the word presents itself to the artist: as a silted-up symbol for his ardent declaiming, signs inside the sign of itself the way feelings mingle with other feelings when lips meet—when the history of earlier encounters, kisses, eye-closing contacts, modify one another amid all that moisture which has not yet turned to spit—and consequently is now a sign which is prepared to establish the most profound relations with others of its sort to shape—what?—a simple sentence like a single berry plucked from its bush to melt into a cautious music in the mouth.

Nominalists endeavor to reduce every class to its referents; they would rather all groups were like audiences at concerts, brought there by common interests, instead of constituting some transcendent entity: the Audience which has no ears; while Realists not only want to stress Sense rather than Reference, the references they prefer are to classes, not to things; and to classes—better yet—that contain names, as my own name might be included in the class, Teacher; but—better yet—only to that title I possess as a Professor, and not to the Billy of my boyhood, or the Willi who has sloppily signed my checks, or the Gassy who demonstrates the accuracy of his name on occasion after occasion. However we choose to think about it, the fact remains that a word is closer to its sense than to its reference, even if we can write or say the word without knowing what it means, as if its meaning were as absent as its object usually is, and therefore producing it without thinking anything, the way I might pick a word at random from the dictionary—'phot,' for instance—and simply say it: "phot . . . phot, phot, phot . . ." before I learn it is a unit of illumination.

Furthermore, the richest words are rarely those that signify the things we encounter every day: 'dog,' 'car,' 'dollar,' 'dinner,' 'teeth,' but rather those whose referents aren't perhaps real at all: 'god,' 'soul,' 'goodness,' 'nature,' 'love'; which suggests that words get their powers from other words—something most Thins have known right along. Certainly it's not simply our devoted cultivation of roses which has made the word so redolent. A wealthy word like 'red' did not inherit from the color. Only when the color left the street and moved into the mind did it begin to make a call girl's profit. Words may issue from things, and ultimately land again on things, but the arc of their flight is neither here nor there, nor are they the same birds which left the branch when they return.

What collects all these meanings like a dusty cloud of lint but the actual word-noise itself, ITS LIFE IN LARGE TYPE, *its presence in the hand?* What acquires this history of use? What appears when 'hillious' is spoken, printed, or written down, if not our friendly and helpful notation, a kind of Fifth Column in the war for reality? Caught between Thicks and Thins, all of whom demand that any system of notation serve their interests first, it counters by betraying both, and finding, in the artist, a champion so note-drunk and loyal to loops and labials he may be knocked out by one of his own gloves. Notation includes not only the requirements for forming letters, or for the spelling and sounding of words, but the ways we express our grammatical rules. These prescriptions direct our reading and our writing eye from left to right along the line, and from top to bottom within the page (although, like the Japanese, others sometimes issue different orders).

When we speak of things and their qualities, we are speaking presumably about our data, the densities of the word; when we speak of substance and their accidents, we are inside a philosophical system which is busy interpreting that material; and when we talk of subjects and predicates, we are dealing with a syntax which may even have points of identity with logical form; but when we place our adjectives in front of our nouns to indicate some sort of modification, or when we insert a verb between two of them to signify an agent's action on an object, we are following the directions of our notational system.

We cannot be confident that our schemes of inscription won't deceive us, and replace the reality we were after with their own. Though it may seem silly indeed to wonder how 'long' came to be a short word when, already, 'short' is, or why 'Mississippi' isn't the name of a snake, as if these △ △ were triangles, and this ★ a star; the fact is that for a long time—and still, in the popular mind—that △ really was one, and not its visualization. For most people, the true triangle is neither the park between three intersecting roads, nor a series of equations, but the Euclidean drawing. We also ought to recall the mischief made by the subtraction sign, which so absolutely resembled the symbol for negative number that a number and an operation were confused; or the case of the law of commutation in which (a b) was said to equal (b a), a not unreasonable claim, and one which certainly seemed to be true of multiplication until Hamilton created quaternions (or did he discover them?).[18] Now one may suspect that commutation is an inscriptional rule of rather wide but not universal application.

Sometimes our notation is inadequate in other ways. If it does not unambiguously report on every element of structure, we may begin to believe that there are hidden grammars, like bones buried in the basement of the language, which we know are there from the way in which we speak and write, but which we will not acknowledge or directly recognize. In short, notation may fail to point out elements in the data, or obscure parts of its organizing structure; it may be itself too flamboyant and distracting, or like Arabic too beautiful for words; it may contribute to the confusion of one thing with another; it may sneak its own elves into Euclid or into the external composition of things. Although without rules of representation there can be no correlation between matter and mind, system and data; nevertheless, without notation, these two cannot be brought together in the same place. It, not the pineal, is the true Cartesian gland. A point must become a dot before a body can be thought to be in position at one. Musical marks (notes, clefs, and staff) revolutionized music, just as those new squiggles did logic. They aid the memory, they facilitate communication; they let us *think*; they

---

18. A quaternion is a four-component number of the form 'a + bi + cj + dk' in which i, j, & k possess the same property as $\sqrt{-1}$. For an account of the significance of these numbers, as well as the confusions surrounding the minus sign, see Morris Klein's *Mathematics: The Loss of Certainty* (New York: Oxford University Press, 1980), pp. 90ff.

also lend conviction. After all, who would believe in zero until it was formed as an 0, and infinity's fallen ∞ suggests the endless curvilinear entrapment it represents in some theories.

"La théorie c'est bon, mais ca n'empêche pas d'exister," Charcot is supposed to have said, but what do things without theory become? *Nausea* contains some suggestions; still it is difficult to know how to assess these mystical "states of nature." The mind makes mistakes with such joy. Its errors cannot be erased without rubbing a hole through the *tabula.* When Hume removed necessary connection from causality merely by observing its rather absolute absence, he nevertheless presumed that, with that glue gone, all would fall apart in pieces of pure sensation, simply because there were no other kinds of ties, and he was left with meaningless juxtaposition like the postage stamps in those bulky unsorted Mission Mixtures. He was still so much under the spell of the spell he had dispelled, it never occurred to him that there might be physical embraces weaker than logical ones, yet stronger than those between distant strangers, the way those jumbled stamps remain stuck to their clipped-off corners. He was in the condition of the man who, hired to exorcise the spirits haunting a house, feels he has done his job by proving their nonexistence. The dialectical tussle between Thicks and Thins has produced many an ironic outcome. Hume left the continuities of experience in ruins, replacing the stream of consciousness with a steady spill of discrete sensations like jellybeans pouring from a jar, and these fell straight into the mouths of the mathematicians, the only people prepared to believe him, not because his impressions were so suitably colorful and fragrant, but because they were so ideally numerical.

The novel, which I said earlier was a fact-infested form, was able, also from the first, to forecast the future of those facts, because so many novels were epistolary then, which meant we were already one-mind-removed from events when we read them; it meant we were clearly conscious of reading *words,* rather than seeing directly through those words to their referents, as if we were eyeing that guilty group of shoes in the hotel hallway which Max Beerbohm drew for Henry James to peer at, his huge head at the height of the keyhole. Later on, most novels would pretend not to have been written at all, but to be life itself, there as soon as you faced the text, if you could summon the spunk for it; but in the pages of *Pamela,* Richardson allows us to recognize how wholly its words are *written,* and how those words reveal their writer as well as the world; even, for instance, in that moist moment when Pamela, deceived, permits the lustful Mr. B into her bed, believing him a maidservant because of his disguise.

> What words shall I find, my dear mother (for my father should not see this shocking part), to describe the rest, and my confusion, when the guilty wretch took my left arm, and laid it under his neck, and the vile procuress held my right; and then he clasped me round the waist![19]

What words shall I find, Pamela wonders, but she does not say her father should not read them, rather that he should not *see* them; and this was the transition that shortly took place in much of fiction, just as I am sure it did for Richardson's readers as well: to read was to see, and to see was to watch Mr. B put his hand in Pamela's bosom. Dream to that tune, ladies! Yes, who wants to read words—mere words—when one can watch such hillious hanky-panky? However, as the novelist's art became artful, the novel's previous attention to detail, its love of ethical, psychological, and sociological analysis, its simpering sentimentalities and lubricious teasing, its dreary derring-do and wild-eyed running up and down on roads, was replaced, without altering anything but the aim of our attention, by *words*—never by mere words, although I've already said so, for words are never mere—in the same radical yet simple way in which Pierre Menard rewrites *Quixote,* so that a brilliant contemporary passage like this one:

> A woman reached her bare arm out of the window to the parrot and gave him a rotten-ripe banana. The parrot, with a little croak of thanks, took it in one claw and ate, fixing a hard dangerous eye on the monkey, who chattered with greed and fear. The cat, who despised them both and feared neither because he was free to fight or run as he chose, was roused by the smell of the raw, tainted meat hanging in chunks in the small butcher's stand below him. Presently he slid over the sill and dropped in silence upon the offal at the butcher's feet. A mangy dog leaped snarling at the cat, and there was a fine, yelping, hissing race between them to the nearest tree in the square, where the cat clawed his way out of danger and the dog, in his blindness of fury, stumbled across the abused feet of the Indian on the bench. The Indian seemed hardly to move, yet with perfect swiftness and economy swung his leg from the knee and planted a kick with the hard edge of his sandal in the dog's lean ribs. The dog, howling all the way, rushed back to the butcher's stand.[20]

---

19. This is Tuesday night during the fortieth day of Pamela's imprisonment in the house of Mr. B.
20. From an early page of Katherine Anne Porter's novel, *Ship of Fools* (Boston: Atlantic–Little Brown, 1962).

can be seen as cinema, with its vivid portrayal of animals in action, or as sensuality and decay, not simply because of the character of its objects, but through its regulated pace and heavy music; or as system, with its reference to the stick/stick-beat-dog nursery rhymes of our childhood, its pecking order allegory, and its foreshadowing of the structure of *Ship of Fools* itself; or finally, as I should hope, as the tense and total interplay, in any fictional model, of all the elements of ontological construction: things, meanings, feelings. Such a turn of attention requires that we focus on the functional components of words and what is done with them when words, themselves, are the very medium of our imagination: when we exploit every aspect of inscription, enlist every scrap of significance, enroll each object or event or property, always in their competitive unity, locked in their relationship like felons, the way members of a family were before divorce was legal, and consequently concerned only with survival, domination, and their success in supplanting all rival realities with their own.

3

METAPHOR   It is Act IV, Scene XII of *Antony and Cleopatra*. Enobarbus is dead. The fleets of Caesar and of Antony are engaged, but Antony's Egyptian allies have again turned tail, as they did at Actium. Antony has gone where a pine tree tops a hill to watch his galleys come to rest like logs in the water, and his war with Caesar sink out of sight like one of his ships. His men desert his cause. Enemies a moment before, the sailors now cast their caps up and carouse like friends long lost. Alone, Antony's embittered soul is speaking to itself:

> O sun, thy uprise shall I see no more:
> Fortune and Antony part here, even here
> Do we shake hands. All comes to this? The hearts
> That spaniel'd me at heels, to whom I gave
> Their wishes, do discandy, melt their sweets
> On blossoming Caesar; and this pine is bark'd
> That overtopp'd them all.

A gloss on this glorious outburst is easy enough, although we leave the poetry behind like a departing plane. The sycophants who once fawned on Antony have taken their flattery to Caesar now, and yap at Antony instead—a tree that's been blazed for cutting down. A vulgar joke, a double pun, combine with a neologism in a complex intermesh of images to convey Antony's anger and contempt. The action of the language is felt immediately, though miraculously, the way the flavor of a complex sauce can be complete in a single taste. However, the construction, the operation of the imagery—that is another matter.

The first thing to observe is that we encounter these metaphors one at a time, although they come at us quickly, like poles we pass on a speeding train; but there is that moment when we are alone with 'hearts,' our overt subject. "The hearts That . . ." Individuals like Cleopatra and those who comprise her court, as well as Antony's allies in general, are the objects of the image. The heart through which they are examined, and which serves, then, as a thick system of related meanings, is so historically rich the word itself can be said to designate a symbol. Certainly it is not the actual muscle which is being so honored. *It* could hardly serve as the seat of feeling. *It* is not red, heart-shaped, and velvety as any valentine. *It* hasn't a history reaching to the ancient Greeks in which it is the pot where passions boil. The very nature of this initial noun has been changed; it has been redefined; it is no longer the same word it was outside the passage, for it has lost its *essential meaning*; peripheral ideas now occupy its center. When Rilke remarked that:

> No word in the poem (I mean here every 'and' or 'the') is identical with the same-sounding word in common use and conversation; the purer conformity with the law, the great relationship, the constellation it occupies in verse or artistic prose, changes it to the core of its nature, renders it useless, unserviceable for mere everyday use, untouchable and permanent: a transformation as it takes place, incredibly, splendidly, sometimes in Goethe . . . often in George.[21]

he was referring to this phenomenon. An ontological transformation has occurred, one which is fundamental to the nature of every art, not literature alone, and one which has many important ramifications.[22]

Following a principle of synecdoche, the rule of representation which is in force here is arrived at transitively: let the organ stand for the entire body; and let the body, in turn, represent the inner life or soul; then the heart can be the soul of the body—specifically, the passionate part. From the very opening of the play, the characters have been seen as emotional centers—that is, as hearts—for instance in this first speech by Philo about Antony:

---

21. Rainer Maria Rilke in a letter to Countess Margot Sizzo-Noris-Crouy, March 17, 1922.
22. I have discussed the idea of ontological transformation in an essay, "Carrots, Noses, Snow, Rose, Roses," in *The World Within the Word*, pp. 280–307.

> . . . his captain's heart,
> Which in the scuffles of great fights hath burst
> The buckles on his breast, reneges all temper,
> And is become the bellows and the fan
> To cool a gypsy's lust.

All the actions of these creatures of feeling—to which they have been explosively reduced—are perceived as acts of spaniels—in particular, the acts of following and obeying. In an instant, that whole deep range of meanings represented by 'hearts' is reinterpreted by 'spaniel'd'; it is transformed and reordered, especially in terms of value. The acts of the courtiers are immediately understood to be unworthy of honest men and women.

There are no doubt good things to be said about spaniels, but they won't be relevant in this context, which chooses, from what *we* know, what *it* wants. Our experiences of such dogs, including our visual memories of them—the way, precisely, they bound after one, their wet affection and overeagerness to bestow love—play an important part in our appreciation of the image; but what is happening when the spaniel serves as our Euclid for these movements is a wholly verbal process; one which is unlike ordinary modification or *extensional* selection, where, among dogs, an adjective picks out the largest long-haired one, or when a verb like 'bites' establishes a correspondingly painful relation between a dog and its victim; because one entire set of actions (bowing, scraping, protesting one's love) is *interpenetrated* by another set (jumping, panting, wagging, licking). It isn't that one set simply replaces another, because we don't forget our courtiers like yesterday's news, and think exclusively of dogs; rather a considerable number of internal, implicitly realized metaphors are produced, as the spaniel's sort of fawning is brought to bear, act after act, detail against detail, upon the behavior of some kowtowing lickspittles. Unlike mathematical or philosophical models, which cause their objects to divest themselves of all their ordinary properties in order to become pure points or transcendental purposes, 'hearts' become 'spaniels' here, *without diminishment*. Although these intricate meanings interpenetrate, it is important which term is the active one, because, on another occasion, I might want to say: "Oh, those spaniels I raised from pups, and who paid court to me with fluttering cuffs . . ."

We also understand just how Antony threw his benisons to his followers, like bones beneath the table, and how he called them to him, scratched their ears and held their paws. The candy image begins as a separate, though subordinate, one; that is, it never forms itself outside of the dominant spaniel metaphor as the heart synecdoche did. The compliments of the courtiers are regarded as Indian-given gifts whose dubious sweetness is being offered now to Caesar; but Caesar, himself, has meantime become a tree, like Antony, whom the spaniels come to lift a leg for; so that the 'dis-' in 'discandy' functions like both the 'dis-' in 'disappear' and the 'dis-' in 'disgorge,' with the consequence that two processes are distinguished, and then united again, as the appearance of flattery on the one hand, and its reality on the other. The wishes which Antony granted (*his* sweets) reappear as piss and vomit (the reality of flattery), and the servilities of the courtiers (*their* sweets) are poured upon Caesar now in the form of melting words and syrupacious deeds (the appearance of flattery). Then the dazzling double pun on 'barked' allows Shakespeare to tie the almost flapping edges of his image down.

Only by making the mind blink rapidly from 'hearts' to 'spaniel'd' and back again could one sustain the notion that a realm of fact where dog-behaving organs were a rule, and the lungs brayed and bowels baa'd as a matter of course, was being represented in this passage. We are in another world here, all right, one in which hearts and spaniels, trees and men, are fused—fused the only way they can be—conceptually, by a process of interpenetrating meanings, and each relation which is established with that interpenetration is itself metaphorical (the courtiers ask for favors the way dogs beg), hence another penetration of one meaning by another, and so on (Philo put up an imploring paw). The total result is an understanding founded on feeling, not on fact. *The fact* is that followers are frequently self-serving and treacherous; *the feeling* is that they are pissy-nervous little yaps.

Like scientific models, every metaphor has a range or scope. The spaniel image controls each word in this speech of Antony's, but the moment Antony begins to think specifically of Cleopatra, its boundaries are overstepped, its influence ceases, other emblems are invoked, other comparisons rule. "O this false soul of Egypt," Antony cries,

> this grave charm,
> Whose eye beck'd forth my wars and call'd them home,
> Whose bosom was my crownet, my chief end,
> Like a right gypsy hath at fast and loose
> Beguil'd me to the very heart of loss.

Cleopatra has been called a gypsy by others beside Antony, and we must understand her under this heading for the entire course of the action.

Philo's opening lines describe her as a gypsy whose lust is first aroused (fanned) and then cooled (again, fanned) by Antony's bellows-breathing heart. At the end of the passage which is our present concern, that word 'heart,' with which it began, pops up once more in the poet's play on the phrase 'loss of heart.' Antony's followers have done just that—lost heart—and Antony has done just that—lost his heart to Cleopatra—so that now he is left alone in the very heart of loss itself. It is a brilliant but characteristic turnaround in the writing.

A metaphor, as we've just seen, may rule openly or serve quietly for the duration of its life, invisibly sometimes, even behind those who are behind the throne, as 'heart,' here, begins with considerable *prominence,* gives itself over to the transformations of the spaniel image, and then reappears, its meaning ironically altered, in the conclusion. We should expect this, because that is the nature of its behavior during the entire work—a work the word 'heart' is truly Queen of.

We must not only have a sense of the foreground or background placement of an image, hence its comparative presence or absence throughout its range; but we must also be able to measure the degree of *commitment* of every metaphor to the model it's made. The commitment of the spaniel image is complete. The courtiers are not this heel-tagging breed on the basis of only one likeness, but many; and not merely many, but with respect to all the actions which the metaphor's *part of speech* renders relevant: Antony's followers eat like dogs, sleep like dogs, pee like dogs, no doubt do it doggie fashion, and so on; but they don't necessarily have long loose silken liver-colored curly hair and floppy ears, a feathered tail, or wet, full, pity-imploring eyes, because our model has been made to serve as a verb which must perforce *act on its object,* not as an adjective which cosmetically calls for its qualities. So when his false friends spaniel'd him, Antony was treed.

A metaphor, furthermore, has a *focus,* in this case indicated by the phrase 'at heels,' which starts off our interpretation at this point in the maze of its meanings, rather than at some other. A focus may be narrow, sharp, or soft, wide-angled, doubled, or fuzzy.

Finally, there is no metaphor which does not reach figuration without flying in the face of some factual commonplace,

The lady's arm lay like a length of snake around my neck . . .

without violating some grammatical rule,

She lady'd her way around the room . . .

or outraging some social norm or prevailing standard,

> Never tip your tie to a lady . . .

and sometimes the metaphor is uppity in the syntactic, semantic, and pragmatic dimensions simultaneously,

> No lady he, Luke lolled inside the lacy confines of his lingerie
> like a shopgirl lingering in her Sunday bed . . .

We must not be misled by words or phrases such as 'looks like,' 'as,' 'way,' 'though,' and 'as if,' into supposing that some simple prosy comparison is being made, because, more often than not, the simile words themselves are being used with metaphorical intent and effect:

> Her hands felt like ice, and soon they had melted in mine.

Change the critical preposition slightly, and another meaning emerges:

> Her hands felt like ice, and shortly they had melted into mine.

Ordinary comparisons simply lack commitment. One might have begun by meaning that the lady's hands were quite cold, but having said something else, something stronger, a new belief is born—one which can carry us this way or that:

> Her hands felt like ice cubes sliding down my back.

If I said that "the dawn was like dusk during the eclipse," we might take my remark to contain a relatively factual comparison, something it certainly could be doing; but its forthright character can be quickly subverted by giving it, for instance, a more Homeric focus:

> The dawn was like dusk during the eclipse,
> its fabled rosy fingers the pale bones of
> a buried corpse.

Finally, not all the metaphors in a literary work are immediately or obviously verbal. The pine tree which Antony goes to stand by is already a metaphor for him. Not only is the pine tree indicated in the text, one can presumably see its painted cardboard outline on the stage. In this case, the cutout designates the tree, which, in turn, stands for the word, which then can be a metaphor for Antony. The road in *Waiting for Godot* is of course an image. It is the image of a road. But what word does the road stand for? If we abide by the lesson we rather perversely wrenched from *Nausea,* things have no meaning unless they stand for—become—signs; for once that path upon the stage is read as a road, and the road we've reached is rendered as the word, the road can keep a different company: with 'tramp,' with 'bicycle,' with 'ditch,' and not simply with a tramp, a bicycle, or a ditch. A particular text can contain a straightforwardly literal description of two objects or events which nevertheless possess a metaphorical relation to one another, as the parallel scenes of cattle sale and seduction do in *Madame Bovary.* However, the figurative relation between them does not exist in some "reality," but is indicated by the placement of the two scenes in the text. In short, although not all the metaphors in a literary work are immediately or obviously verbal, they ultimately are, however subtle their action and connection.

Yet you never can tell. Out of a cloud that merely looks dragonish may come a bolt of lightning like a sudden exhalation of fire.

If we were to use the word 'metaphorical' to describe the relation between a word on the one hand and an object on the other, our use of the word 'metaphorical' would be metaphorical.

The tension we might feel between the two terms of a metaphor in any particular example is exactly that rivalry between data and design I've been speaking of, and, in not a few instances, it is difficult to be certain which word is in command, the interpenetrations of meaning seem so mutual.

We say that Beckett's empty road is an image, but of what we are not so certain. We point to the leafless tree in *Godot,* or at Winnie, buried to her neck in stage clay, or to the objects she hauls out of her shopping bag, and argue that they, too, are symbols; but without the same confidence and security we have with Shakespeare's spaniels, because the object of the image has been suppressed. Sometimes the suppression is momentary, as it is with 'hearts,' sometimes it is permanent, as in the case of *Endgame*'s ashcans; more rarely, the interpretive system itself may shoulder its way into the world it wishes to render, becoming, as we might say, "one of the boys"; as though the fifth apple we counted were to be eaten by its numeral, which then pretended to be red, tart, crisp, and—in the apple's place—enclose a core. Normally we might have said of Gregor Samsa that he was a little no-account man who lived in the cracks of life like a bug between boards, but Kafka causes the image to become the character, which Shakespeare might have done had he allowed Cleopatra and Antony to disappear leaving only their large tumultuous hearts to carry on the action on the stage. In Gregor Samsa's situation, the interpretive system succeeds in abolishing its object, in taking its place. But a bug of what kind, we might ask. Why, a bug in a bed—a bedbug—the sperm that Samsa's name suggests in German, and the immediate meaning of 'bedbug' to the imagination. Hence in Kafka's *Metamorphosis* not only does the interpretive term become the agent of the action, it then receives its own appropriate figuration.

Certain philosophical systems can claim to discover conditions and laws in our life because they have become so enamored of their interpretive systems, where alone such conditions and laws exist, they do not realize that they are dreaming in their dressing gowns and an unconsuming fire is lit; yet it is precisely this ancient belief that in the beginning was the Word (for many a mathematician, probably the word 'One' or the symbols '1 +') which allows them to describe the general principles of creation with such accuracy; and, although the likely truth is that the real world fell out of bed being born and broke like a dish, so that whatever once might have worked no longer does, and whatever was whole once is now in pieces; all the same, like Plato in his *Timaeus* or Leibniz in his *Monadology,* they still approach the cosmos as if it were a fabricated object, designed down to the last detail like a novel by Nabokov, and therefore obedient to every logical and esthetic necessity, and to nothing else. Had God had the wit of Henry James or Alfred North Whitehead, He would have done better by us; as, I am sure, were there one, He would have had, and would have done.

A monad is a spirit aware of a world. The world which any monad more or less clearly apprehends is one for which every element and event has a sufficient reason—a ground in God—so that each alteration is an act of definition—of innermost exfoliation—and would be seen to occur with absolute necessity were we able to grasp that immense whole of which it offers, among indefinitely many, only one point of view. Nevertheless, it promises itself a perspective from which a completeness can, in principle, be inferred with the same sort of condensed immediacy with which we have sometimes experienced a short, hard, sudden noise as a slam, and in that slam heard a violent closing, and from the character and direction of the noise understood what kind of door it was, and then sensed the anger in the arm which swung it shut, felt the feeling in another which created this signal of rejection and departure, the final fate of an affair compressed into a single sound of severance and settlement; so that one hears it, weakens, trembles, knows: we shall have to sell our Miró.

I cannot have in my consciousness the actual consciousness of another, so there is no direct way for me to know if we are seeing or feeling the same things—you causing the doorslam, I hearing it, both inferring and fearing divorce, both lost and out of love in that instant, cutting an aquatint in two with a lawyer's shears—because we are wholly window-less with regard to one another, to use Leibniz's wonderful word; so we must depend upon the harmony (not of our loves but of our lives) pre-established between us by God.

Whether any of this is really true of human beings like ourselves, im-mured in our morbid and measly perspectives, it is a rather firmer fact about fiction. Made of concepts and their connections, of vestigial twitches in the larynx, gray paradigms of sound, the novel moves through the mind like a procession of speech; and as it does so it largely replaces, like music, our own interior life—those little vistas of bed sheet, table, and freeway, our immodest mumblings of self-justification and praise, our low heats and frosts of absent feeling—with its grander avenues of interest, its lucent objects and eloquent emotions; for a novel is a mind like a monad aware of a world; and as we, while reading, live it, we live within a metaphorical model of our own, even though the two may seem as distant as my life is from Sancho Panza's; as different as the careening carriage of the Princess Cassamassima is from the mere point on a pen-ciled path it momentarily may have become for a criminal calculating its interception; and it is the aim of the pages which add up to *Remem-brance of Things Past* or *A Man Without Qualities* to construct a thick conceptual system whose meanings will similarly intercept and penetrate and alter ours—as I fancy I see the dastardly Count Luciano this minute lifting a lacy chemise; for we are the courtiers now who nuzzle our masters, or who break the buckles on our breastplates as our hearts en-large in the heat of battle; and it is natural that we should resist having the details of our lives replaced by others which do not ennoble or enlarge or excite us, or favor a Brand Name Realism over Handke's dislocations or Calvino's shimmering cities.

The narrator's mother in *A Sorrow Beyond Dreams* prefers books which she can profitably compare with her own life.

> "I'm not like that," she sometimes said, as though the author had written about *her*. To her, every book was an account of her own life, and in reading she came to life; for the first time, she came out of her shell; she learned to talk about *herself*, and with each book she had more ideas on the subject.

We needn't narrow our reading eye to such a slit, or look so literally upon the text; nevertheless, it is our world, as we most broadly perceive it, which the novel intersects, interpenetrates, and transforms. Like any metaphor, the novel, too, will have a scope, several undulating layers of meaning, a hierarchy of structures and organizing principles, a focus, its kind of commitment; and even those realistic novels which claim to be comparisons whose accuracy can be verified by careful accountants will often reveal themselves to be more metaphorically like us than promised, and turn us into their terrors and their tears, as that icy hand I mentioned a moment ago was first moist, and then moisture—to disappear into a towel.

If the war within the word is a fierce one, the reader's reluctance to submit to the novel's transforming power is like that of a threatened people. Ordinary readers want their view of the world reinforced; they want to be reassured that wickedness is really wickedness, that all is well in just the way they wish it were, that all is not well in just the way they like to fear; they want every representation to resemble them; they want to wear a text like gardening pants; they want romance, escape, or sameness. Even most critics imagine that it is *Terra Nostra,* or whatever, they are interpreting, when it is *Hopscotch,* or whatever, which is interpreting *them.* To let go of one's own vision of life and let another order alter it; to become a different monad for a moment, often one which will look through every apparent paradise and see only hells; one which will force us out of our worldly interests into a different world's disinterested contemplation; which will not pander or curtsy or gently or easily mean, but one which will mean too much, too precisely, too entirely, with the total commitment of the turtle's snap; above all, one which is perilously perfect in both its pleasures and its pains, necessary to itself as reality rarely is; formful and orderly in a disheartening, inhuman way, cruelly conceptual; one which dares to make beautiful all the causes we curse, and all the brutal ugliness of life as well, when Cinderella'd by the right language; to adopt another mind and find your own is paltry and unworthy: how can this be thrilling? something to be sought after? what is the point past pure humiliation?

Since the novel is made of so-called facts in a so-called system, the reader's readiest ally is always the data, for the data can be domesticated; the data can be $\sqrt{}$'d; the data belong to daily life somewhere or other; the data suggest that the novelist has a wholesome acquaintance with things—is sound, observant, sober—since data don't dance; and the reader rushes nervously through the word in search of some object in the world he has a date with the way Alice's white rabbit dithered down his hole; but the organization of this data—its shaping and subordination, the making of its meanings—is essentially resisted; because it is here that the metaphor is most likely to rearrange the reader's life; not by speaking of farmyards or jungles when the reader walks a city side-walk, or carries heavy water to the elephants, has money, beard, good looks, the pox; but when sentences similar to Gertrude Stein's

It looked like a garden but he had hurt himself by accident.

affright him like a flying saucer; where spaces are created like kites to fly time; where a soul may be pitched like a nomad's tent, a calculus of characters constructed, a voice given tongue; then everything has been rephilosophized, and even ordinary objects seem strange and lack resemblance when we recognize them recombined within a system the way we follow the passage of insult and injury through parrot, monkey, cat, dog, Indian, in Katherine Anne Porter's paragraph—a pecking-order prelude to our voyage on a ship of fools.

Or do we really imagine we are reading about other people?

Or reading about?

Novels which allow me to turn the tables, which permit me to be the metaphor, the model, to find the focus, to fill in and furnish, are accommodating but lousy novels. Their forms have to be as loose as the wires of a weak fence. Bad critics treat good books as if they were lousy novels. Even though their copies were complimentary and haven't cost them, they sprawl on top as if they had paid.

Consider all those who have endeavored to make over Marx, mimic Nietzsche, play the positivist, or prattle phenomenology, and compare them to those critics who have thought they had jaws hinged like snakes, and could swallow masterpieces like small pigs. So in their pride they become hillious for a moment; but Balzac and Flaubert and Mann and Proust, they return alive without the benefit of the whale's belch or woodsman's ax. Slowly the swallowed systematically supplants the swallower. *Mann ist was er isst,* after all, even if it is the letter *S.*

Of the enemies of art (and what is a war without enemies?), perhaps the worst are those who will not read, sense, see, hear, sing, the word. For them it is not even a note. They look down upon a passage of Beckett, for example, as though it were a false trail in the snow; they will not step into such tracks. Yet if the inscription is skimped, *what is real?*

A novel is a mind aware of a world, but if the novel is not performed; if it is not moved as it ought to be through the space of the spirit, the notation notes not; because our metaphors, our theories, our histories, do not merely fall upon their page like pictures sent in black pricks over a wire; they must be enacted, entered into; they must be rolled like drums; they must be marched in columns, formed in hollow squares; they must be sometimes quietly hummed, or possibly panted. (The symbol ' ▨ ' stands for a pant-point.)

> past moments ▨ old dreams back again ▨ or fresh like those that pass ▨ or things ▨ things always ▨ and memories ▨ I say them as I hear them ▨ murmur them in the mud

That's *How It Is*.

> in me ▨ that were without ▨ when the panting stops ▨ scraps of an ancient voice ▨ in me ▨ not mine

> my life ▨ last state ▨ last version ▨ ill-heard ▨ ill-recaptured ▨ ill-murmured in the mud ▨ brief movements of the lower face ▨ losses everywhere

Yes. Right. Losses everywhere. Shortness of breath. But you expect some losses. In a war.

THE SOUL INSIDE THE SENTENCE

1

Since we should listen with our eyes when we read, it is not rough justice if we see with our ears when we hear, but a scale so finely balanced we can set all difference down to dust; therefore let us begin in what seems the best way possible by facing our adversary squarely and providing ourselves with a few sounds put together as beautifully as English prose permits, on a subject that is not amiss our purpose either, but rather its honed and subtle edge.

Certain funeral urns of pagan origin were once unearthed near Norwich, and Sir Thomas Browne, not then of course a knight, confided to a neighboring friend the earnest lessons, as he perceived them, of these tombs. The roundly orchestrated paragraphs of *Urn-Burial* remind us how short life is, how certain death, how deep and incorruptible oblivion, and how always futile it has been to commemorate the soft body's brevities by means of its somewhat sterner bones.

> Circles and right lines limit and close all bodies, and the mortall right-lined circle must conclude and shut up all. There is no antidote against the Opium of time, which temporally considereth all things; Our Fathers finde their graves in our short memories, and sadly tell us how we may be buried in our Survivors. Gravestones tell truth scarce fourty years: Generations passe while some trees stand, and old Families last not three Oaks. To be read by bare Inscriptions like many in *Gruter,* to hope for Eternity by AEnigmatical Epithetes, or first letters of our names, to be studied by Antiquaries, who we were, and have new Names given us like many of the Mummies, are cold consolations unto the Students of perpetuity, even by everlasting Languages.

These sentences have a psychology because they have a soul; and how anything like a soul, even as ethereal as it is by reputation, can contrive to squeeze itself among so many sickly if not lifeless syllables; how any series of ordinary words containing, in this case, Christian commonplaces and the pulpit's platitudes, can rise up from its page, not merely like a snake from its basket, but into immaterial lengths of song, as though the serpent had become the music which entranced it: that rare bit of magic, and its unmasking, is the elusive object of this enterprise.

It is not unfair to make our initial selection from the greatest age of English prose, for that is precisely what we need to confront: greatness; and wonder at it, and in wondering wonder further at the will—the will to create such greatness—like a wondrous wind behind it.

Words are with us everywhere. In our erotic secrecies, in our sleep. We're often no more aware of them than our own spit, although we use them oftener than legs. So of course in the customary shallow unconscious sense, we comprehend the curse, the prayer, and the whoop. We've heard roars of rage as raw as grubbed-up roots, and hunger's whimper from at least the dog. We've digested suave excuses like iced cake, and gotten sick on slander, drunk on lies. With words we follow the metaled links of honest argument and harken with the same ear to the huckster's pitch and the king's command. Because of words, deep designs can be licked from a shallow dish, although not a few false promises, grandly served, are soon flat as a warm drink. Yet they lift our spirits—these poor weak words. They guide and they coerce. They settle fights, initiate disputes, compound errors, elicit truth. How long have we known it? They gather dust, too, and spoil in jokes which draw our laughter like the flies.

Yet how are we to understand an activity which seems as natural as making water; and on the surface so much like the hoot and holler of the crowd as to be quite indistinct from churchy verses, accepted sentiment, songstuff, speeches, gossip, news; when in fact it is rare as eclipses, unnatural as the gait of a classical dancer, and otherwise so far from any point of contact with ordinary rhyme and verbal rattle that we might more acceptably compare Columbus to a requiem or iodine with Indiana. Among the thousands of words and the millions of their combinations, even among the serious meditations of devoted and intelligent women and men, in a life of principled and practiced writing, only occasionally can we observe Beauty on the verge of coming into being— unobtrusively, almost in shame—shall we say the way Aphrodite slipped ashore on the calcified splash of her father's balls?

And what of the desire, then, to manufacture sentences which will persist past all utility, live outrageously beyond their means like exiled aristocracy or reckless *nouveau riche,* outlasting fashion and every novelty of thought or fad in phrasing? sentences in language like a vaulter's limber pole to leap times, to transcend the initial circumstances of their making as well as each succeeding situation which might reasonably require them, as if one set of Last Words might be properly the first learned, and so to welcome, as if summoned, as if always appropriately dressed, every moment after?

I am speaking of sentences, for instance, like this one:

> What a deale of cold busines doth a man mis-spend the better part of life in! in scattering *complements,* tendring *visits,* gathering and venting *newes,* following *Feasts* and *Playes,* making a little winter-love in a darke corner.

Or even more simply:

> Gardens were before gardeners and but some hours after the earth.

Soon the hand which shaped them, and the mouth, too, which spoke what the fingers first formed, is left entirely behind, so that these sentences of Ben Jonson and Sir Thomas Browne are as much ours now as theirs. Only their quality continues to give them a right to be. Displaced to study hall or bus station, uttered under the heart as beneath the breath, they act like anxious tics; repressed, they return: and we protect and repeat them as though they were charms against our insecurities.

In general, work of the highest quality does not come about in a moment, nor has it a single source called genius, talent, or inspiration. The muses were invented as a cover for our ignorance. The factors involved are alarmingly complex, and disturbingly variable. Only in the arts would a man expect to paint on weekends with any prospect of success, or indite verses on the cuffs of his account books. Physics would not be taken up so lightly, or mathematics either. The wider course and spread of events which mold men and women and make for their achievement is like a life of weather in which only a few bolts are likely to startle the blue sky, or snow cool the Sahara; and we know perfectly well that fine work is usually the result of a long process of preparation, plus an intense concentration of skill and knowledge on some special and specific problem. Without the burning glass, a genial sunshine sets not even tinder to smoking.

Since it is not difficult to distinguish a lifetime of athletic activity from one spring spent in training, or that, in turn, from a single contest, it should not be hard to mark the differences between conception and gestation, practice and performance, trigger and load, or measure the small but rarely sparkable gap between what's simply acceptable work and what's rare and accomplished; yet we regularly make a mess of the matter, confusing the perfect poet the poseur is concerned to project with the real artist's ordinary boring imperfections, and refusing to observe the qualitative change of mind which comes between composition and revision, writing and erasing, changing and retaining, or dreaming and doing, the way second thoughts come down between lovers like a drawn shade; as if we did not want to know what it is to think and see and form and feel in writing, to repeat, redo, revise, get on, excuse, backtrack, straighten, set aside; as if it were all one to misjudge, invent, accept, construe, steal, ponder, cut, approve, give up, knuckle under—possibly because they all very often occur in the same time, place, person, and creative gesture; as if writing were one skill, and not twenty; as if it took one kind of mind, and not many.

It should not be terribly difficult, either, to recognize that the kind of character an artist needs in order to get any sort of work done in our world will not greatly explain the character that work has when—in relief, or in pain and disappointment—it does get done at last. The obstacles overcome, the fences taken at a stride or slowly and awkwardly climbed, are left behind. They are the wake of writing, not the hull of the craft.

> For fourteen years I have not had a day's real health; I have wakened sick and gone to bed weary; and I have done my work unflinchingly. I have written in bed and written out of it, written in hemorrhages, written in sickness, written torn by coughing, written when my head swam for weakness; and for so long, it seems to me I have won my wager and recovered my glove . . . I was made for a contest, and the Powers have so willed that my battlefield should be this dingy, inglorious one of the bed and the physic bottle.

This passage tells us, of course, of Robert Louis Stevenson's illnesses and his courage ("Character is what he has," James said), and particularly of his pride, which it hoists like a flag; but in the quotation itself there is a quality which neither the author's personality nor his environment will explain—its doubled-up *W*s, its cadence, its *energy*, its shape—for Stevenson was writing here to Meredith, and he was not going to appear unshaven in such a presence ("Before all things, he is a writer with a style," James said).

When a real inspirational storm strikes, as it did Rilke, it strikes not John Jerk but a genius; it is as prepared for as a blitzkrieg; and it is the summation of a lifetime of commitment and calculation. If we think it odd the gods should always choose a voice so full and gloriously throated, when they could presumably toot through any instrument, we should remember that it is their choice of such a golden throat, each time, that makes them gods.

The miseries of adolescence—loneliness, lack of recognition, status, selfhood, sexual need—prompt many to seek relief in writing, and even in those instances where skills are easily acquired and talent seems plentiful, the passion for the beautiful is soon as dry as paint, and the writer (now in the breastfallen middle of her age) sits silent as a hill, or is content to repeat what previously pleased, or (rich now, famous, sexually successful) allows his former cool and skeptical regard to be as warm and generous as his fatuous admirers' misty eyes, so that, fattened by her own vain estimation, yet Orlando no longer, the writer's weaknesses spread like the flesh, and the odor of the alleged "late manner" (unlike the redolent flowering of pure James) is that of a rancid youth or aged maid; therefore the psychological disabilities which propelled the writer into prose in the first place must remain unresolved, the relief obtained paltry and wretched indeed; the pain which preceded the pain of the present must painfully continue to the last; the mad raw youth must be the old man mad; for what is fame, don't we pretend to believe? but a distracting noise, and sexual pleasure a promise which draws itself away with a toot like a departing train? what is the strength of a steel pen when the soul's grasp on itself is loosening? what pride of prick or cunt's conceit can disguise from the spirit the spirit's repeated humiliations? where can money go to buy more genius, don't we say? in the wet earth, as Browne warns, will wealth keep away the common rot, improve our prose, purchase a plot on Parnassus, when our modest dot of immortality faints like a distant star in a bright and boundless sky?

Then they should cherish their afflictions, one supposes; but, otherwise, writers as persons are surely as various as books themselves; although, again in general, we can expect to find them ambitious, almost by definition, persistent, stubborn, single-minded and selfish, diligent and devoted, fierce and determined—we might say, "obsessed"—for there will be few to encourage and fewer to reward; thus we are likely to find them incorruptible and patient, too, with a passion for perfection—as far as their work is concerned—vain as flowers; yet away from their desks and papers and their plots, they may be lazy cheats and careless liars, inconstant and insecure and simple-minded and vulgar and dense, or vague and evenly agreeable, softly spousy, uncritical and undemanding, kind, sweet, modest (ah, do go on), scheming, mean, tyrannical, plain. They smoke, pop pills, and drink a lot. They commit industriously gray adulteries, complain of editors, the laziness of agents, the foolishness of critics, the fickleness of the public, their own lack of fame, of love, their deplorable lack of money, their conveniently bad health. Envy is as common as the fly. So is bad posture, fat, eyeglasses, genital deficiency. But we could find similar constellations of qualities around every occupation. These collections twinkle but light little, and they come out for the hack as often as the artist.

Alcohol, like illness, may momentarily reduce a writer's level of repression, cigarettes may give the nerves something to do, sex may strengthen a weakened ego, drugs may dull the sense of failure, coffee may produce an illusion of alertness, seasons may supply subjects or encourage moods, energies may ebb and flow through times of day like sunlight among clouds, little rituals may give comfort, anal ordering some security, sensory cues, like those apples whose odor as they spoiled gave Schiller a lift, may stimulate the flow of that saliva which moistens the pen in poets who work like dogs. Creative rites are rites of magic, and, like magic, cannot explain success. Concentration, of course, is necessary. Fears, petty worries must be put aside. And as one's relation to one's work deepens, the level of tension rises, anxiety accompanies accomplishment, skepticism, like a skull, grins at one's approval, and the fear, when things are going well, that the thread will be lost, the onward rush cease, the next word fail to appear, becomes nearly intolerable, as is the thought that it may go on, winding one tight and toward a resolution which will never come; for climaxes in writing are rare, and mostly it is plod, mostly it is routine—the same cold flesh on the same old spouse—mostly it is dull and tense and hard, and rarely does it seem creative.

'Creativity' has become a healthy, even a holy word. Its popularity is recent, its followers alarmingly American. The command has gone out from gurus of every persuasion: be creative! an injunction which is followed by the assurance that it's actually better for you than bowling; and millions have eagerly, anxiously responded. The pursuit and practice of something labeled creativity is now as epidemic as tennis or jogging, and apparently will be as difficult to discourage, now it's here, as trailer parks, poverty, or moviegoing.

These merely social phenomena would be unimportant to our theme if they did not conveniently illustrate a confusion which has crippled most psychological studies of the creative process from the beginning. One common assumption has been that ambition, aim, or intention is psychologically sufficient: that if I regularly stumble over a stick held three feet in the air, I am as much of a vaulter's mind as a vaulter; that if I am in agony over the smudges on my canvas, my agony is as Rothko's or Cézanne's; that if I am struggling to compose a be-my-Valentine, I am as angry and frustrated as Hart Crane was when he hurled his Underwood out a window because it refused to write in Spanish; but if I'm displacing the bar at three feet, it's clear that I haven't encountered the vaulter's peculiar difficulties yet, and if I am fudging my tax returns, I haven't suddenly entered the world of mathematical invention like a Dorothy dropped in Oz. Poker for peanuts or pennies is not the same game as one with limitless stakes, and there are certain driving skills which come into play only at high speeds; so that even if there's a resemblance between walking a fallen log and crossing a piece of structural steel amidst the worries of work, wind, and altitude, the achievements are in no way the same, although, again, exhortations like "careful to keep your balance" are in both cases appropriate and certainly appreciated.

People call themselves poets and painters, and seek help for their failures, as I might come to a psychiatrist to discover the causes of my vaulter's block or to find out why I can't get anywhere in nuclear physics. Indeed, regularly people push through the turnstiles of the critic's day who feel very strongly the need to pass as poets, to be called "creative," to fit themselves into a certain social niche, acquire an identity the way one acquires plants there's no time to tend or goldfish that can't be kept alive, and their problems are important and interesting and genuine enough; but they are not the problems of poets as poets, any more than the child who tiptoes to school on the tops of fences has the steelworker's nerves or nervousness or rightly deserves his wage.

Oftener than ever, artists are inventing their own forms, and when there is no model or master; when there is, in effect, nothing to copy; when a loose scatter of words on a page nicely impersonates a poem; counterfeiting becomes easy, since it is no longer, itself, an art. Mannikins aren't ugly or inadequate people, though they may be ugly or inadequate mannikins, and most of the verses we encounter we do not encounter in poems—neither in good ones nor in bad. Consequently many studies of creative people are not studies of creative people; they are not even studies of people who mimic or imitate creative people; for if I, being as noteless and unmusical as a stone, sat down to compose a symphony, the sounds I made on the piano, the blots I put on my staffy paper, would be child's play, not imitation, and only another child, as ignorant of everything as I am, would be taken in.

If mastering an art were like learning to walk or drive a car, if it were merely a matter of fitting our psyches into the world like a key; or even if it involved cleansing ourselves of unconscious contaminations until we were released to do what was always well within our power—to swim under water, kill the king, maintain an erection—then we could treat creativity as a craft the way Aristotle does, and shelve it alongside the other intellectual virtues; but there are no manuals for the imagination; it does not make love in a well-lighted room; its failures are as hard to understand as its successes are, for if most verse is not yet poetry of any kind, most poetry of every kind is poor from birth, and this poverty is oddly as difficult to achieve by rule, advice, or aim as inherited wealth. When the Duchess of Newcastle writes

> Life scums the cream of Beauty with Time's spoon . . .

she becomes one of the sour immortals, or when, according to legend, Alfred Austin, perhaps without peer among impoverished poets, composed this couplet:

> They went across the veldt
> As hard as they could pelt . . .

he deserved his laureate. To write as badly as Wordsworth is not easy. Even for Wordsworth it was as difficult as when Wordsworth was writing well.

So even when the writer is undeniably great, or at least large, as in the case of Dostoevsky, the creative element is seldom the real concern of the student. The author's works are treated as though they were longitudinal reveries, pipe dreams, couch speech, through which, like a clouded window, the psychophile hopes to catch sight of his beloved, much as medieval theologians peered through the word and works of God toward what was presumably the crystalline source of His Being; except that the manner of these investigations leaves us in some doubt about why they were undertaken, since the genius is soon gone from Goethe, the artist left out of Proust, the poet omitted from Hölderlin, the prophet erased from Blake. Freud was certainly frank enough when he wrote at the beginning of his essay on Dostoevsky that "before the problem of the creative artist, analysis must, alas, lay down its arms."

Among such abandoned arms, do I dare to pick up even a pouch of damp power?

2

At the conclusion of Freud's 1915 paper on the unconscious, while considering with his customary unempirical daring the passage of such material into our awareness, Freud extended the views he had earlier expressed in *Die Traumdeutung* by suggesting that before any idea could become conscious it had first to find a sign, and that consequently the content of the preconscious must consist of thoughts which had found verbal formulation. It is one of the mind's more marvelous moments, and made at least this heart leap up. By pulling at the one end offered us, how many silken scarves, like the tail of a kite so far away we cannot see it, can be drawn from the sleeve of this incredible magician?

Initially, and from the psychoanalytic point of view, we might imagine that just as dreams use the scraps of a previous sleeplessness to piece themselves into being, so our ideas of objects, too, might float up to present view on the backs of our past perceptions of them, but Freud believed instead that

> thought proceeds in systems that are so remote from the original residues of perception that they have no longer retained anything of the qualities of these residues, so that in order to become conscious the content of the thought-systems needs to be reinforced by new qualities.[1]

Our earliest communications may have taken place in silence, through the cozy inferences and the warm smells of touch; all the same, cooing continues to accompany it. The sounds we make as babes, unlike the things we touch when we kick, or smell when we root, or taste when we suck, are among the first sensations we fashion for ourselves like our own pee or poop, or the sense of movement in our muscles. Even now I cannot cry out color and thereby create it, or flavor my saliva with a wine-dark savory, or saddle my nose with leather like a horse; but I can sing, I can chant, I can talk; so I think we can set it down as our first general principle that the satisfactions of babbling are particularly

---

1. Sigmund Freud, "The Unconscious," in *Collected Papers,* IV (New York: Basic Books, 1959), p. 134–5.

intense in our budding poet, because we soon sense that our noises do not simply leak from us like a washerless tap, but that these sounds, which are such dramatically effective parts of the external world, are securely fastened to our will. *They are something we produce.* Surrounded by our own scent, slowly aware of our limbs, we soon swaddle ourselves in our own sounds, as we shall live later with the dearest companion of our life: the voice of consciousness, the words which become the self.

We should never forget, then, that from that very beginning, when the word made the world, the word has been one of the most important "objects" in human experience. We were born into language as into perception, pain and pleasure. We shortly associated it with heads, eyes, lips, tongues, and eventually with the hidden internality of things. In turn, we manufactured our own noise, and long before we knew the meaning words bore, we knew the meanings which bore them, the emotional contexts of revenge and reward in which they were formed.

It is of course the dynamics of speech which allows us to communicate ahead of any understanding: the whisper, mutter, and war cry, the drone, drawl, slur, bark, stutter, scream, or otherwise the various precisions of articulation appropriate to the actor, pedant, or priest, every intonation and inflection too, the rhythm and the pace, every overtone, projection, inner energy, the recognizable return of the same sounds, the total up and down of the verbal path, stress and pause and peace, the facial surround—the smiling and the shouting mouth—these give to the talk they contain an almost gestural expressiveness, symptomatic as a blush on the cheek or blood in the penis, just as the configurations of the parental face and body underlie the emotional life of most lines and shapes.

Language without rhythm, without physicality, without the undertow of that sea which once covered everything and from which the land first arose like a cautious toe—levelless language, in short, voiceless type, pissless prose—can never be artistically complete. Sentences which run on without a body have no soul. They will be felt, however conceptually well connected, however well designed by the higher bureaus of the mind, to go through our understanding like the sharp cold blade of a skate over ice.

Upon the crucifixion of Christ, "cold care and cumbrance has come to us all," the *Piers Plowman* poet writes, and the passion of that simple and immortal line lies as deep inside us as our bones.

The language of science should serve the reality principle; the language of art serves the soul. When Flaubert wrote to George Sand that

"It is hardly necessary that words express ideas. So long as one assembles them in harmonious sequence, the object of art is served," he undoubtedly went too far. Meeting this condition is clearly necessary, but Tennyson, Poe, and Swinburne, among others, have shown that it is not sufficient.

Though he may never understand what he's been taught, a child soon learns that it's not his wants which his parents so persistently oppose, but his method of expressing them—his imperious haste, his tactless greed—and that if he finds the right way, not only will his needs be met, the meeting will be eager. It's not permissible to say you want sexual pleasure from your mom, but you can say you want to be like dad when you grow up, and even dad will pat his little rival proudly on the head.

If we think of ourselves, for a moment, purely in verbal terms, as a function and source of words (appropriate enough for a writer, and nothing less than the truth in the case of fictional characters), our unconscious becomes a voiceless darkness, dark because it's mute, and "the force that through the green fuse drives the flower" is simply undifferentiated instinct, and its trials are those of any leaf reaching for light, or root searching for moisture.

Society civilizes us by stylizing our desires, and it is not, as Gertrude Stein has said, the various facts of life which separate one generation or one culture from another, but the manner of their composition. The suggestion which Freud makes (one that is central to the account of creativity I am in the fuddled process of proposing) is that when thoughts are kept from consciousness by being denied their signs, it is not the thought itself the door is slammed on, but certain expressions of it, so that the ego is required to write and rewrite until its unfriendly editor is satisfied.

If every original desire can be thought of as a secret sentence of the self, then every modification can be regarded as a method of rewriting, initially so that the desire can be allowed expression, and eventually so that the desire can be satisfied.[2] There are six basic elements in such sentences, and it is these which are altered as revision proceeds: (1) the wish itself, originally an undifferentiated lust, a roar of wind through the loins, the belly, and the bowels; (2) the alleged owner of the wish (an "I" which is fronting for an "it"); (3) the strength of the wish measured in terms of the mobilization of the resources of the psyche in

---

2. I have discussed many of these points at greater length in "Anatomy of Mind," in *The World Within the Word,* pp. 208–252.

its service; (4) the valence of the wish, its active or passive character;
(5) the object in the world associated through experience with the reduction of the drive; and finally (6) the organ of the body through which
satisfaction is to be achieved.

Instincts are transformed in accordance with certain quasi-logical
operations until acceptable versions are found. These are compromises,
sometimes, of an oddly ambivalent character, like "yes, we have no
bananas, especially if you like pears" (and, of course, what will be
found acceptable will vary with age as well as other circumstances).
The following exchange between the id and its editors may illustrate,
though crudely and incompletely, a part of the process.

Original Wish: [Diffusion]	I want the pleasure of touching myself.	Infantile Narcissism: Enjoyment of Self in Self.
Original Wish: [Localization]	I want the pleasure of playing with my genitals.	
Denial:	THAT'S MASTURBATION!	
Original Wish: [Relocation]	I want the pleasure of playing with my toes. . . sucking my thumb. . . picking my nose. . .	
Denial:	WHAT HORRIBLE HABITS!	
Introjection: [Same Sex]	I want the pleasure of touching your genitals.	Adolescent Narcissism: Enjoyment of Self in an-other self of the same sex. Bonding.
Denial:	THAT'S HOMOSEXUALITY!	
Introjection: [Opposite Sex]	I want the pleasure of touching your genitals.	Adult Narcissism: Enjoy-ment of Self in another self of the opposite sex. Marriage.
Denial:	ONLY IF YOU ARE OLD ENOUGH! ONLY IF YOU ARE MARRIED! ONLY TO BEGET CHILDREN! ONLY IF X IS OF THE RIGHT CLASS, RACE, RELIGION, ETC.!	
Projection:	You want the pleasure of touch-ing my genitals.	Exhibitionism or Prudery, depending on psychologi-cal use.
Denial:	YOU MATA HARI! YOU VAMP!	

Partial Reversal: [Change of Voice or Role]	I want the pleasure of being touched.	Passivity.
Denial:	TROLLOP! SLUT!	
Full Reversal: [Change of Voice and Valence]	I want the shame of being mo- lested, raped, beaten, etc.	Masochism.
Denial:	BE A MAN! DON'T BE A PATSY! WOMEN REALLY ASK FOR IT. OK, TAKE THAT!	
Sublimation: [Object/Organ Substitution]	I really enjoy working with clay.	Narcissism of Art: En- joyment of Self in things.
Denial:	THAT'S CHILD'S PLAY! TAKE UP ACCOUNTING!	
Repression:	I want the pleasure of touching you with what I most want touched.	Mutual Masturbation or Sexual Intercourse
Denial:	I WOULDN'T LET YOU TOUCH ME WITH CLARK GABLE'S PHALLUS!	
Repression:	I love you.	Romantic Love, or Mutual Masturbation of both Mind and Body.
	That was a very touching thing to say. Say it again, and again, and again.	
Art:	All right. "How do I love thee, let me count the ways . . ."	

We lose a great deal when we civilize our requests. Style alters its object. The tantrum displays the urgency, the dismay, the anger, the bodily involvement, both the power and the impotence—the drama— of the demand. But we learn to ask politely, discreetly, deviously, indirectly. We learn the art of acceptable disguise. Nonetheless, although we may secretly express our voyeurism by exhibiting ourselves, hide our envy behind excessive admiration, our fear of rejection behind a generalized contempt, front our masochism with aggression; still, satisfying one desire by indulging in its opposite makes for a slender settlement. Whatever the public result, sweet Narcissus is the one we care for, whose features we love, whose genitals we want to be in bliss.

Writing, I shall outrageously say, is blissing. But at what remove? And these days, with what sort of amorous engine?

So my guess is that the superego says no, not to the wishes of the id, but to certain formulations of them. Art is an elaborate euphemism for what the soul says is dirt. And the censor may say no so often, with such ancestral severity, that we think the desire itself is being denied. Certainly the primal crime is not the deed, the satisfaction of some disallowed wish, it is the very possession of the desire in the first place, for our psyche believes as Jesus did that if a man looks at a woman with adultery in his loins, he has committed adultery with her in his heart; and if he has committed adultery with her in his heart, he might just as well have committed adultery with his loins . . . never mind the contradiction of his continuing ache. Nonetheless, we will allow ourselves to express any wish we can find a suitable code for. Mother minds if Sally wants to play with her stools (so unladylike and messy), but finger paints are perfectly all right, and so are rolls of clay and lumps of wet sand which look like whatever the cat's made. Mother not only forbids certain acts, in addition she teaches the child in what form her wishes will be found acceptable.

A dream is also in code, but the secrets which the dreamwork tries to hide merely have to be hidden. So long as the superego recognizes the meaning of the message, the message will be sent back like a bad bottle. The preconscious contains thoughts which have passed our severest, although least sophisticated, censor, but our disguises aren't costumes we can doff, they become us. A prince we may be, but the prince is a frog.

Although, in practice, it has been the psychoanalyst's special vice to push aside composition in search of content, the unity of style and meaning is a profound social and psychological truth. There may be, in principle, many ways to cook a goose, but the method we choose and fix on, by becoming our only one, defines us, as we define it. The way we keep the Sabbath *is* the Sabbath. Means join their ends and become ends enlarged—coated with custom. Ego and superego are not enemies in this enterprise. If we watch, in fact, how our wants are rewritten, we shall see soon enough that they sit at adjoining desks in the editorial office, and teach the same lessons.

3

In the following little drama, we can witness, distantly within our hero—Frank—a desire struggling weakly for expression.

I WANT MY MOMMY!

The superego will blue-pencil this desire at once if its meaning is indecent, but even if all that is wished for is a little comfort and assurance, the ego will cross it out if the superego doesn't: you are thirty-three, a big boy now, in fact a little fat, and besides, what will people think? What people think, how they reward or punish us, are realities every bit as compelling as a bee sting or a painful burn. By and large, it is not inhuman nature which causes us psychological distress, but that ever present hell (as Sartre said) made up of other people.

First Desk: *The Superego and its Wastebasket, the Unconscious.*

The desk of the first censor is occupied by Ma, Pa, several Step-Uncles, Foster Parents, God, the Orphanage, and Immanuel Kant. Its nays are categorical. The remaining desks (and I shall count six more) are staffed by real officials. Some are salesmen; some have managerial ambitions; some are good at PR; and each is alert to the responses of the world; each is skilled at procrastination, pass-the-buck, and run-around, as efficient bureaucrats must be: full of facts, suggestions, cautions and precautions; on the lookout, naturally, for Number One; each the internalization of means and standards; serving the pleasure principle but governed by reality—a reality which shifts from desk to desk almost kaleidoscopically, at one moment crassly material, vulgar, local, and grasping, and at another moment devoted, sacrificial, universal, and ideal.

Of course, if Frank wanted his mother's body the way he enjoyed it when he was a baby, then the superego will have already said: you mustn't say that, even to yourself. We will notice that when the ego denies something, it always tries to be "reasonable," and reminds Frank that his mother is seventy-five or that she is not now nursing or wouldn't in company open her dress; whereas the superego, a notorious dogmatist and fanatic, simply says: no. In any case, the censor must have something to go on: a text. The desire must be recognized as a forbidden one before its employment can be terminated. With his id at his elbow, Frank tries again. He has noticed that his hostess, Carol Cozycott, has a gently rolling chest like the hills of Ohio and his dear mother of memory. Her hair is similarly long and dark, and her nose has a crease across it like a dog-eared page. She'd be a suitable substitute.

I WANT CAROL!

Second Desk: *The Ego and its Wastebasket, the Preconscious.*

The first curious thing about the process of revision is that not only do we remain unaware of our initial version, we are also ignorant of the character of the writer who holds the pen (Frank doesn't know he has a fixation on this kind of contour; he believes it to be a fact that some breasts are sexier than others). Carol is your best friend's babysitter, the official at the second desk reminds Frank; you better not think about her now; perhaps another time in a quiet daydream, preferably in the tub or on the john. So the thought ("I want Carol") is thrust into the preconscious like a dirty postcard in a pants pocket.

Third Desk: *The Ego and its Second Wastebasket, Discretion.*

But Frank still wants his mommy and Carol still has her cleavage. Her pie, Frank can't help noticing, is treacly. No matter. His mother's molasses pies were always treacly too. He'd better try to choke down another piece. The truth is, he probably doesn't remember his mother's molasses pie, and the identification of the two women remains obscure, but Frank has been well trained, and the censor at the third desk hardly has to raise his eyebrows, because Frank isn't any more likely to say "choke" aloud than he'll let out his canary. Instead, Frank says:

"Carol dear, may I have a little more of your lovely pie, please?"

The soul of discretion, Frank does not even use the word 'piece,' and, as one, all the editors cry:

"Good boy! It's a print!"

This example is wrongly simple, not to say squalid; nevertheless, it may enable us to discern and describe the several stages through which Frank's wish for a little maternal comfort has passed on its way to his reward: a few more calories and perhaps a little heartburn . . . also, of course, Carol's good regard.

During the first stage, deep in the unconscious like a man in the dark, the wish bumps about searching for signs. If it finds none, it cannot become conscious. It follows, since the wish may be sent back again and again, that the larger the number of employable signs, and the greater the range of transformational types, the better the chances are that the wish will find a formula. A lifetime of reading will stock the unconscious with a lifetime of signs and expressive possibilities.

I should like to suggest that all sub-basement sentences of this sort contain, first of all, an id without an identity (the id does not call itself Frank); that they invariably refer to primary processes; that they are always put in the passive voice, and involve a narcissistic unity of world and body. In short: It wants (to receive) pleasure from, let's say, the body's maternal breast through the body's mouth. I want to stress this now because I believe that one aim of writing well is a narcissistic satisfaction which depends upon taking in, disarming, and reconstituting a world by means of language. This activity is largely oral and involves, most deeply, the fusion of the ability to make one's own sensory environment with the passive gratifications of the breast, though, of course, one aggressively sucks while being passively fed, and passively listens to one's own active babbling.

We enter the second stage when the initial formulation is refused and the wish cannot penetrate the preconscious. It may be that the regular occupants of the preconscious must at one time have lived in the light, if only briefly, like flying fish, so that the way to the preconscious is through consciousness, as we reach Monaco through France, but at present this is one problem whose solution we can, with pleasure, refuse to consider.

These initial revisions are crude and drastic. Passive attitudes may become active as an itch, or our desires may suffer full reversal, pain replacing the requested pleasure, or all sorts of substitutions may be made in our orders so that we come home with pot roast instead of ham, or the soul may resort to euphemisms as enthusiastically as an undertaker.

It is not a calm colloquy: the id demanding, the parent saying no. It is push against shove. Suppression is prolonged, tense, angry, often violent, and at any time later in life it will be as it was in the beginning—the sufferance of this so-called superego who acts and orders only for our Good as Papa Doc once did in Haiti, benevolent and brutal—because our supervisor will often be sly, devious, frequently dishonest, occasionally desperate, certainly inconsistent, divided (as Mother and Father issue different orders or are split to be conquered or strike one another with the sweet fat of an infant like the hard flat of a hand), and in this allegedly safe and soft and sweet environment attitudes will grow hopelessly ambivalent at the same time the emotional gain goes up, as if two stations were coming in at once, and these broadcasts will become insistent, obsessive, incessant, until static covers everything like dust. Increasingly, heads will ache, eyes burn, stomachs sour, hearts fail, backs break, bodies faint, while wants turn perversely grandiose in the face of every objection, annoyance following nuisance to hotels of irritation like bees back to the hive; and squalling meets suggestion, and resistance meets rebuke, and pout answers pleading, until the child draws another child out of the parent's heart (the real sibling rival at last) to confront it, total war is declared, the crib is grasped and shaken like a sieve by terrified angered hands, and then it will be wee bawling baby against big brawling bully, with odds favoring the baby by two to one.

The censor snaps his pencil, promises pain, outrages the omnipotent aspirations of the id: say please, say thank you, say uncle. Forbidden to refuse food, the child may throw up (and what can you do about that, mommy, but buy a new bucket and mop?); punished, its nose bleeds (so there, daddy-o, you brute!); it develops allergies (especially to milk), becomes asthmatic, pees in drawers filled with silks, on platters, in planters like a cat, poops in its pants or on the vinyl, has earaches, dawdles, talks too much or absolutely not, stutters to remind you how you've terrified it, or mumbles to make you ask, what? destroys its toys or picks its nose or fights, or rubs its crotch or whines and wheedles, or cries at the sight of strangers, dogs, or beetles, makes lewd suggestions as if in all innocence, at bedtime needs lights and unsettles your sleep with its dreaming, throws up in cars or at birthday parties, becomes overexcited, plays with matches, develops a cry like a shaken saw, swears precociously, spits, has a permanently runny nose, scabs on knees and elbows, dirt like a clown's comical cosmetic around its mouth, holds tantrums in shops the way some hold public meetings, darts into the street and pushes over bicycles, filches pennies, is a victim of inexplicable frights, fads, and manias, is peevish, pouts, enjoys meaningless disobedience or extended sulks, or pesters the grownups like bees at a picnic, but disappears when called and hides when sought, can be sugary and solicitous, docile and loving, yet when no one is watching, scratches, pinches, hits, kicks, and bites.

We must make no mistake: childhood is a civil war, a state of nurture, if I dare to say it, where every child is the enemy of every child, including pets and plants and father, father's job and father's car, family hobbies, habits, little tics, mother's migraines and her playing cards, everybody's dreams and everybody's love affairs, not excluding meter readers and other intruders, a rabble of relatives, well-meaning friends, frets and parental worries as numerous as starlings raisining their evening trees. There are crimes committed, wounds inflicted, guilts as frequently felt and multitudinous as fleas, misunderstandings too, misconceptions, masturbation, false success, reliefless ease.

This war has no victors, no peace table, no medals, no quarter. It must be fought to a draw or everyone loses. And it is the sword swung then, usually so useless against the swift sandal and the quicker sling, which sharpens that pen which one day shall be mightier. Nor does the struggle cease with death, for when we fall we are buried in the bodies of our children, as Sir Thomas Browne suggests, where we shall shortly be forgotten, yet where we—unforgiving as the Furies, unrelenting—in that deep forgetting find our final victory; since, like a tumor, we make our presence felt where we can walk about unrecognized, unlike the ghosts which haunt the conscience of the guilty and need belief to be.

Well . . . not final victory. There's nothing final in it, really. Nature knows nothing of ends like these. Its patterns contain few figures of closure or purposive designs. Its course proceeds as randomly as crowds of cars upon a freeway—a thousand shots and not a single aim, countless plots and not one point. We are merely conduits of culture, of half- or quarter-truths, elusive meanings and iron measures: that hammer which fell so often angrily from my father's shaping fist struck my sons more severely than the soft white metal I was mistakenly believed to be.

During the third stage, which we now reach once more like a wave, a number of reformulations are made until an acceptable one is found and the thought reaches consciousness. It is possible at this point that the psyche develops a partiality for certain forms of revision, habitually sublimation, for example (blanket for body, bottle for breast), or reversal, or introjection, or the euphemisms of repression; for we notice that some writers throw bits away and begin again, some patch and piece, some pare but some accrete, so that if a sentence is wrong, a setting, or a scene, getting it right means making it longer, or scrubbing it clean, or starting over; just as when we have blundered socially, saying or doing the wrong thing, some of us must follow the foot in our mouth with its ankle, others blush furiously and fall silent, others deny having uttered the offending sentences, as if misquoted by their own ears, and produce new ones, more fashionable, more politic, amusing, or more daring.

Fourth Desk: *The Class Historian.*

A thought which reaches consciousness may not be allowed to stay: it may strike us as unimportant, or as unpleasant, or as distracting and inappropriate to the present moment. Later, we say . . . later; and during its wait the memory (for it is now that) undergoes alterations. We know how anecdotes are removed from storage like old clothes, spotted, brushed, and pressed, let out or taken in, and we carefully lace the sleeve of our personal history with lies, which really are revisions, until eventually a formula for the past is settled on which (flattering or not) somehow suits us by concealing our nature. We can bear to remember the war, our childhood, first love. Misery has become amusing. As students of Freud, we know that these fictions are often more revealing than the facts, just as the coat which is cut to conceal our belly may display our taste and pretentions nakedly to every eye. Such reinterpretations of the past, which Proust performed so consciously, comprise stage four.

Fifth Desk: *The Town Crier.*

During stage five, the wish, acceptable to consciousness, is inspected, and usually rewritten once more to satisfy the demands of public utterance. There are those who, it's said, say the first thing that pops into their pretty heads (like rattlebrained incompetence, it is a trait assigned, by the common consent of men, to women). They appear to hide nothing, and to be charmingly frank and direct. The child is often like this and will winningly ask the fat ugly woman why she is, or want to know of the cripple what's cracked, or of a leg how it came unstuffed.

Sixth Desk: *The Teacher's.*

What we say when we speak in public won't bear much writing down. We hem and haw, backtrack, repeat, use preformed phrases which have fallen out of the mouths of radios or slid off screens, piece our speech together out of sentence fragments, and instead of punctuating pop our cheeks or suck our teeth or wiggle our eyebrows and sometimes fingers. The moment one begins to write words down instead of sailing them into invisible dissolution in the air, one feels the censor's presence, now a new one: a grammarian, conscious of spelling, parsing, construing, phrasing, all proper forms. Do I indent three spaces? how do you address a bishop or spell "yours truly"?

All previous stages, which this argument has dragged us through, were ones in which the word was made by the mouth (even if unspoken), and if our parents have, by this time, trained us to express our savage lusts liked cowed adults, both in speech and in behavior, they have had no control over our writing. Puppies still, we go to school to be paper trained. We leave our box. This was not always the case, of course, but now it is a generally accomplished fact, and a terribly important one. We take our first formed sentences home as we do our first scrawly drawings or an injured bird we've found in the street. There our parents help or hinder, encourage or frighten us, but that step into the written, reading world is the first free one. There were once scarcely any adolescents with hair upon their genitals and a head upon their shoulders who didn't realize, reading away in their door-covered rooms, that escape lay over and through the word, just as in the books they were devouring, liberty was always just beyond some bordering mountains, across a river, through a few trees. Nowadays, television and movies have tried to replace those walls with their tinted images, but they have so far had the kind of success we associate with billboards plugging the sun in Florida.

The average person, taught to write, writes little in a lifetime, and, with the possible exception of a few letters of love, apology, or sorrow, would never consider the composition of sentences which should transform his soul into syllables to possess the slightest interest. But what of the million fledgling writers who remain? What, when they scratch away, pen poems to one another, push stories into print the way a shy son or daughter is pushed by the parent into a room of strangers . . . what, when they establish periodicals whose life is so brief their period comes promptly after *The* . . . what do they want?

Seventh Desk: *Editors, Publishers, the Public.*

There are many pressures to publish, most of which ruffle the surface of our psychology like wind, but the principal one, I've been suggesting, is the desire to have one's wants (that is to say, the deep self itself) not merely accepted—oh no—applauded, deliriously praised: how marvelous of you to have thought that! how searching! how sensitive! how wise! how expressive! The soul where desires of such a sweet and eloquent nature dwell must be likened to a land flowing with silk, thighs, and money . . . and so on through every rich adverb and glowing etcetera. Yet how battered the instincts are by this time; what tedious vicissitudes they have gone through to reach ink; how altered, as Bottom was . . . translated into an ass!

To hurdle the barriers briefly once again: at the first desk sits accident, blind as justice but weighing nothing, grasping piggishly at whatever comes, exercising censorship only through eagerness, as the worser apple is eaten if it's nearer the mouth. At the second is the categorical THOU SHALT NOT of the Mosaic Law, while at the third we hear the incessant yes of the ego—*yes, yes, yes, but*—a devious Uriah Heap and treacherous sycophant who always counsels the id to work within the system. Then at the fourth is perched, as on a stool, a lying, smiling historian in the pay of the Home Office, who hopes for a knighthood or annually expects election to the Royal Academy. The fifth editorial advisor wheels and deals, Frenching the phone, a sophist trained in the spirit of Dale Carnegie, wrapping remarks to look like Cuban cigars or Belgian candy, and selling the staler ones—a real steal—at two for a doll. Wielding a ruler, her hair in the requisite bun, the English teacher is next, guarding the grammatical proprieties like a treasure. At last we reach the general public, which may not be so general after all: one's class at school, a small community or neighborhood, a few science fiction fans, subscribers to the Masterpieces of the Month Club, the no longer quite so vast audience for poems, plays, and tales. As we proceed, the presence of our editors is more openly felt, their demands become better known, but their hold is also relatively weaker, the standards spongier and sometimes vacillating, inconsistently applied, increasingly unclear. Except through chance and circumstance, the approval of the crowd is hard to obtain, harder to hold, and requires, like drink, progressively larger amounts for its effect, since its plaudits are cheap and fickle, uneducated and anonymous for the most part, or neurotically loyal as fans sometimes are, local and circumscribed to the point of being pinched.

Obviously our editors are internalized representatives, arranged roughly in rings, of all those agencies which, during our formative years, inflicted pain or permitted pleasure because of our way with words.

Of course men and women want money, power, glory, and the love of other men and women. But why try to obtain it by writing? It's a mug's game, and only a few are driven to lengthen the line of desks. For most, it is enough that they get their piece of pie or piece of Carol. Dreiser chose to achieve his aims by writing, but not by writing well; John Locke by expressing rather carelessly a lot of liberal sentiments and dull truths; De Sade through shock; Heidegger by pedantry and obfuscation; Mill by specializing in superficiality like a decorator of cakes; but who but a lardhead would want to seek renown through the placement of eyebrows and noses, the manufacture of metaphors, the management of rhyme? Not promising. Foolish on the face of it. Foolish deeper down and foolish deeper in.

Yet psychologically the art of fine writing is very close to the art of becoming civilized, even human. It parallels, if it doesn't ape, the transformations of the instincts into acceptable acts of expression. And the final stage—the grandeurs and intimidations of style ("Gravestones tell truth scarce fourty years")—signals, like psychoanalysis itself, a return to early urges and their effects. This return is not nostalgic and nothing like regression, because it is a return armed, a conscious and controlled effort to rewrite the instincts in accord with another kind of standard which requires the withdrawal and capture within the self of what has been excellent in the writing of the past; the digestion, over decades of feasting and fasting, of the efforts of others bent on the same improbable errand. It is, as in the case of Stephen Dedalus, the search for a verbal parent, an authority made of authors, a Leviathan which when constituted will prove as unremittingly hostile, implacably severe, impossible to please, equal, or even emulate, as any other God the Father, and who will henceforth receive, like mash notes written with a poisoned pen, all our scribbler's inner ambivalences: his love and fear and jealousy, her hope and hate and hallelujah.

As far as writing itself goes, although that section of the soul which makes the money, makes the love, or makes the garden grow may remain relatively unaffected, a fine writer must accomplish five fundamental psychological tasks: (1) he must replace his present editorial staff, as far as possible, with a single, rich yet precise, wide though discriminating sense of taste, drawn from all his reading but preferably from the most inclusive tradition of excellence he can assimilate; a sense to which he gives the power of a parent; (2) yet he must not give up in the face of the parrot who will now speak to his muse: "Not good enough, not good enough, awk! not good enough"; but gain its eventual approval for his own individual transformations; (3) he must displace, in so doing, the reality principle from world to word, so that with words and their formal structures he can (4) overcome the intense destructive urges which are the basis for his desperate creative activities; for superlative writing is love lavished on the word in order to repair a world which revengeful fantasy has destroyed, as well as to persuade its agreeable aspects to remain unchanged, because if they indicate a desire to depart, they will be savagely attacked too, bombed into oblivion; and (5) he must compose his work in such a way that the full features of infantile life are brought up to date without the sacrifices of expression demanded by his former bosses: the complete child must come forth in the whole man or woman who invests and shapes a successful style, in a manner exactly contrary to the situation I described earlier in which an angry teasing child reduces the adult to another angry teasing threatening child, and this use of the earliest urges by the most sophisticated can be achieved only if the powers that be can be persuaded to pull back, approve and praise, because only then can forgiveness be received in the peace and blessing of the great lines; only then will the psyche believe that its impulses aren't satanic, that all is not lost, that the self has not been left alone amid the debris of its own demolishment, the ashes of its anger.

I want to devote my remaining pages to a brief description of these tasks.

4

One of the fundamental facts of psychic life is that we want to wound and heal, eat and have, condemn and save, preserve and destroy, at the same time. Nothing would suit us better than the blow whose bruise blooms, or the bite whose indentations decorate, and this ambivalence only weakly names the state, since we recognize the love in those who love us by the degree of damage they are willing to sustain without causing us grief to have done so. Guiltless, we savage the peach to its pit, for what sweeter compliment can we pay anything to surpass swallowing it? May I have another piece of your lovely pie, please? The primal and still ultimate rejection is the retch. And would we not fall in love with a vengeance, if it wreaked vengeance? and wouldn't revenge be richer if it led to love, for hate is finest when it elevates and saves. I love peaches, yet the snake I fear and flee from prospers. Strange. Suppose each time we broke our favorite plate it grew more beautiful and complete; then to smash, again to smash: what a total pleasure!

At least one important theory of art has concluded that, though the world be without purpose, or justice, or meaning (as far as reason can confidently ascertain), the unified objects which art makes of these spoiling fragments renders things finally as they ought to be, for even if every actor suffered and then died during an Elizabethan tragedy (and sometimes that nearly happened), and the motives of men were mercilessly laid open like an ox that's been flayed so we might see the blood they had their baths in, the effect is not one of gloom or dismay, but of energy, wholeness, perfection, joy.

Remember Baudelaire's description of the carrion—flies at picnic upon a decaying vulva—Hamlet's little speech to Yorick's skull, or Rilke's rhetorical wonderment about his mother: did I come out of that hole in the wallpaper? or if I may be forgiven a moment of bad manners, this brief passage from a story of my own, in which the narrator (only in thought, of course) excoriates a harmless old neighbor woman who often comes to visit him, the outburst leading to an unexpected and involuntary epiphany:

> For I am now in B, in Indiana: out of job and out of patience,
> out of love and time and money, out of bread and out of body,
> in a temper, Mrs. Desmond, out of tea. So shut your fist up,
> bitch, you bag of death; go bang another door; go die, my
> dearie. Die, life-deaf old lady. Spill your breath. Fall over
> like a frozen board. Gray hair grows from the nose of your
> mind. You are a skull already—*memento mori*—the foreskin
> retracts from your teeth. Will your plastic gums last longer
> than your bones, and color their grinning? And is your
> twot still hazel-hairy, or are you bald as a ditch? . . .
> bitch . . . . . bitch . . . . bitch. I wanted to be
> famous, but you bring me age—my emptiness. Was it *that*
> which I thought would balloon me above the rest? Love?
> where are you? . . . love me. I want to rise so high, I said,
> that when I shit I won't miss anybody.

The emptiness which Beckett describes for us, for instance, is full. His plays are what the world would be, absurd as it is, if it were yet well-spoken; but we must imagine that when God said, let there be light, He had a bad cough (look if you can at the light as it falls on Beckett's stage, pitiless and blank and even as a shroud), and when He saw what He'd made was good, His voice failed, and other words both made and judged it. Every work of art is such a judgment, such a justification of the Great World's Ways. What else did Dante do but settle scores and square accounts and make awards and set things straight? As Kafka says, the writer does not copy the world, or explain it, but declares his dissatisfaction with it, and suffers.

Some of the cases I've cited will seem extreme. After all, praise, as Rilke maintained, is the thing; but only some things in this life can be unambiguously, unironically, celebrated. The poet wanders among the animals and flowers, in landscapes finds his freedom, amid luminous skies lets his soul soar like a kestrel; for what *is* the way I want the world? wholly in my power; and the more powerless I may have found myself, as in growing up we all find ourselves, the more completely, as a writer, will I rest within the word, because as difficult as its management is: listen! I speak and these friendly syllables surround me; they have never done me any harm, for even when I ascribe them to my enemies, make up villains in a tale to torment victims I have also fabricated, the words they speak are mine, the sentiments indeed are mine, coming from every corner, the villainies as well . . . ah, yes, those *especially*.

I am present in every disguise, every twist and transformation (Proteus, in changing, cannot escape his nature as a changeling); and if I write well enough and dispose my voices artfully, *I can say anything;* only then can one dare to speak the truth about one's self, off the couch and out of an office, onto an engraving. I can, in those conditions, lay my heart bare, as Baudelaire hoped to do, not merely because unburdening is a blessing, but because I want to be blessed as the Son was by the Father, blessed first by those books which are my friends and gave me my values and taught me how I ought to live, and then, perversely, by the world, precisely because I am the sort of total sinner who wants not just the tree but the tree toad, not just the rainbow or the pot of gold, but the whole kit, the entire kaboodle. Then after every plaything—the choir of heaven and the furniture of the earth—has been grabbed up and stuffed in my toy box, and while I sit securely on its lid with that insufferable smile of possession, rattling my heels, I expect the pleasure and praise of an emptied universe to approach me like applause.

No. That's inexact. I don't want the world to be mine (my motorcar, my wife, my house, my gloves, my dog), I want it to be *me* the way my mother's body was before her treachery, and the nipple came away in my mouth like a handle in a surprised hand breaks from its satchel, or a button spits out its cloth.

Well, we all settle our claims out of court, for there is no judge; and we settle for less, much less . . . much . . . much . . . much less, until we settle for smidgens, seconds, leftovers, culls: the writer settles for words he can't own (suppose I owned 'and' and it cost you to use it?); accepts a grammar he can't claim (and half of it hidden anyway, only Chomsky knows where); approaches traditional forms which merely shrug at his existence and he has to run to catch like a late commuter; takes on themes as fucked over as a two-buck whore would be in the days when haircuts were two bits; and looks out on a world of *les autres* who have as little claim to the language they mispronounce as he has.

Moreover, the psychological satisfactions of writing: the payment of reparations, the release from guilt, the pleasures of attack and destruction, the implicit approval of the masters, the consequent acceptance of the self, and so on—these results are often felt no farther than the borders of the artist, and as she rises from her worktable to placate her baby-husband or her baby-baby, she is merely another frazzled mum, more than generally resentful, not simply because she must leave her work, but because she must leave herself.

Among the maladies which character and circumstance combine to guarantee we shall surely suffer is the clamorous confusion of overmany and mixed motives. Remember all those interfering editors? They all want to have the last word about our words. None cares to be bypassed, and even though the writer may have discovered that the most direct way to the self is through a style as convoluted as that of Joyce or Lyly or De Quincey or Proust, or through one so Shakerlike and pure it's suddenly as though the page were awash with clear creek water and the reader could measure plainly every resting fish and count every rounding pebble; nevertheless, we are a multiple; we want the approval of both Plato and the public, the ghost of our father and the ghost of Henry James, and the ghost of Miss Tish, too, who wouldn't let us punctuate with dashes, and Carol, whose pie we really don't want another treacly piece of; so that the writer struggles with more than words, he competes with his obsessions, his screens, his weaknesses, with family lies, with strange expectations, with tastes twisted by neurosis, beliefs he wears like loud neckties, with alcohol, anxieties, with impotence, with menopausal flushes, hysterical pregnancies, manic states, sexual rage.

Everywhere, then, we encounter an overestimation of the word—those knuckles of our knowing. And what, then, is a sentence but a fist?

It is not simply that the writer thinks of his daily life largely as an excuse for speech and a source of language (that birds are blessed because they suggest their names); or that he has put lines about love and suffer-

ing, composed of sounds and thoughts responsive to him, in place of the
body of his beloved, since she turns her back and will not warm; it is not
simply because he can chastise his enemies in secret and safety, or spill
his guts and sell them in a store; it is basically because he has himself
become the word: he is its source; his id is now its energy; his ego is a
mediator between the words which want to leap like salmon out of his
soul and the words already there on the page, the project already begun,
the life being formed out of leftover alphabets, exhausted genres, un-
spared parts from the remaining whole of literature, a presence which
shadows that page like a long cloud across the sun; his creative superego
is meanwhile seeking sanction—yea or nay—in the qualities of the great
texts, searching above all for that quality most prized, most rare, most
praised: that they shall not quickly pass away.

We should not leave the table without one last taste of our topic, this
time Jeremy Taylor. Full of faults—forced conceits, unregulated repetitions, occasionally confused imagery and a little local awkwardness of
gait—this passage pushes its problems roughly aside to become sublime.
The qualities it possesses, the soul inside this sentence, all the finest
writing strives for: energy, perception, passion, thought, music, movement, and imagination; yet what will it tell us: that life is hard; that we
are fragile; that time is short? goodby.

> We are as water; weak and of no consistence, always de-
> scending, abiding in no certain place, unless we are detained
> with violence; and every little breath of wind makes us rough
> and tempestuous and troubles our faces; every trifling accident
> discomposes us; and as the face of the waters wafting in a
> storm so wrinkles itself that it makes upon its forehead fur-
> rows deep and hollow like a grave, so do our great and little
> cares and trifles first make the wrinkles of old age, and then
> they dig a grave for us; and there is in nature nothing so con-
> temptible, but it may meet us in such circumstances that it may
> be too hard for us in our weaknesses; and the sting of a bee is
> a weapon sharp enough to pierce the finger of a child or the
> lip of a man; and those creatures which nature hath left with-
> out weapons yet are they armed sufficiently to vex those parts
> of man which are left defenseless and obnoxious to a sun-
> beam, to the roughness of a sour grape, to the unevenness of a
> gravel stone to the dust of a wheel, or the unwholesome
> breath of a star looking awry upon a sinner.

Nearly everyone writes about the brevity of life: in elegies, odes, meditations like Browne's, in treatises, in anatomy texts, in stories, plays, and

preachments like Taylor's—life would be long indeed if we were to listen to a millionth part. Then how shall one man or woman, among so many, say the same thing so originally, so forcefully, so beautifully, we'd recognize their pen print anywhere? ". . . the unwholesome breath of a star looking awry upon a sinner."

The sentence, then, if it is to have a soul, rather than merely be a sign of the existence somewhere of one, must be composed by our innermost being, finding in its drive and rhythm, if not in its subject, the verbal equivalent of instinct; in its sound and repetitions, too, its equivalent feeling; and then perceive its thought as Eliot said Donne did, as immediately as the odor of a rose—fully, the way we see ships at anchor rise and fall as though they lay on a breathing chest.

In Sir Thomas Browne's day death came early, often in the morning of a life, before the hair was combed; then the image in the shaving mirror often grinned like a skull, though its owner wasn't grinning; and the spirit which only one day past had moved the body so vigorously through its braggadocios, its fucking, its sighs and singing, its drunkenness and piggery, might suddenly seem lost and wan in the new sun, so that the world which might be clean of mist by noon might also be free of both this pale glass shadow and its affrighted soul; consequently, the Elizabethan interest in death, or rather, their concern about the fragility of life, is scarcely surprising; and yet while Sir Thomas Browne tells us how futile it is to preserve our bodies, bones, or ashes; how brief and inarticulate the speech of those stones which like jawless teeth irrupt the lawns of our cemeteries, what is he quietly doing but fashioning a monument for his psyche which heaven will not have matter for or space or skill to build? because, in so saying what he's said, he becomes as immortal as may be, and comes as near to realizing the one real wish of us all as other wills and wishes will allow—no more is permitted; and which one of us would be unwilling to lie down among such sentences as though they were boughs for our burning? because Browne, and all those like him, did not merely bring these books of his, these eloquent passages, their memorable lines, into being; he brought himself into existence on the page, as it were through a hole in the word; although, as he would require us to observe, what are these urns which have lasted a thousand years when we measure them up the leg of eternity? do they extend so far as the knee, the cuff? do they reach the lace of the shoe, the tongue? possibly as far as that?—no—but if we cannot have an everlong life, perhaps we can create a soul, within some substance elsewhere and other than ourselves, which it would be a crime on the world's part to let die.

TROPES OF THE TEXT

I have argued elsewhere[1] that the novel is a mind, like a Leibnizean monad, metaphorically aware of a world; that it apprehends things only through thoughts; that it is dangerously divided into particular facts and their generalizing figurations, just as, in the interior of every word, there is a war between meaning and referent concerning who shall rule. These oppositions have been given many different titles over time. The list of ten dualities which the Pythagoreans drew up now seems mild and incomplete compared with Hegel's elaborate charts and tables, even though their list was charmingly cast in the shape of two triangles: the plus side headed by Unity, or the radiant One; its dark, downwardly pointing pubic shadow by Plurality, or the many and the minus. Perhaps the most convenient opposition to consider, concerning the novel now, would be that between the empirical realist, for whom the novel is in one way or another a report upon the world, and that of the rationalist, for whom the novel is an intense interior, formed like a flower from within, and opening out only into absence.

It has always seemed to me, from the esthetic point of view, although the empiricists have a case to make, that the rationalists come closer to the truth; and in the same essay I've already alluded to, I repeated my belief that the novel's relationship to the world was fundamentally figurative. I said that the novelist created a metaphorical model, a text which, in effect, reinterpreted the history and common understanding of the reader's world and life—any reader's, anywhere, and any life through any time—as if it were composed and laid out like another text. We are all familiar with the kind of kaleidoscope which has no colored chips, itself, to shuffle about, but contains in its tube only mirrors and an eyepiece through which any aspect of the world is shattered and rearranged according to a new geometry.

---

1. In the third essay in this volume, "Representation and the War for Reality."

One consequence of this view is that if the novel is a metaphor for life as it is lived at this time or that, by this person or other, there will be some legitimate differences in the meanings which emerge from the interaction of the author's text and the imaginary one of the reader's. The "Pierre Menard" effect will be real and acceptable. The kaleidoscope turns you and me and all of us into formally the same but qualitatively different patterns.

But from the English novel's earliest beginnings, at any rate, there has also been a tendency to think of the text of the novel, itself, in terms of some trope. That is, the novel attempted (without any real intention to deceive, of course) to pass itself off as a factually normal and truthful piece of prose. The trope of the text was always another type of text. I am not a novel, it said; look, I am an autobiography. I am not a novel, I am another fabulous travel tale; I am a volume of titillating letters; I am a fascinating history, a shocking report upon the ravages of the Plague; I am the cautionary, edifying, intimate diary of a seducer.

In honest fact, however, what am I? I am made up. I am made up to resemble the journal kept by a man in prison, an exchange of *billets-doux,* the biography of—of all people—a foundling; and what depths of insignificance will I flatter my public by sinking to next? At any rate, I am not myself, but some other fellow, someone solid, informative, real.

To establish this trope in the mind of the reader, the novel would often closely imitate the rituals, the style and form, of such works as possessed a satisfying and virtuous utility; and I suspect it is because of this imitation of factual modes that fiction, at first, seemed bent on realism—a serious misapprehension which novelists soon believed themselves, and hastened, by their practice, to reaffirm as the truth. Our commodity culture was at that time but an erotic moan from the depths of some machine, but the force of the *Zeitgeist* was great enough to pull fiction up from its roots in Rabelais and Cervantes, and carry it away into the bourgeois world like so much else. The trope allowed the fictional text to imagine that it was not fictional, and therefore, even more importantly, to pretend that its relation to the world was literal, and not simply literary—a deception ardently desired by both reader and writer alike.

The romance announces, openly and frankly enough, its fundamentally fictional character. It often uses allegory's apparatus to touch ground. But the "new" novel, like the New Learning, had to justify its serious perusal by decent, no-nonsense people.

The title page of the original 1748 edition of *Clarissa Harlowe* shows us how Richardson, not content with one ameliorating metaphor, doubled the trope by advertising his novel as

CLARISSA.

OR, THE

HISTORY

OF A

YOUNG LADY:

Comprehending

The most Important Concerns *of* Private LIFE.

And particularly shewing,

The DISTRESSES that may attend the Misconduct
Both of PARENTS and CHILDREN,

In Relation to MARRIAGE.

Published by the EDITOR *of* PAMELA.

VOL. I.

LONDON:

Printed for S. Richardson:

And Sold by A. MILLAR, over-against *Catherine-street* in the *Strand;*
J. and JA. RIVINGTON, in *St. Paul's Church-yard;*
JOHN OSBORN, in *Pater-noster Row.*
And by J. LEAKE, at *Bath.*

M.DCC.XLVIII.

This is a history given to us in a series of letters, Richardson says in
his preface, and to aid in our acceptance of this complicated metaphor
for the text, he carefully omits the name of the author from both preface
and title page, slipping "S. Richardson" in as the printer (which, of
course, he was); he dates and identifies each letter; some are signed; he
edits others, not omitting cross-references; and he appropriately varies
both style and tone to suit the personalities of his correspondents, and

the different occasions which inspire them to take up their pens—which they do with unflagging facility.

These letters are not only sent and received, they are copied, shown to others, discussed, secreted, intercepted, forged, stolen, and slyly altered. In short, the trope closest to the text—that it is a collection of letters—is assiduously maintained and exploited. The remoter trope, although it is the governing one on the title page, is far more loosely pursued, and most of the formulas we might find in the biographies of the time are absent.

Why all this folderol, when we know perfectly well that these letters are imaginary? We know who the so-called editor of *Pamela* is, and we have been eagerly awaiting his next book. We can count, and we can consequently wonder how Lovelace, between 6 A.M. and midnight of June 10, could manage to write 14,000 words while also living through many of the adventures he is writing about. Is our amazement removed by Richardson's smooth suggestion that Lovelace is writing in shorthand? Of course, most of the letters are far too long to be letters in any ordinary sense, and many of them open out into dramatic scenes full of dialogue and emotional badmintons. Thus the original action is often set forth in a *playlet* which is then rendered within the body of a *letter,* which, with many others of its sort, is given to the reader as a *history,* and which is received by the reader, nevertheless, as a *novel.*

The readers' and the writer's complicities mesh, and the reason for this complicated pretense of deception finally becomes clear. By establishing such a set of tropes for the text, the writer invites the reader to enjoy the considerable immorality of examining other people's mail. Now the reader can spy on a romantic yet real world, because letters are part of the real world. The characters must feel actual also, for wraiths and figments don't write letters, only creatures like the readers themselves do that. Moreover (and because, at the same time, it is openly understood that this work is a fiction), the reader need not assume the serious and responsible scholarly posture she might have felt required to take were she studying the correspondence of General Lovelace, late of the Crimea, and an account of his exploits during, as Joyce would say, the penisolate war; nor does she have to feel the guilt which would be appropriate if these were the letters of a neighbor or a friend. The trope pays handsome dividends, safely increasing the vicarious pleasure we may take in this lengthy seduction, and saving us, at the same time, the embarrassment of having been actually present at any of these happenings; for otherwise wouldn't we risk being overcome by the simpering sentimentality of such scenes as Clarissa Harlowe's death, when she expires like a tubercular soprano:

> Bless—bless—bless—you all—and now—and now (holding
> up her almost lifeless hands for the last time)—come—O
> come—blessed Lord—JESUS!

The death of Lovelace is not a bit less melodramatic.

Lydia Pinkham's Vegetable Compound was a medicine which many American women at one time took for their nerves and for other typically feminine ailments. Its active ingredients were opium and alcohol, but it successfully disguised itself inside a medical metaphor, so that it was perfectly all right and socially acceptable to nip on it a bit. Richardson's novels are similarly—although far more subtly—packaged. The romantic, the erotic theme, was the real reason for reading Richardson, but the titillating salaciousness of his work, which is considerable, is hidden behind the other ingredients (prominently listed, one must notice, in the author's preface, as "vehicles of instruction," as though printed on a bottle label). In a strictly analogous fashion, the letters conceal from frank view the fact that the reader is amusing herself with an idleness of immense duration, a fiction of a thousand pages. Richardson, no doubt a victim of his own unconscious duplicities, gives the game away when he writes:

> . . . considerate readers will not enter upon the perusal of
> the Piece before them, as if it were designed *only* to divert and
> amuse. It will probably be thought tedious to all such as *dip*
> into it, expecting a *light Novel,* or *transitory Romance;* and
> look upon the Story in it (interesting as that generally is al-
> lowed to be) as its *sole end* . . .

Although Richardson is aware of the problems which such a form forces upon him (in particular, how it slows the narrative flow), he did not choose his form because it presented to the artist some challenging difficulties, or even because it offered itself as the only way his tale could be told. When Henry James undertook his story "A Bundle of Letters," the letter seemed to him more than merely a helping hand; rather it was the very body of the work itself.

Richardson chose the letter because he loved letters and liked to write them; because he had got up a book of sample letters which had had a good sale; because it was the one medium of written prose which his readers might also have practiced; because it encouraged a more familiar style than one frequently encountered, and hence put his readers more at their ease; and because, both in real life and on the purely fictive page, the letter was a formidable instrument of seduction, yet one which was socially acceptable and shielded the writer from certain criticisms. The novel, to Stendhal, may have been a mirror dawdling down a road, but to Richardson, the novel was that same mirror, up all night after such a dusty day, reflecting upon what it had reflected.

Defoe pretends, in his preface to *Moll Flanders,* that

> The world is so taken up of late with novels and romances, that it will be hard for a private history to be taken for genuine, where the names and other circumstances of the person are concealed, and on this account we must be content to leave the reader to pass his own opinion upon the ensuing sheets, and take it just as he pleases.

"As he pleases" is perfect, and how much it would please me to imagine that this ill-bred moniker, "Moll Flanders," is actually the cover for a lady well known to us all. Swift follows the pattern devised by Defoe for his *Robinson Crusoe,* elaborating a little on the prefatory lie by inventing a cousin for Gulliver who edits the texts, eliminating a lot of tedious materials concerning winds and tides.

If Henry James's story is convenient here in permitting me to underline the difference between a text that is actually made of letters, albeit fictional ones, and a text like *Clarissa,* which is such a collection metaphorically (or the difference between *David Copperfield,* which is an invented autobiography, and *The Autobiography of Alice B. Toklas,* which is a figurative one; or that between *Robinson Crusoe,* which passes itself off as real, and *Gulliver's Travels,* which is *Crusoe* at a masquerade); the differences between the mirror and its meditations allow me to stress the contesting elements of essay and story in the early novel. This *mythos,* or story, or what is sometimes said to be "the plot," is frequently alleged to be the most primitive and therefore (though this is a dubious inference) the basic element in fiction. More correctly, we might call it the *chronicle element,* as it appears so prominently in Froissart or Bede—a simple stringing together of events: a Goldilocks.

But rarely are fictions made up merely of actions; fictions characteristically move over rails which belong to different, even opposing, realms of Being—the world of matter in motion (the realm of the referent), and the spaceless sphere of the mediating mind (the realm of meaning)—so we must recognize immediately that we are riding in a strange train if it passes along such a track. Hence story and essay, early on, combine, for there is no escaping the fact that the actions of the story are always *seen,* however neutral that observing eye pretends to be. The same bone that sockets the eye holds the brain. That aspect of the drama which Aristotle called *dianoia* must be dealt with from the first, and therefore narrative techniques (the telling of the story) and expositional devices (the exfoliation of meaning) can never be completely severed from one another.

Traditionally, stories were stolen, as Chaucer stole his; or they were felt to be the common property of a culture or community, as the story of the prodigal son still is, or the myth of Oedipus, the history of Cleopatra, or again, that tale of Goldilocks. These notable happenings, imagined or real, lay outside language the way history itself is supposed to, in a condition of pure occurrence, since they might equally well be danced or painted, mimed or sung. Nowadays they may be filmed. And even when they were realized in words, dramas or epics might be made of them. In fact, as often as many of these tales were told—passed about as ordinary anecdote or gossip is in the guise of folk news—they were rarely written down or put in plain prose.

When ordinary people replaced divinities and princes as the principal objects of our interest, it became expected that the writer would invent his chronicles too, or steal them in an acceptable way, as James did, listening in on the whispers of society. The meanings which went with these myths were also highly standardized, and only later was it thought necessary for the culture to provide them. Like plots, these meanings can be danced, sung, filmed, or played, so neither can be regarded as basic to fiction itself. Nothing is yet fixed in a specific set of words.

There is a third element, equally primitive, and that is talk. The most elementary tale will contain at least a smidgen of talk, thought, and action. Most of the talk is in formulas; it is ritualized: the magic words are "open sesame"; the giant always cries "fee, fi, fo, fum"; the wolf huffs and puffs as he says he will; riddles are like revolvers—you solve them or you're shot. These formulas are the first true phrases of literature because the sentences are sacred; they must not be altered; order is everything. Again, only later is the writer expected to invent these sacred sentences.

Richardson did not pose philosophical questions. He did not ask himself, in so many words, what a letter was. He knew letters facilitated his interest in moral analysis, in sentiment and idea, and one is tempted to say that he simply set about writing his marvelous imitations; however, he understood, in particular, one formal element so well the Postmodernists have not yet proceeded as far as he dared to; indeed, the logical complexity of *Clarissa* approaches the infinite like light. Letters are written, dusted, folded, sealed, enclosed, and Richardson cared about envelopment. As the thousands and thousands of the novel's words approach a million, we can begin to understand how he thought of it.

Held as if prisoner by Lovelace, the distraught Clarissa tries to write first to her friend Fanny Howe, next in her confusion to her father, then to her heartless captor, but finds herself unable. She tears apart pages or crumples them and throws them on the floor. It is there they are found and borne to Lovelace by the maid. Lovelace calmly copies some of them into his own letter: Clarissa's crumpled pages, her scratched-out letter, the letter torn in two, have become, inadvertently but irretrievably, bits of letters in a letter, her hand now held in Lovelace's hand as though offered, not refused.

James, on the other hand (and it makes him modern), is less carried away by the psychological insistence of one element. He carefully considers the interior, formal character of the letter in order that he may successfully structure his text. In addition, he expands on the letter's communal sense of itself, if only through a titular hint. The letters, as I said, are real enough, but the "bundle" they make is quite imaginary. And here, at last, is a trope for the text which is not another text. One dull day, we might suppose, poking through things in the attic, we come upon a bundle of letters tied together with the inevitable faded pink or purple ribbon. The bow is soon pulled, and the letters read in the order of their stacking. The word "bundle" suggests something like this; it hints at an environmental frame, even if it is only a ribbon, which holds these letters together; but we are going to be disappointed if we believe that James took his title very seriously, because the letters are from six quite different, quite unrelated people, and how all of them were recovered from the distant countries they were sent to, and tied together here, remains a mystery. James himself would be quite nonplussed by this complaint; nevertheless, the fact remains that, although he declares his story to be a bundle of letters, it is not.

The old conventions have broken down. We can no longer be so cavalier. If we are painting *The Portrait of a Lady* or *A Portrait of the Artist as a Young Man* or *The Portrait of Dorian Gray,* then a painting must emerge. In the case of Wilde's novel, for instance, no trope for the text is intended, because the book is about a portrait; it never pretends to be one. The portrait, however, is a symbol for its subject's soul. Nowadays we must think about what a portrait is, or a bit of correspondence. Our burdens are great. Often our groans can be heard like the hoots of owls in the night.

Since a letter is written in the absence of its recipient—indeed, because of that absence—and even if writer and receiver share adjoining rooms—it is like a soliloquy intended to be overheard. An exchange of letters involves a strange exchange of talk—talk that is not talk—responses that are delayed, or not made at all. This lapse of time between letters: the posting of them, the transportation of them, the receiving of them, the reading of them, the thoughts about them, the mental answers which are composed but never sent, the postponements of reply, the various procrastinations, the feelings of inadequacy which overcome some, the love of the "I" which faithful letter writers generally have a surfeit of, the final composition of the response, sheets torn up, whole letters cast aside, the mailing finally, after one or two have lain in a pocket or a purse for several days (as forgotten as a wad of foil or crayon kicked under the car's seat, a bus token or ticket stub), then the sluggish progress of the post from B back to A, the Saturday delivery— slow—the smeared address because of Tuesday's rain, the paper cut received by its recipient when opening it, and so on: all these elements are left out of epistolary novels (although not always out of Richardson's), and for good reason—their model is *not* the letter, not the business of correspondence, but the later, usually posthumous, collection of them into a volume. So Richardson annotates and footnotes like a proper editor. Who cares about the envelopes? Or that passionate epistle I composed in my head and never sent, although today I am no longer sure whether I did or not? Yet how could one write an epistolary novel now without thinking of the palsied hand holding the pen, the machine whose keys stick, the canceled stamps? the baby-blue or soiled canary paper, the little stickum'd return address in the corner, *par avion,* the passionate lines of xxxxs and oooos?

The traditional novelist's commitment to the textual model is no wider than a grin. Neither James nor Richardson is really that interested in *letters*. Both are interested in the peculiar, personal, past-tense, meditative manner letters allow; in the analytic, essaylike exposition of events and feelings they facilitate. Letters aren't overcome by the rush of immediacy, but they aren't dried-up history either. However, the contemporary writer is increasingly concerned with the nature of inscription, with notation, with the space of the page; in the question of where the text starts, stops, overslops; where, if you like, the frame is, the city limits are. Faulkner's texts become intrinsically entangled. What is the connection, in this respect, between *The Sot-Weed Factor* and *Humphry Clinker*? between Barth's recent *Letters,* all of his earlier novels, and those which Richardson has composed? Could a novel like *Letters* have been brief when *Clarissa Harlowe* is so long? Richardson has no room for 'letters' on his title page, although it is Barth's entire title (it forms an acrostic, stands for the alphabet as well as the profession); and when Richardson says, in the first sentence of his preface, that what follows is a history "given in a Series of Letters," he does not stoop to a pun, whereas, for Barth, the pun is principal. He begins bent. Although Clarissa and Lovelace are characters whose realization depends upon the letters Richardson writes for them, many of the people in Barth's massive erasure of the genre are people from his other books, and so *begin* as fictions, they do not merely *end* as such. The dates still matter, but they matter so very differently: 1969 and 1812 line up easily in Barth's Borgesean collection of parallels and correspondence, where all texts are calmly contemporaries and reach out of their covers to caress or kick one another, to shake fists, shake hands, or admonish with a shaken finger. *Clarissa Harlowe* is not Samuel Richardson's life in letters, but in a very significant sense *Letters* is John Barth's *L* in *L*.

Theodore Dreiser wrote as if words had little resonance, no sound, no shape, as if their inscription were invisible, and he employed a syntax as uncomplicated and casual as a wad of cotton. He is a preliterate novelist, and indeed we do soon wish to pass through his words to the world he is asking us to imagine. The pornographer is preliterate in the same way; the dirty deeds he lets us look at lead us to overlook the dirty window through which we are watching them, except, of course, for the dirty words he may use, which retain their unclean interest. Henry James feels a larger obligation, and plumps his page like a pillow, for he is literate to a fault like the golden bowl's. Joyce worries about the color of the cover for *Ulysses,* since he is transliterate. And after all, if alliteration is important, why not the relation of closed spaces to open ones in a type face? Why shouldn't the long sounds in short words astonish? Why should the implications of one materiality lie idle while another is worked and worn out? These days, the text is oozing out into the very shapes of the letters themselves (another ambiguity which Barth did not neglect), out into the space of the print, into the nature of the page—in placement, drawings, type size, binding, cover—into all the other items of attribution and copyright and dedication which may have once been safely "out of the book." Nothing is now safely out of the book.

And when we bring pieces of the outside world into our work—a sample of shirt cloth, maybe, or a bit of tablecloth, a coffee stain, as I have done—don't we do it in order to demonstrate what little reality these scraps and stains have until they become signs?

Transliteracy is our aim: a place beyond the asterisk, if not beyond the stars. And an artist who does not seize upon the possibilities and exploit them; who is not on the lookout for more regions of control, more lands and peoples to occupy and conquer, will never be entitled Tamburlaine, or have a Christopher Marlowe to write bombulating speeches for him: "Now clear the triple regions of the air, and let the majesty of heaven behold their scourge and terror . . . ," and so on. The transliterate notice that Harlowe and Marlowe rhyme, and it sets them to wondering why.

Yet when readers read as if the words on the page were only fleeting visual events, soon to be gone like flies, and not signs to be sung inside themselves—so that the author's voice is stilled—the author's hand must reach out into the space of the page and put a print upon it that will be unmistakable, uneradicable. With lipstick, perhaps. And if, in their new-found yet unearned arrogance, the critics ululate at the death of the author—one more god gone—we shall merely remind them that we were never myths, rode our lovers to death long since, and before they drew breath, and shall henceforth create texts so intelligent they will read themselves.

One such, Rainer Maria Rilke's novel, *The Notebooks of Malte Laurids Brigge,* also has a metaphorical identity. *The Journal of My Other Self* was the title he abandoned for this less explicit and directive one, although the novel does retain a number of journal-like characteristics. By giving up the idea of a daybook, however, Rilke gained a certain freedom from Time. The novel pretends to be made up of two notebooks of very nearly the same length. By calling them notebooks Rilke prepares us to expect a work composed of independent paragraphs and short sections, which is what we get. It also lets him end the work abruptly, when the second notebook is filled, and raises several questions not put to every book that comes to hand: why did Malte begin these notebooks in the first place (a question which the novel answers easily enough), and then, why does he stop? or has he stopped? perhaps a third notebook has been lost? (here the answers are far from obvious, and remain conjectural).

The text's resemblance to any actual notebook is a slight and fragile one, however. Nothing could be less "notelike" than these poetic paragraphs, these vivid vignettes; nothing is less "jotty"; and even though they are mostly memories, these lines of Malte's, they are not reminders to remember, as a note is; they are not jogs to rouse a sleepyhead; they *are* the memories, the moments, themselves. Indeed, we know that Rilke included several of his letters, very little changed, though not identified, in these notebooks. When Lovelace appropriates one of Clarissa's letters it is one thing (a fiction has stolen from a fiction), but when Malte writes down Rilke's prose—what then? It is not a miracle that the eye of Malte, looking through the author's eye, catches sight of those letters and is moved to copy some of them into his life. Such plagiarism happens all the time. The notebook is a trope for the text, then, the way the travel memoir is a trope for Swift, or letters were for Richardson.

In Rilke's case, however, this trope, referred to with suspicious openness in the title, is only the overt likeness. There are at least two other tropes for the text, and they provide a model for our understanding of the fundamental form of the work. The two images are cooperative, not contrasting, one adding a slightly dynamic dimension. The first is represented by the celebrated Unicorn Tapestries on display in the Cluny Museum in Paris. The tapestries are described on the final pages of the first notebook, and in the opening pages of the second; thus these wall hangings, and Rilke's wondrous prose about them, are the novel's hinge; they bridge the gap between the two notebooks. It is not coincidental that the parable of the prodigal son, with which the novel closes, is also represented in a tapestry at Cluny, though it is not one of the ones described. The other image is made of the lace which Malte's mother takes out of a chest and unrolls for him—unspools really—and in which he sees strange designs and mysterious worlds. Unspooling lace, a great wall hanging composed of emblematic creatures almost floating in space: these are the governing figures for the form of *Malte Laurids Brigge,* and they explain the spatialized, relatively static, almost embroidered scenes, thoughts, and fancies which make up the *Notebooks,* and suggest how we may easily pass back and forth among its sections.

Our covert tropes are described by, and function importantly in, the text itself (which does not always happen), and this creates a curious reflexive situation. The Cluny tapestries certainly exist outside the text, and are not themselves a text, yet their description constitutes a text which is part of the text troped. Young girls can be found standing before them, bemused, as Rilke says, until they bring forth their pads and begin to draw, perhaps, one of the happy animals. Part of our way through this work would have been made easier had Rilke chosen to title it *The Sketchbooks of Malte Laurids Brigge.*

What do these metaphors do, and why have some authors chosen to imagine their work in this way? There are two principal problems for any artist who is presently working in the field of fiction. The first is the problem of Form—a perennial headache—for every fiction has at least, by my lazy count, seven structural levels. The second problem, more contemporary in the pressures it exerts, is the difficulty of finding a new and adequate notation for the novelist's investigations, one which will permit new effects, new meanings to be articulated.

The first structural level is the tripartite, preliterary stage of *mythos, dianoia,* and *logos,* of which I have already spoken. The story of Goldilocks is made up of a highly patterned series of events, its repeated verbal formulas, and its moral, or presumed point. The second consists of the linear level of presentation, where narrative, dramatic, and expository designs are decided upon. If the first level can crudely be called the Tale, this is its Telling. In my version, Goldilocks is explaining to her mother why she was roaming around in the woods, how she came to tear her dress, and what she saw there that has excited her so much. The deep theme of sibling rivalry will only gradually be revealed. The third is the level of inscription, where these plans are put into particular words, thus into selected sounds, sequences, syntax, shapes, symbol, and other sibilants. It is what we do when we write: we write. Before this stage is reached (if you do not begin here and discover your story as you scribble along), you have only that awful object with which acquaintances, knowing that you are an author, are always presenting you, as though with a gift, namely, "a good idea for a novel."

If the novel is a mind aware of a world, then its ontological status, at the fourth division, is complex and troubled. As mind, it is meaning, and belongs in a Platonic nowhere; as the world that mind is aware of, it is object, matter, extension, creatures, things—metaphorically observed, of course, and dreamed as only possible; then as writing read and sounded, it is both spatially simultaneous and yet present only in its sounded moment like music. The printed text exists as a whole, all at once, as the rooms, stairways, and floors of a building do; and our first reading is like our first visit to the Palace of the Popes at Avignon, perhaps, where an informed and garrulous guide leads us here and there as seems best: one step, one hall and doorway, one religious relic, at a time; but it remains a building whose relation to the clock—like the Escorial—is only phenomenological. Novels are books and books are buildings, and therefore they exist like other built objects—they are a space in space. The temporality of *Finnegans Wake* is, first and foremost, circular like the text which establishes it; the game of chess requires a squared-off field, and gets it in Nabokov's *The Defense; Terra Nostra* collapses time like a punctured balloon; the numbered rectangles requisite for hopscotch are laid out in Cortázar's novel; and the logarithmic spiral in Barth's "Perseid" winds itself triumphantly around a pillar, so that, in a certain sense, pieces of the text can properly be said to be above and to the left or right of others. The colon [: : : : : : :] in Goytisolo's work not only announces the beginning of a list—so: it is also two fingers thrust in the eye, like one of the aggressive gestures of the Three Stooges. These tropes for the text, these spatializations, center themselves in the field of the page—in the ontology of the *printed* or *written* word.

However, the printed word is but a surrogate for the spoken one, and only those works, like Dreiser's, in which the results of real reading are too cacophonous, and where haste, like running through the rain, is called for, should be thought of as silent. Silence, indeed, is the last aspect of the word, the one we use when we read, not aloud, but to ourselves, creating shadows of sound with incipient muscularities—bringing the concept (stripped naked of flesh, deprived of bone) as near to Plato's conception of it as can be and have life. Here is the true source of the word; it is in the silent speaker, as Beckett has seen and insisted. Although the written word has become increasingly important for thought and the clear and simple conveyance of information, the spoken word will remain basic for every literary use because it is the word we learned as infants, which has those reservoirs of early feeling, which we still use to talk to ourselves, and which constitutes any close human exchange.[2]

Nowadays, of course, a text will bring written and spoken words together like butter and honey on a biscuit. When, in *Letters,* John Barth presents us the formula for the "Swan-Geese" folk tale which he says Professors Propp and Rosenberg have discovered,

$$\gamma\beta\delta \text{ ABC} \uparrow \left\{ \frac{[\text{DE Neg F Neg}]^3}{\text{DEF}} \right\} \text{GHIK} \downarrow \text{Pr [DEF]}\ ^3\text{Rs}$$

of course we are only supposed to stare like a visitor at the zoo at some outlandish animal, just as we are to register the word "RESET" as an indication of the computer's presence in the passage; but all around this unintelligible formula, as around the charts and diagrams and graphs, the language mills as down a millrace, and would the wheel turn if the water passed without a sound?

The same author's extraordinary novella "The Menelaid" consists of a containing "frame tale" and six other stories, neatly nested in the Chinese fashion, inside it. The quotation marks we use to indicate indirect address [I said he said *she* said], and logicians use to differentiate between words in the object language [look at the cow, Billy], words themselves [Billy, write the word 'cow'], and words in the metalanguage ["cow" is what we call 'cow,' Billy, whereas 'cow' is what we call cows], are used, in turn, by Barth, whenever something is said in one story which is also simultaneously said in another, so that, at one point, Helen severally answers—and I quote—" " ' " ' " ' "Love!" ' " ' " ' " " We are

2. Some justification for my view that the spoken word is primary is provided in the essays "The Soul Inside the Sentence," "On Talking to Oneself," and "On Reading to Oneself" in this volume. Plato's point of view, and the true source of the word, are the subject of "The Habitations of the Word."

suddenly able to look down through story after story as though we were peering down an elevator shaft, to see the space below. "The Menelaid" is pierced with these moments, as with spears.

We can imagine stories told in code, with a template of word-sized holes forming one page, and an uninterrupted text another. With the template down, the text will tell a different tale.

So notations differ radically in what they aim at. Some, like plans, maps, sketches, exhibit marks and spaces designed to disclose to us other spatial relations: wires, river, rooms; while those of a more narrowly literary kind, however spatially indited, are marks made to be felt; they signify an exceptional set of silences or sounds, as we reenact the pauses in *Waiting for Godot* or the panting in *How It Is* or try to fully mouth the pages of *The Golden Bowl*.

If all these elements seem outrageously heterogeneous, remember that the writer's wrestle with the word is not any different than Descartes' with the world. A rose is a rose is a rose is not a rose garden.

On the fifth floor (we are nearly to notions, rugs, and blond mod furniture) we find the phenomenological: the work as it is actually read or experienced. Ontologically, for example, the music of the read work is conceived as continuous, like those nonstop readings of *The Making of Americans* which occur occasionally at Concept Carnivals and New York Book Fairs. However, the motion of the text depends on the reader (one reason for Richardson's strategies of stimulation: they keep the reader reading—when will the hand that's just held the pen slip down a bodice?); but every author realizes only too well that readers answer the door, go to the bathroom, doze, skim, skip, peek ahead, reread, misread, get sick, mislay, forget, lend. Not only is the reader who is implied by the ontology of the text indefatigable but he or she (actually there is little energy left for establishing a sexual identity) must often have a perfect memory. Fielding allows us to forget pages of details, just as we forget things in life, but Joyce's texts roll up behind themselves like a wave, so that every past page continues to weigh upon every succeeding one, as, in fact, the future pages do, as if something were bending them back, constantly affecting the Now with the Not-Yet. The textual metaphor for Joyce's *Ulysses* may be Homer's *Odyssey*, but his nontextual metaphor is the twenty-four-hour day—the day that is to replace the reader's day, the day the reader will need to give up in order to live through Joyce's fiction, reading continuously, going to the bathroom only when Bloom does. It is the day, of course, that is a small model for the whole of life. It is that day, like most, which is half dark and perfectly Manichean. The trope for *Finnegans Wake,* on the other hand, is the lifetime night-

mare—the whole of history undertaken in blackness, in sleep, in confusion—so that the replacement of the reader's existence with the lifeline
of the text is total.

But *Finnegans Wake* dictates the phenomenology of its visitors as
well, precisely because it expects nothing but visitors. Its Viconian structure is repeated on almost every page, the general point is made again
and again, the levels of allegory and analogy and insinuation and inference are stacked up in sentence after sentence like a waiter's plates. Here
the reader's interest cannot be sewn to some story like a button to a coat,
the narrative thread is too weak for that and far away; so it doesn't
matter where you begin, or whether you come or go. *It* is all there anyway, even if you aren't.

Sometimes elements of the text which we associate with one level
make their persistent way up or down to another: such are the ubiquitous
colons of Goytisolo's *Makbara.* They soon cease to be punctuation and
become guns going off. The catalogues they announce are not by Sears
& Roebuck. Notation, too, can find its way into our nightmares. How
about, on death lists, the little lines that do the crossing out?

Sometimes texts, like many of Gertrude Stein's, anticipate the brief,
bewildered, even hostile, attention they will receive from their readers,
and mimic, or mock, or in other ways duplicate it. Furthermore, the con-
temporary text is not made for *a* reading, for one does not read *Count
Julian* or *Terra Nostra* or *Paradiso* or *The Lime Works* or *The Passion
Artist* or *Invisible Cities* or *The Green House* or *JR* or *The Tin Drum* or
The Autumn of the Patriarch (to cite only a few significant contemporary novels); one does not read *A Public Burning, Degrees,* or *A Bad
Man* the first time in order to read it, but to ready oneself to read it.
Only the common run of novels expects the one-night stand. Fielding
and Richardson require a fresh and interested eye, but the events themselves should intrigue it, the situations should excite. Joyce and Beckett
and Barth and Borges expect a jaded eye, one already blackened by its
most recent round in the ring, chary of further blows, not a bit innocent,
for whom all the action, the incidents, the tension and suspense, are
well known and over and dead and gone. The steamy sex sits in a cold
pot now; and only perfection, complexity and richness of meaning,
depth, resonance, a resourcefulness surpassing Ulysses'—however dis-
gruntled the mood, however sour the tone—only feeling, song itself,
satisfies . . . suits.

If it is astonishing to us now that innumerable readers, mostly women,
ill prepared for Richardson's genius, we might suppose, would eat their
way through the pages of *Clarissa,* what are we to expect will be said

when such appetites are served *JR, Terra Nostra,* or *Letters* (to mention once more three great works of the twentieth-century imagination). To begin them at all is foolhardy. To quit early is to lie to your friends. These works require everything; they expect nothing. They are, and are symbols of, the art of our time. Perhaps their length will eventually be forgiven them, their difficulty overcome; perhaps even their art will be forgiven; but who will forgive the cultivation they require, their intelligence?

The sixth level, often put last, is the form which negates form, as Beckett's novel *How It Is* negates in its final pages all the pages which have gone before. *Letters* consistently betrays its own trope.

Shapelessness may be the general enemy of shape, but every particular form has its own undoing, its forceful opposite, that condition which it is continually not being. In the mosaic pattern on the floor of a pilgrim church, there is often found the outline of a maze, and amid the ordered garden which surrounds a luminously laid out palace, a labyrinth of hedges may be encountered. Beneath the vaulted nave of the cathedral lie those other vaults, its lifeless opposites, the crypts. Penelope undoes during the night what she has woven during the day, and Prometheus' liver nightly repairs itself for the daily visit of the vultures. If there is no insubstantial shadow, there is no substance which has cast it. Home is the aim of the Odyssey, but not getting there constitutes the story. The circularity of *Finnegans Wake* encloses a zero, and out of that mountain of meaning an idle hen scratches, as out of a midden, a meaningless message.

Lovelace's letters regularly threaten to become endless, and hence to be no longer letters. *The Good Soldier*'s saddest story is told to somebody, but to whom? It is like a letter which has lost itself in monologue, just as Beckett's plays always threaten to reverse the history of the Greek theater and progressively eliminate, first the third, then the second, actor.

My seventh and final area of organization is, of course, the trope of the text. As we know, an author may not be aware of these levels, or may describe them differently, or choose to ignore them, in which case their condition is somewhat analogous to a hotel's suppressed thirteenth floor: not on the elevator indicator, full of splayed beds, broken television sets, irremediably soiled sheets and no longer resilient mattresses to which bellboys and chambermaids repair to revitalize the dust and warm the dark. In other words, these are levels of opportunity. In the game of life, it may be that opportunities are best avoided, or politely declined, so that we can hold on more tightly to what we have, but in the serious business of art, opportunities are enemies unless seized.

The novel, this inherently loose and baggy monster, to re-aim James's words, must be disinherited of disorder, and there is simply so much to do, so many ends, like flies, to tie, so many bases to touch, so many details which must be made essential, so many *mots* to be beaten or flattered into being *juste,* that tropes for the text have been increasingly employed, not only to organize certain levels better (which the trope may have a tendency to single out) but to dissolve genres (one of Borges' fictions will say it is an essay, one of his essays will suggest it is a story), to establish connections between texts through the trope, or to try to fasten all the levels together, to form forms. Katherine Anne Porter's brilliant little story "The Grave" uses its title as a headstone. The reader enters the text as the children in the story enter those holes from which the coffins have been removed. The reader comes away from the text with symbols, just as the two children find the engraved ring, and silver dove, a coffin screw. And the reader experiences that same sudden epiphany of meaning that Miranda does, as the graves of memory open, and the past is retrieved. The trope organizes the entire work, even our experience of it.

The trope sometimes begins in sameness, and then careens toward difference. This book is full of letters, it says, and then we find that it is not. Equally often, it begins its work at a distance—the text is a grave, it says, a sphere, a building, a box—and then approaches like the villain in a horror movie: closer and closer.

The trope which any text proposes for itself contains its unholy ghost, just as Katherine Anne Porter's grave is an absence, a past, from which a recollection, a recognition, a renewal arises, and, indeed, is the emptiness to which it will retire, which it will fill again.

A novel of mine, *Willie Masters' Lonesome Wife,* regards its text as the body of a woman of generous morals and much misuse, so that I once felt it might be appropriate to provide those who thought to enter it with a condom which would serve double duty as a book mark, so safeguarding their journey. But the symbol was too sexist, the publisher too chary. Let them take their chances. No one warned *me.* Long ago I contracted the Verbal Disease.

My present novel, *The Tunnel,* is dominated by the trope of its title. The text is at once the hollow absence of life, words, and earth, which the narrator is hauling secretly away; then it is the uneasy structure of bedboards, bent flesh, rhetorical flourishes and other fustian forms, which shapes the passage, and which incontinently caves in occasionally, filling the reader's nose with noise, and ears with sand and misunderstanding; while finally it is the shapeless mess of dirt, word-dung, and desire, which has to be taken out and disposed of. Every tunnel invokes Being, Non-Being, and Becoming in equal portions and with equal fervor. This is the last example I shall force upon you, and a cautionary instance, for now and then the trope itself will be in such need of a proper bringing up, be itself such a symbol of flight and connection, concealment and search, that it brings its wretched employer nothing but confusion, nothing but Postmodernism, nothing but grief.

is used 3381 times in James Joyce's *A Portrait of the Artist as a Young Man,* and occurs on 7170 occasions in that same author's *Ulysses,* from which we can conclude that the latter is a much longer book. It appears oftener than 'a' and oftener than 'an'—although its frequency lags far behind 'the' (as regards ubiquity always the winner)—and it easily outdoes 'or,' 'of,' 'it,' 'oh!,' as well as every other little word which might be presumed to be its rival, even 'is,' even 'I.'[1] Some snoop[2] has reported that of the number of words we use in ordinary correspondence, nine words ('I,' 'the,' 'and,' 'you,' 'to,' 'your,' 'of,' 'for,' and 'in'), at one time at least, comprised a fourth of the total, whereas in telephone conversations 'and' barely makes the top ten in frequency of use.

Words that get heavy, one might say almost continuous, employment, are invariably short. Suppose 'and' were as long as 'moreover'? It would soon *mean* "moreover," and drop to an ignominious rate of three in *A Portrait,* to a sad two in *Ulysses,* a frequency which will scarcely seed a satisfying life. And if 'and' were spelled, say, like 'Mesopotamia,' would it receive any use at all? And what would happen to the ideas it represents, if we were too busy to think them, or to all the various ands in the world we could no longer trouble ourselves to designate? That ceaselessly constant conjunction of which Hume spoke would now be noted only rarely: when we were forced to remind ourselves of the connection between Punch moreover Judy, or Mutt mesopotamia Jeff.

Such is not its plight, or ours, however. On word lists, the occurrences of 'and' are merely numbered, never cited. The dictionary contains it only as a courtesy, and out of a traditional conceit of completeness. No

---

1. *Word Index to James Joyce's Portrait of the Artist,* compiled by Leslie Hancock (Carbondale, Ill.: Southern Illinois University Press, 1967), and *Word Index to James Joyce's Ulysses,* compiled by Miles L. Hanley (Madison, Wisc.: privately printed, 1937).
2. The Bell System, of course. H. L. Mencken, *The American Language, Supplement Two* (New York: Alfred Knopf, 1948), p. 352.

one is going to look up 'and.' We do not "look up" manhole covers when we visit the city. So it is a squeak we are used to. It passes through the ear, the eye, the mind, unheard, unseen, and unremarked. It can copulate as openly as birds do, the way park ducks wanton on their ponds. Indeed, pigeons are more heatedly complained of, for 'and' leaves no poop on public shoulders. As a word, 'and' is an amiable nothing. It hasn't even a substantiating, an ennobling function like 'the,' which has caused many a philosopher's hackles to rise.

Joyce singled out 'the' and gave it pride of final place in *Finnegans Wake,* although one might argue that while 'the' has the last word in the body of the text, it acts only to buckle the belly of the book together, and that the pride of penultimate places is actually given to 'a,' ordinarily a halt word, a rhyme chime, a mere space maker, the shallowest exhalation: "A way a lone a last a loved a long the . . ." where it interrupts the ells as they likker across the tongue: "lone last loved long riverrun, past Eve and Adam's, from swerve of shore to bend of bay . . . a . . . a . . . a . . ." Just a few lines earlier, 'and' had been allowed to perform an equally rocking rhythmical function: "And it's old and old it's sad and old it's sad and weary I go back to you, my cold father, my cold mad father, my cold mad feary father . . ." It is worth noticing how 'old' slips into an 'O' like a woman into a wrapper: "And it's old and O it's sad and O it's sad and weary . . ." just as the C-sound it picks up later will reinstruct our ears so that we hear, in retrospect, "And it's cold and cold it's sad and cold it's sad and weary . . ." Of these musical methods, of course, Joyce was a master.

The anonymity of 'and,' its very invisibility, recommends the word to the student of language, for when we really look at it, study it, listen to it, 'and' no longer appears to be 'and' at all, because 'and' is, as we said, invisible, one of the threads that holds our clothes together: what business has it being a pants leg or the frilly panel of a blouse? The unwatched word is meaningless—a noise in the nose—it falls on the page as it pleases, while the writer is worrying about nouns and verbs, welfare checks or a love affair; whereas the watched word has many meanings, some of them profound; it has a wide range of functions, some of them essential; it has many lessons to teach us about language, some of them surprising; and it has metaphysical significance of an even salutary sort.

'And'

is produced initially with an open mouth, the breath flowing out, but then that breath is driven up against the roof, toward the nose, even invading it before the sound is stoppered by the tongue against the teeth. The article 'a' can be pronounced "aw," "A," "uh," "aah," or nearly forgotten, while 'the' is "thuh" or "thee," depending on position and status; but 'and' is only and always "and," although its length, like many such words which contain the outrush of a vowel, is relatively indeterminate: "aah-nn-duh"—where the "duh" is like a lariat lassoing the next word, filling the voice stream, allowing one's thought to continue, inhibiting interruptions: "pahst Eeev anduhAahdummz . . ." In Middle English, and often among the vulgar since, the word has appeared in reduced circumstances, either as a conditional: an' it please your lordship, I'll drop me drawers; or as a common conjunction: an' here an' there the bullets went an' never touched me nearly. Hollywood nosh nooks, back in the thirties, bobbed it even farther: "Dunk 'n Dine," their signs said, "Sit 'n Eat." There was also the nautical "spit 'n polish," and that enigmatic putdown "shit 'n shinola."[3] Nothing rivals the erosion which 'and' in Spanish has had to suffer. My sources affirm that it was '*Yolanda*' in its early great romantic days, whereas now it goes about as the vulgar, hardly heard '*y*.' We live in evil times.

Although the sound "and" and the word 'and' may appear and reappear in sentence after sentence, both in spoken and in written form, there is no single meaning (AND) which remains tethered to the token. The word is, perhaps, no sneakier than most words, but it is sneaky enough, hiding itself inside other sounds, pulling syllables up over its head. It is, of course, the principal element in 'randy,' 'saraband,' and 'island,' a not inconsiderable segment of 'Andorra,' 'Anderson,' 'antediluvian,' 'Spandau,' and 'ampersand,' whose elegantly twisted symbol [& — &] (the so-called short or alphabetical 'and' made by intertwining the 'e' and 't' of 'et') also contains it. 'Ampersand' has been reported to be a slovenly corruption of 'and per se and,' which would suggest, when the symbol is used, that it wishes to upset any implied balance or equality in favor of the leadoff term: *Dombey and Son* would mean "Dombey and equally his son," while *Dombey & Son* would mean "Dombey in himself and, in addition, his son." 'And' also lurks about in words like 'spanned,' and in apparently innocent commands like 'please put the pan down, Anne,' as well as in many allegations or simple statements of fact, for instance, that 'panders and pimps and pushers, panhandlers and prostitutes, stand like so many lamps on the streetcorners.'

---

3. "He don't know shit from shinola" and "He don't know the difference between shit 'n shinola" both refer, I take it, to the condition of one's footwear, since Shinola is a shoe polish.

Not only are there more 'ands' about than immediately meets the eye, the word by itself in the open is manifold in its meanings, and not in the way that most words are ambiguous either: 'bank' variously signifying a calculated bounce or guarded vault or sloping river edge; 'rank' signifying something overripe or of military station; 'tank' referring to an armored vehicle, a cylinder for gas or certain fluids, an approximate measure. 'And' is ambiguous the way prepositions are, not straightforwardly but curvaceously, almost metaphysically, multiple. Think of the differences designated by the same, seemingly simple, 'on' in (1) 'the poorhouse is on fire,' (2) 'the seafood is on the table,' (3) 'her panties were hanging on the line,' (4) 'their lacy patterns turned him on,' (5) 'now his mind was mainly on Mary.'[4] Such words are constantly in transit between meanings, their very indeterminacy an invitation to their contexts to seize and to shape them; and if 'bank' were like that, we should sense how we might slide down some weedy slope into the till, or how we might count on a good bounce from our rubber check.

Initially a preposition itself, and derived from 'end,' the idea of fronting or facing a boundary, the word suggested an opposition, a standing of something next to but over against something else, such as 'up' with 'down,' 'high' next to 'low,' 'peace' over against 'war.' Later, as various words collapsed into and became 'and' ('ond,' 'ant,' 'enti,' 'anda,' 'undi,' 'und,' 'unt,' 'et,' et cetera) its function as a relatively neutral conjunction increased. Now not even Proteus can match the magicality of its many metamorphoses.

A single example from Gertrude Stein's "Melanctha" should be sufficient to show our small word's true and larger nature.

> She tended Rose, and[1] she was patient, submissive, soothing, and[2] untiring, while the sullen, childish, cowardly, black Rosie grumbled and[3] fussed and[4] howled and[5] made herself to be an abomination and[6] like a simple beast.

['And' #1] "She tended Rose, and she was patient, submissive, soothing . . ." This is the adverbial use of 'and.' The expression is to be read: "She tended Rose, and [in doing so] she was patient, submissive, soothing . . ." It is not so much that 'and' is an adverb here; rather it determines the nature of application to the verb 'tended' of what follows it. We have no grammatical category for this operation.

['And' #2] ". . . she was patient, submissive, soothing, and untir-

---

4. I discuss the ambiguous character of the preposition 'of,' citing fourteen different uses without presuming to have mentioned all of them, in "The Ontology of the Sentence, or How to Make a World of Words," *The World Within the Word*, pp. 308–338.

ing . . ." This 'and' begins as the 'and' of balance and coordination. That is, we have 'soothing' on the one hand balanced logically and grammatically with 'untiring' like two weights on a scale. Both words belong to the same part of speech; both are about the same length; both designate qualities of the same logical order, although soothed is something the patient is supposed to feel, while untiring is something the nurse is, and, more important, looks. But when 'soothing,' as a word, is not alone; when it is joined, on its side, by two others; then the balance goes out of whack, and the nature of our 'and' begins to alter.

$$\underline{patient, \ submissive, \ soothing} \ \underset{\triangle}{\underline{untiring}}$$

The 'and' we now confront means "finally." It may even mean "and in particular" or "above all." Death, Donne tells us, is "a slave to fate, chance, kings, and [finally] desperate men." This 'and,' then, moves from one meaning to another like a pointer on that imaginary scale it has suggested. It begins by intimating equality and balance, but both its position in the series (last) and its separation from the rest ('and' acts as a barrier) increase its importance, as if it were significant enough by itself to weigh as much as the other three. Principally, however, this second 'and' indicates the approaching conclusion of a list the way certain symphonic gestures ready us for the culmination of the music. "I love your lips, nose, eyes, hair, chin, and hollow cheeks, your big bank account and bust, my dear." Balances are delicate and easily tipped. The social status of a word, its force, its length, its history of use: anything can do it. Syntax sets up the scale, but semantics puts the weights in the pans. The following are out of balance: (1) "the bandit shot my son, stabbed me in the arm, and called me names," (2) "what bitter things both life and aspirin are!," (3) "I've boated everywhere—on the Po and on Pawtucket Creek," (4) "you say your marriage suffers from coital insufficiency and greasy fries?," (5) "yeah, my wife kisses her customers and brings their bad breath to bed."

Between the words 'patient' and 'submissive' in the Stein sentence, only a comma intervenes, but that comma stands for an 'and' whose presence is purely conceptual. It is 'and' become ghostly and bodiless. It is that famously fatuous gleam in Father's eye. Indeed, one could easily write another essay on the germinal, the spermatic character of this seedy wormlike bit of punctuation. The comma resembles the law, and can command our conscience without a policeman. The absence of the officer is essential to its effect, however, for "she was patient and submissive and soothing and untiring" is another sentence entirely, and not a very forceful one.

To the logician, who is at least patient and untiring, if not soothing and submissive, a connective like 'and' or its sometime substitute, the comma, asserts the joint dependency of every element in the pursuit of truth. The logician is outspoken and prefers everything laid out on the bed like clothes for a trip. She (Melanctha) was patient; and she (Melanctha) was submissive; and she (Melanctha) was soothing; and she (Melanctha) was untiring, too—at once and altogether. One can hear what a wearisome way to go at things this is; and for some of the same reason we like our workaday words short and preferably snappy, we fold our ideas over whenever we can—wad them up—and indicate the folds with commas. The logician's assertion of mutual dependency of parts where truth is concerned is paradoxical, and tells us a good deal about 'and,' because 'and,' whenever it interposes its body, separates each quality from the others and insists that we examine them one at a time, as if they might display themselves on different days or places (as if we were saying that Melanctha was patient on Tuesday, when she wore her bright blue dress, and untiring on Wednesday in her red riding habit, and submissive on Sunday, when she put on her smart pink smock); as if being patient and untiring were conditions which never interpenetrate or affect one another.

The logician's 'and' is indifferent to grouping and order. It is all the same to it whether (1) "Bill has a boil on his nose and water in the pot" or (2) "water in the pot and a boil on his nose" or whether (3) "Bill has a boil on his nose, water in the pot, and a plant on the sill," or (4) "a boil on his nose and water in the pot, a plant on the sill with its window on the world." To our logician, if Melanctha was soothing, then she was soothing, and while we know that she was soothing, we also know she failed to soothe, for Rose Johnson behaved like a simple beast. She was, in good biblical fashion, an abomination. Soothing that is not soothing is not exactly the same as soothing that succeeds and soothes. It is much more likely, in fact, to be infuriating. Who, after all, enjoys being placated? there . . . there . . .

'And'

plays a major role in the meaning of many words familiar to the logician like 'yet,' 'but,' and 'although,' although 'and' is not all of any. "Bill has a boil on his nose, but a window on the world" suggests that "Bill has a boil on his nose, and nevertheless throws open a window on the world."

'But' is often an 'although' and 'although' is frequently an "and despite."
"Bill has water in the pot, although his plant is on the sill."

In short, in addition to its full appearance as a word, 'and' can make itself felt simply as a sound, as in the expression 'canned ham,' or it can constitute the underlying meaning of another connective like 'but,' or it can exert itself invisibly, as a recurrent idea, a rule of organization. Counting the commas which are stand-ins for it, there are eleven 'ands' in Gertrude Stein's sentence.

['And' #3] ". . . while the sullen, childish, cowardly, black Rosie grumbled and fussed . . ." Our second 'and' drew a list to a close. This third 'and' occurs immediately after the commencement of such a series. Certainly 'and,' here, suggests that 'grumbled' and 'fussed' are in balance, but 'fussed' will soon be paired with 'howled,' and momentarily find itself in a tray belonging to two different scales. As we pass along the list, accumulating the 'ands' of 'grumbled and fussed and howled and made herself an abomination . . .' we must constantly shift our weight, first grouping 'grumbled' with 'fussed,' then 'fussed' with 'howled,' and finally, with four characteristics at last in place, comparing the first pair of bad behaviors with the second set.

grumbled   *fussed*   howled   *made herself to be an abomination*

The specific thing that 'fussed' does is to add itself to 'grumbled,' and the idea of addition, like those of balance, equality, difference, and co-ordination, is basic to our word, which is often a $+$ sign. "Rosie grumbled and [in addition] fussed." Additions, of course, can be of many kinds. Sometimes they merely lengthen a list: (1) "Darling: remember to buy Kleenex and coffee and new strings for your mop." Sometimes, however, they alter its character, change its direction, either mildly, as (2) "I love your lips, nose, eyes, hair, chin, and fallen bosom" does, or more radically, like (3) "Duckie, don't forget catsup, kohlrabi, and some conniption, a large can, you know, the kind in sugar syrup."

Every addition implies that somewhere there's a sum. You can't add one number to another—8 to 4, for instance—if the 8 has disappeared by the time the 4 has come round to be counted. However, ordinary actions are like that. I must stop hopping if I'm to skip, and halt all skipping if I'm to jump. My present footstep cannot find the others I have made, even their sound on the sidewalk is gone. So 'fussed' adds itself to 'grumbled' only in the mind of some observer for whom the sum is one of aggravation. To Melanctha, Rose Johnson grumbled, and (in addition) fussed, and (to top it off) howled. Since Rose did not fuss because she had grumbled, her actions, as external events, merely follow one another in time, and replace one another in space, the way Hume indicates our impressions do; and this notion of a simple "next!" is another which is fundamental to the meaning of 'and.'

Certain things cannot be added to others because they are already there by implication. To lamb stew you cannot *add* lamb. Nor is there any sense in saying that "In addition to being triangular, their love affair had three sides." Thus, because it is a defining list, in "sullen, childish, cowardly, black Rosie," the commas do not replace a plus.

When, however, we try to add salt to sensation or affection to a mitered joint, either we exhibit a woeful lack of knowledge about English and the English-Speaking World, or we are marvelous makers of metaphor: (1) "his stew absolutely sparkled with salt and sensation"; or (2) "they made an affectionate and mitered joint"—cases where it is probably the 'and' itself which is metaphorical, pretending that it can conjoin "right and life," "he and whee," "solicitude and shrimp." These cases are rare because most writers ignore 'of,' 'and,' 'but,' 'because,' 'why,' 'not' as possible transformers of reality, but that does not mean they are unimportant. Boundaries, outer edges, extreme cases, define.

Generally, 'and' designates only external and unnecessary relations; it deals with incidentals, separables, shoes that slip on and off; but not when it means something like "equally true." "A triangle has three sides and [it is equally true that] the sum of its interior angles is 180°." To return to the metaphorical 'and' for just one more moment: "A triangle has three sides and [it is equally true that] each one of its sides is after an angle."

['And' #4] ". . . Rosie grumbled and fussed *and* howled . . ." This is the 'and' of increasing emphasis. "Rosie grumbled and [in addition] fussed and [what's more] howled." It has not lost its coordinate qualities (indeed it is now operating as a pivot between two pairs), and it remains an additive 'and' too, but it is now in a place of weight as well. This usually requires that it occupy the last place in any series of conjunctions, and that the items of the set (in this case, names of actions) show a corresponding rise, swell, or increase in scope and importance. You might get away with "Rosie fussed and grumbled and howled," because it is difficult to regard fussing as any more serious or annoying than grumbling, but you would never find much sanction for "Rosie howled and grumbled and fussed," unless, of course, you had a special use for that kind of comedown.

Malory's celebrated lament for Lancelot uses 'and' to create a brilliant anaphoric series:

> Sir Launcelot . . . thou wert never matched of earthly
> knight's hand; and thou wert the courteoust knight that ever
> bare shield; and thou wert the truest friend to thy lover that
> ever bestrad horse; and thou wert the truest lover of sinful
> man that ever loved woman; and thou wert the kindest man
> that ever struck with sword; and thou wert the goodliest per-
> son that ever came among press of knights; and thou wert the
> meekest man and the gentlest that ever ate in hall among
> ladies; and thou wert the sternest knight to thy mortal foe
> that ever put spear in the rest.

Omit the 'and' in "knight's hand" and the eight other 'ands' which follow
it, and you will lose, among other things, the sense of contrast between
qualities which the conjunction heightens: the sense, throughout, of characteristics coexisting despite one another: "fire and ice," "snow and
sand," " 'and' and 'but.' "

['And' #5] ". . . and made herself to be an abomination . . ." Our
fifth 'and,' since it appears in series with 'ands' #3 & #4, begins by
signaling that it is another addition with emphasis. Indeed, it starts to
withdraw some of #4's culminating force, for it is seen, now, not quite
to culminate. However, the expression which follows the fifth 'and' is not
a single verb, which its normal coordinating function would lead us to
expect anyway, but an entire clause. Furthermore, while 'howling,' 'fussing,' and 'grumbling' are intransitive verbs, 'making' is not. I said a moment ago that addition implies a sum, and here it is: the summarizing,
totalizing 'and.' "Rosie grumbled and fussed and howled and [altogether]
made herself to be an abomination . . ."

['And' #6] ". . . and like a simple beast." Our final explicit 'and'
does not occur in a balancing position. Although it is in series, that
series, as we have moved through it, has been undergoing transformations. 'Fussed' is added to 'grumbled,' then 'howled' is emphatically
attached, and these add up to 'abomination.' Now this sum is interpreted
and explained by resorting to the 'and' of equivalance, to the 'and' of
"that is to say." "She made herself to be an abomination and [that is to
say] like a simple beast."

We can summarize the six different functions of the spelled-out 'ands'
in Gertrude Stein's admirably instructive sentence this way: "She tended
Rose, and [in doing so] she was patient, submissive, soothing, and [finally]
untiring, while the sullen, childish, cowardly, black Rosie grumbled and
[in addition] fussed and [what's more] howled and [taken altogether]
made herself to be an abomination and [what is the same thing] like a
simple beast."

So far, we have considered these 'ands' as if they existed in relative isolation, in terms of their local impact upon one another, and not in terms of the total effect of their use. But six 'ands' have surfaced in this sentence. Each one comes between its companions like a referee. Within most prepositional phrases, for instance, the sense of things follows the reading eye from left to right as seems proper. "Look → at the little dog → in its cute pink angora sweater." Because, in such formations, the so-called minor and undominant connectors come first, meaning moves toward 'dog,' then 'sweater' like a drain, although with all those adjectives piled up in the second phrase, the drain begins to clog. But our 'ands' part their elements while retaining them. They divvy, weigh, and order. They spread their objects out like dishes on a table. "And look at the little dog, and at its cute and pink and fuzzy angora sweater." Innocence is thick as custard here, because 'and' is an enemy of ordinary subordination. It appears (although this, as we saw, is somewhat illusory) . . . it appears to be unspecific and sloppy, to replace definitely understood connections with vaguely indistinct ones; hence it is frequently found in unstudied and childlike speech, or in regressive and harried circumstances. "I saw a snake and it was long and black and slithery and fork-tongued and pepper-eyed and slimy and evil and a cliché in the grass." Although such a sentence generates plenty of forward motion, most of it is due to the breathlessness implied by the repeated use of the conjunction, and not by its separative and spatializing function.

Gertrude Stein's sentence achieves its slightly breathless quality this way, but its innocent simplicity is only apparent. If one wants the child to grow up to be a man, the 'ands' may be ruthlessly removed. "I saw a snake. It was long. It was black, slithery, fork-tongued and pepper-eyed. It was slimy, evil. It was a cliché in the grass." More often than not, minimalism is mere mindlessness.

In the following example, Ernest Hemingway, Gertrude Stein's anderstudy, is working for a kind of fuddled bewilderment and frightened energy by a deliberate misuse of the word. The narrator in the story "After the Storm" has just knifed a man in a bar.

> Well, I went out of there and there were plenty of them with him and some came out after me and I made a turn and was down by the docks and I met a fellow and he said somebody killed a man up the street. I said "Who killed him?" and he said "I don't know who killed him but he's dead all right," and it was dark and there was water standing in the street and no lights and windows broke and boats all up in the town and trees blown down and everything all blown and I

got a skiff and went out and found my boat where I had her inside of Mango Key and she was all right only she was full of water. So I bailed her out and pumped her out and there was a moon but plenty of clouds and still plenty rough and I took it down along; and when it was daylight I was off Eastern Harbor.

These 'ands' do not establish parallels or connections; they suggest chasms. Between one act and another—between turning a corner and meeting a man—there is nothing. These 'ands' condense or skip. They insist upon the suddenness of everything, the disappearance of time, the collision of distant spaces. Of course these are the 'ands' of nervousness, too, of worry and sleeplessness, of sheep leaping fences one after another. They cause events to ricochet.[5]

'Ands'

are almost essential for excess. They are perfect if you want to make big piles or imply an endless addition. One 'and' may make a tidy pair, closing a couple like a lock: *War and Peace,* ham and eggs, *Pride and Prejudice.* Add another, however, and the third 'and' will begin to alter the earlier ones the same miraculous way the squashed and flattened condition designated by 'mashed' is lent the fully contrasting sense of 'heaped' simply by putting it near the word 'potato.' No one is any better at this energetic mounding than the Dickens of *Dombey.* Here is part of a long passage describing the ruination of a neighborhood by some new laid railroad tracks. It implies he is not telling us the half of it:

> There were frowzy fields, and cow-houses, and dunghills, and dust-heaps, and ditches, and gardens, and summerhouses, and carpet-beating grounds, at the very door of the railway. Little tumuli of oyster shells in the oyster season, and of lobster shells in the lobster season, and of broken crockery and faded cabbage leaves in all seasons, encroached upon its high places. Posts, and rails, and old cautions to trespassers, and backs of mean houses, and patches of wretched vegetation, stared it out of countenance.

There is the 'and' that enumerates things and conditions, as here, and helps to fork them into heaps; and there is the 'and' which multiplies

---

5. Frederick Busch discusses a part of this passage and makes some similar points in "Icebergs, Islands, Ships Beneath the Sea," in *Insights I; Working Papers in Contemporary Criticism, a John Hawkes Symposium* (New York: New Directions, 1977), pp. 51–52.

names and descriptions, creating a verbal heap instead, as we frequently find in Rabelais, master of all middens, and of every excess the celebrant, and extoller, and rhapsodist.

If we momentarily return, now, to the first 'and' of Gertrude Stein's set of six, we can see that it attaches the entire remainder of our sentence to the initial "She tended Rose . . ." This 'and' is adverbial, as we saw, informing us how well and kindly Melanctha took care of Rose, but it is adversarial in addition, setting Melanctha's conduct sharply over against that of Rose (who becomes "Rosie" when we learn of her low-class ways). So our specimen is made of that opening clause ("She tended Rose . . .") and a closing phrase (". . . like a simple beast") that precisely balances it, while between these two segments three four-term series are sung, one that belongs to Melanctha, and two that belong to Rose and describe first her character and then her behavior. At this point we encounter an 'and' (also active in the sample from Dickens) that has its home within the rhetorical structure itself, for it is as if the sentence's shape said that Melanctha was patient and Rose was sullen; Melanctha was submissive and Rose was childish, and so on, employing the 'and' of simultaneity, of "while." "Gricks may rise and Troysers fall . . ." Joyce writes, using the same connective. Sullen Rosie grumbled, the rhetorical form also says; childish Rosie fussed; cowardly black Rosie howled and made herself to be an abomination and like a simple beast— a structure that invokes the 'and' of consequence and cause. "I bought some stock in IBM and the bottom of the market parted like a wet sack."

Dickens, by repeating "oyster shells in the oyster season" and "lobster shells in the lobster season," not only collects these two kinds of shells in the same place, his 'and' identifies two rhetorical formulas in which these four little tumuli of shells and crockery and cabbage leave are given to us. So there are 'ands' that vary in their meanings, and 'ands' that differ in terms of the kinds of objects they connect: things, inscriptions, concepts, or syntactical shapes and rhetorical patterns.

In the single sentence I took from Gertrude Stein, we have now found six overt 'ands,' each with a different dominant meaning, five covert 'ands,' which hid themselves unsuccessfully under commas, and two 'ands' that were implied by the form. Nor does this list (itself an 'and'-producing format) even remotely exhaust the various senses, sometimes several at the same time, these thirteen 'ands' possess, nor did my account even minimally describe the interaction between different meanings which any one written or spoken token might represent, or do more than suggest something of the dynamics of switching and sliding sentences, as readings were anticipated, accepted, revised, rejected, retained.

And we have only to glance again at the passage from Hemingway to find meanings for the word we haven't yet examined. You may recall the peculiar formation: "Well, I went out of there and there were plenty of them with him . . ." This is the 'and' of consequence, in this case inverted so that it becomes an 'and' of tardy explanation, the 'and' of belated "because." The narrator got out of there because the man he knifed had plenty of friends with him.

'And'

sometimes means "in company" or "together with," as "the passengers and all their luggage were hurled from the plane."

'And'

sometimes means "we may call these things by the same name, but the differences among them are often important and profound," as "there are doctors and doctors." This use may be regarded as a particularly pronounced example of the differentiating, or "over against," 'and.'

'And'

sometimes means "remember all the incidents, events, ideas, that came before, or just before, this," as in the famous opening of Pound's *Cantos*.

> And then went down to the ship,
> Set keel to breakers, forth on the godly sea, and
> We set up mast and sail on that swart ship,
> Bore sheep aboard her, and our bodies also
> Heavy with weeping, and winds from sternward
> Bore us out onward with bellying canvas,
> Circe's this craft, the trim-coiffed goddess.

'And'

is sometimes used in the spirit of "you might not believe it, but . . ." and as if in answer to an unspoken question. (1) "And yes, we did set up mast and sail on that swart ship." Or (2) "at the half we had a ten-point lead, and we still lost by two touchdowns." Or (3) "and we ate human flesh!"

Often the dangled or uncoupled or shaved 'and' expresses surprise or indignation. It is an emphatic form of the remember-what-came-before 'and.' "And you talk to me this way, after all I've done for you?" Here the 'and' of consequence has suffered a familiar disappointment. Or, "so Peking; and do you now go to Moscow?"

There are several rather antique 'ands': the 'and' of "four score and seven," the 'and' of "I'll love you forever and ever," or "we'll get together by and by." More ancient is the 'and' that sometimes substitutes for "times," as "they crowded aboard the ark two and two," or "the room was only ten and ten," now rarely resorted to, and replaced by 'by.'

There is the 'and' that turns the initial member of a coordinate pair into an adverb. In "the fire kept them nice and warm," "nicely warm" is meant. But 'nicely warm' is not a synonym because the 'and' allows the fire to keep them nice, as if at any moment they might dry out and get tough, or evil, or mean. There is also the 'and' which replaces the infinitive: "Why don't you come up and see me sometime?" Again, this is not simply a mindless replacement for the apparently more precise: "Why don't you come up *to* see me?" because 'and' equalizes "coming" and "seeing" and removes the rather insistent statement of purpose—especially important here, where seeing is probably only the first—shoeless—step.

Around some expressions there hover an astonishing number of ghostly forms, whiffs, sibilant suggestions, vague intimations, and these, as well as the more overt relationships which the reader is expected to grasp as a matter of course, help give them a feeling of classic correctness. Mae West's notorious invitation, "Why don't you come up and see me sometime?," with its careful softening of a command into a question, alters the cliché—"You folks come back and see me soon, you hear?"—basically by only one word—'up'—and that change suggests "bedroom" to my bad ear, while 'come up' suggests "erection," 'come' suggests "climax," 'see me' "seize me," and "seed me," and so on, so that the 'and' it contains hums like a tuning fork between all these fainter and further thoughts and their terms. Mae West's seductive delivery, of course, lets us know how we are to hear her invitation, but 'up' is the verbal pointer that prepares us to flush these remaining meanings within range of our gun.

Logical and grammatical form—the fact that 'and' is a connective, and not an article, an adjective, or a noun—limits somewhat the meanings that our word may assume, but only somewhat, and there is little in these formal dispositions that can tell us in advance of experience what 'and' means. We can't even know whether we are going to be dealing with a preposition, a conjunction, or a strange kind of adverb; yet the ordinary reader is able to distinguish one use of 'and' from another with an ease that never causes us any astonishment: the syntax takes shape simultaneously with the meanings it shapes.

For we know what it is to take care of someone. We know what it is to be patient. We have seen patient caring, and the irritable, impatient kind (we can even imagine impatient patience, as if one were in a hurry to get this period of placid absorbency and affable putting-up-with over with), so that when the words call our experiences together in a sentence, the ensuing arrangement, and completed meaning, are the result of our memories of life and our understanding of language. Patience has a history as a human condition that I've encountered before and occasionally enjoyed; and the word 'patience' has a career as a concept and a mark that I have, myself, seen and heard and written down and uttered. It is the same, to a degree, with all words. That is, I remember their meanings; I remember my encounters with their referents; and I remember the company of other words that the ones in question have commonly kept. However, when I remember these things, I do not do so serially, one fact or feeling, one usage, at a time, as if I were thumbing through an index or flipping through a file. These memories have been compacted and their effects summed, although I may recollect my mother's patience during one trying time with particular distinctness, or recall the famous "now patience" passage in *Finnegans Wake* more readily than others. My mind remembers the way trained muscles do, so when I speak and read as well as I walk and bike, then we can say that I have incorporated my language; it has become another nature, an organlike facility; and *that* language, at least, will have been invested with meaning, not merely assigned it. I may have just learned that *"ne plus ultra"* signifies an ultimate or utmost point; nevertheless, the phrase will still stand aside from its referent like politeness at a doorway; but when, for me, idea and object fuse with their sign, then the sign is valuable like the coin it resembles; it is alive, a unity of mind and body that can be taught to sing, to dance.

The suggestion that we use the language of ordinary men normally is a good one, not simply because we shall reach the ear and understanding of ordinary men that way (which remains unlikely), but because such words are rich with history, both in our life and in theirs, and shine throughout with smoothness like stones that have, for vast ages, been tossed back and forth in the surf of some ancient shore, becoming eloquent, as pebbles made the month of Demosthenes hiss and seethe and roar. 'And' is such a polished orb. Think of the places it has been, the shoulders it has rubbed, the connections it has had, the meanings it has absorbed, the almost limitless future which yet awaits!

And

if we were suddenly to speak of the "andness" of things, we would be rather readily understood to refer to that aspect of life which consists of just one damned 'and' after another. 'And' is a truly desperate part of speech because it separates and joins at the same time. It equalizes. Neither ham nor eggs are more or less. In a phrase like "donkeys and dragons" the donkey brings the dragon down, while in the combination "sweet cream and a kiss" the thick milk begins to resemble champagne.

And

so what? The inner order of the 'and' is the list, to which we must now turn—that field where all its objects at least implicitly rest. Here is a brief list of lists: (1) the list which is made up of reminders, shorthand commands—get X, do Y, √ Z—such as the grocery or shopping list, the list of things to get done before leaving for Europe, before ignition and liftoff, before embarking upon a prolonged affair; and (2) there are want lists, Christmas lists, and so on, much the same; then (3) there is the inventory, and (4) the catalogue, (5) the bests and the worsts, restaurants deserving two stars and three forks, (6) statistical tables and other compilations, (7) directories, (8) almanacs, (9) hit lists, (10) dictionaries, (11) deportation orders, and (12) delightfully sheer enumerations. Some lists are as disorderly as laundry—that is, only somewhat—or as chaotic as one made for marketing, ordered only as items pop into the mind, or as supplies run out, and having no real first, middle, most, or honest end. Sometimes particular items will be underscored or starred. Certain 'ands' (the 'and' for emphasis, for instance) often operate like an asterisk. Other arrangements are neutral and simply for convenience, as book lists are often alphabetical. The factors of '8' could be listed in any order without real prejudice, although I prefer '1 + 2 + 4 + 8' to other, more slipshod renditions. Occasionally a book dealer will shelve his books according to author only, instead of by title or subject matter, and then the catalogue's alphabetical simplicity and the structure of the corresponding state of affairs in his shop will be the same.

Among the organizing principles of lists, then, are (1) things simply come upon, either the way they are remembered, as a guest list may be composed, or as found, for instance, when the police inventory your pockets before putting you away; (2) items listed in accordance with some external principle, often so that things can be easily located—for instance, numerically, alphabetically, astrologically, regimentally, cartologically, hermeneutically; and (3) as dictated by the order of things themselves, like a book's table of contents, or vice versa, as when the library's catalogue shelves the books, and commands their connections. We must suppose that God's list of things to do (on the First Day— Light, on the Second Day—Land, on the Third Day—Life, and so on) possessed a hidden internal principle, and there may be other self-generating lists of this kind.

Lists are juxtapositions, and often employ some of the techniques of collage. The collage, of course, brings strangers together, uses its 'ands' to suggest an affinity without specifying what it is, and produces, thereby, a low-level but general nervousness. It is one of the essential elements of a truly contemporary style. Lists—full of 'ands' as they are— remove things from their normal place, not as an artist might, by picking up a piece of paper from the street to paste upon a canvas (as the Romance maintains), but by substituting for such found objects their names, and then rearranging those. As a consequence, lists are dominated by nouns. Here is a little list of words of the sort that rarely appear on lists: 'always' is never there, or 'nevermore,' or 'if' (although there is the expression "don't give me any 'ifs,' 'ands,' or 'buts' "), less than occasionally 'subjugation,' 'halfheartedly,' 'oh yeah?,' or 'Lithuaneousness.' Even some nouns, like 'junta,' manage to stay quite away. However, adjectives of a usefully descriptive kind, those quiet, unassuming servants of nouns, frequently appear: 'yellow cheese,' 'large eggs,' 'fresh milk,' 'bitten nails.'

'And'

also always has one or two or more nouns hanging around. There are two basic configurations, although there are many variations. The first

consists of two balloons held in one fist: . "A long and succulent squash." The second is the simple scale I remarked on earlier: . "My ear is full of water and wax like a new car in the rain."

That part of punctuation most associated with lists is therefore the colon, for presumably everything that follows *it* is a list. As we know, the colon is frequently an abbreviation for "namely," or "for instance." "There are thirteen ways of looking at a blackbird: [namely] on Sunday, in the yellowing woods, with a faithless friend, following a thin fall rain, and so forth."

Lists sometimes suggest or supply alternatives, not necessarily exclusive, for example, ways of getting spots off tea trays, or means of travel which avoid Cleveland. They supply possibilities: the people who could ride on the cow catcher, the games you could play in a stadium: roller skating up and down the ramps, playing checkers on an empty seat, hide-and-seek. If I am drawing up a list of physical attitudes or comportments surprisingly suitable for modeling clothes or for sex, although there is an implicit 'and' standing between each (while leaning wearily against your partner like the man with the hoe, as though sitting slowly down upon a hassock), it is not expected that you will put all of these to use one after another as though loading groceries in a cart. These 'ands' resemble 'or' more than they resemble themselves.

Lists have subjects. They are possessive. Lists are lists of. There is the list of foodstuffs needed for the ascent of Everest; there is the ruck one finds in a rucksack, items up for auction in an auction barn, wines and prices; while the little leaflet, the roster sheet, the penciled-in dance card, the back of an old envelope on which a list has been made: each of these symbolizes the table top or field or sorting tray, rucksack or room, where we may imagine these items have been assembled. This is sometimes called "the site."

Since a list has a subject to which its items are constantly referred (as every explicit 'and' has: 'ear' for 'water' and 'wax,' 'squash' for 'long' and 'green' and 'succulent' and 'bottle-nosed'), it suppresses its verb (to buy R, to remind one of S, to count T, to store U), and tends to retard the forward movement of the mind. We remain on the site. While the early 'ands' of a series propel us onward, the later ones run breathlessly in place; thus the list is a fundamental device for creating a sense of overflow, abundance, excess. We find it almost invariably so used in Rabelais, and often in Cervantes. Why name one thing when you can invoke many? Why be merely thirsty, why simply drink, when you can cry out with Grangousier: "I wet, I dampen, I moisten, I humect my gullet, I drink—and all for fear of dying of aridity!" Here, however, our list is not one of alternative actions, but of additional *words*. I could say "moisten my gullet"; or I could say "dampen my gullet"; but, by the swollen tongues of all the sophists, I shall say both, and more, in order to suggest the greedy great gulp of life I am presently consuming. Who, indeed, could be satisfied to say, of the breasts of their beloved, simply that they are as white and soft as a hillock of junket? *"Rühmen, dass ist!"*

Rabelais is also full of lists of rapid talk, dialogue which does not advance the subject at all, but rather fills it, as drink does the bladder. Topers sail away in a wind of words, they do not hitchhike the highroads. Then there are the slanging matches, bouts of bad-mouthing: you, sir, are a sickly snerd; and you, sir, are a vulgar gurp; and you, snerd, are a suckalini; and you, gurp, are a loony goofballoof! One remembers, with fondness, the two whores and their name-calling contest in *The Sot-Weed Factor*. But the entire world is on a diet. Those whose tongues are not dry and starving are recommending a puritanical prose, small bites of life, small spoons of dehydrated water.

Lists, then, are for those who savor, who revel and wallow, who embrace, not only the whole of things, but all of its accounts, histories, descriptions, justifications. They are for those who like, in every circumstance, to Thomas Wolfe things down, to whoop it, Whitmanly, up. 'Ands' spew out of Wolfe as if he were a faucet for them.

> And before and after that, and in between, and in and out, and during it and later on, and now and then, and here and there, and at home and abroad, and on the seven seas, and across the length and breadth of the five continents, and yesterday and tomorrow and forever—could it be said of her that she had been promiscuous?

Even the jeremiad is a list, and full of joy, for damnations are delightful. Lists are finally for those who love language, the vowel-swollen cheek, the lilting, dancing tongue, because lists are fields full of words, and roving bands of 'and.' Think of the many American masters of this conjunction: Faulkner, Hemingway, Stein, Melville:

> Now when these poor sun-burnt mariners, bare-footed, and with their trowsers rolled high up on their eely legs, had wearily hauled their fat fish high and dry, promising themselves a good £150 from the precious oil and bone; and in fantasy sipping rare tea with their wives, and good ale with their cronies, upon the strength of their respective shares; up steps a very learned and most Christian and charitable gentleman, with a copy of Blackstone under his arm; and laying it upon the whale's head, he says—"Hands off! this fish, my masters, is a Fast-Fish. I seize it as the Lord Warden's."

Perhaps 'AND' should be sewn on the flag. Life itself can only be compiled and thereby captured on a list, if it can be laid out anywhere at all, especially if you are a nominalist.

List making is a form of collecting, of course, conservative in that sense, and dictionaries are the noblest lists of all; but lists are ubiquitous in literature. It is not merely Walt Whitman who is made of them. They are as frequent a rhetorical element as 'and' is a grammatical one. We could scarcely write much without either.

When do we have a list, however, and when not? There is no limit, presumably, to the length of lists so long as they have one, for the idea of a list implies the possibility of a complete enumeration. I may not have completed my list of all the cars with Delaware license plates which have stopped at my gas station, but an end is in sight, for my cancer is incurable and the station will soon close. I cannot make a list of all the odd numbers, only the ones, say, I like. There are an infinite number of numbers which no one will ever name. My mentioning five trillion and seven, now, will not make a dent in it. A daunting thought. It is sometimes naïvely supposed that those unnamed numbers will be either unimaginably huge (galaxies of googolplexes) or terrifyingly tiny (pi, pied), but there are almost certainly neglected numbers of no particular distinction hidden in the shadows of others, which chance has simply skipped. Another daunting thought. Or what of those lists of numbers which only spell out a name (of an insurance policy, for instance) and which aren't really functioning as a number at all? To exist so inexactly: another daunting thought.

So lists must be *of a length*. When Rabelais tells us what little Gargantua did between the ages of three and five, the entire chapter becomes an enumeration of the characteristics and qualities, the deeds, of this Herculean tyke.

> Fat? another ounce of wind and he would have exploded. Appreciative? He would piss, full-bladdered, at the sun. Cautious? He used to hide under water for fear of the rain.

However, when we write nothing but "Kleenex" on the flap of our envelope, we haven't a list yet, though we may have begun to make one; it awaits the 'and.' "Kleenex, cauliflower" is only a pair, and pairs are opposed to lists, and close upon themselves like clapping hands (though I wonder what sound this pair would make when they came together?), while "Kleenex, cauliflower, catnip" is simply a skimpy plurality. Alliteration actually makes the three items seem more numerous than they are, so I think that with four such we can say our list has truly begun. When I wrote down 'catnip,' I did not add it to a list, for there wasn't a list yet (I was, however, *making* a list); but now that we have one, various things can be said to be *on* or *off* it, or eligible for inclusion or summarily blackballed. The phrase "fate, chance, kings, and desperate men" forms a list. Notice, however, that until there was a list, 'fate,' like 'catnip' previously, was not on it; but that, once the list was made, 'fate,' we see, was always on.

There may be lists which exist mainly in an ideal realm, and which are consequently rarely realized. Maybe I've made a list of what I need to get at the grocer's: "Kleenex, chicken wings, Twinkies, thick-skinned fruit"; when actually what I really need are lemons, vitamins, and thighs. I've forgotten Chuckie's cat food, too, so my list isn't even a list of what *I* want. I really need Rye Crisp and secretly bottled water. When I initially collect the qualities which create a character, don't I often discard some and add others, as if, all along, I am searching for the *right set*? "Fate, chance, kings, and desperate men" is certainly a correct collection, and therefore it is a complete list. There are no more openings. My complete grocery list may include items which I cannot afford or which are unavailable anywhere in the Northern Hemisphere. So it may contain needfuls I know nothing of.

There are some lists one wants rather desperately to be on: the Honor Roll, or the Not Nasty But Nice, for instance; but some should be shunned, like the Lord High Executioner's little list of people who surely won't be missed, or that other roll call way up yonder for which one does not wish to be eligible just yet.

Although the list by itself is a small democracy, and usually lacks hierarchies (the one thousand and three women on Don Giovanni's are, presumably, all loved equally by the list, if not by the Don), when the list occurs in a literary work, these conditions change, and the order of items becomes especially important. "Ah hah!" Holmes exclaims, "our suspect has put down 'catnip' just ahead of 'Kleenex'—did you notice that, Watson?" Of course, like Holmes's cases, works of literature suffer from an excess of the essential.

The normal democracy of lists is connected with the coordinating and balancing functions of 'and,' as well as its additive and merely enumerative character: "How do I love thee, let me count the ways . . ." yet even though the 'ands' of emphasis, or of "finally," or "in sum," introduce certain small subordinations, the importance of every 'and,' and the elements it connects, even its pecking orders, remains substantially the same.

I've pointed out that listing things, or inserting an 'and' between them, can be done only by replacing the things in question with their names, and thereby transforming their relations. If you are moving, and have made a list of your belongings so that the insurance company can repay you when the wagons are lost crossing the mountains, the spatial relation between these objects (between hairbrush and table, table and footstool,

footstool and rug) will be replaced (as it just was) with a simple serial relation between indifferent nouns which find their rest, now, only on a yellow sheet. The rug on which I lay as a baby to have my naked picture taken will be listed in the same way as yours—"one woolly rug/ worn spot in center"—though it was there you lost your virginity, and he laid one tan hand beneath the frillies of your tennis dress, and—. Nothing but a list can restore such moments to us. A list can calmly take apart a chair and reduce its simultaneous assemblage to a song: "back, leg, cushion, square feet, embroidery, grease spot, saggy spring, slight scratch, small tear, lost tack." If I cut up an action for inclusion on a list, I shall have to divide it the way the flight of Zeno's arrow was divided, and a continuum will become an enumeration. "He ran rapidly forward, leaped, and comfortably cleared the first hurdle" makes three acts out of what was once one, and these segments can be moved about like beans. "Landing awkwardly on his left leg, already sore from last night's impromptus, he knew his run had been rapid enough for his leap at least to clear the hurdle." What has been divided, here, is no longer an action, but a memory. Indeed, I can cut up the action in a lot of ways, slicing "He ran rapidly forward" into a stride with the right foot, a stride with the left, and so on, even becoming microscopic: "shove off right, lift, swing, extend, plant, pull," etc., and in this way never reaching, any more than Achilles does, the hurdle. The camera is such a list maker, because a film is essentially a series of stills, temporally arranged and uniformly flashed so as to restore continuity at the price of illusion.

Jorge Luis Borges, who has made some of our more memorable lists, refers at one point to a "certain Chinese encyclopedia" in which it is written that

> animals are divided into (a) belonging to the Emperor, (b) embalmed, (c) tame, (d) sucking pigs, (e) sirens, (f) fabulous, (g) stray dogs, (h) included in the present classification, (i) frenzied, (j) innumerable, (k) drawn with a very fine camelhair brush, (l) *et cetera,* (m) having just broken the water pitcher, (n) that from a long way off look like flies . . .

and Michel Foucault, who claims this passage and the laughter it provoked were the initial stimulus for his book *The Order of Things,* says we cannot imagine the kind of place where these creatures could be brought together and sorted out. The site is impossible to conceive. He says that the encyclopedia, "and the taxonomy it proposes, lead to a

kind of thought without space, to words and categories that lack all life
and place, but are rooted in a ceremonial space, overburdened with complex figures, with tangled paths, strange places, secret passages, and unexpected communications." We read the congregation of these riddling
words, but is there anywhere a sack which will sometime fill with such
groceries?

'And'

always raises this issue as if it were a flag for waving. 'Bread' and 'honey'
meet at the breakfast table as easily as husband and wife; they are both
with us in our world, and cause scarcely a blink; but what keeps 'carrot'
and 'cruelty' together besides 'c'? Every list has a length, a purpose, an
order, its own entrance requirements, its own principles of exclusion, its
site. Foucault has not felt the point of the Chinese encyclopedia's list, so
he cannot conceive of its site, but Borges does not mean merely to confound and delight us with this crazy classification; for, at another level,
it represents a well-chosen series of logical mistakes. It is a collection of
examples, and is not to be taken any more literally than, let's say, remarks about the cross and the crown should be thought to be simply
about crowns and crosses.

The Chinese world, we traditionally think, is upside down? Very well.
So is this list. The classes it names aren't workably exclusive, but badly
overlap: birds belonging to the emperor might be tamed or embalmed,
and if so, they are certainly "included in the present classification." Live
dogs, stuffed deer, mythological monsters, are grouped so aggressively
they challenge the presumably overriding importance of other distinctions—that between the real and the imaginary, for instance, or the alive
and dead. Still, as widely as its net is thrown, there are too many holes
in it: most wild animals will easily elude its cast, and it omits mention
of those animals whose names have never been used to characterize football teams. The groups are too specific in some cases, too general in
others. It offers us categories which cannot be applied, others which are
vague, wholly subjective, or disastrously self-referential. In short, each
example attacks some part of the logical structure of the list, and this is
what, wonderlandlike, it is a list of. It may seem to suggest that there are
more things in heaven and earth than are dreamt of in our taxonomies,
but Borges provides us with a possible reality behind that appearance.
The site of this list is in an introductory text in logic—somewhere in the
chapter on classification.

One can sense what 'and' is up to also by examining writers and passages which use it sparingly, or exclude it altogether, as Beckett characteristically does, especially in later works like *How It Is,* because it is precisely the dissolution and denial of identities he wishes to stress. When, very rarely, the word appears, either it stands between terms only verbally different ("with me someone there with me still and me there still") or 'and' is used to equalize life and death ("the voice stops for one or the other reason and life along with it above in the light and we along with it that is what becomes of us"). On the other hand, you find little use of the word in writing which states subordinations clearly and precisely, as often is the case in the hierarchical prose of Henry James.

Can one word make a world? Of course not. God said: *"Es werde Licht,"* not *"Licht"* alone.[6] But when an 'and' appears between any two terms, as we have seen, a place where these two "things" belong together has been implied. Furthermore, the homogeneity of chaos, *"ohne Form und leer,"* has been sundered, for we must think of chaos, *'Tiefe,'* not as a helterskelter of worn-out and broken or halfheartedly realized things like a junkyard or potter's midden, but as a fluid mishmash of thinglessness in every lack of direction, as if a blender had run amok.

'And'

is that sunderer; it divides into new accords; it stands between *"Himmel und Erde"*; it divides light from darkness.

'And'

again moves between sea and sky and their several waters, so that a new relationship arises between them, one that is external and unencumbering, although intimate as later Eve and Adam will be. Dividing earth from ocean, grass from earth, summer from winter and night from day, is again: 'and.'

'And'

those that crawl are otherwise than those that fly because of it. Finally, of course, between Himself and Himself there came a glass, a gleaming image: God and man, then. And among man, the male and the female; and within man, the soul and life and mind and body, were sorted and set, as though in left and right hands, beside but separate from one another.

---

6. It is my suspicious conviction that God speaks only German.

'And'

then God went away to other delights, *"an Reiz und Kraft,"* leaving us with our days and nights and other downfalls, our sites and lists and querulous designs and petty plans, our sentiments and insatiables and dreamlands, with the problem of other minds, with the spirit's unhappy household in the body, with all those divisions among things which 'and' has bridged and rivered, with essences and accidents and linear implications, with all those bilious and libelous tongues, pissing angels, withheld rewards, broken promises, all those opportunities for good and evil, sex, marriage, world wars, work, and worship—and with 'and' itself—'and': a sword which cleaves things as it cleaves them.

'And'

then some.

CULTURE, SELF, AND STYLE

> *Culture is one thing, and varnish an-*
> *other. There can be no high culture*
> *without pure morals. With the truly cul-*
> *tivated man,—the maiden, the orphan,*
> *the poor man, and the hunted slave feel*
> *safe.*
>
> —EMERSON's *Journal*
> for December 1868

1

Like a wreath, "culture" is a word we place upon the brow of a victor. It would be a little late now to try to pick it clean of prejudice and praise, to make a neutral scientific word of it by scattering the laurel leaves, defoliating the bays. It knows very well who and what it is; it has gone to Groton and has advanced degrees; it has studied Bach and had long lingering love affairs, punctuated by the pleonasms of poetry; it has trudged through the Pitti Palace amidst the sweat of August days with a doggedness habitual among those who persistently seek the high C; it has suffered hangovers from history, been disappointed, betrayed, seen Spain ablaze; it has had what we call an "upbringing"; it will never be the same—the same simple word it once was when it was the verb 'to till.'

Yet when I read Emerson's journal entry, does the phrase "without pure morals" pass so smoothly by, or has the chalk squeaked, and sent a shiver through us? How naïve, how innocent, of Emerson—who has denied the Fall of Man but has been a witness to the Civil War; who thinks Goethe represents a cultivated nation; and whose holocausts are all in the Book of Revelation—to regard culture in these terms. How provincial of him, too, to believe not only in purity but in morals. There, among the Concord prudes, he dares to assert the nobility of man, and to

185

cry out, expansively, for "initiative, spermatic, prophesying, man-making words."

Matthew Arnold felt he had to defend the term from those who thought culture consisted of the standard smatter of classical Greek and the composition of twiddly little critical reviews, so that it consequently meant a condition of smart-assed self-indulgence in what was essentially a shallow and trivial spirit. But when Arnold, for his part, insists that the aim of the man of culture is "to make reason and the will of God prevail," however prudently he proceeds to note our fallibility concerning the knowledge of God's will and the dictates of Reason, and even when we learn that God is something like the aims and order of Nature, the word 'prevail' still carries a cold chill to the chest where they say the heart hides, because cultivation sometimes goes in narrow rows, and to give power to the scholar or the connoisseur, to persons whose work lies literally in and under their own hands, is to give it to those who are likely to have a wholly false sense of it, when power is directed toward others, because political affairs cannot be worked like words or conducted like an orchestra. Perfection, which Arnold held to be an essential element in culture, is not a sensible political pursuit, nor is a scorn for the practical an ideal attitude, or that lingering envy of the active, so often found in round-shouldered souls, the best goad.

Once the property of stuffy moralizing men of letters (Emerson, Arnold, Eliot), the word is now shared by anthropologists and sociologists with about the same grace and good feeling as quarreling kids. In *Notes Toward a Definition of Culture,* Eliot does not carry his exposition very far before he cites E. B. Tylor's *Primitive Culture,* and Frazier and Weston were, as we know, intimates of his mind. If we want to know what a culture is, shouldn't we examine it in its earlier and allegedly simpler forms, both to be found in history and at the edges of the present world?

Anthropologists or not, we all used to call them "natives"—those little, distant, jungle and island people, and we came to recognize the unscientific snobbery in that. Even our more respectable journals could show them naked without offense, because their pendulous or pointed breasts were as inhuman to us as the udder of a cow. Shortly we came to our senses, and had them dress. We grew to distrust our own point of view, our local certainties, and embraced relativism, although it is one of the scabbier whores; and we went on to endorse a nice equality among cultures, each of which was carrying out its task of coalescing, conserving, and structuring some society. A large sense of superiority was one of the white man's burdens, and that weight, released, was replaced by an equally heavy sense of guilt.

No more than we might expect a surgeon to say, "Well, dead, but good riddance," would an anthropologist exclaim, stepping from the culture just surveyed as you might shed a set of working clothes: "Goodness, what a terrible way to live!" because, even if the natives were impoverished, covered with dust and sores; even if they had been trodden on by stronger feet till they were flat as a path; even if they were rapidly dying off; still, the observer could remark how frequently they smiled, or how infrequently their children fought, or how serene they were. We can envy the Zuni their peaceful ways, and the Navaho their "happy hearts."

Besides, the sores were caused by disease, impoverishment by a climate change, and general debility by colonization and imperial tyrannies. None of it was ever the culture's "fault."

It was amazing how mollified we were to find that there was some functional point to food taboos, infibulation, or clitoridectomy, and if you still felt morally squeamish about human sacrifice or headhunting, it was clear from those qualms that you were still squeezed into a narrowly modern and European point of view,[1] and had no sympathy, and didn't—couldn't—understand. Yet when we encountered certain adolescents among indolent summery seaside tribes who were allowed to screw without taboo, we wondered whether this enabled them to avoid the stresses of our own youth, and we secretly hoped it hadn't.

Some anthropologists have released the moral point of view, so sacred to stuffies like Eliot and Arnold and Emerson, from every mooring (science and art also float away on the stream of Becoming), calling any belief in objective knowledge "fundamentalist," as if it were the same as a benighted biblical literalism, and arguing for the total mutability of man and the complete sociology of what, under such circumstances, could no longer be considered knowledge, but only *doxa,* or "opinion."

> It is part of our culture to recognize at last our cognitive precariousness. It is part of our culture to be sophisticated about fundamentalist claims to secure knowledge. It is part of our culture to be forced to take aboard the idea that other cultures are rational in the same way as ours. Their organization of experience is different, their objectives different, their successes and weak points different too. The refusal to privilege one bit of reality as more absolutely real, one kind of truth

---

1. This is truly the age of the sophist, not simply because it is an age of media, persuasion, and the domination of the "masses," but because the pragmatism and relativism convenient to doing business under such circumstances (as the sophists in Plato's time also seized the opportunity) have been made into general philosophical principles. Kuhn's understanding of science, Foucault's of history, the Marxist attack on the Enlightenment, so-called "deconstruction," and so on, are all examples.

more true, one intellectual process more valid, allows the
original comparative project dear to Durkheim to go forward
at last.[2]

It *is* a part of our culture to recognize these things, a vital point to
which I shall return, but the characteristics Mary Douglas cites do not
necessarily lead to the liberal cultural relativity which, with rhetoric and
a curious conviction, she recites, since a man who stands precariously
upon a swaying wire may still be standing there, and to be sophisticated
about the difficulties of obtaining certainty may merely make you, like
Descartes, all the more resolute, though wary, in your pursuit of it;
that our "objective" knowledge may be only probable does not make it
impossible; that others have other goals does not minimize or subjectify
mine; nor is it entirely without irony that one observes how, after thirteen hundred years, someone is still uttering the propositions of Prota-
goras, Proclus, and Prodicus with such moral fervor. If anthropology
teaches us about the diversity of cultures, the history of philosophy instructs us on the eternal recurrence of arguments and points of view, and
those disciplines which encourage a "sociology of knowledge" should not
remain silent about the connections between the attitude expressed by
"you are right and I am right and everything is quite correct" and the
social and economic interests of the singer. If, as Nietzsche said, meek-
ness serves the servile, what does this modest "standpointism" serve?

We remembered our missionaries, too, and how they had belabored
many a naked, native babe in the woods with our beliefs, and tamed
savages the way the jungle itself was leveled to make roads; how Chris-
tianity converted treacherous yellow gooks into serving maids and house-
boys who could be trusted with our bowls and Bibles, table water, knives.
On our boats we brought them smallpox, syphilis, psalms, sin, our alphabet, and beads. First we conquered and then we Schweitzered them, and
it's not clear which was worse. Now, of course, we come in smoothly
smiling corps of peace, with medical marvels and plant poisons and trac-
tors to terrorize and tame the earth. We teach. Our opinions are all about
techniques. We carry economic notions in our carpetbag of tricks, en-
gineering information and industrial disease.

Our historians, considered as students of the cultural past, had been
hauled up short as well. They had been too patronizing, or too idola-
trous. We saw in the German worship of the Greeks a dangerously

---

2. Mary Douglas, *Implicit Meanings: Essays on Anthropology* (London: Routledge and
Kegan Paul, 1975), pp. xvii–xviii.

sentimental worship of themselves. The smug sense that men were pretty much alike, and likely English anyway, down deep, clouded even the customarily clear-eyed views of Hume. It did not come as a surprise that Mind marched toward the Absolute *auf Deutsche,* or that the West was like an aging lecher casting about for virgin lands and populations to debauch. Optimism cockadoodledoo'd in the face of the farmer's ax, and pessimism dove like a loon into an empty lake.

Our habit was to expect too much, and then to mope at the little we felt we received. Schiller expects great things from the French Revolution, and when he doesn't get them gets cross. Emerson watches America disappoint him with a wrathful and finally a weary eye. Because the sixties didn't permanently alter the nature of man, life, and the state, the seventies were sullen.

So formerly we were ardent aristocrats or racists or patriots or profiteers or priests, or we were sorry we were white and had motor cars, and hoped the refrigerator hadn't ruined our palate with frozen peas, the electric razor our Samsonite get-up-and-go, and TV our intelligence. We couldn't study other cultures fairly because of the biases of our own; and we couldn't understand ourselves because, as de Tocqueville's success had presumably shown, we were too close to ourselves for clarity, too concerned with ourselves to be dispassionate, too intimate for innocence, too much in hate and love. Culture, in short, has had a bad conscience. Writing about it confesses to a past or present prejudice.

But the fact that there are social causes for our ideas and attitudes surely should not surprise us; it is a truth which ought to be at least gently embraced; there are psychological and economic ones as well, sexual, culinary, and numerous other claimants; nevertheless, if our language is indeed the limit of our world, then we must find another, larger, stronger, more inventive language which will burst those limits like the paper hoop the clown breaks, and not lie unburning, weightless, unashamed upon some doltish tongue or commonplace page; since a culture remains imprisoned within itself so long as it is content with its pat, traditional ways—so long as it rests on *those* laurels, wears *that* wreath—because its finest wines will soon sour, its herds decline, a moral blindness like that which gripped Thebes will settle like a plague upon it, if the city—the country—the culture is not soon passionately and persistently concerned with acts and ideas that, while having causes and conditions, to be sure, transcend them in search of justifications, in search of some rational ground for change; and it is just here that knowledge of the startling and perplexing variety of life creates the sophist's salutary doubt about the universal rightness of *this* hearth and heaven, *this* flag and spear, so that we seek for something that rests on a better base than our own bones and local being, but rather on an anatomy we all share: our heavy, swollen, bilateral brains—the home of the human, if there is any.

With a truly cultivated man the hunted slave feels safe. In response to our gods, we may pull the hot heart out of a bleeding chest only so often and remain right. A culture morally and functionally fails which does not let its crazies, its artists and its saints, its scientists and politicians, claim, on occasion, a higher law than its own congresses can pass, traditions permit, or conscience conceive.

There *are* truths. However often and long we lie about it, reason is never a gun in the street.

Culture is one thing, varnish another. In Port Moresby I saw men and women who had presumably ventured down from their tribal homes in the hills, squatting along the road with a can of Coke in one hand and a little cellophane-covered cupcake in the other. The local hotel where I stayed was staffed by young men in dress suits and bare feet, and there were TVs in every room, just as there are in Australia, although there was no transmitter on the island and a gray screen was all you could receive.

Many of the people spoke Melanesian pidgin, a language which perfectly expresses the collision of cultures. The diet of the natives was soft, Western, and sweet, yet one had to feel their Stone Age stomachs turning: *Bel i tantanim,* they might have said in that lingo which is all broken habits and bent psyches, merchandise and trading, a mélange due to men who *bilong longwe ples.*

I felt what I thought they should feel not because I had a basket of facts to sell to any passing hypothesis like fruit along the highway, but because I had always been convinced that culture was not something men created like a quarter candy bar or corner cupboard; it was not one of those external goods—glory or money—against which Aristotle has so eloquently argued. You could not even imagine it away, as Hobbes thought, putting war and a state of nature in its place. It had no onset, like puberty, and man hadn't evolved into it as you might take stairs to another floor. Nor did it seem to me that humanity was a creation of culture the way management, the coach, and the team define a linebacker: so completely within his task, if they have their way, all off-field life is left out. Rather the relation was as Socrates suggested in the *Crito:* that of son to father or arm to man, both instrument and organ, integral yet not supreme; or, as I should prefer, as the tongue I wag stands to the language it cannot help but wag in, if it wants to wag at all.

Culture not only contains our written and spoken languages, it is itself a larger language: a set of rules and directives, orders and ordinances, which enable our actions to become significant, which bind us together in the same system of signs. In short, culture creates a grammar—a malleable syntax—to smooth and straighten the stammer of life. We learn this language, so it is not a part of our natural growth the way breasts are, or body hair; and although there are many kinds of culture, and many languages, around the world, it is necessary that we learn at least one, else we remain inhuman, incomplete, unformed. Greeks may have been provincial when they identified the human—the civilized—with themselves, and thought of the Persians as barbarians; but they were right to recognize that one had to be something: a Cypriot or Spartan, a Cretan or Corinthian; because a culture makes our natural abstractness concrete; it causes consciousness to become French or Javanese or German, and only when consciousness is fully formed and furnished is it fully human; so any sense of the self that does not see that self as a literal *embodiment* of society—of tradition and time, climate and space, condition and aim—is woefully inadequate.

Culture is no less natural to man than any other organ, and it has grown together and alike with the body and the brain to its present size and complexity, its elastic capabilities, its diversified effects. So if one is going to think of culture as an implement or an enemy, then it is a tool which is attached to us like a nipple or a phallus; it is within us like a defect in the genes.

We are born defenseless, we always say—naked—without the teeth of the tiger, the poison of the snake, the instincts of the spider, or the chameleon's camouflage; and it is true that nature is not nearly definite or directive enough, neither about our own human nature nor about nature's nature. If we spilled ourselves directly, there would be nothing but a blot, and that would be precisely because our nervous systems are too complex for simple reflex, for bell and slaver. The anteater is one word. His craving for ants is concrete, and he usually has the sense to be born near the tents and tepees of his taste. Our stomach is abstract, our thirst is general, our longings as vague and universal as the atmosphere. We would copulate with Black and Brown, with animals and moist mud, with hands and mouths, with the appropriate hollow and pointed parts of vegetables and trees. We wake to a world we cannot understand, but the levels of life beneath us have no need for understanding. They do not make things up. They do not play in bands. They do not look for their life in the stars. They do not thumb through arty books for advice on how to fuck.

Here now: we have all this hair on our heads. It gets dirty. It knots. An ape would know how to groom it. We could just let it flop. We could just cut it close and scrub it a lot. Consider this, from an imaginary encyclopedia:

> The female of the human species, just after the age of puberty has passed like an embarrassed blush, when the hair is at its healthiest and full of zing, cuts it all off to weave a wallet for her marriage money. How clever of this creature, whose body chemistry at her first menstruation incites this behavior at just the right time.

Clearly, nothing like this can be seriously said of us. However, that does not mean we take no interest in our hair. On the contrary. How we cut and comb and dress it, how we fangle it up or tease it, wig it or dye, becomes a significant part of our cultural language. The stimulus with its response is replaced by a sign with its significance.

Indeed, we can count the steps which establish a style. If we did our hair in honey one day, in grease another; if we put it up in the morning for a while, and let it down at night, only to alter everything in an instant like the dispersal of a cloud; if we sometimes cut it when we were grieving and other times weighted strands with stones; if, in short, we had no habits, had no principles of selection, no order of action, only acts which were random and willy-nilly—then we would have no language, because our behavior would not fit into a system; it would be inhuman; that is, it would be without significance beyond its immediate provocation, as we might bind up our hair because it gets in our eyes when we hunt. Yet the question quickly comes: why not cut it short instead? why tie it up? with a leather band? in a compound knot? around a feather or a bone? or bury it beneath a hat?

Similarly, if we ate, when hungry, whatever was conveniently at hand: onions one day, nectarines the next; if we always took the brisk straight way to the satisfaction of our needs, as if nature peeled the grapes it hung above our heads—we could not say we had a culture, because culture fills in the blanks, narrows choice, decides, defines; it makes our actions like a line of type.

One might want to say that ants, bees, baboons, have a society, yet until their behavior did more than merely feed or protect or propagate them, but had, in addition, social significance and sensitivity, one could not correctly speak of the presence of culture.

Still, if we want to compare a culture to a language, then we must be prepared to set out over a terrain not so much untraveled as trampled into featureless confusion, and with the disturbing knowledge that our guide is a metaphor already overworked and mutinous; so if our interest is in the price a self has to pay to become a self in such a system of unwhistled signals and covert sighs; if our concern is for the place of the self, its purposes and possibilities, among society's conventional symbols, habitual signs—then it might be more advantageous to study, not the simple, but the complex; not the crude and rudimentary, but the highly refined; not the common, but the special—culture in its finest expression, its fullest realization—rather than the cheap kitsch that clutters the street, embarrasses the eye as it shames the feelings, sweet-cakes and Cokes the stomach, and affrights the mind.

2

Early in the development of Henry James's late novel, *The Golden Bowl,* we accompany an impoverished and clownishly named Italian prince, Prince Amerigo, on a shopping expedition with the lovely Charlotte Stant, an Italian-born American who is infatuated with him. The meeting is clandestine, and its purpose is the purchase of a gift for Maggie Verver, the woman whom the Prince plans to marry. At last they arrive in the antique shop where they will be shown a goblet cut from a single crystal and covered skillfully in gold, a gilding which not only enhances the beauty of the bowl but also hides a flaw in the quartz. However, first the dealer sets out a few smaller items in this singular sentence:

> Of decent old gold, old silver, old bronze, of old chased and jewelled artistry, were the objects that, successively produced, had ended by numerously dotting the counter, where the shopman's slim, light fingers, with neat nails, touched them at moments, briefly, nervously, tenderly, as those of a chess player rest, a few seconds, over the board, on a figure he thinks he may move and then may not: small florid ancientries, ornaments, pendants, lockets, brooches, buckles, pretexts for dim brilliants, bloodless rubies, pearls either too large or too opaque for value; miniatures mounted with diamonds that had ceased to dazzle; snuff-boxes presented to— or by—the too questionable great; cups, trays, taper-stands, suggestive of pawn-tickets, archaic and brown, that would themselves, if preserved, have been prized curiosities.

Whatever it was that compelled Henry James to write fiction; whatever fancies or feelings he had which he felt he had to express; the fact is that the blank page yields him nearly every freedom. Facing it, the author can only be impressed by its duplicitous generosity. Allowing everything, it facilitates nothing. James does not have to write; he does not have to write fiction; he does not have to write a novel; he does not have to write *The Golden Bowl,* and in a style that will cool off his tepid supporters; yet he must imagine that he must. The sentences he composes with such consummate attention to detail, such musical skill, such morally perceptive art, do not answer any questions; they furnish no one with useful schoolboy information; nowhere do they urge the instant purchase of gelid pastes and chemical powders; nor do they comprise a cry like "ouch!" however prolonged. No one is addressed. The novel's composition has no occasion, no external justification. It counts as cultural surplus. Its existence is arbitrary in that sense; it has been wholly *willed.* Yet James has no novel in his head which his words then make sensible. The work works to fashion itself in the same moment it is shaping Henry James and James is devising it.

The passage of which I have quoted part is an important piece of the book, and is in the language and conventions of the European novel; it is also in the language of late James—well in. It is written in the tradition of Austen and Eliot, in English of the upper class, in English with a few American singularities and tones; so if we were to distinguish, as Saussure did, between a language considered as a whole and a particular speech or bit of writing in it, we should be obliged to notice that our specimen is an example of more than one tongue, or rather that, at the very least, it is a language within a language which is yet within another, and so on. The English language is mighty and general; Jamesian English is particular and special. *The Golden Bowl* itself is unique.

As we enter the sentence, we observe first of all that the sounds of the words, normally rather arbitrary and accidental properties of what we want to convey, are the object of the greatest care, and that patterns are produced quite different from the ones which syntax requires, and these organize and direct its course. The letters 'o' and 'l' predominate, as they do in the phrase "the golden bowl." The word 'old' is reiterated, as it ought to be in a shop full of antiques, and the metals are announced which have always named the legendary ages of man: "old gold, old silver, old bronze." The shopman is playing a game with the Prince and his companion, exactly as James is with us. He is making his moves, and each object he displays is defective in some slight way. He shows them "dim brilliants, bloodless rubies," "diamonds that had ceased to dazzle." The expression "small florid ancientries" is itself, and aptly, just a little florid. The pauses, the hesitations in the passage, mimic the movement of the tradesman's hand, which touches the various brooches and pendants and pearls "briefly, nervously, tenderly." The action of the language and the action of the hand lie on parallel and resembling planes. The shopkeeper lovingly offers Charlotte and the Prince a counter full of things. James lovingly gives us a list of words: "cups, trays, taper-stands." As readers we are placed in the position of the Prince. He sees these bibelots. We read these words. The one *is* the other. The Prince's instructed eye, and James's immaculate judgment, wittily remark the vulgar limitations of the stock, as the rich list continues, wrapped in the elegant warmth of its own sound, the delightful shimmer of its irony:

> A few commemorative medals, of neat outline but dull refer-
> ence; a classic monument or two, things of the first years of
> the century; things consular, Napoleonic, temples, obelisks,
> arches, tinily re-embodied, completed the discreet cluster; in
> which, however, even after tentative reinforcement from sev-
> eral quaint rings, intaglios, amethysts, carbuncles, each of
> which had found a home in the ancient sallow satin of some
> weakly-snapping little box, there was, in spite of the due
> proportion of faint poetry, no great force of persuasion.

James returns to his brilliantly reflective form as one still hungry goes back to the buffet, but now the concern of the sentence is the nature of the Prince's and Charlotte's attention:

> They looked, the visitors, they touched, they vaguely pre-
> tended to consider, but with scepticism, so far as courtesy per-
> mitted, in the quality of their attention.

A style could scarcely be more a mirror of its own effects; and the wonderful result is that our picture of the Prince and his companion is held within the words like an image in clear, unruffled water, where the deep bottom of the stream lies brightly on the surface as though it were a reflection fallen from above and not one which has risen from below. In the next breath, James is defining the moral nature of his indiscreet couple's discreet perception, the exactness of which is fully adequate to the scrupulosity (at this point) of the principals in question.

> It was impossible they shouldn't, after a little, tacitly agree as
> to the absurdity of carrying to Maggie a token from such a
> stock. It would be—that was the difficulty—pretentious with-

out being "good"; too usual, as a treasure, to have been an inspiration of the giver, and yet too primitive to be taken as tribute welcome on any terms.

The nervous nicety of word, the salesman's hesitant manipulations, the shift of both our attention as readers and that of the characters, and finally the quality of their sensitivity and ours, of course, as we follow and affirm it, not to omit the author's deeper discriminations as he composes the entire scene, are combined to provide us with an almost daunting example of what a culture crystallized within a style can do.

A sentence is a length of awareness. Henry James makes us conscious of that. Its pace, its track, its jittery going back, its gush, its merciless precision—whatever the qualities are—its pruderies, its pride in its own powers, its Latinate pomposity or raucous yawps, constitute a particular expressive presence. Still, we must take account of what this swatch of unvoiced sound—this mind in its moving—is made of: language and custom and cultural object, history and belief, status and sensation, thought and need, feeling and dream.

It is entirely appropriate that what the Prince and Charlotte are shopping for is a symbol: an object that shall convey, in its worn and somewhat aged elements, a complex geometry of human implications and recognitions, glimpses which pass through the gloriously gilded surface, and the clear ring of the crystal, toward its half-hidden inner flaw, that weakness waiting to show itself in any human whole. Henry James's characters live in a system of social relations so complex and connected, so culturally developed and refined, that his sentences can keep up only by being equally complete in the plump ripe resonance of their meanings; for if his famous injunction—to be one on whom nothing is lost—is to be matched by his art, then no element of language, at the level of either worldly referent, abstract concept, or material sign, can be overlooked; just as a gesture, mute as a wave in a waste of ocean, becomes, in the right place, an anguished sign of parting—a conveyance of private feeling into public knowledge—or, as Rilke writes, perhaps the motion of the wave is like "the tremor of a plum-tree and the bough a startled cuckoo has set free."

Observing a birthday, celebrating Christmas, keeping the Sabbath holy, are activities which are fairly free of natural law. They are like the blank page. They await definition. We needn't eat three meals a day, either; we needn't have an egg for breakfast; we needn't be so finicky about the time it cooks; we needn't put it in a faience cup, the small end up; we needn't crack it with a silver knife; we needn't accompany it with coffee, taken black. We needn't, but there are cultural constraints against roast duck with cherries, against pemmican and raw snake, against *coq au vin,* before we really are unslippered and awake.

Even the simplest society has to keep its members in some sort of rhythmic step. And ours? When would we open our restaurants? what would they dare to serve? would we eat from our hands, from a trough, out of wooden bowls, off china plates? furtive and alone as in a public john? in friendly bunches? in hostile bands?

Culture draws an apparently arbitrary and vagrant line between our desires and their eventual satisfaction, setting up arbitrary obstacles like a row of hurdles in front of a dash man. Freud sometimes felt it was a substitute reality, at once false and overdemanding, because culture is totally nosy; it is not a neighbor but the neighborhood; it cares about everything: about the character of containers, furnishings, clothes; about the difference between a cup and a mug, a grin and a sneer, a chaste kiss and a lewd one, about the social superiority of wine to beer. Its judgments stratify as well as any high-rise. It considers chartreuse a dime-store hue, something to wear with painted toes and teased hair, and not a color to swallow coffee from, since it seems to sicken that thick and normally lightless brew. It wants silent sips. It interposes objects and implements between ourselves and our food. The head should not be bent too narrowly above the bowl or the rice shoveled roughly in. It wants to disguise and supplement the brutality of our biology. We are in no hurry. We are well off. We know where our next meal is coming from. We shall, therefore, be calm, witty in our conversation, and not stick our tongue into the custard. Culture is upwardly mobile. Thus its requirements go on and on.

One does not whistle between bites or, while still at table, talk about catching the syph in Singapore or getting sick and throwing up in Saigon. There are also definite limits to the permissibly sleazy and obscene. One does not spit, shout, or gargle. One does not come to dinner nude, or in a blood-spattered butcher's apron, or without shoes. One smiles a lot. Talk is correct, and silence is suspect and rude. At other guests one does not throw wet pellets of bread. On the other hand, one does display charm and wit, qualities as social as the obscene or the syph. One pays the host and hostess a compliment on the warmth of their hospitality, the wisdom of their wines, the excellence of their food, but one does not lick the platter clean.

Yet as we watch that devious, wandering, hazardous line develop, we can see the unfolding form, the slow unbudding beauty of it, because our coffee is more than coffee now, to the right nose; it is part of a social ceremony, a ceremony which allows us to discern much in saying more: color and region and richness of bean, the cup in our palm like a warm hand as we shape another metaphor and sexual sign; and held in common, too, the deep taste, the heartening smell of the blend, the stimulating effects of the caffeine.

James feared that democracy might render society too featureless for fiction; but the human mind demands division and difference, hierarchy and opposition, just as Saussure insisted language does, in order to establish the identity of its words and semantic strategies. A grimace, a gesture, a sign (for instance, the one that means money, or is a goodby wave, or a small *moue* of disappointment) must be able to mark itself off from any other of its kind ('honey' from 'money,' 'phony' from 'funny,' or so-long from the fanning hand which says "hi, there! here I am!" or that small dip in the spirit from the wrinkled nose which tells us it smells the fat in the fire). We learn to read the natural world in the same way, because our culture instructs us about the manifold meanings of river and mountains, valleys and plains, of cypresses and fountains, of yews and plane trees and bays. In a sense, culture has completed its work when everything is a sign, and every element of every sign is also a sign. That is the secret of Swedenborg, if anybody cares.

Consider the quietly beautiful opening of *A Farewell to Arms:*

> In the late summer of that year we lived in a house in a village that looked across the river and the plain to the mountains. In the bed of the river there were pebbles and boulders, dry and white in the sun, and the water was clear and swiftly moving and blue in the channels. Troops went by the house and down the road and the dust they raised powdered the leaves of the trees. The trunks of the trees too were dusty and the leaves fell early that year and we saw the troops marching along the road and the dust rising and leaves, stirred by the breeze, falling and the soldiers marching and afterward the road bare and white except for the leaves.

The parallel between fallen troops and fallen leaves is obvious enough— the dusty road and the clear stream—but the parallel can be drawn because falling leaves are already richly invested items. The novelist treats nature like a page of the person, and does so without in the least having to attribute to it human cares and needs. The house "looked" across the river; the river has boulders in its "bed"; dust "powdered" the leaves. The novelist has never had any other subject than society in the fullest sense. If we want to know what Virginia Woolf's words are about (normally a naïve question), we must answer that they render cultural signs, configurations which she also manipulates with the same artful concern for sensuous meaning, systems and design, as her sentences. 'River' does not mean "river" in this passage; it means all the things that rivers mean. James, Mann, Chekhov, Joyce—Faulkner, Melville, Flaubert—Beckett, Tolstoy, Proust—they invent, they imagine, they compose in two languages—two tongues—simultaneously. This is not to pretend that Beckett is a novelist or yet a playwright of manners in the old sense, or to suggest that the writer's real job is to give us the lowdown on our chapfallen civilization, that "old bitch gone in the teeth"; yet what are the objects which Winnie hauls out of her capacious black bag at the beginning of *Happy Days,* but leftovers from our markets and our shops, fragments from our life—the insanely misproductive commercial world? There is a toothbrush, pair of spectacles, mirror, lipstick, nearly empty bottle of red medicine, a feathered brimless hat, a magnifying glass, revolver. In other words: violence, self-love, vanity, a concern for appearances, distortion and blindness, sexual allure, fear. Upon some of these objects—the bottle, the brush—there is writing, and Winnie tries to make it out:

> Loss of spirits . . . lack of keenness . . . want of appetite . . . infants . . . children . . . adults . . . six level . . . tablespoonfuls daily . . . —the old style!— . . . daily . . . before and after . . . meals . . . instantaneous . . . improvement.   . . . .

> Fully guaranteed . . . . . . genuine pure . . . Fully guaranteed . . . . . . genuine pure . . . Fully guaranteed . . . . . . genuine pure . . . . . . hog's . . . setae.

A brush that scrubs the teeth with hog's hair, a syrup that soothes: they talk; they mean almost too much, now that they've become pure props. Winnie is already half archeological as she lies there buried beneath a wooden earth to above the waist; and shards from old pots could not have been dug from the ground with more meaning than her pistol is drawn out or her parasol waved. As relics, like the clichés which Winnie mouths, they resonate without first ringing; they are memorabilia become memory itself; and through the fertility of this sterile *dreck,* Beckett demonstrates once again the true immortality of *things* . . . an immortality which lies in the manifold inescapabilities of signs.

Our expressions, choices, gestures, not only turn us inside out, they regulate and organize our mind, just as the body, which must learn not merely to run, but to hurdle as well, develops new habits for its muscles, new expectations from its movements, new perceptions of the cinder track, new hurts, new fears.

Imagine, for a moment, that I have chosen to express my distress at the death of a friend by weighting down lengths of my long hair with stones. Not only does meaning—my mourning—spread like a metaphor through every strand of my behavior; my actions are, themselves, an analysis of my emotion. What was purely mine is, in that sense, shared; and what was purely private is, at the same time, felt as a feeling among friends. Of course, if it became customary to grieve in this fashion, I'd have invented a style; but in the beginning I would have to consider carefully the cultural significance of long hair, of braids, death, grief, and stones; in short, the internal harmony between my actions and my feeling; because how else could the meaning of my performance be read, *prima facie,* without some aptness of imagery, some contextual congruence, some intrinsic directions?

Eventually, of course, I might only need to mimic my original motions, while my feelings were on vacation, or even buy an already weighted, oiled, and braided mourning wig; however, every additional detail, every fillip (deciding on imitation stones wrought artfully of gold, for instance, determining the thickness of the braid, the nature of the tie, the bow, the proper pattern to be formed by parted hair across the field of the skull, and so on, the substitution of sad small bells for the stones— as a paper bag and talc might stand in for sackcloth and ashes—and as the ritual grows, the angle of the bowed head, the darkly mascaraed eyes, the shuffling gait, the periodic moan), any alteration would revivify the significance of the whole; it would, in effect, revise the feeling I was claiming, and, with my ritual worries, celebrating.

We wear our rue with a difference, and I would wear my wig in my own way, too. The fact that culture completes us as persons by creating a common consciousness, so that the little round ornate ivory plate I ritually touch my tongue to signals my satisfaction with my food, and will serve to say I'd like to lick the platter clean; this fact does not have as an inevitable consequence the disappearance of my individuality behind a costume of convention in the instant I raise that ornate ivory dimpled dish to gaze at my features, and *blanc* meets *blanc* like the juice of two grapes; for even if each table setting has one, and even if each person feels obliged by custom to complete the gesture, nothing prevents me from being a Nureyev of this little rite, since only I may know how far one ought to stick the tongue out, whether to dart it, or loll, where to hold the gleaming plate, what expression to put on my otherwise empty face. Of course, it is true that most people are not so immediately discernible as separate selves in any society—no more than are deer in their herds—and that anonymity is as rampant as heart disease, and hypocrisy is epidemic; nevertheless, a closer look will always discover a Bambi, find on the leader scars left by teeth and spears.

Most patches of English, like patches of sky, are like other patches of English. Lawn is like lawn, weeds are like weeds to the discouraged eye. Only variations in subject matter or location serve to distinguish them, and, even on that count, not always very well; yet if we pretend that a paragraph of Henry James is one expression of the Jamesian manner, in its late and tangled entirety, the way his style, in turn, is an example of the English language in pressed, in extended, use; why, then, it might profit us to go on and suggest that my mourning rite, my cow-belled hair and blackened ears, are attached to me as I am attached to the larger body of my culture.

It is a mixed attachment, certainly, of kind and of degree, because my ears belong to me more firmly than their blackening. Hair can be cut, but not so easily its habit of growing. I can leave some of my history behind me like wrappings of my lunch blown down the highway—I can leave *some*—and some of my upbringing, too, and friends, and job. I can give up living in the city, taking the Times. I can shed habits like taking tea at bedtime, observing the holidays, or having sex only after washing down the car in the park. I can shed some. But the habit of acquiring such habits can't be washed off like dust. I can flee society at full speed; indeed, I can utter a loud vow of silence, but I can't forget the language I refuse to speak.

Each of us has the capacity to compose sentences in the English language, even novel ones are easy for us ("George, please put the pastrami back in the glove compartment"); a very few may be able to write as well as Henry James or the Hemingway of that passage; but none of us can mimic the precise moves of their minds without mockery, or ape the qualities of their style without becoming one, or try to reach the special level of their artistry without falling into parody and ridicule along the way. Their work cannot be successfully counterfeited, even by another genius. *The Beast in the Jungle* could not possibly be by Beckett. *Happy Days* could not possibly be by Barth. Out of the same long list of words we all use, with the same rules available, the same sounds, each artist achieves an intrinsic uniqueness, and this is because what the culture can accomplish, by and large, is in their care, and, through their skill, perfected. "Perfection." It is Matthew Arnold's word.

Yet in one sense this perfection is not perfection at all, but its opposite. If I make a bowl so beautiful that no one dares to use it, I have
separated it from its kind, as I might cut out a stallion from its herd; I
have denied it its function, which might have been that of serving me
my mashed potatoes. Because images line its side as on Keats's urn, it
has become wholly cultural.

James's language no longer communicates in the ordinary sense, because it communicates too much, too carefully; because it is conscious
of its own character, as the highest culture must be, if it is ever to be
critical of itself; and these sentences are incredibly critical; they demand
the impossible: they want every element related, every relation enriched,
every meaning multiplied, every thought or sensation they contain, every
desire or revelation, every passion, precisely defined and pushed to its
finest and fullest expression. That is why they are celebrations—these
sentences—not informations, placations, injunctions, improvements,
vacations for the body or the mind. They are, indeed, as particular and
well wrought as we are, for we, in our way, are works of art and celebrations, too; because of the consciousness we possess, our power of dis-
crimination, our general command of fact, and the fact that with us the
orphan, the maiden, the hunted slave, is safe; our sense, then, for the
natural and the moral law, our tact, our taste for Poussin, Corbusier,
and Bach: are not these capacities and conditions—so fragile and easily
snuffed out—are they not the most men and women in their mutual
history have made of themselves?

Ah, but to speak so—isn't that to betray the smug provinciality I
warned of earlier? What a bouquet made of old blooms from jolly old
Bloomsbury! what pampered, rose-sniffing estheticism! what familiar decay: the lesbians of Pierre Louÿs play with their pillows and sing songs
about breasts and eyes and scented hair. But to speak in this way is not
to talk about decay; it is to talk about excellence.

"Human beings are too important to be treated as mere symptoms of
the past," Lytton Strachey once wrote. "They have a value which is independent of any temporal process—which is eternal, and must be felt
for its own sake." Lytton, however, is just a skinny bent plant in Virginia Woolf's garden, a debunking brat who peeked up Queen Victoria's
skirt: feminist, socialist, pacifist, pansy—back when it was painful to be
even one of these. To have culture within a culture can bring you to
such a pass.

Consciousness is all the holiness we have. It ought to move ever upward, and not always on hot air; it ought to become continuously more
inclusive, more knowing, more self-regarding, as though Paul Valéry

held the mirror; it ought to be tender and plastic; its thoughts and figures ought to dance; it ought to be more searching, more rambunctious,
more daring, more intense; and yet our only record of that accomplishment lies in a few golden bowls, a few songs and sentences (it may seem
like many sometimes—crammed shelves, full museums, packed record
racks—yet there are only a few, really, relative to the rest), just a few
chants and fugues, a scattered number of buildings and bridges and
tombs, some sacred places and performances, here and there a spread of
paint upon a wall so sublimely shaped it makes us ashamed of our eyes
and fingers, our own slow skills; and then some historians, too, wealthier
in their accounts than the events they recite, as well as a set of imagina-
tive and ambitious theories, so sharp, so clear and clean and crisply
designed, it's as if the mind had whistled in its wonder at the world.

We can be as relative as almost anyone would want. We can recognize
the beauty and sadness in Beckett, in Kazantzakis and Kawabata
equally; but if we want to say that cultures "work us up" in any way in
the manner of the masters, then we shall have to distinguish between
trash and art, the kitschy and the classic, and single out in men and
women, too, those who have taken a shortcut to their completion.
About the right life, style has much to teach; method—blessed method—
much. It is a way of arriving at and discerning value. The cultures I
should like to count as highest, then, are those which enable the people
they shape not only to see deeply in, but to see widely without; to become
as individual, as conscious, as critical, as whole in themselves, as a good
sentence. Not so simple. Certainly not easy, and easily put off. "The
people are not ready for freedom," it is routinely and apologetically pronounced. Yet freedom is earth and air: half of the elements.

It is simply not enough to live and to be honey-happy, to hump and
hollar, to reproduce. Bees achieve it, and they still sting, still buzz. To
seek the truth (which requires method), to endeavor to be just (which
depends on process), to create and serve beauty (which is the formal
object of style), these old "ha-has," like peace and freedom and respect
for persons, are seldom aims or states of the world these days, but only
words most likely found in Sunday schools, or adrift like booze on the
breath of cheapjacks, preachers, politicians, teachers, popes; nevertheless, they can still be sweet on the right tongue, and name our ends and
our most honorable dreams.

There is, then, meaning contemplated, meaning we repeatedly return
to, meaning it is as good to hold in the mouth as good wine; and there is
also its opposite, and here the analogy with language may help us find
the enemies of culture which culture itself creates, because language al-

lows anonymity as well as distinction; it has its signs which say GENTS, its fast foods, its wetting dolls, its drively little verses which sentimental sogs send as sops to other sogs, endless paragraphs and pages and entire books which anyone could have written and probably did: guidelines and directions and directories and handbooks and all sorts of reports and memos and factual entries and puffy bios of politicians and punks, stars of stage, screen, field, and whorehouse, and petty lies and dreary chat and insinuating gossip and the flatterous tittle-tattle of TV talk shows, with their relentlessly cheery hosts, and vomitous film scenarios and wretched radio gabble and self-serving memoirs and stilted forms and humiliating applications, contracts, agreements, subpoenas, creditors' threats, and private eye/romantic/western/spy and sci-fi/fantasy films and fictions, and dozens of dirty gumshoe did-him-ins and wise guy all-abouts, how-tos, and why-nots, and fan mags and digests and Hardy Boys and Nancy Drews and clubby hobby gun and body beautiful books and the whole copiously illustrated pulp and porno scandal pushers from the hard-core soft-on press; and indeed machines might have made them, and one day will, with the same successful sameness as sheets of toilet tissue, similarly daisied, similarly scented, similarly soft, are presented to the uniformly smiling crack of all those similar consumers.

Even that is not the triumph of our culture's bottom end: it is the glassy plastic drinking cup. Scarcely an object, it is so superbly universal Hegel might have halloed at it. Made of a substance found nowhere in nature, manufactured by processes equally unnatural and strange, it is the complete and expert artifact. Then packaged in sterilized stacks as though it weren't a thing at all by itself, this light, translucent emptiness is so utterly identical to the other items in its package, the other members of its class, it might almost be space. Sloganless—it has no message—often not even the indented hallmark of its maker. It is an abstraction acting as a glass, and resists individuation perfectly, because you can't crimp its rim or write on it or poke it full of pencil holes—it will shatter first, rather than submit—so there is no way, after a committee meeting, a church sup or reception (its ideal locales), to know one from the other, as it won't discolor, stain, craze, chip, but simply safeguards the world from its contents until both the flat Coke or cold coffee and their cup are disposed of. It is a decendental object. It cannot have a history. It has disappeared entirely into its function. It is completely what it does, except that what it does, it does as a species. Of itself it provides no experience, and scarcely of its kind. Even a bullet gets uniquely scarred. Still, this *shotte,* this *nebech,* is just as much a cultural object, and just as crystalline in its way, as our golden bowl, and is without flaws, and costs nothing, and demands nothing, and is one of the ultimate wonders of the universe of *dreck*—the world of neutered things. It *is* perfect. That is Arnold's word.

Nevertheless, the perfections of this plain clear plastic cup perversely deny it perfection. Since it is nothing but its use, its existence is otherwise ignored. It is not worth a rewash. It is not worth another look, a feel, a heft. It has been desexed. Thus indifference is encouraged. Consumption is encouraged. Convenience is encouraged. Castoffs are multiplied, and our world is already full of the unwanted and used up. Its rim lies along the lip like the edge of a knife. That quality is also ignored and insensitivity encouraged. It is a servant, but it has none of the receptivity of artistic material, and in that sense it does not serve; its absences are everywhere. Since, like an overblown balloon, it has as much emptiness as it can take, it is completely its shape, and because it totally contains, it is estranged from what it holds. Thus dissociation is encouraged. Poured into such a vessel, wine moans for a certain moment, and then is silent; its color pales, its bouquet fades, it becomes pop; yet there is a pallid sadness in its modest mimicry of the greater goblets, in its pretense to perfect nothingness, in its ordinary evil, since it is no Genghis Khan, or Coriolanus, but a discreet and humble functionary, simply doing its job as it has been designed and directed to do, like the other members of the masses, and disappearing with less flutter than leaves.

Our culture hesitates between these two polarities of pure end and even purer means, between utility and consecration, and it dreams of men who are worthy to be ends in themselves, who will take any trouble to be free of the shackles of ease and convenience, who truly treasure the world; and it desires men who will be willing to be mowed down in anonymous rows if need be, used up in families, in farms and factories, thrown away on the streets of sprawling towns, who want to pass through existence so cleanly no trace of them will ever be found. It is not an easy dilemma, because, of itself, use is as innocent as aspirin, and the damage it does, it does not: we do. Yet use is naturally annihilation. Ideally, it is to disappear without remainder. Confronted by its pale translucent face, can the maiden, the orphan, the poor man, the hunted slave feel safe? Only so long as their safety has its uses. Only until the stock gives out. Not when there is no difference between plastic cup, its instant coffee, and swallowing mouth.

ON TALKING TO ONESELF

Dinner, let us imagine, has reached its second wine. We are exchanging pleasantries: gossip, tittle-tattle, perilously keen remarks. Like a fine sauce, they pique the mind. They pass the time. A thought is peeled and placed upon a plate. A nearby lady lends us a small smile, and there are glances brilliant as the silver. Patiently we listen while another talks, because everyone, our etiquette instructs, must have his chance to speak. We wait. We draw upon the cloth with unused knives. Our goblets turn as slowly as the world.

At this moment, you are reading. I am absent. Still, I shall pretend to talk. Shall you pretend to listen while you read? I shall pretend to be speaking though I write. Is this a late wet lonely night? Who knows where a voice is from, any more than we know a fly's home, when it lands on type? or where your ear is, perhaps this instant barely lifted from a pillow to listen for a noise in the house? Our present circumstances—it may be I have no present circumstance—could they be more different?

I want to talk to you about talking, that commonest of all our intended activities. Talking is our public link with one another: it is a need; it is an art; it is the chief instrument of all instruction; it is the most personal aspect of our private lives. To those who have sponsored our appearance in the world, the first memorable moment to follow our inaugural bawl is the awkward birth of our first word. It is that noise, a sound that is no longer a simple signal, like the greedy squalling of a gull, but a declaration of the incipient presence of mind, that delivers us into the human sphere. Before, there was only energy, intake, and excretion; now a person has begun. And in no idle, ordinary, or jesting sense, words are what that being will become. It is language which most shows a man, Ben Jonson said. "Speake that I may see thee." And Emerson certainly supports him: "Man is only half himself," he said, "the other half is his expression." Truths like this have been the long companions of our life, and so we often overlook them, as we miss the familiar mole upon our chin, even while powdering the blemish, or running over it with a razor.

Silence is the soul's invisibility. We can, of course, conceal ourselves behind lies and sophistries, but when we speak, we are present, however careful our disguise. The creature we choose to be on Halloween says something about the creature we are. I have often gone to masquerades as myself, and in that guise no one knew I was there.

Not to speak—to be gagged, isolated, put away out of earshot—is in its way to be removed from the world—to be shouted down, censored, rendered mute. And not to be spoken to, to be sent to Coventry, hasn't that always been felt to be as hard to carry as a cross? When we wish we were elsewhere, but are powerless to leave, we sulk. To whom I will not talk, my actions say, is not.

Plato thought of the soul as an ardent debating society in which our various interests pled their causes; and there were honest speeches and dishonest ones; there was reason, lucid and open and lovely like the nakedness of the gods, where truth found its youngest friend and nobility its ancient eloquence; and there was also pin-eyed fanaticism, deceit and meanness, a coarseness like sand in cold grease; there was bribery and seduction, flattery, browbeating and bombast. Little has changed, in that regard, either in our souls or in society since; for the great Greeks were correct: life must be lived according to the right word—the *logos* they loved—and so the search for it, the mastery of it, the fullest and finest and truest expression of it, the defense of it, became the heart of a life-long educational enterprise.

To an almost measureless degree, to *know* is to possess words, and all of us who live out in the world as well as within our own are aware that we inhabit a forest of symbols; we dwell in a context of texts. Adam created the animals and birds by naming them, and we name incessantly, conserving achievements and customs, and countries that no longer exist, in the museum of human memory. But it is not only the books which we pile about us like a building, or the papers we painfully compose, the exams or letters we write, the calculations we come to by means of mystic diagrams, mathematical symbols, astrological charts or other ill- or well-drawn maps of the mind; it is not simply our habit of lining the streets with wheedling, hectoring, threatening signs, writing warnings on the sides of little jars and boxes, or with cajoling smoke defacing the sky, or turning on the radio to bruise with entreaty every ear, or the TV which illustrates its lies with clowns and color; it is not alone the languages we learn to mispronounce, the lists, the arguments and rhymes, we get by heart; it is not even our tendency to turn what is unwritten into writing with a mere look, so that rocks will suddenly say their age and origin and activity, or what is numb flesh and exposed bone will cry out that cotton candy killed it, or cancer, or canoodling, the letter C like a cut across an artery; no, it is not the undeniable importance of these things which leads me to lay such weight upon the word; it is rather our interior self I'm concerned with, and therefore with the language which springs out of the most retiring and inmost parts of us, and is the image of its parent like a child: the words we use to convey our love to one another, or to cope with anxiety, for instance; the words which will convince, persuade, which will show us clearly, or make the many one; the words I listen to when I wait out a speech at a dinner party; words which can comfort and assuage, damage and delight, amuse and dismay; but, above all, the words which one burns like beacons against the darkness, and which together comprise the society of the silently speaking self; because all these words are but humble echoes of the words the poet uses when she speaks of passion, or the historian when he drives his nails through time, or when the psychoanalyst divines our desires as through tea leaves left at the bottom of our dreams.

Even if the world becomes so visual that words must grow faces to save themselves, and put on smiles made of fragrant paste; and even if we all hunker down in front of films like savages before a divinity, to have experience explained to us in terms of experiences which need to be explained; still, we shall not trade portraits of our love affairs, only of ourselves; there is no Polaroid that will develop in moments the state of our soul, or cassette to record our pangs of conscience; so we shall never talk in doodles over dinner, or call up our spirit to its struggle with a little private sit-com or a dreary soap. Could we quarrel very well in ink blots, or reach a legal understanding in the video arcade? Even if the world falls silent and we shrink in fear within ourselves; even if words are banished to the Balkans or otherwise driven altogether out of hearing (as the word 'Balkans' has been), as though every syllable were subversive (as indeed each is); all the same, when we have withdrawn from any companionship with things and people, when we have collapsed in terror behind our talcumed skins, and we peer suspiciously through the keyholes of our eyes, when we have reached the limit of our dwindle—the last dry seed of the self—then we shall see how greatly correct is the work of Samuel Beckett, because we shall find there, inside that seed, nothing but his featureless cell, nothing but voice, nothing but darkness and talk.

How desperately, then, we need to learn it—to talk to ourselves— because we are babies about it. Oh, we have excellent languages for the secrets of nature. Wave packets, black holes, and skeins of genes: we can write precisely and consequentially of these, as well as other extraordinary phenomena; but can we talk even of trifles: for instance, of the way a look sometimes crosses a face like the leap of a frog, so little does it live there; or how the habit of anger raisins the heart, or wet leaves paper a street? Our anatomy texts can skin us without our pain, the cellular urges of trees are no surprise, the skies are driven by winds we cannot see; yet science has passed daily life like the last bus, and left it to poetry.

It is terribly important to know how a breast is made: how to touch it in order to produce a tingle, or discover a hidden cyst (we find these things written of in books); but isn't it just as important to be able to put the beauty of a body in words, words we give like a gift to its bearer; to communicate the self to another, and in that way form a community of feeling, of thought about feeling, of belief about thought: an exchange of warmth like breathing, of simple tastes and the touch of the eye, and other sensations shortly to be sought, since there is no place for the utopia of the flesh outside the utopia of talk?

It can't be helped. We are made of layers of language like a Viennese torte. We are a Freudian dessert. My dinner companion, the lady who lent me her smile, has raised her goblet in a quiet toast. It is as though its rim had touched me, and I try to find words for the feeling, and for the wine which glows like molten rubies in her glass; because if I can do that, I can take away more than a memory which will fade faster than a winter footprint; I can take away an intense and interpreted description, a record as tough to erase as a relief, since without words what can be well and richly remembered? Yesterdays are gone like drying mist. Without our histories, without the conservation which concepts nearly alone make possible, we could not preserve our lives as were the bodies of the pharaohs, the present would soon be as clear of the past as a bright day, and we would be innocent arboreals again.

Of course we could redream the occasion, or pretend to film our feeling, but we'll need words to label and index our images anyway, and can the photograph contain the rush of color to my face, the warmth which reminds me I also am a glass and have become wine?

We dream in images, and might we not learn to sleepwalk while awake, think in diagrams and maps and coded color schemes? but the images of sleep are symbols, and the words we make up while awake outline our dreams and render clearly their declarations. The phrase "a photographic history" is a misnomer. Every photograph requires a thousand words.

I remember because I talk. I talk from morning to night, and then I talk on in my sleep. Our talk is so precious to us, we think we punish others when we stop, as I've remarked. So I stay at peace because I talk. *Tête-à-têtes* are talk. Shop is talk. Parties are parades of anecdotes, gossip, opinion, raillery, and reportage. There is sometimes a band and we have to shout. Out of an incredibly complex gabble, how wonderfully clever of me to hear so immediately my own name; yet at my quiet breakfast table, I may be unwilling, and thus unable, to hear a thing my wife says. When wives complain that romance has fled from their marriage, they mean that their husbands have grown quiet and unresponsive as moss. Taciturnity—long, lovely word—it is a famous tactic. As soon as two people decide they have nothing more to talk about, everything should be talked out. Silence shields no passion. Only the mechanical flame is sputterless and quiet.

Like a good husband, then, I tell my wife what went on through the day—in the car, on the courts, at the office. Well, perhaps I do not tell her *all* that went on; perhaps I give her a slightly cleaned-up and economical account. I tell my friends how I fared in New York, and of the impatient taxi which honked me through the streets. I tell my students the substance of what they should have read. I tell my children how it used to be (it was better), and how I was a hero (of a modest kind, of course) in the Great War, moving from fact to fiction within the space of a single word. I tell my neighbors pleasant lies about the beauty of their lawns and dogs and vandalizing tykes, and in my head I tell the whole world where to get off.

Those who have reputations as great conversationalists are careful never to let anyone else open a mouth. Like Napoleons, they first conquer, then rule, the entire space of speech around them. Jesus preached. Samuel Johnson bullied. Carlyle fulminated. Bucky Fuller droned. Wittgenstein thought painfully aloud like a surgeon. But Socrates talked . . . hazardously, gaily, amorously, eloquently, religiously . . . he talked with wit, with passion, with honesty; he asked; he answered; he considered; he debated; he entertained; he made of his mind a boulevard before there was even a France.

I remember—I contain a past—partly because my friends and family allow me to repeat and polish my tales, tall as they sometimes are, like the stalk Jack climbed to encounter the giant. Shouldn't I be able to learn from history how to chronicle my self? "Every man should be so much an artist," again Emerson said, "that he could report in conversation what had befallen him." Words befell Emerson often. He made speeches in public and on paper, wherever he was, and until his mind changed, he always meant what he said. Frequently his mind changed before he reached any conclusion. In his head his heart heard the language of the other side.

Talk, of course, is not always communication. It is often just a buzz, the hum the husband makes when he's still lit, but the station's gone off. We can be bores as catastrophic as quakes, causing even the earth to yawn. Talk can be cruel and injurious to a degree which is frightening; the right word wrongly used can strike a man down like a club, turn a heart dark forever, freeze the feelings; nevertheless, while the thief is threatening to take our money or our life, he has yet to do either; and while talk mediates a strike, or weighs an allegation in the press or in committee, or considers a law in Congress or argues a crime in court; while a spouse gripes, or the con man cons, while ideas are explained to a point beyond opacity by the prof; then it's not yet the dreadful day of the exam, sentence has not been passed, the crime has not yet occurred, the walkout, or the war. It may sound like a balk, a hitch in the motion, a failure to follow through, but many things recommend talk, not least its rich and wandering rhymes.

Our thoughts tend to travel like our shadow in the morning walking west, casting their outline just ahead of us so that we can see and approve, or amend and cancel, what we are about to say. It is the only rehearsal our conversation usually gets; but that is one reason we fall upon cliché as if it were a sofa and not a sword; for we have rehearsed "good morning," and "how are you?" and "have a nice day," to the place where the tongue is like a stale bun in the mouth; and we have talked of Tommy's teeth and our cold car's stalling treachery, of our slobby dog's affection and Alice's asthma and Hazel's latest honeybunny, who, thank god, is only black and not gay like her last one; we have emptied our empty jars over one another like slapstick comics through so many baggy-panted performances we can now dream of Cannes and complain of Canada with the same breath we use to spit an olive in a napkin, since one can easily do several thoughtless things at once—in fact, one ought; and indeed it is true that prefab conversation frees the mind, yet rarely does the mind have a mind left after these interconnected clichés have conquered it; better to rent rooms to hooligans who will only draw on the walls and break the furniture; for our Gerberized phrases touch nothing; they keep the head hollow by crowding out thought; they fill all the chairs with buttocks like balloons; they are neither fed nor feed; they drift like dust; they refuse to breathe.

We forget sometimes that we live with ourselves—worse luck most likely—as well as within. The head we inhabit is a haunted house. Nevertheless, we often ignore our own voice when it speaks to us: "Remember me," the spirit says, "I am your holy ghost." But we are bored by our own baloney. Why otherwise would we fall in love if not to hear that same sweet hokum from another? Still, we should remember that we comprise true Siamese twins, fastened by language and feeling, wed better than any bed; because when we talk to ourselves we divide into the self which is all ear and the self which is all mouth. Yet which one of us is which? Does the same self do most of the talking while a second self soaks it up, or is there a real conversation?

Frequently we put on plays like a producer: one voice belongs to sister, shrill and intrepidly stupid; a nephew has another (he wants a cookie); the boss is next—we've cast him as a barnyard bully; and then there is a servant or a spouse, crabby and recalcitrant. All speak as they are spoken through; each runs around in its role like a caged squirrel, while an audience we also invent (patient, visible, too easily interested, readily pleased) applauds the heroine or the hero who has righted wrongs like an avenging angel, answered every challenge like a Lancelot, every question like Ann Landers, and met every opportunity like a perfect Romeo, every romance like a living doll. If we really love the little comedy we've constructed, it's likely to have a long run.

Does it really matter how richly and honestly and well we speak? What is our attitude toward ourselves; what tone do we tend to take? Consider Hamlet, a character who escapes his circumstances and achieves greatness despite the fact his will wavers or he can't remember the injunctions of his father's ghost. He certainly doesn't bring it off because he has an Oedipus complex (we are all supposed to have that); but because he talks to himself more beautifully than anyone else almost ever has. Consider his passion, his eloquence, his style, his range, his wit: "O what a rogue and peasant slave am I," he exclaims; "now could I drink hot blood," he brags; "to be or not to be," he wonders; "O," he hopes, "that this too too solid flesh would melt," and he complains that all occasions do inform against him. For our part, what do *we* do? do we lick our own hand and play the spaniel? do we whine and wheedle or natter like a ninny? can we formulate our anger in a righteous phrase, or will we be reduced to swearing like a soldier? All of us are dramatists, but how will we receive our training? where can we improve upon the puerile theatricals of our parents, if not here among the plays and perils of Pirandello and the dialogues of Plato, the operas of Puccini and the follies of most faculties (among the many glories of the letter 'p')?

If we think awareness is like water purling gaily in its stream, we have been listening to the wrong James, for our consciousness is largely composed of slogans and signs, of language of one kind or other: we wake to an alarm; we read the weather by the brightness of a streak on the ceiling, the mood of our lover by the night's cramp still clenched in her morning body; our trembling tells us we're hung over; we wipe ourselves with a symbol of softness, push an ad around over our face; the scale rolls up a number which means "overweight," and the innersoles of our shoes say "hush!" Thus, even if we haven't uttered a word, we've so far spent the morning reading. Signs don't stream. They may straggle, but they mostly march. Language allies itself with order. Even its fragments suggest syntax, wholeness, regularity, though many of us are ashamed to address ourselves in complete sentences. Rhetorically structured paragraphs seem pretentious to us, as if, to gaze at our image in a mirror, we had first to put on a tux; and this means that everything of real importance, every decision which requires care, thoughtful analysis, emotional distance, and mature judgment, must be talked out with someone else— a consequence we can't always face, with its attendant arguments, embarrassments, counterclaims, and lies. To think for yourself—not narrowly, but rather as a mind—you must be able to talk to yourself: well, openly, and at length. You must come in from the rain of requests and responses. You must take and employ your time as if it were your life. And that side of you which speaks must be prepared to say anything so long as it is so—is seen so, felt so, thought so—and that side of you that listens must be ready to hear horrors, for much of what is so *is* horrible—horrible to see, horrible to feel, horrible to consider. But at length, and honestly—that is not enough. To speak well to oneself . . . to speak well we must go down as far as the bucket can be lowered. Every thought must be thought through from its ultimate cost back to its cheap beginnings; every perception, however profound and distant, must be as clear and easy as the moon; every desire must be recognized as a relative and named as fearlessly as Satan named his angels; finally, every feeling must be felt to its bottom where the bucket rests in the silt and water rises like a tower around it. To talk to ourselves well requires, then, endless rehearsals—rehearsals in which we revise, and the revision of the inner life strikes many people as hypocritical; but to think how to express some passion properly is the only way to be possessed by it, for unformed feelings lack impact, just as unfelt ideas lose weight. So walk around unrewritten, if you like. Live on broken phrases and syllable gristle, telegraphese and film reviews. No one will suspect . . . until you speak, and your soul falls out of your mouth like a can of corn from a shelf.

There are kinds and forms of this inner speech. Many years ago, when my eldest son was about fourteen, I was gardening alongside our house

one midday in mid-May, hidden as it happened between two bushes I
was pruning, when Richard came out of the house in a hurry to return
to school following lunch, and like a character in a French farce, skulking there, I overheard him talking to himself. "Well, racing fans, it
looks . . . it looks like the question we've all been asking is about to
be answered, because HERE COMES RICHARD GASS OUT OF THE PITS NOW!
He doesn't appear to be limping from that bad crash he had at the race-
way yesterday—what a crash that was!—and he is certainly going
straight for his car . . . what courage! . . . his helmet is on his head,
fans . . . yes, he is getting into his car . . . not a hesitation . . . yes,
he is going to be off in a moment for the track . . . yes—" and then he
went, peddling out of my hearing, busily broadcasting his life.

My son's consciousness, in that moment, was not only thoroughly
verbal (although its subject was the Indy 500, then not too many days
away, and although he could still see the street he would ride on), it had
a form: that given to his language and its referents by the radio sports-
caster. As I remember it now, the verbal tone belonged more to baseball
than to racing. In any case, Richard's body was, in effect, on the air; his
mind was in the booth "upstairs," while his feelings were doubtless
mixed in with his audience, both at home and in the stands. He was
being seen, heard, and *spoken of,* at the same time.

Later this memory led me to wonder whether we all didn't have
fashions and forms in which we talked to ourselves; whether some of
these might be habits of the most indelible sort, the spelling out of our
secret personality; and, finally, whether they might not vitally influence
the way we spoke to others, especially in our less formal moments—in
bed, at breakfast, at the thirteenth tee. And for men and women, might
they not very likely come from those areas of greatest influence or ambition in their lives? I recognized at once that this was certainly true of
me; that although I employed many styles and modes, there was one
verbal form which had me completely in its grip the way Baron Mun-
chausen was held in his own tall tales, or the *Piers Plowman* poet in his
lovely alliteration. If Richard's was that of the radio broadcast, as it
seemed, mine was that of the lecture. I realized that when I woke in the
morning, I rose from bed as though at the end of a night of sleepless
explication, already primed to ask the world if it had any questions. I
was, almost from birth, and so I suppose by "bottom nature," what Gertrude Stein called Ezra Pound—a village explainer—which, she said,
was all right if you were a village, but if not, not; and sooner than sun-
rise I would be launched on an unvoiced speechification on the art of
internal discourse, a lecture I would have given many times, though
rarely aloud.

I have since asked a number of people, some from very different back-
grounds, what shape their internal talk took, and found, first of all
(when there was not a polite amused smile which signified unalterable
resistance), that they agreed to the important presence of these forms,
and that one type did tend to dominate the others: it was often broadcasting—never the lecture—though I once encountered a sermon and
several revival-style pray-makers; it frequently took place in the court-
room where one was conducting a fearless prosecution or a triumphant
defense; it was regularly the repetition of some pattern of parental exchange, a rut full of relatives and preconditioned response; the drama
appeared to be popular, as well as works of pornography, though, in this
regard, there were more movies shown than words said—a pity, both
modes need such improvement. There were monologues such as Brown-
ing might have penned: the vaunt, the threat, the keen, the kvetch, the
eulogy for yourself when dead; there was even the bedtime story, the
diary, the chronicle, and, of course, the novel, gothic in character, or at
least full of intrigue and suspense: Little did William Gass realize when
he rose that gentle May morning to thump his chest and touch his toes
that he would soon be embarked on an adventure whose endless ramifications would utterly alter his life; otherwise he might not have set out
for the supermarket without a list; otherwise he might not have done that
extra push-up; he might better have stayed in bed with the bedclothes
pulled thickly over his stupidly chattering head.

In my little survey, oral modes beat written ones by a mile. Obviously. They could be spoken. And the broadcast, with its apportion-
ment of speaker into "speaker," "spectator," and "sportsman," had a
formal edge over most of its competition.

There were, finally, important differences as to sex: no woman ad-
mitted she broadcast her life as though it were some sporting event,
especially not the "sporting ladies" who regularly reenacted a role they
imagined their mothers had starred in: giving sex and getting money.

Yet I should like to suggest (despite the undeniable sappiness of it)
that the center of the self itself is this secret, obsessive, often silly, nearly
continuous *voice*—the voice that is the surest sign we are alive; and that
one fundamental function of language is the communication with this
self which it makes feasible; that, in fact, without someone speaking,
someone hearing, someone overhearing both, no full self can exist; that
if society—its families and factories and congresses and schools—has
done its work, then every day every one of us is a bit nearer than we
were before to being one of the fortunates who have made rich and
beautiful the great conversation which constitutes our life.

When Richard rode his bike to school, the rider rode, the radio approved, the world around the ride applauded his progress. We know, in truth, that it is often otherwise; that sometimes these elements are enemies, and external conflicts become internal ferocities. What might be a neutral or friendly triangle—speaker, hearer, overhearer—is habitually filled by surrogates for ourselves, for our parents and our peers, scapegoats and villains and victims, and sometimes even by judges, juries, and the police. Then we cannot talk to ourselves for fear of being overheard. But I suspect that tyrannies, and tyrannical conditions, although they frighten many into a public silence which stills the inner self as well, produce an intense, far-ranging, wildly explosive and productive internal confrontation: that initial stage in the composition of dissident and revolutionary works. The adversary attitude can move a lot of freight—some of it even along the right track.

And everywhere here in my present absence—in your, the reader's silence, where you, or something of you, sits among the scattered numbers of listening chairs like a choir before bursting into song—there is the subversive murmur of us all: our glad, our scrappy, rude, grand, small talk to ourselves, the unheard hum of our humanity; without which—think of it!—we might not be awake; without which—imagine it!—we might not be alive; since while we speak we live up there above our bodies in the mind, and there is hope as long as we continue to talk; so long as we continue to speak, to search for eloquence even over happiness or sympathy in sorrow or anger in revenge, even if all that is left to us is the omitted outcry, Christ's query, the silent condemnation: "My God, my God, why have you left me alone?"

ON READING TO ONESELF

I was never much of an athlete, but I was once a member of a team. Indeed, I was its star, and we were champions. I belonged to a squad of speed readers, although I was never awarded a letter for it. Still, we took on the top teams in our territory, and read as rapidly as possible every time we were challenged to a match, hoping to finish in front of our opponents: that towheaded punk from Canton, the tomato-cheeked girl from Marietta, or that silent pair of sisters, all spectacles and squints, who looked tough as German script, and who hailed from Shaker Heights, Ohio, a region noted for its swift, mean raveners of text. We called ourselves "The Speeders." Of course. Everybody did. There were the Sharon Speeders, the Steubenville Speeders, the Sperryville Speeders, and the Niles Nouns. The Niles Nouns never won. How could they—with that name. Nouns are always at rest.

I lost a match once to a kid from a forgettable small town, but I do remember he had green teeth. And that's the way, I'm afraid, we always appeared to others: as creeps with squints, bad posture, unclean complexions, unscrubbed teeth, unremediably tousled hair. We never had dates, only memorized them; and when any real team went on the road to represent the school, we carried the socks, the Tootsie Rolls, the towels. My nemesis had a head of thin red hair like rust on a saw; he screwed a suggestive little finger into his large fungiform ears. He was made of rust, moss, and wax, and I had lost to him . . . lost . . . and the shame of that defeat still rushes to my face whenever I remember it. Nevertheless, although our team had no sweaters, we never earned a letter, and our exploits never made the papers, I still possess a substantial gold-colored medallion on which one sunbeaming eye seems hung above a book like a spider. Both book and eye are open—wide. I take that open, streaming eye to have been a symbol and an omen.

Our reading life has its salad days, its autumnal times. At first, of course, we do it badly, scarcely keeping our balance, toddling along behind our finger, so intent on remembering what each word is supposed to mean that the sentence is no longer a path, and we arrive at its end without having gone anywhere. Thus it is with all the things we learn, for at first they passively oppose us; they lie outside us like mist or the laws of nature; we have to issue orders to our eyes, our limbs, our understanding: lift this, shift that, thumb the space bar, lean more to one side, let up on the clutch—and take it easy, or you'll strip the gears—and don't forget to modify the verb, or remember what an escudo's worth. After a while, though, we find we like standing up, riding a bike, singing *Don Giovanni,* making puff paste or puppy love, building model planes. Then we are indeed like the adolescent in our eager green enthusiasms: they are plentiful as leaves. Every page is a pasture, and we are let out to graze like hungry herds.

Do you remember the magic the word 'thigh' could work on you, showing up suddenly in the middle of a passage like a whiff of cologne in a theater? I admit it: the widening of the upper thigh remains a miracle, and, honestly, many of us once read the word 'thigh' as if we were exploring Africa, seeking the source of the Nile. No volume was too hefty, then, no style too verbal; the weight of a big book was more comforting than Christmas candy; though you have to be lucky, strike the right text at the right time, because the special excitement which Thomas Wolfe provides, for instance, can be felt only in the teens; and when, again, will any of us possess the energy, the patience, the inner sympathy for volcanic bombast, to read—to enjoy—Carlyle?

Rereading—repeating—was automatic. Who needed the lessons taught by Gertrude Stein? I must have rushed through a pleasant little baseball book called *The Crimson Pennant* at least a dozen times, consuming a cake I had already cut into crumbs, yet that big base hit which always came when matters were most crucial was never more satisfying than on the final occasion when its hero and I ran round those bases, and shyly lifted our caps toward the crowd.

I said who needed the lessons taught by Gertrude Stein, but one of the best books for beginners remains her magical *First Reader.* Here are the opening lines of "Lesson One":

> A dog said that he was going to learn to read. The other dogs said he could learn to bark but he could not learn to read. They did not know that dog, if he said he was going to learn to read, he would learn to read. He might be drowned dead in water but if he said that he was going to read he was going to learn to read.
>
> He never was drowned in water not dead drowned and he never did learn to read. Are there any children like that. One

> two three. Are there any children like that. Four five six. Are
> there any children like that. Seven eight nine are there any
> children like that.

There turn out to be ten, each with a dog who says he is going to learn
to read, and shortly the story gets very exciting.

Back in the days of "once upon a time," no one threatened to warm
our behinds if we didn't read another Nancy Drew by Tuesday; no sour-
faced virgin browbeat us with *The Blithedale Romance* or held out *The
Cloister and the Hearth* like a cold plate of "it's good for you" food. We
were on our own. I read Swinburne and the *Adventures of the Shadow*.
I read Havelock Ellis and Tom Swift and *The Idylls of the King*. I read
whatever came to hand, and what came to hand were a lot of naughty
French novels, some by Émile Zola, detective stories, medical adventures,
books about bees, biographies of Napoleon, and *Thus Spake Zarathustra*
like a bolt of lightning. I read them all, whatever they were, with an ease
that defies the goat's digestion, and with an ease which is now so easily
forgotten, just as we forget the wild wobble in the wheels, or the humiliating falls we took, when we began our life on spokes. That wind I
felt, when I finally stayed upright around the block, continuously re-
affirmed the basic joy of cycling. It told me not merely that I was moving,
but that I was moving *under my own power*; just as later, when I'd passed
my driver's test, I would feel another sort of exhilaration—an intense, ad-
dictive, dangerous one—that of command: of my ability to control the
energy produced by another thing or person, to direct the life contained
in another creature. Yes, in those early word-drunk years, I would down
a book or two a day as though they were gins. I read for adventure, excitement, to sample the exotic and the strange, for climax and resolution, to
participate in otherwise unknown and forbidden passions. I forgot what
it was to be *under my own power, under my own steam*. I knew that
Shakespeare came after Sophocles, but I forgot that I went back and
forth between them as though they were towns. In my passion for time,
I forgot their geography. All books occupy the same space. Dante and
Dickens: they cheek by jowl. And although books begin their life in the
world at different times, these dates rarely determine the days they begin
in yours and mine. We forget simple things like that: that we are built
of books. I forgot the Coke I was drinking, the chair, the chill in the air.
I was, like so many adolescents, as eager to leap from my ordinary life as
the salmon are to get upstream. I sought a replacement for the world.
With a surreptitious lamp lit, I stayed awake to dream. I grew reckless.
I read for speed.

When you read for speed you do not read recursively, looping along the line like a sewing machine, stitching something together—say the panel of a bodice to a sleeve—linking a pair of terms, the contents of a clause, closing a seam by following the internal directions of the sentence (not when you read for speed), so that the word 'you' is first fastened to the word 'read,' and then the phrase 'for speed' is attached to both in order that the entire expression can be finally fronted by a grandly capitalized 'When . . .' (but not when you read for speed), while all of that, in turn, is gathered up to await the completion of the later segment which begins 'you do not read recursively' (certainly not when you read for speed). You can hear how long it seems to take—this patient process— and how confusing it can become. Nor do you linger over language, repeating (not when you read for speed) some especially pleasant little passage, in the enjoyment, perhaps, of a modest rhyme (for example, the small clause 'when you read for speed'), or a particularly apt turn of phrase (an image, for instance, such as the one which dealt with my difficult opponent's green teeth and thin red hair—like rust on a saw), (none of that, when you read for speed). Nor, naturally, do you move your lips as you read the word 'read' or the words 'moving your lips,' so that the poor fellow next to you in the reading room has to watch intently to see what your lips are saying: are you asking him out? for the loan of his *Plutarch's Lives*? and of course the poor fellow is flummoxed to find that you are moving your lips to say 'moving your lips.' What can that mean? The lip-mover—Oh, such a person is low on our skill scale. We are taught to have scorn for her, for him.

On the other hand, the speeding reader drops diagonally down across the page, on a slant like a skier; cuts across the text the way a butcher prefers to slice sausage, so that a small round can be made to yield a misleadingly larger, oval piece. The speeding reader is after the kernel, the heart, the gist. Paragraphs become a country the eye flies over looking for landmarks, reference points, airports, restrooms, passages of sex. The speeding reader guts a book the way the skillful clean fish. The gills are gone, the tail, the scales, the fins; then the fillet slides away swiftly as though fed to a seal; and only the slow reader, one whom those with green teeth chew through like furious worms; only the reader whose finger falters in front of long words, who moves the lips, who dances the text, will notice the odd crowd of images—flier, skier, butcher, seal—which have gathered to comment on the aims and activities of the speeding reader, perhaps like gossips at a wedding. To the speeding reader, this jostle of images, this crazy collision of ideas—of landing strip, kernel, heart, guts, sex—will not be felt or even recognized, because these readers are after what they regard as the inner core of meaning; it is the gist they want, the heart of the matter; they want what can equally well be said in their own, other, and always fewer words; so that the gist of this passage could be said to be: readers who read rapidly read only for the most generalized and stereotyped significances. For them, meaning floats over the page like fluffy clouds. Cliché is forever in fashion. They read, as we say, synonymously, seeking sameness; and, indeed, it is all the same to them if they are said in one moment to be greedy as seals, and in another moment likened to descalers of fish. They . . . you, I . . . we get the idea.

Most writing and most reading proceeds, not in terms of specific words and phrases, although specific ones must be used, but in terms of loose general sets or gatherings of synonyms. Synonymous writing is relatively easy to read, provided one doesn't drowse, because it lives in the approximate; it survives wide tolerances; its standards of relevance resemble those of a streetwalker, and its pleasures are of the same kind.

If any of us read, "When Jack put his hand in the till, he got his fingers burned, so that now he's all washed up at the Bank," we might smile at this silly collision of commonplaces, but we would also "get the drift," the melody, the gist. The gist is that Jack was caught with his hand in the cookie jar and consequently was given a sack he can't put his cookies in. Well, the stupid mother cut his own throat just to get his necktie red. Jack—man—wow!—I mean, he fucked up for sure—and now he's screwed—man—like a wet place—he's been wiped up! Punctuation dissolves into dashes; it contracts, shrinks, disappears entirely. Fred did the CRIME, got CAUGHT, now feels the PAIN. These three general ideas, like cartoon balloons, drift above the surface of the sentence, and are read as easily as Al Capp.

Precise writing becomes difficult, and slow, precisely because it requires that we read it precisely—take it all in. Most of us put words on a page the way kids throw snow at a wall. Only the general white splat matters anyhow.

When I participated in them, speed-reading matches had two halves like a game of football. The first consisted of the rapid reading itself, through which, of course, I whizzzzed, all the while making the sound of turning pages and closing covers in order to disconcert Green Teeth or the Silent Shaker Heights Sisters, who were to think I had completed my reading already. I didn't wear glasses then, but I carried a case to every match, and always dropped it at a pertinent moment, along with a few coins.

Next we were required to answer questions about what we claimed we'd covered, and quickness, here, was again essential. The questions, however, soon disclosed their biases. They had a structure, their own gist; and it became possible, after some experience, to guess what would be asked about a text almost before it had been begun. Is it Goldilocks we're skimming? Then what is the favorite breakfast food of the three bears? How does Goldilocks escape from the house? Why weren't the three bears at home when Goldilocks came calling? The multiple answers we were offered also had their own tired tilt, and, like the questions, quickly gave themselves away. The favorite breakfast foods, for instance, were: (a) Quaker Oats (who, we can imagine, are paying for the prizes this year, and in this sly fashion get their name in); (b) Just Rite (written like a brand name); (c) porridge (usually misspelled); (d) sugar-coated curds and whey. No one ever wondered whether Goldilocks was suffering from sibling rivalry; why she had become a teenie trasher; or why mother bear's bowl of porridge was cold when baby bear's smaller bowl was still warm, and Just Rite. There were many other mysteries, but not for these quiz masters who didn't even want to know the sexual significance of Cinderella's slipper, or why it had to be made of glass (the better to drink from, of course). I won my championship medal by ignoring the text entirely (it was a section from Vol. II of Oswald Spengler's *The Decline of the West,* the part which begins "Regard the flowers at eventide as, one after the other, they close in the setting sun . . ." but then, of course, you remember that perhaps overfamiliar passage). I skipped the questions as well, and simply encircled the gloomiest alternatives offered. Won in record time. No one's got through Spengler with such dispatch since.

What did these matches, with their quizzes for comprehension, their love of literal learning, tell me? They told me that time was money (a speed reader's dearest idea); they told me what the world wanted me to read when I read, eat when I ate, see when I saw. Like the glutton, I was to get everything in and out of the store in a hurry. Turnover was topmost. What the world wanted me to get was the gist, but the gist was nothing but an idea of trade—an idea so drearily uniform and emaciated that it might have modeled dresses.

We are expected to get on with our life, to pass over it so swiftly we needn't notice its lack of quality, the mismatch of theory with thing, the gap between program and practice. We must live as we read; listen as we live. Please: only the melody . . . shards of "golden oldies," foreplays of what's "just about out" and "all the rage," of what's "brand new." We've grown accustomed to the slum our consciousness has become. It tastes like the spit in our own mouth, not the spit from the mouth of another.

This trail of clichés, sorry commonplaces, dreary stereotypes, boring slogans, loud adverts and brutal simplifications, titles, trademarks, tags, *typiques,* our mind leaves behind like the slime of a slug—the sameness we excrete—is democratic: one stool's no better than another to the normally undiscerning eye and impatient bowel. 'To be all washed up' is not a kingly expression which 'over the hill' or 'past his prime' must serve like a slave. Each cliché is a varlet and a churl, but there's no master. Each one refers us, with a vague wave of its hand, to the entire unkempt class. The meaning we impute to our expressions is never fixed; our thought (and *there* is a self-important term), our thought moves aimlessly from one form of words to another, scarcely touching any, like a bee in God's garden. The fact is that Jack has had it. We all know *that*. He's run the course. And now he's been zapped. Why go on about it?

There are three other ways of reading that I'd like to recommend. They are slow, old-fashioned, not easy either, rarely practiced. They must be learned. Together with the speeder they describe the proper way to write as well as read, and can serve as a partial emblem for the right life.

That seems unlikely, yet they apply to all our needs, our habits: thinking, seeing, eating, drinking. We can gulp our glass of wine if we please. To get the gist. And the gist is the level of alcohol in the blood, the pixilated breath one blows into the test balloon. It makes appropriate the expression: have a belt. It makes dangerous the expression: one for the road. We can toss down a text, a time of life, a love affair, that walk in the park which gets us from here to there. We can chug-a-lug them. You have, perhaps, had to travel sometime with a person whose passion was that simple: it was *getting there*. You have no doubt encountered people who impatiently wait for the payoff; they urge you to come to the point; at dinner, the early courses merely delay dessert; they don't go to the games, only bet on them; they look solely at the bottom line (that obscene phrase whose further meaning synonymous readers never notice); they are persons consumed by consequences; they want to climax without the bother of buildup or crescendo.

But we can read and walk and write and look in quite a different way. It *is* possible. I was saved from sameness by philosophy and Immanuel Kant, by Gertrude Stein and her seeming repetitions. You can't speed read *Process and Reality* or *The Critique of Pure Reason*. You can't speed read Wallace Stevens or Mallarmé. There is no gist, no simple translation, no key concept which will unlock these works; actually, there is no lock, no door, no wall, no room, no house, no world . . .

One of my favorite sentences is by Gertrude Stein. It goes: "It looked like a garden, but he had hurt himself by accident." Our example is actually two sentences: "It looked like a garden" and "He had hurt himself by accident." Separately, and apart, each is a perfectly ordinary, ignorable element of proletarian prose; but when they are brought together in this unusual way, they force us to consider their real, complete, and peculiar natures. The injury, we may decide, although it looked self-inflicted, planned, kept up, was actually the result of an accident. How much better we feel when we know that Gertrude Stein's sentence has a gloss, because now we can forget it. The fellow was actually *not* trying to defraud his insurance company, although at first it looked like it.

Alas for the security of our comfort, her sentence is not equivalent to its synonymous reading—this consoling interpretation. It cannot be replaced by another. It cannot be translated without a *complete loss of its very special effect*. It was composed—this sentence—with a fine esthetic feel for "difference," for clean and clear distinctions, for the true weight and full use of the word. If, when we say we understand something someone's said, we mean that we can rephrase the matter, put it in other words (and we frequently do mean this), then Gertrude Stein's critics may be right: you can't *understand* such a sentence; and it has no value *as a medium of exchange*.

We can attempt to understand the sentence in another way. We can point out the elements and relations which, together, produce its special effect. For instance, we can call attention to the juxtaposition of an event which normally happens in a moment (an accident) with a condition which is achieved over a long period of time (a garden); or cite the contrasts between care and carelessness, the desirable and undesirable, between appearance and reality, chance and design, which the two sentences set up; and note the pivotal shift of pronouns ("It looked . . . but he had . . ."). We might furthermore comment on the particular kind of surprise the entire sentence provides, because after reading "It looked like a garden, but . . ." we certainly expect something like "but the plants had all sprung up like weeds."

The isolation of analytical functions in the sentence is accomplished by comparing the actual sentence with its possible variations. What is the force of the phrase, "by accident"? We can find out by removing it.

It looked like a garden, but he had hurt himself with a hammer.

We replace 'hurt' with 'injured' in order to feel the difference a little alliteration makes; what the new meter does; and to understand to what degree, exactly, 'hurt' is a more intimate and warmer word, less physical in its implications, yet also benignly general and vague in a way 'wounded,' for instance, is not.

We can try being more specific:

It looked like a rose garden, but he had hurt himself by slipping on the ice.

We can also see, if we look, how lengthening the second sentence segment spoils the effect of the whole:

It looked like a garden, but he had nevertheless managed to hurt himself quite by accident.

The onset of the surprise must be swift, otherwise everything is ruined. Suppose we extend our example's other arm:

It looked, as well as I could make it out through the early morning mist, like a garden, but he had hurt himself by accident.

We can make other substitutions, sometimes rather wild ones, in order to measure the distances between resemblances:

It looked like a flower box, but he had hurt himself by accident.
It looked like a Dali, but he had hurt himself by accident.

It looked like a garden, but he had dug himself up by accident.
It looked like a garden, but he had hurt himself by post.

It is important that we keep our sentence's most "normal" form in front of us, namely: "It looked very intentional, but he had hurt himself by accident." By now, through repetition, and by dint of analysis, the sentence has lost its ability to shock or surprise, and like a religious chant has surrendered whatever meaning it might have had. On the other hand, in a month's time, out of the blue, the sentence will return to consciousness with the force of a revelation.

What we've done, in short, is to reenact the idealized method of its conscious composition. We have made explicit the nature of its verbal choices by examining some of those which might have been made instead, as if we were translating English into English.

If synonymous reading is to be contrasted with antonymical reading, which stresses untranslatability, difference, and uniqueness; then analytical reading, which looks at the way words are put together to achieve certain effects, should be contrasted with synthetical reading, which concentrates on the quality and character of the effect itself. Synthetical reading integrates every element and *responds*.

Imagine for a moment a consummate Brunswick stew. In such a perfect dish, not only must the carrot contribute its bit, but *this* carrot must contribute *its*. As we sample the stew, we first of all must realize we are eating just that: stew. This knowledge gives our tongue its orientation; it tells us what to look for, what values count, what belongs, and what (like bubble gum) does not; it informs us about the *method* of its preparation. We assure ourselves it is stew we are eating by comparing our present experience with others (or we ask the waitress, who tells us what the chef says). That is, this stew has a general character (look, smell, texture, flavor)—a "gist"—which we then may match with others of its sort. So far we are engaged in synonymous eating (as disgusting as that sounds). One bite of stew, one bowl of chili, one flattened hamburger patty, is like another patty, bowl, or bite. Clearly, for the rapid eater or the speed reader, consciousness will not register much difference, and the difference that does appear will be, of course, in *content*. I've eaten this bowl of porridge, so that bowl must be another one.

But the educated and careful tongue will taste and discriminate this particular stew from every other. Tasting is a dialectical process in which one proceeds from general to specific similarities, but this can be accomplished only through a series of differentiations. Antonymical tasting (which also sounds disgusting) ultimately "identifies" this dish, not only as pure stew, but as Brunswick stew, and knows whether it was done in Creole style or not, and then finally it recognizes, in this plate's present version of the recipe, that the squirrels were fat and gray and came from Mississippi where they fed on elderberries and acorns of the swamp oak. One grasps an act, an object, an idea, a sentence, synthetically, simply by feeling or receiving its full effect—in the case of the stew that means its complete, unique taste. I need not be able to name the ingredients; I need not be able to describe how the dish was prepared; but I should be a paragon of appreciation. This quality, because it is the experience of differentiation within a context of comparison, cannot be captured in concepts, cannot be expressed in words. Analytical tasting has a different aim. It desires to discover what went into the dish; it reconstructs the recipe, and recreates the method of its preparation. It moves from effects to causes.

Reading is a complicated, profound, silent, still, very personal, very private, a very solitary, yet civilizing activity. Nothing is more social than speech—we are bound together by our common sounds more securely than even by our laws—nevertheless, no one is more aware of the isolated self than the reader; for a reader communes with the word heard immaterially in that hollow of the head made only for hearing, a room nowhere in the body in any ordinary sense. On the bus, every one of us may be deep in something different. Sitting next to a priest, I can still enjoy my pornography, although I may keep a thumb discreetly on top of the title: *The Cancan Girls Celebrate Christmas*. It doesn't matter to me that Father McIvie is reading about investments, or that the kid with rusty hair in the seat ahead is devouring a book about handicapping horses. Yet while all of us, in our verbal recreations, are full of respect for the privacy of our neighbors, the placards advertising perfume or footware invade the public space like a visual smell; Muzak fills every unstoppered ear the way the static of the street does. The movies, radio, TV, theater, orchestra: all run on at their own rate, and the listener or the viewer must attend, keep up, or lose out; but not the reader. The reader is free. The reader is in charge, and pedals the cycle. It is easy for a reader to announce that his present run of Proust has been postponed until the holidays.

Reading, that is, is not a public imposition. Of course, when we read, many of us squirm and fidget. One of the closest friends of my youth would sensuously wind and unwind on his forefinger the long blond strands of his hair. How he read: that is how I remember him. Yes, our postures are often provocative, perverse. Yet these outward movements of the body really testify to the importance of the inner movements of the mind; and even those rapid flickers of the eye, as we shift from word to word, phrase to phrase, and clause to clause, hoping to keep our head afloat on a flood of Faulkner or Proust or Joyce or James, are registers of reason: for reading is reasoning, figuring things out through thoughts, making arrangements out of arrangements until we've understood a text so fully it is nothing but feeling and pure response; until its conceptual turns are like the reversals of mood in a marriage: petty, sad, ecstatic, commonplace, foreseeable, amazing.

In order to have this experience, however, one must learn to perform the text, say, sing, shout the words to oneself, give them, with *our minds, their body*; otherwise the eye skates over every syllable like the speeder. There can be no doubt that often what we read should be skimmed, as what we are frequently asked to drink should be spilled; but the speeding reader is alone in another, less satisfactory way, one quite different from that of the reader who says the words to herself, because as we read we divide into a theater: there is the performer who shapes these silent sounds, moving the muscles of the larynx almost invisibly; and there is the listener who hears them said, and who responds to their passion or their wisdom.

Such a reader sees every text as unique; greets every work as a familiar stranger. Such a reader is willing to allow another's words to become hers, his.

In the next moment, let us read a wine, so as to show how many things may be read which have not been written. We have prepared for the occasion, of course. The bottle has been allowed to breathe. Books need to breathe, too. They should be opened properly, hefted, thumbed. Their covers part like pairs of supplicating palms. The paper, print, layout, should be appreciated. But now we decant the text into our wide-open and welcoming eyes. We warm the wine in the bowl of the glass with our hand. We let its bouquet collect above it like the red of red roses seems to stain the air. We wade—shoeless, to be sure—through the color it has liquefied. We roll a bit of it about in our mouths. We sip. We savor. We say some sentences of that great master Sir Thomas Browne: "We tearme sleepe a death, and yet it is waking that kills us, and destroyes those spirits which are the house of life. Tis indeed a part of life that best expresseth death, for every man truely lives so long as hee acts his nature, or someway makes good the faculties of himself . . ." Are these words not from a fine field, in a splendid year? There is, of course, a sameness in all these words: life/death, man/nature; we get the drift. But the differences! the differences make all the difference, the way nose and eyes and cheekbones form a face; the way a muscle makes emotion pass across it. It is the differences we read. Differences are not only identifiable, distinct; they are epidemic: the wine is light, perhaps, spicy, slow to release its grip upon itself, the upper thigh is widening wonderfully, the night air has hands, words fly out of our mouths like birds: "but who knows the fate of his bones," Browne says, "or how often he is to be buried"; yet as I say his soul out loud, he lives again; he has risen up in me, and I can be, for him, that temporary savior that every real reader is, putting his words in my mouth; not nervously, notice, as though they were pieces of chewed gum, but in that way which is necessary if the heart is to hear them; and though they are his words, and his soul, then, which returns through me, I am in charge; he has asked nothing of me; his words move because I move them. It is like cycling, reading is. Can you feel the air, the pure passage of the spirit past the exposed skin?

So this reading will be like living, then; the living each of you will be off in a moment to be busy with; not always speedily, I hope, or in the continuous anxiety of consequence, the sullenness of inattention, the annoying static of distraction. But it will be only a semblance of living— this living—nevertheless, the way unspoken reading is a semblance, unless, from time to time, you perform the outer world and let it live within; because only in that manner can it deliver itself to us. As Rainer Maria Rilke once commanded: "dance the taste of the fruit you have been tasting. Dance the orange." I should like to multiply that charge, even past all possibility. Speak the street to yourself sometimes, hear the horns in the forest, read the breeze aloud, and make that inner wind yours, because, whether Nature, Man, or God, has given us the text, we independently possess the ability to read, to read really well, and to move our own mind freely in tune to the moving world.

THE ORIGIN OF EXTERMINATION
IN THE IMAGINATION

As I drive my new car from the dealer's lot I notice another, much like mine and almost as new, parked in front of the body shop, a pronounced dent in its right front fender. I feel a pang of sympathy, the sort of pang one has while reading the evening paper and learning about a beaten boy, or of the difficult death of a despondent woman, or the sale of a favorite shortstop. The pang passes. It passes because we can't be continually panging. We are not rugs so widely indiscriminate and underfoot, we welcome the world's walk. It was one of the easy ones—the production of this pang—for I could see the dent directly from my own uninjured vehicle. My imagination had hardly to hear its name before I was in that other driver's seat. And so it passed as pangs do, but the thought remained: Drive carefully, you don't want a dent like that in this car—your car—itself as pure and perfect as the middle water of the bucket. The pang has passed, but the memory of that dent remains. It fixes itself in my consciousness. It troubles my sleep. All night men with hornhard hooves dance upon the hood of my chest. In the morning I walk around my car to see whether the night air has sharpened itself and slit a tire, or the moon belted a bumper with a particularly heavy and malevolent beam. In time, the image of the dent passes; I cannot recall its contours; I cease to dream of hailstorms or adolescents with ball-peen hammers; but the thought does not go away; I continue to think, to remember, to repeat: Drive carefully, you don't want a dent in your car. Although it is near new, as new, like new now, and not new, I remain inconsolably fearful and anxious. I hate every syllable of my repeated admonition. I would like to put its words out of my mind, to forget them, to lose their spelling like small change down a grate. But I also wish to bear their cautionary message near my heart. I hate the sentence, but remembering its meaning is good for me. It keeps me careful.

I avoid looking at parked cars because all I see are signs of wear, mis-guidance, age. Junkyards are not nice places. 'Junkyard' is not a nice word. Fences ought to be put up around them: the places, the word, the thought. Pansies can be planted along their perimeters. In Manila every vacant lot is soon filled with the cardboard and box-wood shacks of the poor. Mattresses, as worn as if half the population had been begotten on them, fall everywhere upon the open ground like exhausted bodies. Marcos has wearied of driving the poor away, collecting them in open fields far from the city. He just puts up a high fence, and the poor disappear in peace. We should do that to dents and other disfigurements. Scratches are unclean. They fester in the air. And so I avert my eyes, and it is then that some dame pushes the door of her parked car into the path of mine.

There comes a time when the fear of something becomes more un-bearable than its object. Now that, at least, is gone. The worry, the wait-ing, is over. I no longer have to dream of or imagine my dents. I have one. I take immediate steps to have it repaired, of course, but I must wait for parts. The robots in Japan are broken, asleep, or on strike. The injured vehicle, its purity punctured, waits in the drive as I sleep. I dream of tortured metal, of spoons bent by the power of pure thought, of scars restored to the blood of their wounds. What had been a consciousness made up of worried expectation has become a consciousness of immedi-ate catastrophe. And it remains immediate—day after day—for don't I dwell on it, take its image away from the fender where it was born to nurture its details, relive my remorse? The freshly dead dog us; their corpses fill our thoughts like stool packed in the bowel. In this shift from an anxiety about the future to a depression brought on by the present, there is an element which I wish to single out: while I still awaited the worst, the worst, nonetheless, was not; and so long as I could confine my imagination to the mode of expectation, I was clearly safe. Long after he is breathless from it, the smoker believes he is only "running the risk" of lung cancer, and the alcoholic believes that if he isn't careful and doesn't begin to cut down he may become a hopeless drunk, and he thinks that on the day he dies of his last drink.

Expectation projects the imagination forward in time, and it does so always with a double and doubtful valence; for if one expects the best, there remains the possibility of its loss, and this possibility is sometimes numbing, sometimes courted, sometimes celebrated; and if one expects the worst, it remains wonderful, titillating, even exhilarating, that the worst is yet to come. Put off till tomorrow only that which you cannot put off today. On what other grounds does Bertrand Russell so happily confront the eventual demise of life?

Brief and powerless is Man's life; on him and all his race the slow, sure doom falls pitiless and dark. Blind to good and evil, reckless of destruction, omnipotent matter rolls on its relentless way; for Man, condemned to-day to lose his dearest, tomorrow himself to pass through the gate of darkness, it remains only to cherish, ere yet the blow falls, the lofty thoughts that ennoble his little day; disdaining the coward terrors of the slave of Fate, to worship at the shrine that his own hands have built; undismayed by the empire of chance, to preserve a mind free from the wanton tyranny that rules his outward life; proudly defiant of the irresistible forces that tolerate, for a moment, his knowledge and his condemnation, to sustain alone, a weary but unyielding Atlas, the world that his own ideals have fashioned despite the trampling march of unconscious power.

Thought looks into the pit of Hell, and is not afraid. In fact, it is fun so fearlessly to face an end we're—so far—far from; but when Bertrand Russell wrote "A Free Man's Worship" didn't he expect to die himself before that pitiless sure doom arrived?

Whether or not we accept Bishop Berkeley's famous formula, to be is to be perceived, there is a profound psychological truth in it. Things do tend to exist for us only as they impinge upon or occupy our consciousness, and if it is not the things themselves we encounter, then at least we must deal with their effects. Absence makes the heart grow fonder only if an image is not absent; only if around a surrogate a halo of obsession forms. Out of sight, out of mind, is more to the point; but even here "out of sight" has to mean "out of life." In the simplest way we can classify experiences as those we welcome and would continue if we could, and those we dislike and would expunge if we had the power, with a large number left over toward which we have a ticket taker's sovereign indifference. When we say that unwanted experience is unwanted, we mean that its death is desired, although not necessarily willed, because we may understand very clearly the unpleasant consequences of our wishes, were they to be carried out. Drugs, distraction, counterirritation, amputation, divorce, exile: all have been employed at one time or other to annihilate unpleasantness and pain.

Late in his life Freud suggested that an organism, when assaulted by some stimulus (and it is always felt as an affront, an invasion of privacy), regularly responds either by flight (as my hand jerks back from the flame), or, when that avenue is closed, by actions aimed at its mastery and reduction (I blow the match out; I encase my hand in an asbestos mitten). Some stimuli can be annulled by movement, but there are others which have to be overcome, smothered with sleep, or assuaged by pungent unguents, beaten, dungeoned, pensioned off; while still others, like thirst and hunger and hope, return and return like a tubercular cough. The instincts, which are never satisfied and constantly torment us, require that we go out into a world of pain and danger in order to find the water which will dampen them, the fuel our fires feed on, the friend who will alleviate our lust. Again, we may wish to quarrel with Freud's assumption that life is fundamentally inertial—that life resents life and longs to abolish itself—but his views do nicely specify the two tacks we take when we wish to eliminate a sensation. You can spit out the hot soup or pour cold water down your throat after it, down toward the emptiness which the soup is supposed to fill.

I want to begin by thinking of annihilation as it occurs in consciousness. I want to consider the basic act, not of murder per se, or some other sort of destruction, but its psychological equivalent: its out-of-mindness.

Things have a life, a presence, a value in consciousness which they can possess nowhere else, and Henry James's admonition—that we try to be someone on whom nothing is lost—is more than a Bloomsbury nicety, a pleasant social aim, a leftover passage from G. E. Moore's *Principia Ethica*; it is a profound obligation. Perhaps it was Rainer Maria Rilke who felt this obligation most intensely, because it is his poems which repeatedly suggest that the world rises up in each of us, invisibly, as we walk and look about; that our organs are instruments of transformation by which an otherwise vain beating of the air becomes a song. However we try as philosophers to account for it, the world is, to some degree, from some awkward, stupid, or elegant point of view, invisibly, impalpably, inaudibly within us all. It is not only a world transformed—from what we might suppose was its material mode—into a simple mental one; it is in addition infused with feeling; it is redolent with meaning; any percept is like a piece of exotic cargo, caught up and carried on toward its life in a new land like Columbus in his ships.

If we depend upon the world, need what it pours into us to be a cup at all, the world as well awaits us—awaits our seeing, as Rilke said, our tongue, our touch—and we are obliged by the nature nature's given us to bring these other beings into the condition of consciousness that is our own. We must mind matter, and not merely the way mother minds her baby. We must rearrange it rationally; we must make it shed its dust and solidify as spirit, and of course we must care. When we fail to see whatever is plainly put before us; when we deny the existence of certain concepts, and will not entertain them; when we refuse to draw necessary inferences, and continue to cherish our beliefs long after their infamous, false, and misleading nature has been disclosed; when we are indifferent in our responses, callous in our concerns, capable of counting only half the heads that comprise the company of mankind and discounting the others; when we look the absolute necessity for peace straight in the face and still prefer to organize for war; when the full horror of the inhumanity in man has hit us and we feel no smart and show no bruise; when our evils go unspoken, unconfessed, cynically rewarded: then we are polluting, distorting, maiming, killing consciousness, that space which should be most sacred to us; again, not alone on account of our own precious awareness, which, after all, is all we are; but on account of the conscious and unconscious world of others—of persons, of plants, of water and institutions, atmosphere and animals, of man-made and mineral *things*—for each one of us is an other too, a flesh in flower for a fellow being, possibly; and certainly I want to be, in Rilke's phrase, a high tree in your ear; I want to be not merely a presence half lit in the presence of myself, but, like one of the Magi's gifts, a present to yours.

And at the moment I want my car to go down the road unscathed, healing itself in the sunlight.

We are familiar, certainly since Plato, with the various ways we cover one consciousness with another, as if by turning up the radio we would no longer have to hear the screams. There are sensations of all kinds waiting in the wings for their chance to come on stage: that almost grainy irritation at the end of the big toe, for instance, gnats rising like steam from a drain on a sudden spring morning, a small mole growing in the eyebrow of my right eye, little rattle in the refrigerator, look on your face as if having heard glass break. So I can have my car fixed and forget it; I can collect dents (here is one from a bus I sideswiped in Baltimore— it was May, I remember—the kids were eating ice cream); I can lose it among the familiar, see it so often I no longer need to remember it as damage (like those dark green vans, those long trains full of groaning old clothes, that singular smoke stench, a bomb burst as pretty by now as our image of Old Faithful—it would make a handsome postage stamp); but then shouldn't we adore these signs of life and experience? everyone grows old, life is like that, full of trouble and death, war is here to stay, omelettes are made with broken eggs, and if we eat we shit; anyway, dents give the car character, now it can be identified easily if stolen; well, actually, the car was made that way, came with that crease from the factory, because it is a subtle part of the design; you've heard of those sculptures which rush their way toward beauty according to a timetable? how sensible of me to have purchased a preburst balloon, a predented fender, now I shan't have to suffer its breaking, its crumpled displeasure.

If we threw back all those covers, Plato thought, we would suddenly see, quite nakedly, the Forms and all their intricate relations; but we don't want to see them; past a certain period in our growing up, the thought of our parents naked is an embarrassment, just as my students are embarrassed, walking by my house, to see me mowing the grass. The trouble with the truth, apart from the fact that it is so, is that the truth keeps returning like the dog you've dumped in the country; it seeps through the walls like damp; it creeps through cracks and is quicker than a roach, tougher than a rat. What? still there, old ghost? after all the poison I've put out? after all the official exorcisms? those coats of cosmetic I've had professionally applied? is that former face still there, its features seared off, still staring at me through its hollow sockets—an absence of eye that sees me still? Suddenly I need another argument for God; I require a vetted regiment to put down another threatened loss of confidence in the State; I need more advanced arms to resist reason; I need new enemies and further dark intentions in order to aim death like a gun barrel at my head; old hatreds need to be refurbished, memories for injuries restored, suspicions re-formed, confirmed like hotel reservations, with penalties for late arrival. The bugs are about, you see, the queers, the cranks, the wimps; blacks are congregating again on white corners; the Jews are overcharging for the use of the JCCA pool; in the middle of our song of war some sap is singing in the key of peace. It's just that there are an increasing number of kinks in things; there is always a fresh infestation of failure, always so much to be overlooked, to be forgotten, stepped on like a butt in the street; what is the phone number of those exterminators?

We can cover up. We do a lot of that. We can repress, forget, mislay, lose, jog our minds loose; but covers get uncovered occasionally; a breast pops out of its bra. The repressed returns continually; that name on the tip of our tongue, which we never wanted to remember anyway, suddenly explodes like a fart in the mouth; the purloined letter comes back in the mail —it had insufficient postage, incorrect address; or an old flame turns up to burn the toast; or a banished anxiety returns from exile with an army.

Suppose I blow my nose with your hands: an enormous rearrangement. And we can alter everything by means of a little close thought about it, especially when our thought turns dialectical. There will be, in such a case, the "thing" in the process of being thought about (mass murder, maybe); our thought in the act of being about it (I wonder how many Jews had to be killed before the number became holocaustic); and ourselves engaged in attaching our thought to that something, or representing that something to ourselves. Let us look at an instance:

A husband is having unkind thoughts about his wife. She will never remember to put the caps back on medicine bottles; she kicks off her shoes in the middle of the floor; she won't pick up her towels; she leaves her dresser drawers at precisely the point to which they were initially drawn, etc.; but while he is thinking these things he is also observing the cap of the toothpaste tube, now on the floor, and remembering that he always begins this particular litany of little complaints in the early morning, just after brushing his teeth, when he must hunt up the cap for the tube, which is sometimes on the floor, sometimes in the sink, sometimes in a corner of the medicine cabinet; and being of a more reflective turn of mind than most, he furthermore notes how all these complaints have to do with the way his wife leaves things open, or on (like the lights he now adds to the list), or out of place, or where they were last employed; all of which are thoughts about her, but equally about him, as he picks up the towel and recaps the tube and covers the aspirin securely again; and he concludes that his wife is a person who leaves a trail, a path, like someone who wishes to be followed, and that he is the sort who conceals where he has been: books, plates, pen, papers, doors, shovels, shoes, put back where they were, as if nothing had happened, as if nothing had passed or changed. But the man's thoughts turn sour only when he realizes that he is not only an obliterator, a concealer of his trail, but a follower too, for even now he is closing his wife's dresser drawers, erasing the prints of her passage as well as his own.

I have a dream. I dream that a carefully selected section of an appropriate city—a particularly foul and eloquent ghetto—is suddenly sprayed with polyurethane to the clear depth of several inches, so that the exact character of the pesthole is retained: the bugs in the bed, the people in their tatters, the turds overflowing the toilets—only black folks after all, fixed forever in attitudes of dismay, as if they had been Pompeii'd—and the world could parade by our National Ghetto Museum, where only whites may apply as guides.

I have a suggestion. I think one of the better death camps should be reactivated, and the condemned of the world sent there for execution so as to keep the memory of our former work alive for a more enlightened future.

The example I examined—of the husband who follows his wife's trail—juxtaposes two patterns of behavior which his thought vibrates between; that is, between the ideas he has about his wife and himself, and the actual form (he begins to discover) of his marriage. Before our thought becomes truly dialectical, however, these different elements which our imagination has just joined, almost metaphorically, must be measured for their mutual dependence, not simply on one another, but on their very opposition. Our man cannot follow his wife's trail unless she leaves one, but the crucial dialectical element is their tense, felt, dynamic opposition. Dialectical thinking concentrates on just that internal tug and begins to generalize it.

The husband becomes aware of the commonplace fact that his wife cooks, while he cleans up, both after meals and after parties; that he puts back her books, hangs up her coat, not only holds her chair, but tucks it back beneath the table, too. If, at a party, she makes a catty or cutting remark, he moves quickly to repair it; if she spills something, he mops it up; if she breaks something, he mends it. He recalls a parallel hypothesis which helps to structure Henry James's novel *The Sacred Fount*. It is the possibility that among couples one will always be drawing strength and life from the other, who will be surrendering it. Our husband realizes that he has in his possession a dialectical principle— that of Do/Undo—and that this principle, *now that it has been brought clearly forward in consciousness,* will act to alter, to interfere with, or overdevelop, behavior. Cleaning up will take on meaning, not only because it is being seen in the light of this hypothesis, but because it is being grouped with other actions. A pattern has been discerned in the way this couple lives. True dialectical change has begun.

So the husband notices how his wife leaves things out and around and about: the door off the latch, the bread package open, handbag in the hall; but being a person of stolid common sense, he simply assumes what he believes in fact he knows, that his wife is still acting like the spoiled brat she was when she was a spoiled brat, and that she simply expects him to pick up after her the way her parents did. And as he does so, returning her violin to its case, he understands their respective roles to be those of Father/Daughter.

The wife has very strict rules for the children, however. They must pick up all their clothes, their toys, the schoolbooks and papers, and put them carefully away in places she has designated. They live in rooms full of labeled boxes, sorting trays, and hooks and hangers. The husband, for his part, has a study aslope with mislaid accounting forms and business papers. He gets ink on his thumb and ash on his vest. But no one picks up for him.

Patterns disclose themselves in our behavior, our thinking, in which the elements are still other patterns: in this case, patterns of putting away and picking up, of leaving the past as it was, or canceling, as far as one can, its effect. Perhaps we should never allow ourselves to recover from a war. What sort of sickness is it which leaves us healthier than before? Perhaps we should design a war we can't recover from. Anyway, we have found at least two explanations for what is commonly called neatness—or its lack—in our little example. Both explanations clearly internalize important social principles. The first is that things have their place and things should be in their place, and if an individual is not prepared to practice the proper self-discipline (that is, mirror the society in the self), what is called "a mess" will ensue. If one possesses the right status, influence, sufficient power, someone else can be got to clean up the mess and put things to rights. The second explanation points out that neatness is an enemy of history. It desires to hide events behind a façade of unchanging normalcy. The gun that has been cleaned and returned to its case has not been used. Things are as they were, and they were—thank god!—just as they ought to be. To be a neat orderly person is to reproduce in one's personal life the image of a social ideal.

Perhaps it is not such a good idea to continue to mirror in the self a society systematically engaged in suicidal self-deception.

Any thoughtful rearrangement of forms, especially a dialectical one, tends to retain too much to be entitled a real effacement. If we invert a musical motif, we can reinvert it; if we reperceive our social relations in a fresh way, we can often deperceive them, too. Relations have resiliency. Things have a habit of bobbing back. It is an old story. We put a cheap crook in prison where he learns accomplishment at our expense. We are forced to knock him off eventually, but he somehow (it's amazing, for he's such a squit) has family, friends. Ideas, feelings, have associates too. We can liquidate the whole damn clan, of course, and all its even loose connections, but the chronicle of their exploits will remain. It's a bloody business . . . running a bloody business.

To extirpate is another matter. To forget forever. To get rid of a diseased and contaminating mind the way we've rid ourselves of the pox; to kill the King, to scald our hands clean of his royal blood; no longer to remember the murder in sleep or madness; to kick it out of history; rub it out of every chronicle, plow up the city, salt the fields, pi the type, break the press, smash the font—that's the ticket we want to buy—an Auschwitz that goes up in smoke itself when its work is finished; not merely a bit of consciousness obscured by noise, or run away from, or pressed into the past until it turns to coal, or is altered cleverly into its opposite; but oblivion secure and certain. Urnless and immortal. Of course, for this task, at least for a time, there will have to be a ministry in the mind which knows, which recognizes its enemy and relentlessly pursues it; which keeps the gorge down.

Our problem is: How can we finally forget Man?

So long as the consciousness we speak of is simply a consciousness of nature and the external world, like that of Nietzsche's quietly grazing cows, or as we imagine the tiger's is (and through whose eyes, as Rilke writes, perceptions pass the way they've first squeezed themselves between the bars which bind and stripe his body, only to carry the sight of us deep into his heart where we die, even if as an image), then we can concentrate on avoiding the objects whose presence is offensive, or, at a push, we can remove or destroy them. We have uprooted mountains, felled streams, sawed valleys into smooth logs with this intention.

But when consciousness becomes conscious of itself, it is no longer enough to retract our reach, give away unwanted wedding gifts to the Good Will, transmit plague like a wireless message, drop canisters of disease, because the contaminant is now in the mind itself; the contaminant is in the social structure of our thinking; the contaminant is in the inner form of our life, as though its soul were twisted, for you can't write a love lyric with the limerick; and although we do lobotomize ourselves, there is naturally a limit to it; and although we subjugate our feelings like a race of conquered people, it takes all our energy, our whole will, our entire time. Still, as I've said, we can try. We can erase the object and forget its image. But when the offending agent isn't an object we can drown like a cat, or a thought which we find offensive and, like a yawn, suppress; when it is in fact a feeling or belief or memory in the mind of another; worse, when it is the way another thinks, the indwelling form of an alien self, a renegade society, a hostile *style*: then what? how do we get at that?

That dent I spoke about has dented me, and I've become demented. I have denied the real dent by allowing it a falsely hyperbolic status: a plate cracks and the world ends. What am I really mourning for: purity? permanence? perfection? My wife has heard my whines, has listened to me shake my fist, and now my little *idée fixe* has become obnoxious to her. While she sleeps, her dreams know what I am dreaming. Her thoughts are filled with that silence in which mine shout. In short, what has become annoying to her now is the quality of my consciousness: what she hates is what is going on in my head, and only indirectly what is going on in hers. We are familiar with the feeling. The deprecator, the bully, the flatterer, the snob: we know what is going on in them. Worse, it is intolerable to be around one who, like a spouse, knows you for a fornicator and a liar, a failure, a really silly twit. From what does our hatred of adolescent boys so naturally stem? not from their snickering; not because we know they are measuring one another through their pants, and through their practice of punch-up braggadocio; rather because of their childish mimicking of the myth of the male mind; because their behavior signifies a worse condition of consciousness than their vulgar errant gestures directly display: one that is frightened, prurient, silly, churlish, ignorant, leering, eager to see but reluctant to understand, infinitely cheap and coarse, conformist and unclean. They will stare for hours at a photograph of anything violent, naked, or female, even at a truckload of lifeless women, their bodies as white and loose as a scatter of broken swans. Unfortunately, too many of these little boys, having got older by remaining the same age, are heads of state, generals of armies, captains of industry. So it is certainly not the soft mouths sucking up sodas in those happy ads which cause us to smile, avert our thoughts, decline sex, and deprecate youth; it is the knowledge of what that fizzing pop is bound for—souls their owners wish were simple as enamel pans.

When Thomas Hobbes wrote that the laws of the state and the proclamations of the sovereign bound one only *in foro externo* (to the acts they required), because the King could compel compliance; but could never bind *in foro interno* (that is, to the desire that such acts take place), because the King could not reach so far into the heart; he was perhaps being naïve about the power of propaganda even then, and the insistence of people that we all share the same beliefs. Nevertheless, the distinction remains important because in the everyday sense of it we all feel rather helpless before the structure and quality of another person's consciousness. I hate *what* my wife is thinking, and she hates *how* I'm going about it. Furthermore, we both feel trapped. There is no easy way to avoid ourselves, even when our bodies in the bed act like two hills. In fact, the sight of one another now sets both of us off on trains of thought neither wishes to take. Is a reconciliation possible? When the dent is repaired, presumably I will shush, and soon all will be well again; but she will remember with concern my obsessive care for my car—what does it bode?—and when a nick shows up in a piece of our good china, she won't tell me, fearing a recurrence of that damn denticity of mine. Perhaps we can both forget the matter and get in tidy tune again, or better, perhaps we can understand the whole business so well and thoroughly we won't have to forget anything. Generally, however, such "understandings" are illusory. Democracies thrive on illusions of this "understanding" sort. Tyrannies erase their differences by erasing differers. Let us examine a case or two, for which a slight change of style may suggest an additional point.

It frequently happens that a married pair, their relationship broken by irretrievable blows and kept in those resulting bits and pieces by the implacable hostility of the spaces they have placed between the fragments; it frequently happens that a married pair will quarrel, and when they do (for often there is a glacial silence between them instead, longer than any ice age), it frequently happens that this married pair will quarrel over trivial, childish matters: washing habits, hiccups, handbills, spare change; well, it often happens that a married pair will quarrel over issues far from the facts which form the basis of their anger or resentment, and we might psychoanalytically suppose that these small peeves were surrogates for the fundamental ones; that they were playing checkers with beans, perhaps, but playing checkers still; when actually the points of contention have been chosen, and made minute, made minor, so that later, after the fussing and fuming has subsided, they can be seen as of no moment and without merit, as laughable, as ridiculous; and thus it frequently happens that a married pair, their relationship broken beyond repair by any rhyme, will quarrel over the noise their bled-white life together made while it was bleeding, only to make up amid tears and caresses, forgiving one another in illusion, and, beneath their marital and mortuary sheets, concealing those wounds which remain untended and unhealed and unforgiven.

The quarrels unions have with management often have the same falsely placating structure.

The alternatives, however, may be flight, murder, civil war, or divorce.

Certain diseases are so persistent and painful, you never feel the organ failure that kills you.

Another example. At church bazaars and birthday parties everyone wins in the games, except that at church bazaars what everyone wins is a donated (that is, thrown away) trinket which the "winner" doesn't want—in short, a sop. No one, here, is under the illusion of having won. The illusion being fostered is that losing is not punished.

Another example. Having deprived black people of a decent education, we advance them through the system anyway, turning out into their world (certainly whites won't have to suffer their services) incompetents who will confirm the secondary status of their race.

Another example. It might be argued that, although busing violates the traditional ideal relationship of school to neighborhood and is terribly inconvenient and expensive and often promotes only friction, it does do at least three things: (1) it allows blacks to believe something is being done for them; (2) it allows liberals to believe they are doing something for blacks; (3) it safeguards the continued segregation of the neighborhoods by quarantining integration inside the school. However, when liberals and conservatives quarrel over busing, we have another instance of the false squabbles which must precede every illusory reconciliation of the sort already noted.

We may regard these devices and the others which resemble them as "social sophistries" because they produce patterns of behavior and belief which are as deceptively based as the convictions created by fallacious yet persuasive arguments. The parties agree to help one another obscure their real concerns, mainly because, if the depth of their differences were known, they wouldn't be able to live together. Mediators faithfully repeat their favorite cliché: all is well so long as we're still at the table, talking together; but they omit to observe that it is the talking itself which is the concealment; that the bargaining is simply a bluff, because they don't have anything to trade.

Except lies. And just as the mark connives with the con man to make the mark a mark, and the dearly beloved desires to be daydreamed out of imperfection into excellence, and the believer at all costs and hazards and botheration strains to believe (it really doesn't matter what: remember that great passage in Hobbes? the list of what people have regarded as gods, and worshiped in the past, which ends with a leek that's been deified?). I, myself, know that somewhere there is still a piece of the first car, which, if placed against mine, would undent it forever; and I tell my wife, who thinks that notion not even amusing, that she should simply write down all the dumb things she believes, beginning with her idea that she will smell better if she doesn't smell at all, and concluding with her confident conviction that large portions of California won't one day soon slide into the sea; which just shows that what people *won't* believe is equally astounding; well, she wants to argue with me, but I tell her that arguing about a thing like that suggests that the conclusion is in doubt, when, in fact, about the end of the world, for instance, the argument is over; we don't need any more data; it's no longer, if it ever was, a matter for reason; which catastrophe will befall us first is the real question; but my wife simply sticks out her tongue (so pretty in the old days); and then I tell her that I now realize what the first catastrophe will be: it will be a universal plague of lies; yes, we beg our bamboozlement from everybody: spouses, friends, salesmen, advertisers, politicians, clergymen, priests, physicians, teachers, salesmen, advertisers, spouses, friends— please, we prefer Plato's Cave, it's got good movies, double features, everything will be all right when we all have our own guns, believe in scientism, complete our bomb shelters (the defense, eventually, catches up); everything will be all right when I get that dent removed, that memory of your adultery excised, that little piece of tissue under the scope. Deception is the business of life and business is good, never better. The church hasn't shut up shop. The UN hasn't closed its mouth. The Foreign Office is open. Germany has voted to let us move in our missiles. Nary a politician has choked on a lying tongue or been poisoned by his own spit.

My father was very wary of hospitals, and wisely, it seemed to me; but he wore a copper bracelet on his wrist as a cure for his arthritis. The bracelet doesn't hurt, he told me, the hospital might. My father was mistaken. If the understanding anywhere is lamed, the mind limps.

Immanuel Kant once wrote that to will an end was equivalent to willing at least some means thereto, whereas merely to wish for an end was only to dream the length of one's desire while leaving the means alone. In our society, where the murder of the mind is as common and everyday as the comics, in which the lie sets the standard for truth, in which falsifying ameliorations are epidemic; one thing at least ought to be clear, as the pattern of our public acts betrays it: Among us, war is willed, while peace is only wished.

If a spy has a bit of secret information in his head, I can remove it by removing him. So? one spy? what is one spy? two spies? three? And if my wife were weary of the way I thought about things, of the checkered covers I insisted our car wear, the false fenders and extra bumpers, the dark glasses, the wig, my calls to the Triple A, the horoscopes I've had drawn up for my Honda, she could take classes in ceramics, go to her mother's, phone her lover, drive her damn Chevrolet to Canada, even without the driver's door which got knocked off when she opened it onto traffic. But when I notice my neighborhood being infiltrated by a foreign people who don't even know what a bidet is for; when it is not one or another of them that has done me damage, but the very mode of their being, the continued condition of their consciousness; when a considerable part of their history is an awareness of me, my guilt, my criminality, of what I have done to them; when they seem to exist only to bear witness to the fallen character of man; when they refuse to couch their consciousness in my language; when they will not even pretend to fit in— they might, for instance, at least eat the same foods, celebrate the same holidays, wear basic beige and sport spiffy arm bands from Bill Blass— but continue in stubborn contrariness to insist, while being stepped on even, on their superiority to my shoes (although, I must admit, a good many are attempting to pass, very suspicious types, these, and bear watching; once you could tell by their names; shifty, several have tried to gain admission to my club); and when, in addition to all this, in addition to their presence, their food smells, their clannishness, their circumcisions, they are successfully competing with me for wealth and women and other articles of exchange, for power and other positions where one can exercise inflexibility; what then? what then?

Who is this *émigré* you are complaining about? who is the fellow? is he the Chink? the Red Menace? the Turk? the Slav? the Jew? Oh no. No one special. Merely our fellow man.

Ah. Well, then. The dumb bunny deserves it. Puff to you, boy.

Boo-oo-oo-oom.

And that is the origin of extermination in the imagination.

THE HABITATIONS OF THE WORD

Plato's *Phaedrus* has seemed to some critics to have too many subjects; to be drawn first in this direction and then that, as if those uncooperative horses that it has created, flown, and thereby caused to be celebrated, were pulling apart its pages. Is it about love, or about oratory, the scholars ask; is it a vision or a recitation, an allegory or an exercise? It is at least all of these, but I should like to believe that this extraordinary dialogue is fundamentally concerned with the local habitation of the name, and with the nature of honest eloquence—the speech which is just, the speech which can be believed—and that it goes about its business by providing us with a classification, by means of model and example, of the various residences of the word, at all times seeking the best address.

When we ask ourselves what a word is we may be wondering whether it is a complex set of sounds or a more or less regular march of marks which have come to have a special significance because of all the contexts they've been used in, each one shaving its sense more closely as if polishing the skin, or we may be inquiring about the word's relations or roots, or puzzling ourselves concerning the unenviable middle place it takes between thing and thought, object and idea; but I wish to ask the word a few questions about its native state instead: *I want to know where it is from.*

The *Phaedrus* opens with a curious exchange between Socrates and Phaedrus concerning a new composition by the noted rhetorician Lysias that Phaedrus has heard only that morning. Obviously intended as a display piece to demonstrate the orator's art by taking a difficult, if not perverse, point of view, Lysias' speech argues that an impersonal lust presents, in principle, a better suit of the favor of a beautiful boy's body than love can; that selfish pleasure is a more reliable motive and provides a more secure environment for its object than passion does. Socrates shows an immediate and ironic interest in this subject, wishing only that Lysias had proved a similar superiority for poverty and age, not excluding Socrates' other debilities.[1] The immediate implications of Socrates' little joke are certainly serious ones, namely that Lysias' composition has a use; that it might be employed by anyone who had the orator's leave or had paid his fee, and had a nice young man in mind; for it was out of just such an expectation of payment that Lysias had written his brief for the defense in the case of two men who had loved the same boy and come to blows over him; and again for a similar quarrel over the purchase of a slave girl; and yet another time for the prosecution of a guardian, guilty of embezzlement; or when money had tempted his pen to the defense of a farmer accused of cutting down a sacred olive grove. In one case only, as far as we know, did Lysias himself speak what he had written. On that occasion he prosecuted Eratosthenes for the execution, without trial, of Lysias' own brother, Polemarchus.[2]

When Socrates asks Phaedrus to repeat the oration for him, Phaedrus protests, calling himself an amateur (presumably with respect to the feat of memory it would require to fulfill Socrates' request), and complaining that he should not be expected to reproduce in a moment what it had taken such a wonderful writer weeks, in the inspired labor of his leisure, to create. Socrates then pretends to believe his friend can do just

---

1. Socrates is certainly familiar with the sort of paradoxical twist involved here because he has already argued in the *Lysis* (205d–206a) that it is unwise to praise the youthful object of your affections: first, because encomia which are any good get noised about, and you will be more deeply and publicly shamed if you are rejected; and second, because beautiful boys are vain, and difficult to snare, so that singing their praises will only increase their inherent conceit and the difficulty of their capture. There is, of course, a good deal of hard-boiled truth in this, just as there is in Lysias' similar bit of persuasion—calculations distinguished especially by their cynicism, general correctness, and lack of customary hypocrisy.

2. See *The Murder of Herodes and Other Trials from the Athenian Law-Courts,* compiled, edited, and translated, with an introduction, by Kathleen Freeman (London: Macdonald, 1946). Lysias and Polemarchus are the sons of Cephalus, a wealthy shield maker, whose business and estate are despoiled by the Thirty Tyrants. It is at the house of Cephalus, before these tragic events, that the discussion described in the *Republic* is presumably held. Lysias inherits nothing but these crimes, and must make his living by his pen. It is typical of Plato to set the time frame of his dialogues very artfully, so that his readers will be able to place the fate of the speakers, as it were, above their heads as they talk. The *Symposium* (which resembles the *Phaedrus* very closely in several elements of structure, as well as in subject, not least in its devious "Conradian" opening) is particularly poignant in this respect, for most of the participants in Agathon's victory celebration will end in political exile, disgrace, and death. The *Phaedrus* takes place at a moment when the debate between Alcidamus and Isocrates concerning the superiority of the spoken over the written word was especially intense. See the excellent account by Paul Friedländer in *Platon: Seinswharheit und Lebenswirklichkeit,* Pt. 1, Ch. V, and translated, with, one suspects, as far as the title goes, an intention to mislead, as *Plato: An Introduction,* trans. by Hans Meyerhoff (New York: Pantheon, 1958).

that. He suggests that Phaedrus has already badgered Lysias into repeating his speech; more than this, that he has begged the loan of the manuscript in order to study it closely, commit it to memory even; and that
Phaedrus has made his way just now beyond the city's walls in order to
rehearse what he has memorized—to release into the indifferently receptive country air the winged words which he has so earnestly and carefully caged.

As it turns out, Phaedrus *has* borrowed the manuscript, and has it,
held in his left hand, hidden under his cloak. He has it held in his left
hand because this speech, these words, one will later realize, belong to
the black horse of desire, the left-handed horse whom the charioteer
must check if the soul is to rise.

Socrates insists on hearing the entire work—respoken, not silently
reread—rather than the summary Phaedrus was hoping to give him, and
by that gift to demonstrate, if not his command of the art of verbal memory, at least his ability to recall in the right order the principal points of
an oration, an art which, much later, Cicero and Quintilian would call
a memory for *res* (things: i.e., objects, subjects, important points in a
discourse), instead of the more strenuous and particular one for *verba*
(words got by heart). It was the memory for "things" which was so important to the sophists, jurors, politicians, and those parts of the public
who felt it necessary to be able to return to mind, whenever they wished,
the shape and substance of what had been said on some previous occasion; whereas it was the memory of the word, precisely as it stood among
others, that largely concerned the poets and the rhapsodes and certain
of the rhetoricians.[3]

In order to perform Lysias' allegedly eloquent composition, Socrates
and Phaedrus seek out some shady spot and settle on one near the banks
of the Illissus.[4] Their conversation is rich in allusion and reference; no
god's name is taken in vain;[5] no uttered word lies idle; yet Plato's art-

---

3. See particularly the first two chapters of Frances A. Yates's *The Art of Memory* (Chicago, Ill.: University of Chicago Press, 1966). If, according to Plato's Egyptian story,
Theuth invented the art of writing, ancient tradition says that it was Simonides of Ceos, a
poet frequently cited by Plato, who invented mnemonics. It is, of course, this art which is
most immediately threatened by the hieroglyph.

4. The river which Paul Valéry has turned into the incessant stream of Time in his own
dialogue between Socrates and Phaedrus, the *Eupalinos*.

5. On their way to the river they pass a place where, as Phaedrus incorrectly surmises,
Boreas is said to have made off with the lovely Oreithyia, one of the daughters of the then
King of Athens. Boreas had been in love with the tempestuous Oreithyia for some time,
but her father kept putting Boreas off with false promises and postponements. Angry at
having wasted so much of his time on mere words, Boreas became his impatient nature
again, and one day swept the maiden away in a coil of air while she was dancing on the

istry, never greater than in this dialogue, and equaled only by the philosophical poetry of the *Phaedo* and the *Symposium,* provokes the paradox of his prose; for this dialogue is to be a defense of the word which simply flies sincerely forth from an open and unencumbered heart, whereas the language which so eloquently states that case possesses qualities which are possible only to words which are not merely written, but *composed.* My shopping lists, my address book, my checks, my sick child's school excuses, are written; my lies, my love letters, my legal briefs, my limericks, my *longueurs,* are composed.

We have scarcely begun the dialogue; we have yet to hear Lysias' speech (to read the hearing of it, that is); and already various forms of the word have begun to proliferate. We encountered, first of all and quite naturally enough, the *written* words of Plato, which comprise and create the occasion and conditions of the dialogue; then we meet the *spoken* ones which Plato says were uttered by Socrates and Phaedrus; next there are those *composed* by Lysias, *borrowed* by Phaedrus, and *read aloud,* possibly *performed* by him rather than *memorized* and taken to heart.

---

banks of the Illissus, wafting her to a rock near another stream, where, hidden behind a dark cloud—as Robert Graves describes it in *The Greek Myths,* 2 vols. (Baltimore, Md.: Penguin Books, 1955), Vol. I, pp. 170–172—he took the pleasure of his lust. Eventually Boreas made Oreithyia an honest woman, not merely a wronged one, and she bore the god twin sons, the Argonauts Calais and Zetes, who, when they reached manhood, suddenly grew wings. The Athenians had built a temple to Boreas, and revived his worship in the city, because his winds, at their request, had scattered the Persian fleet. Oreithyia is to be identified with Eurynome, the goddess who in a whirling dance created the world, and who caught the North Wind, and formed it with her fricative hands a phallic coil of air, the serpent Ophion, who promptly wound himself around her with the predictably pregnant result. In addition, Oreithyia is probably another name for Athene the Filly, goddess of the local horse cult, as Graves suggests. Certainly the other stories in which Boreas is featured involve horses, for he lives in the stable of Ares on Mount Haemus, and once, disguised as a stallion, covered twelve of Erichtonius' mares (presumably not all at the same time), although, on Homer's authority, it was once widely believed that mares could conceive by turning their rears to the wind; and, indeed, it was the wind again which was capable of entering a woman's womb in a gust that bore one of her ancestors toward another life. It was perhaps such an egg of air—an abortive flatulence—which Socrates fears might be the sole result of his midwifery in the *Theaetetus.*

It is, of course, Phaedrus who wonders whether the story might be true, while Socrates, though aware of the prevailing skepticism concerning the myths, finds it hardly feasible to pooh-pooh every fantastic tale that comes along, and reduce each one to a commonplace (although he jocularly does just that), because there are so very many of them. It would be like spanking ants. So he would not send away the harmless ones to be debunked, but would prefer to accept them as they innocently present themselves, and worry rather about the myths dwelling in himself which he feels he must discover and expel. It is no doubt true that Plato wishes to dissuade us in advance from any desire we might have either to deride or to overallegorize the tales that Socrates himself will shortly be telling; but any pretty story would have sufficed for that maneuver. The Boreas story is chosen because of the kind of myth it is, and because of the rich connections it makes with the material soon to be brought before us.

Lysias' speech, although given life and spoken by Phaedrus, although approved by his breath, has not been made his; it has not been given residence in his head, which is doubtless, a wise thing; for what is it to take a guest of this kind into the interior of the soul, from whence words rise like a sudden spring; what is it to offer your hospitality to the opinions and passions, the rhythms and rhetoric, of another, perhaps far from perfect, character and mind?

Socrates declares that he can make up a better speech than Lysias',[6] accepting even the rules of the game and the assumption of the debate: namely that it is better for a youth to yield his body to one who desires but does not love him, than to one who does both (especially when the love in question is a blind and selfish passion); but Socrates is reluctant to make good on his boast, and one reason surely is, although several are evident, that the words will not be his: he must pretend to be a vessel which is filled by another, possibly by the muses whom he invokes, though even this is doubtful, for would the muses be inclined to sing on such a subject, insincerely and to a false point? Not only that, but Socrates will have to match his wholly *improvised* and *unwritten* speech against Lysias' cleverly contrived and carefully composed one. Socrates' oration is masterfully made up on the spot by a character whose very figure, as well as every known word, has been artfully imagined by Plato over years of passionate dedication. It is a so-called *unwritten* work which has been written and rewritten, we can be sure, more than once; its alleged lack of composition has been composed and recomposed; its off-the-cuff character has been indelibly inked on the page.

Socrates further guards himself against the anger of the gods (for his words cannot help but blaspheme the real Eros, who is said here to be one of them) by inventing a lover who, while pretending to be free of love's passion the better to satisfy it, will simply pronounce the words which Socrates makes up for him. Neither Socrates nor the mask that Socrates holds out in front of him believes the words being mouthed. Whose words, then, are they? Literally, they belong to no one. The first

---

6. Which ought to be easy to do if Lysias' speech, as R. Hackforth thinks, is poorly put together. See *Plato's Phaedrus* (Cambridge, England: Cambridge University Press, 1952), p. 31. But only if we are unsure of Plato's artistry can we make this complaint, or wonder whether it is really by Lysias, as Taylor and Wilamowitz believe, or was made up by Plato, as Shorey and Hackforth think. Plato never does—and never would—give that much space to worthless writing. Just as Agathon's speech in the *Symposium* is an instance of bombast brilliantly brought off, so Lysias' speech is a superb example of rhetorical opportunism. Coleridge warned Wordsworth not to imitate a dull and garrulous discourser by being dull and garrulous, and Plato has triumphed over time to take his advice.

two speeches of the *Phaedrus* are exemplary orations, models, specimens, or types. Without any actual occasion to bring them into being, representing no actual mind, they belong to the art of eloquence, to rhetoric in the abstract; they are words quite free of responsibility to anyone. It is no wonder that Socrates feels uneasy in their presence.

In normal discourse, and especially in societies which depend principally upon the spoken word to establish and maintain community, the real origin of one's words is a serious, even critical matter. We are always forced to ask of any politician what his words mean; whether he stands behind those promises his mouth so glibly made; whether his stated intentions are really his; whether his promises weren't broken in the moment of their manufacture, as if a large crack were a part of the mold. Our presidents rarely write even their own lies, so in what sense are the lies theirs? The reader or listener must return the word to its proper habitation; the word must be sent on the same pursuit as the soul, in search of *its* truth: the sincerity of its source.

It has long been our habit to quote the words, and hence to adopt, or temporarily to borrow, the views of others. In debate I may attribute to historical figures convictions which they might have expressed on some famous occasion, although I was not present to hear them, as Thucydides did in his history, or Plato did when he composed the *Phaedo*. Again, I may cite Homer or Hesiod to give the weight of their authority to my otherwise airy opinions. I implicitly say, by so doing, that I assent, not only to the sense of their sentences, but also to their style. The breath of my lungs unites us in a common course or cause. But where do these words have their home now? Where do they reside? Are they part of my soul's very flesh and blood? Have they been the words that have nourished me from the first and formed my self and established my character, been the bone of my bones, as the very diction and verbal rhythms of the King James Bible shaped the souls of the early settlers of this country— its meanings, sounds, and meters reinforced by every family reading?

Suppose I could repeat every line of a poem as well as a recording; it nevertheless might be no more important a piece of my past than an anecdote might be, only a folly I recall for the amusement of my friends. As a child I had to *commit* to memory (please note the word, which suggests that memory is a lunatic asylum), and learn to recite in a way deemed impressive, "The shades of night were falling fast/as through an Alpine village passed/a youth who bore mid snow and ice/a banner with a strange device/Excelsior!" and I have since then simply happened to retain in some back room of my mind Auden's immortally awful couplet, "This is the night train crossing the border/bringing the cheque and the postal order"; but these words have never taken up residence, as we say, in my heart, nor have they fathered or nurtured other lines, sentences, further feelings or thoughts of any significance. Our hellos and goodbys, our concerns for one another's health, our hope that all and sundry will have a nice day: these utterances, too, do not proceed from us any more than the dullest actor's lines do; they are as social as the dress suit, and are rarely homemade. It is Plato's point, of course, that almost the entire meaning of "I love you" depends upon what organ or area of the body is energizing the production of the words.

That dull actor, indeed, may perform his greatest service simply by saying his piece and setting free its words instead of draping some interpretation like a coat over its shoulders, because it is likely that the language has more meaning than his inflection can convey, his gestures circumscribe.

Then what of those passages that do follow us home: the sentiments and sentences which we adopt? What is the fate of some of my favorite lines of Rilke: *"Kannst Du Dir denn denken, dass ich Jahre/so—ein Fremder unter Fremden fahre/und nun endlich nimmst Du mich nach Haus,"* sunk like a ship inside me for so long, concealed now by what sort of sea-growth, or preserved by the salt and thus not a day older, or worn by being repeatedly given tongue? And I murmur to myself, "a stranger in a world of strangers," taking warmth and comfort from this cold conception. Then when Rilke is remembering, at the behest of Busoni, the enchanting lines of his poem "Song of the Sea," for instance, and fervently reciting them, they are words which have gone from his soul long since to return to another region of being, for surely the place they were when he wrote them is not the place they are when he remembers and recites them. Nor are they the words that Busoni hears.

I can also recall the expressions of others as though to confront them in court; not in their own persons, of course, but by means of their immortal residues. Yet only lovers memorize the flattery they have spoken to one another; only spouses allow their sharp outcries of complaint to inscribe themselves upon their souls in an unerasable state. Generally, the word must be written down, set adrift from the self, before it can be returned to another starting point in the loins, the lungs, the larynx, or the lips of a stranger.

And when some lines of yours have set another's mouth to moving, making that sense with those sounds: is that not better than a kiss?

However, when a noble thought is implanted on a page, it can be harvested by rascals. What are the words of the Lord doing coming from that foul infidel's face? And when I quote some immortal lines as if I were in inner harmony with them,

> We do not prove the existence of the poem.
> It is something seen and known in lesser poems.
> It is the huge, high harmony that sounds
> A little and a little, suddenly,
> By means of a separate sense. It is and it
> Is not and, therefore, is.

whence does my conceit and confidence come, since I could never have created its controlling notion, set that sort of thought afire, let that kind of song escape from the dirty shaded cage I call myself? How can I ever make divine lines mine?

Wittgenstein surely must have felt that the understanding he sought with such intensity was being carried away by his auditors in little bags and sacks as though they had purchased it; that what was a process for him had become a product for others; and what could Socrates do to remind his disciples that the *logos* they loved was the *logos of his life*, and altered as he did, and grew, as he hoped, toward the light; that wisdom was not something which could be handed round like the mashed potatoes, but was found by means of a vocalized internal investigation, a search of the soul? for the soul would move the body wisely only if its words were wise, since it is solely through these dubious but essential diagrams of sound that the rational spirit speaks.

It is the journey to the truth which convinces the traveler that he has arrived. To be dropped on the top of Mount Everest by helicopter is not to gain the glory of the peak.

Often, of course, the words of others, which I have dragged squalling into my oration like someone else's children, have little substance of their own, but take their authority from the famous, and often imposing, figure of their father. God's word frequently walks lamely enough for the ordinary man to claim it. Because I say so, Zeus thunders. The orders come from me, the Führer screams. It is not the meaning and weight and arrangement—the argument—of the words themselves which persuades. The Sybil's riddles, the Oracles' ambiguities, say: Believe me, because I am in touch with divinity. The highly organized harangues of the politicians say: Believe me, because I can give you what you want, and tell you what you want to hear; my tongue shall lick your ear. The carefully measured considerations of the philosopher say: Believe me, because I am wise; but can the philosopher be wise before his words are? and worse, where in those words can we find the Forms? where is the deep resemblance in these syllables which will spur us to recall and spell out the unspellable Ideas? The well-wrought verses of the poet, too—the periods of the orator, the sophist's sleights of speech—each says: Believe me because I am clever, resonant, beautiful; but the beauty of any such display of talent, and exercise of skill, for Plato, rests on whether its eloquence stirs others to theirs; and because the beauty of the truly Beautiful depends on whether it manages to be an adequate manifestation of the ultimate Good at which Truth aims.

The great value of the Platonic myths has never been, it seems to me, the support they give to certain tenets of Plato's philosophy, or their ability to float us over difficulties like benign clouds; but the conviction they create of being true *somewhere,* as if the truth were a bee in a black bag: you can hear it; you know that it's there; but it certainly isn't easy to find; furthermore, it may sting if you succeed.

We are fallen angels, Plato tells us; we were once winged, and now we live in the sty of our bodies, and move these bodies to and fro, restless as caged bears, aimless and confined. We must regrow those wings, harness our two horses, and climb the heavens in a path trod flat by the chariots of the gods: turn, as the soul of the world itself turns, until we can see beyond the bounds and body of the earth, with its neighboring stars and local sky, into that space which holds the unextended formulas of Being. Then, drawn there by its winged steeds, its base nature in harness with its best, the soul sees the unseeable. These horses are the emblems of our organs of regeneration. The sight of Beauty feeds them. Certainly the image of winged phalli is not uncommon in Greek iconography.[7] In the *Theaetetus,* "seeing" is described as a kind of intercourse in which emanations from the eye and the object intermingle to give birth to twins: the object becomes white, for example, while the eye is filled with "seeing." The imagery of the cave in the *Republic* is explicitly sexual, as is the nearly pornographic account of the union of the soul with the idea of beauty embodied in a boy which we receive in the *Phaedrus.* The soul, to fulfill the functions which Plato's metaphors have imagined for it, must be hermaphroditic. It is phallic in its responses to beauty, becoming engorged, rising, pursuing its object; and in its failures, too, flaccidly falling. But it is female at that point when the Forms fertilize the soul. What is brought to birth in Meno or in Theaetetus, later, is the Ideas which have been laid there by their earlier intercourse with a beauty beyond the stars. The black horse—the dark unruly

---

7. K. J. Dover, in *Greek Homosexuality* (Cambridge, Mass.: Harvard University Press, 1978), reproduces a vase (R 414) on which a woman is shown carrying a penis in the form of a bird, and a pitcher (R 259) depicts a horse whose head becomes penile. Dover discusses them on p. 133. Many of the penises on these vases have eyes (R 414, B 370, for instance).

phallus—desires, if we may so speak, to unite with the body, to enter it and there to realize its seedful dreams; whereas the pale phallus seeks to reproduce creatively, by bringing the Forms into their full fruition in the mind.

In any case, the favored sense is sight. The ear does not replace the eye at any point or passage. We do not sniff eternity or touch the Forms as if they were megaliths, and if they nourish us, it is with the lover's eye that we devour them. So that when our wings wither like Icarus', close to the sun, and we fall to earth again; and when grass grows over everything we know as though it were now in a grave; the soul retains the mark, the scar, the image of what it has seen: not in a set of sentences, not in sounds sent like a message from outer space; but somehow in something like a perception . . . Oh, mental to be sure, not colored in, not an outline either, yet *visual:* a memory of the mind's eye.

Before we suppose that Plato has simply fallen prey to a figure of speech, and is here in no better shape than the poets to fight his way past appearance, we must recall two important points. First, as we moved through that famous classification of realities called "the divided line" in the *Republic,* we systematically rubbed out materiality, not in the direction of images, shadows, reflections, and illusions, which is the downward turning point of Things, but in the direction of the abstracted outline of objects, arriving finally at the drawings which engross the geometer: triangles, circles, squares; that is, we took away from the visual everything we dared to, and left only those minimal qualities behind which were yet necessary to keep the thing *in sight*. The taste and sound and touch and smell and inner warmth and secret kinesis of things have no representations at all in mathematics. We see the fingers we count on, the pebbles we count with, the rebus we arrange, the drawings we place upon the ground or upon the page. Second, however, and on the other side, we must remember that when we "see" the Forms, we simply grasp systems of internal relations, and nowhere in the world of actual sight do we see those either.

It is not with the eye that we speak what we have seen, and if our chief receptive action is the mind's gaze, our chief transmitting organ is the silent tongue of thought. Seeing in this sense/saying in this sense: both blind, both mute: for when in my favorite daydream I am recollecting how you looked that sunny afternoon, your body like a streak of light across the bed, what am I seeing? what is the image I have thrown upon that blackboard on the back of the lid? and when I attempt to describe the reflections of the flower stems, the way the water became green when they were thrust in the vases, what gets uttered so it can be heard outside the hall of the head?

The ladder we are called upon to climb in the *Symposium* is composed of aggressively heteronomous rungs, so that, again, we shall be able to see what all lovely things have in common, whether we are considering a body or a body of laws, a theorem or a theory; whether we are casting our eyes upon a noble youth, or have paused—thunderstruck—on the threshold of perfect Beauty; because we shall have seen a common unity through a lens of difference, in as much as it is precisely the differences between philosophical systems of thought, for instance, and the poets' hymns and songs, between a pair of well-appointed breasts or youthful buttocks and the Palladian design of a pantheon, which pull the concealing flesh away to leave the bones. And the adaptation of parts to a purpose, the harmony of elements which properly proportion a whole, the idea of order as it disposes itself in the Idea of Order itself—none of these things, while visible, can ever be directly seen. Beauty is not present *to* sight, but it is always available *in* it. The natural world is beautiful in this sense because, as the *Timaeus* tells us, it is the purest, most perfect and complete, *qualitative expression of quantitative law*.

When Ideas and things separate, the word is torn in two. The Platonist drives the referent of any term—the water jug, the wagon, the motorcycle—away from its meaning, its narrow definition as well as all its additional and more elusive senses. And that wicked black horse, like materialists, realists, sophists everywhere (as Plato would suppose), wants only the sweet grass in the meadow, the lively frolic, the nuzzle, the mare in heat, and would make the word swerve to serve them, conjure them up, combine; whereas the idealist, who rides the white horse if he does not wear the white hat, moves into the world of meaning like a tramp into a rich flat; there is nothing for the beggar here; here is calm connection, clean towels, fresh sheets, and wholesome sense.

Consider the task of the Demiurge, the shaping principle which Plato calls on to create the world in his dialogue the *Timaeus*. The Demiurge must mold a referent to resemble an Idea; he must implement laws with instances; he must make a form which expresses a formula—a midge, a monster, a mother-in-law, inconsolable motion—which mimics its meaning, the principle of its being; but he must do so by *working around the word;* the word is the absent guest; it is hiding out somewhere (in the soul, as I'll suggest), and there does not at first appear, on the *Phaedrus'* extensive list of words spoken, borrowed, recited, or remembered, or among those composed, purchased, or performed, anywhere any one resembling the word of God, whose elemental utterance stilled chaos and brought light.

In Genesis we are nowhere told whether God shouted as the King will in *Hamlet,* whether he pleaded, whispered, hissed, or calmly commanded, or whether he created the word 'light' by his act of uttering it; whether there was already a divine language for God to draw upon, although Adam appears to have made up the names he confers upon the animals. In any case, in this myth at least, the word preceded the world. It is clear in this case, too, that the creative power of the word lay not in itself, but in the authority of the voice which gave it life, for you or I might have said the same thing, and deep night and chaos would have gone on calmly troubling the void; unless—and here is a thought—unless it was that any creature (you or I or the snake itself) who said the first word would, by that drawing of an imprisoned sword from its tree, its stone, like a sound drawn out of silence, have become King, Creator, Overlord.

Plato's Demiurge translated the eternal Forms into colorful, scented, and sounding things; he spun a triangle to create a cone, and spun a cone to shape a sphere; however, the Demiurge did not render Reality in words. He was a sculptor, a builder, an architect, if you like, but not a poet, not a philosopher. And his task was not less than impossible if the relation between Reality and the image he was to make of it was supposed to be one of resemblance. How could he model the world of Becoming and base it on Being that way? How could he picture permanence in change, drag an Idea down into the dirt and retain anything of its pristine features, its former splendor, its generality? The Demiurge could only represent with exactitude the numbers of things, because the three members of a lovers' triangle, the Three Bears, the three persons of the Trinity, the three coins in the fountain, all embody the Idea of the number three quite perfectly. Three turtledoves do not roughly approximate or simply imitate three, they *are* three and therefore one more than a pair. But the doves multiply in a bird's way; they cannot be factored; they cannot be calmly subtracted from five gold rings in order to reach two French hens as a remainder.

Suppose, though, that we wanted to use three items of anything to represent, not three, but perhaps plurality in general; that we wanted to move from One and Two to Many. How soon would we recognize that ⬚⬚⬚ is Egyptian for flood; that is, heaven + three water jugs? or that 〰〰〰 is water, or one wave × three? or that ʃʃʃ is hair; or one hair in triplicate? Finally, how readily will we figure out that /// (three slanted strokes) is the sign of any plurality?[8] And if we follow a Pythagorean pattern, how much more rapidly do our resemblances disappear to leave us puzzled:

---

8. Karl Menninger, *Number Words and Number Symbols: A Cultural History of Numbers* (Cambridge, Mass.: MIT Press, 1969), p. 17.

♥   ♥ (four pebbles)   ┊ ⌐ ┊ (a square)   (the no. 4)   (the idea)
♠   ♦   = ┊ ⌐ ┊   = 4   = JUSTICE

So, as the soul passes on its journey between the rude world below
and the polished Forms above, it has to take a peek in both directions,
as Plato suggests: "[Our] understanding is a recollection of those things
which our soul beheld aforetime as they journeyed with their god, looking down upon the things which now we suppose to be, and gazing up
to that which truly is" (*Phaedrus,* 249c, Hackforth's translation). With
the left eye the charioteer must look where the black beast is pulling it,
and see, for instance, injustice down there like jaundice in a pale face;
then, with his right eye, he must look past the powerful shoulders of the
white horse to where the Idea of Injustice lies like a gleaming shadow
among Harmony, Wholeness, Order, and their Negation. He should not
be surprised at seeing that shadow there, either, because the knowledge
of any evil is a necessary thing, and an important good. The charioteer
must match Heaven's own bedstead with the bed he will shortly lie in,
because only in that way can his sagging canvas cot recall to his mind
the true notions of Rest and Recumbency which go some distance to
define it. And if that is the case with the Demiurge's impeccable designs—that they cannot resemble the truth sufficiently to lead us alone
from portrait to model; that, as fine and well intentioned as he is, the
Demiurge cannot paint, say, Woman well enough so we would know her
without a name affixed to her fig leaf—then in what worse case do we
find ourselves when we describe the fair sex in words—ah, always so inadequately, so unfairly!—for in what way does 'Woman' resemble
women? Even if Plato's metaphor is ultimately inexplicable—that we
"see" both Being and Becoming at the same time—he knew words well
enough not to choose *them*. Plato never suggests that we read Reality in
the bright light of the Good. He always insists that we *see* it; perhaps as
I say I see some computations. I ask my accountant: "Let's see your results," or "Would you look over these figures?" Yet if the Forms are formulas made of figures (and therefore easy to "see"), where is the facilitating resemblance between H_2O and water, or 5,280 and a mile? How
do I get, on any mimetic basis, from one to the other?

Plato has apparently provided us with three methods for gaining
knowledge of the Forms. The first requires that we separate the influence
of the body and lower parts of the soul upon reason, for by concentrating
upon the least sensuously contaminated subjects, like geometry and
mathematics, we shall be able to reason clearly, free from the prejudices
of perception and the biases of desire. The second suggests that we use
the visual world to remind us about what we saw on our journey to the
invisible one; that we match phenomenon and Form as we once—wall-

eyed—beheld them—together like ill-assorted twins. Finally, we should attempt to achieve accurate definitions of things (and this is the method which seems to require words) by careful collection and the formation of genres, along with the division of each collection by means of specific differences into enduring species. As we do so, we must arrive, we might suppose, at those combinations of words which lie nearest the signs made in the soul by the Forms. These three methods are not exclusive, of course, and they could be combined, or be otherwise necessary or helpful to one another.

One and the same vocabulary, as far as its sounds and marks are concerned, will conceal this double reference to Being and Becoming. On the one hand, the word 'woman' will refer to Franny and Helen and Olga and Ruth, whose forms merely imitate the divine, and, on the other, it will designate an Idea whose embrace is even more to be desired; so if I dare to add a line or two to the majestic myth that Plato has given us in the *Phaedrus,* I should simply say that as we rode higher and higher behind our horses in the van of the gods, and saw to one side of us, as though resting at the base of a great cliff, the upturned face of the world: perfumed, rouged, and screaming; while on the other side, in a relentless glare of clarity which is the look of the Good, appeared the timelessly tiered figures of the Forms; and again, as we advanced as it were along this Pythagorean fold between meaning and things, substantial shadow and insubstantial substance, we drew a line in language from one to the other: 'horse,' 'cloud,' 'cavern,' 'firmament,' 'justice,' 'desire,' we sang as we rode: 'peace,' 'perimeter,' 'cabbage,' 'cube.' From that time on our words, as if drawn by those harsh or handsome horses, sink down in the direction of things and their disconnections, to pornograph among the passions, or they rise as if winged toward meanings, ideas, regions of pure relation. (See diagram.)

The Pythagorean Double Triangle of Ten.
One triangle is the false reflection of the other.

Is it not for this reason that the orations of the sophists, apparently employing terms like 'youth' and 'love' and 'desire' and 'pleasure' just as Socrates would have to if he spoke on the same subject (for no one has a lien on a word), are speeches which lie as low as valleys and slowly fill with fog? They intend to speak the same lubricious lingo as their listeners, for their listeners have damp souls, damp as drains, and they long to be turned in the direction of denotation, as if the word were a wind directed at the world, and they were a vane.

Throughout the dialogue, Plato has distinguished words from words, though their shells seem the same: 'love' in the speech of Lysias, 'love' again in Socrates' mock argument on the same theme, 'love' once more in his mighty oration, and so on. Words about love are quoted, improvised, read, analyzed, scorned. Socrates speaks the word sometimes as though inspired, as though he were lending his breath to another spirit. He also uses it, and his discourse about it, to reach the ultimately wordless and wholly unutterable.

'Love,' as it rests on the bright side of the soul, signifies the upward displacement of desire toward a longing for knowledge, for a reunion with the Forms. In this condition, we are like a youth or a young woman in search of our heavenly bride or bridegroom. Such an elevated word must be spoken, for who could imagine that on the soul's journey, holding those reins, controlling those contrary horses, we have taken along a gooseneck lamp, a desk, and an ink horn? Of course, the soul has no one to speak to but itself, in the beginning. The flight of the Alone, as Plotinus represents it, is of the Alone to the Alone. Correspondingly unpicturable is the reflection of the Ideas within the silent mirror of the self.

So at the center of the spirit is the unvoiced word, the living word of reason perhaps, if you are a Platonist, but it is the rooted word, in any case, the early word, the first word, the word as worm. These original words come from, and have their home in, the realm of Forms, for they were sounded in sight of them, as though by a trumpet; yet we must not forget that their early roots (as Plato himself rather wildly suggests) grow in both directions. Although the image of the charioteer divides our task in three, it is not an entirely accurate picture of the Platonic soul (that great conception which I have turned into a metaphor for the word and its true home), because, of its three faculties, two draw us in the direction of the world, and the one representing reason must then enlist the energies and perceptions of both the other two to do its business. In the lower depths are the instincts, the hungers, the mouth, the gut, the penetrating penis; at the middle level lies sensation—sight, smell, and so on—pleasure, pain, passion, and whatever credit the Greeks gave to the idea of the will. Neither can be called white.

Nor would any of the soul's faculties recognize, in the word 'love' alone, as a sound, any resemblance to either its idea or its condition, but only to 'glove' and 'shove' and other sounds, equally senseless and arbitrary; nor will *'lieben'* brings us any closer to its object. Love has no phonemes, no spelling, no pronunciation, only stages, disappointments, and degrees. Love is the transformation of a reproductive energy, and that notion, now that it has found a word like 'love' (although its English body is a short one and without any special distinction—suppose the word for this mostly misguided exhilaration were 'ululation' instead, or 'cornucopia,' or 'Ohio'?), can be seduced into other occupations, stolen, put in compromising contexts, made to say the opposite of what it was meant to mean.

When lust uses the language, or when our passions speak urgently and plainly, the meaning of 'love' is first phallic and engorged, then moody and romantic. Thus there are at least three root meanings of 'love' (and three for almost every word and every discourse), one for each division of the soul. At least that is one kind of cut through things, one kind of classification. Two of these 'loves,' as I've said, look down at the world the way the dark horse does, at objects of sense, at acts of consummation; they celebrate the referent; the one remaining looks up at the bodiless copulations of the verb 'to be'—toward the abstract, the purely inferential, the eternal. Two of these 'loves' aim at reproducing their likeness in their partners: the first father sees his image reflected in his son; the second sees himself reflected in the objects his infatuation has created; while the third brings Beauty to birth in Beauty, in theory realizes yet another theory. One copulates, one courts and caresses, one contemplates. That is yet another cut, another kind of classification.

In any case, all three sources of the word are ours, and reflect our specific condition, because it is upon that curtained internal stage that the great debate between reason and the passions, the body and the mind, between things and their meanings, begins. Here, no one can make a speech in your place. Here, no words have been hired for the season. The speakers refuse to give up their rights. And there are more than a few of us, I suspect, who have been repeatedly dismayed by our spirit's petty divisions, the crossness of our purposes, the shameful politics played by all the parties in the kingdom of the ego. What shall the "I" who represents us mean when it makes its noises, when it whispers "I love you"? Will we have a clue we can regard with confidence if the object of our endearments is an enterprise? a doctrine? a bible? a boy? No wonder Socrates is fearful that we shall freeze our meaning, end the distressing debate with a blow that breaks the argument. At one moment we believe our beloved must be good and true because we desire her so (and there are some philosophers, like Hobbes, who think that all our tunes are played in this key); at another moment, however, our desires languish behind our controlling passion like a courtly lover, our penis all poem, as we look longingly up at the pedestal where our fair one stands, as cold and polished on her stone as though carved by Canova, and as worthy of worship. In Lysias' speech, which Phaedrus recites for us, desire enlists reason to gain its ends and pushes passion aside like dirt beneath a broom. In Socrates' mocking rejoinder, passion hides itself behind desire in order to make convincing a similar case; but in the famous final oration of Socrates (and it is fully an "oration"), energy and feeling are joined to order and idea to produce a metaphysical climax not entirely lacking its own passionate outcry and genital spasm. Here, the mind cares; the mind comes.

The word is like the soul itself, that intermediary thing which moves between the realms of Being and Becoming; and if my additions to the myth are not altogether unseemly, then it will be the lower parts of the *logos* as well as the *psyche* that remember the world, and the upper one which gazes on or connects itself to the Forms; and unless these separate aspects of ourselves and our language speak to one another, respond to one another, there will be no match of "thing" to the Form it is said to resemble, no string will stretch from significance to subject, for I argued that such resemblance could not be read from the thing itself, nor predicted from the Form in its featureless silence.

Lust, romantic attachment, and intellectual dedication have traveled together in that company of the gods, and that is how they come to know the nature of their rivalry. Moreover, only they can speak to one another with any chance of success, since it is indeed true that although they use the same marks, they do not use the same meanings. There are at least three languages in any language, as I've said. And only when reason leads do the words have energy, passion, and profundity in the right proportion. Only when, we might say, paraphrasing Plato, each tongue does its own job well, and the word is borne along equally, but in good order, by all of them, has the philosopher become a proper poet; one whom, alone, we will allow to sing of the immortal Forms as Plato has.

Words which I speak to you, if you are to remember them, must be taken more deeply into the self than those which I write down, and which you can keep about your person like your tobacco, ticket stubs, or pipe. The spoken word can be questioned, because behind it there is a speaker. The spoken word is alive in a context of life: the breath, the pause, the intonation, the look of the mouth, the eye, the posture of the body, gestures of arm and tilt of head—all contribute to its meaning, confirm its ownership. The written word emasculates memory—Plato's worries on this score have proved to be correct—and the written word which is no longer a surrogate for the real one—first voiced to the self and then to the world—is a murderer of meaning. Technical terms, jargon, diagrams, the Latin names of plants, Germanic obfuscation: none of these belong to the discourse of the soul.

Furthermore, the written word comes forward as the completion of a process, not as the process itself. It quietly omits the context of composition, of discovery. It admits no doubts, no alterations, no unmeant obscurities. A field of rejected alternatives lies invisibly about the chosen word or phrase like dead around the boy who still holds the standard, but we don't realize a battle has taken place; that blood has been shed, ideas denied, feelings changed, accidents allowed to stand; no, the completed sentence stretches itself out in the sun with ease and assurance: its figure is full, even fulsome; it already has a tan. And when many completed sentences lie together to form a treatise or a novel whose composition took many years, and went on in spite of illness, through love affairs, bankruptcy, and divorce, *they*—these sentences—will still pretend that the same author authored all of them; that they came, as they are printed, simultaneously into being; that their source was as ceaselessly constant and continuous as π. The completed text cannot be questioned and makes no reply, yet it invites overthrow; it calls for interpretation the way a stalled motorist might innocently call on a mugger or a rapist for help; and here comes the critic, eager to replace whatever words he finds in front of him with his own, and the mind that made them with his own mind too, concealing every evidence of creativity with his own conceit. Perhaps, grown bolder, greedier, more desperate, he will try to take the work away from its feckless writer by insisting that a text is actually a pastiche of quotation, a piece of systematic plagiarism, and the writer merely a sluice through which language streams.[9] He will argue that the text's only home and true destination is the reader, which is a little like asserting that the true home of the bath water is the drain, when one means only that "down the drain" is what will become of it.

Indeed, the spoken word is addressed to someone. I can see my words touch the thought, the feelings, of another. These words were made for *you,* shaped on this occasion for *your* sake, never again to be used; whereas the printed word is like a shoe which is supposed to fit every foot in society like an elastic sock. The written word repeats itself as woodenly as any signboard; it addresses itself to "whomever," and even when it finds itself in a private letter, the word can be worse than overheard: it can be stolen, reproduced, counterfeited, defaced, defamed.

---

9. For more on this point, see the final essay in this volume, "The Death of the Author."

The expression "to write something down" suggests a descent of thought into the fingers whose movements immediately falsify it. Consider what happens when the Form for the Triangle is displayed in a diagram: △. This triangle receives an extension it didn't have before, because the Form Triangle is not triangular; it is not spread out in space like a piece of breakfast toast: yet how many schoolchildren still think that these figures are triangles through and through, and calculate each hypotenuse as if they were measuring the length of a giraffe's neck. Yet further off from any element of imitation is the word itself. Similarly, the factors of a number like 8, when written out $(2 \times 2 \times 2 \,\&\, 8 \times 1)$, must stand in line like customers at a ticket window, and an idea—complex and total and together—finds its elements laid out like the parts list for a bicycle.

Plato clearly foresaw what would happen when doctrines of depth, subtlety, and importance went abroad as innocent print. I once heard a drunk in a college tavern recite a simple and beautiful poem of Blake's. It had no home in that slack wet mouth. And the subtleties of subtle texts are immediately ignored; the complexities are erased by reviewers who regard them irascibly, and importance is equated with popularity.[10]

Of course, when I have to tell you orally what I think and mean, I cannot think, perhaps, as profoundly, or simultaneously mean as much; but I shall have to be clearer if not clear; I shall never be able to say, "let x," or utter an arrogant *"aufgehoben,"* or commit an act of narratology.

What Plato did not foresee, quite, was the degree to which the written word might become as anonymous as an assassin; how it might establish a vast industry; how words would appear along roadways and on walls and the sides of buildings, not written, but *posted,* and addressed to whoever chanced to be passing. Words are stuck on bumpers, stenciled across chests so they can bounce with the breasts. He could not have imagined the multiplication of the written word, the printed word, the printout word, the painted word, the filmed and photographed word, the day-glow, lit-up word, the sky-written word, the repealed, and stricken, and canceled, and censored and snipped-up, crossworded word, either, and its consequent devaluation, or the total trivialization of speech and conversation in addition.

Roland Barthes celebrates the death of the author—another little god

---

10. "Beware," he tells Dionysios in the *Second Letter,* "lest these doctrines fall among the ignorant. For there is hardly anything, I believe, that sounds more absurd to the vulgar or, on the other hand, more admirable and inspired to men of fine disposition" (314a). Paul Friedländer is excellent on this entire issue, especially in Chapter V, "The Written Work," of *Plato: An Introduction,* pp. 108–125.

gone—by quoting a passage from "Sarrasine" to support his claim, and it bears repeating because it also supports mine.[11] Balzac is commenting on the appearance of a castrato disguised as a woman: "This was woman herself, with her sudden fears, her irrational whims, her instinctive worries, her impetuous boldness, her fussings, and her delicious sensibility." Barthes asserts that this sentence has no particular source or origin, no voice, and he is surely right. The castrato, of course, must exhibit these commonplaces in his own person, otherwise he will not appear to be the "real" thing—woman herself—for the real real thing in such a society is seldom seen. Certainly a sentence of such blatantly platitudinous blather has no "author" behind it, unless, as Barthes seems to think, cliché can hold a Bic. But he is not dismayed by this anonymity; rather, for him "writing is the destruction of every voice, of every point of origin." Such a possibility worried Plato, whose practice in prose shows us the way to avoid it, but it did not worry many of the sophists, who encouraged the sale of words like alligator shirts, nor does it bother many of them now, who embrace the individual, and the individuated sentence, only to crush its pretense to humanity, its singular style, and return it in anonymous pieces to the collectivity—itself a word almost too ugly to utter. An edict can be signed by some "authority" who thereby stands behind it and takes responsibility for it, but a style stands within every syllable and says: I have imagined this; believed this; thought this; and so I have put myself and my mark on it.

This voice, these authors, the idea of the individual, the distinct value of consciousness, are all creatures of Capitalism, according to Barthes, which strikes me as an odd thought, even for a falsehood, since it was the Greeks who created the soul, discovered the self, ennobled men, and sought a distinctly human good. But facts are the pets of the positivists, those descendants of the evil Enlightenment (who themselves are descendents of the Greeks). Facts bark but will not bite—not to worry—though facts will shed on the sofa, sometimes piss elsewhere than their pan. It seems that facts have foregone the French for the time being, gone out of style along with Reason. Truth with an enlarged initial, Truth (the systematic side of the sentence, if facts are stamped on the other), Truth to the ancient Idealists (who are Capitalists to the core, one must suppose), to them Truth was merely a god to be sought out and reverenced, and not, as it was for the sophists, an annoying inconvenience.

---

11. I discuss Barthes, Balzac, and "Sarrasine" at greater length in the essay which follows this one, "The Death of the Author."

In the small myth in which Plato expresses his reservations about writing, the disadvantages he cites are certainly real and correct, as far as they go; but writing, as I've mentioned, has freed the mind (as it did Plato's) to consider far more complex matters than it ever could while operating orally, and if it has hastened the atrophy of our memory, it has saved us the trouble of holding in our head much that was not worth holding there.

Although the written and the printed word greatly impersonalize—indeed, standardize—our verbal tokens, they also objectify language, and hence the thoughts and feelings it contains, in an important way. Because what is written is always "out there"; because it is public and comparatively permanent and can be examined by many at relatively the same level of access and privilege; it is far easier to hold people to what they have said, and to expect a higher standard of care to be set, because, although the author is not present in the moment to produce the text, he is not dead (unless he is a committee, a bureau, an anonymous source, a corporate "spokesperson," an advertising agency). Print is a medium which encourages a greater scrupulosity of expression, and permits more refinement of idea, than the purely spoken (unless it is employed by a committee, a bureau, an anonymous source, a corporate "spokesperson," an advertising agency, a member of Congress). Of necessity, style becomes increasingly individual as the medium becomes a largely inexpressive and neutral one (unless it is employed by a committee, a bureau, an anonymous source, a corporate "spokesperson," an advertising agency, a member of Congress, a general of the army; then the medium's inexpressive and neutral qualities are exploited). It is the oral tradition which had to employ a shortened vocabulary, standardized epithets, and other mnemonic devices which encouraged its own kind of anonymity. The writer must make up for the loss of the spoken context, of the meaningful emotional environment of the uttered word, by emphasizing, and bringing under control, the few physical elements left. Above all, the written word must be so set down that it rises up immediately in its readers to the level of the ear, and becomes a vital presence in their consciousness. It asks, that is, to be performed; to be returned to the world of orality it came from; it asks to be said, to be sung.

Imagine that I was drawn to your body as a lover is drawn; then you would see that when I touch you I want it to carry my love to your heart; but that means that my feelings must be allowed to flow into my fingers; and that means that you must allow my finger to move along your nerves like a voice within a wire; then the sound of your heart will be, as well, the sound of my voice, and the sound of my voice—not as simple sound, not because it's mine, and not because my accent is so wondrously unique, but because it contains the touch of the true word—will circulate as one blood between us. This is what honest oratory, this is what poetry, is all about.

Even if our doubts about the existence of the Forms were multiple and enormous (as mine are), there is, unquestionably, an inner speech, a speech which represents our consciousness as it goes babbling on, and this internal talk cannot be replaced by writing. We may not be able to find our way past the last word to reach a wordless realm, as Plato desires us to do, but if we fail, we shall very likely find ourselves left with the spoken word as the only medium of real thought, although a few diagrams or mental pictures may sometimes supplement it, and machines make easy many wearisome computations. However rapidly our fingers move as we type our thoughts immediately into some machine, they were in unwritten form first, and will always be so.

Finally, the language we learn is a spoken one. It is speech which contains all our childhood fantasies, all our primitive and original impulses, our horror shows, our "mother-meanings," and whatever trips past the Forms we may have taken. And it is the sound of these early words, in the total context of their production, which gives them their emotional power, and connects them so closely with our basic desires.[12] The dark horse is stabled in the child. So the poet, the rhetorician, the philosopher, who thinks of a page as merely a page, and not as a field for the voice; who considers print to be simply print, and does not notice the notes it forms; whose style is disheveled and overcharged with energy or overrun with feeling, or whose frigid and compulsive orderings make the mouth dry; the author who is satisfied to *see* his words, as though at a distance like sheep on a hillside, and not as concepts coasting like clouds across his consciousness; such a writer will never enter, touch, or move the soul; never fill us with the feeling that he's seen the Forms, whether or not there are any; never give us that ride up the hill of Heaven as Plato has, or the sense that in accepting his words, we are accepting a vision.

---

12. I have argued this point in the essay in this volume called "The Soul Inside the Sentence." Other aspects of this question, which sometimes seems the single subject of the volume, are examined in "On Talking to Oneself" and "On Reading to Oneself."

THE DEATH OF THE AUTHOR

Popular wisdom warns us that we frequently substitute the wish for the deed, and when, in 1968, Roland Barthes announced the death of the author, he was actually calling for it.[1] Nor did Roland Barthes himself sign up for suicide, but wrote his way into the College of France where he performed *volte-faces* for an admiring audience.[2]

Many of the observations that Barthes makes in his celebrated essay are suggestive, opportune, and even correct; but none of them quite drives home the stake. The reasons for this are complex. The idea of the death of the author does not match the idea of the death of god as perfectly as the current members of this faith may suppose, because we know—as they know—that there *are* authors; and we know—as they know—there *are no* gods. The death of the author is not an ordinary demise, nor is it simply the departure of belief, like an exotic visitor from the East, from the minds of the masses. The two expressions are metaphors which are the reverse of one another. The death of god represents not only the realization that gods have never existed, but the contention that such a belief is no longer even irrationally possible: that neither reason nor the taste and temper of the times can condone it. The belief lingers on, of course, but it does so like astrology or a faith in a flat earth—in worse case than a neurotic symptom, no longer even *à la mode.* The death of the author, on the other hand, signifies a decline in authority, in theological power, as if Zeus were stripped of his thunderbolts and swans, perhaps residing on Olympus still, but now living in a camper and cooking with propane. He *is,* but he is no longer a god.

Barthes is careful to point out the theological overtones of his announcement.[3] Deities are in the business of design; they order oftener

---

1. "The Death of the Author," in *Image, Music, Text,* essays selected, edited, and translated by Stephen Heath (New York: Hill and Wang, 1977), pp. 142–148.
2. Jonathan Culler, *Roland Barthes* (New York: Oxford University Press, 1983), p. 119.
3. "The Death of the Author," in *Image, Music, Text,* p. 149.

than generals; the robes the painters put them in are juridical. God handed down the tablets of the law to Moses; and Jane Austen or Harriet Beecher Stowe hands down texts to us. While it is by no means necessary to put the author's powers and responsibilities in religious terms, Beckett's schoolboy copybooks are treated like tablets, too, and attract the scribes and the pharisees as though they'd been brought from a mountain. When John Crowe Ransom, in clearly secular language, praises Milton's "Lycidas" as "a poem nearly anonymous," he means to applaud the degree to which Milton has freed the poem from its poet, and consequently from the danger of certain legal difficulties.

> Anonymity, of some real if not literal sort, is a condition of poetry. A good poem, even if it is signed with a full and well-known name, intends as a work of art to lose the identity of the author; that is, it means to represent him not actualized, like an eye-witness testifying in court and held strictly by zealous counsel to the point at issue, but freed from his juridical or prose self and taking an ideal or fictitious personality; otherwise his evidence amounts the less to poetry.[4]

In this case, the disappearance of the author coincides with his arrogance, his overbearing presence. Joyce has Stephen Dedalus state the aim exactly:

> The personality of the artist, at first a cry or a cadence or a mood and then a fluid and lambent narrative, finally refines itself out of existence, impersonalizes itself, so to speak. The esthetic image in the dramatic form is life purified in and reprojected from the human imagination. The mystery of esthetic, like that of material creation, is accomplished. The artist, like the God of creation, remains within or behind or beyond or above his handiwork, invisible, refined out of existence, indifferent, paring his fingernails.[5]

The dramatist's curtained disappearance is not complete enough for Barthes. He knows that *"Madame Bovary—c'est moi!"* remains true despite Flaubert's celebrated detachment. He knows how the deity of tradition took delight in concealing himself. Hunt as hard as you cared to, he

---

4. "A Poem Nearly Anonymous," by John Crowe Ransom, in his collection of essays, *The World's Body* (New York: Charles Scribner's Sons, 1938), p. 2.

5. Stephen says this during a one-sided conversation with Lynch in the middle of the final chapter of *A Portrait of the Artist as a Young Man*. Lynch shortly follows this with the wry joke that God must have hidden himself after perpetrating Ireland.

could easily elude you if he wished. Still, such difficulties did not dampen the desire of the faithful to find him, or weaken in any way their belief that he was there. Zeus may have hidden his passion in the shape of a swan, but we are not obliged to believe that Leda felt simply some feathers. Circumstances have kept Shakespeare's life a secret from us, yet he has been hunted like a criminal. In volume after volume, his unknown character is cleverly constructed like a ship in a bottle. So Roland Barthes wishes to slay a spirit, dispel an aura. It is the demise of just that confident, coldly overbearing, creator—that so palpably erased and disdainfully imperial person of the artist—that he longs for.

It is apparent in the quotation from Joyce that when the work of writing has been done, the essential artistic task is over. The freedom from himself which the artist has given to his composition is the indifferent freedom of the Rilkean *Dinge,* an object which exists like a tree, a hat, or a stream, and like the stream scarcely needs canoes or campers to complete it; yet it is a thing whose modulated surfaces betray the consciousness it contains, and which we read, as we read words, to find the hand, the arm, the head, the voice, the self which is shaping them, which is arranging those surfaces—this second skin—to reflect an inside sun, and reveal the climate of an inner life. In the old theological mode, we thought to find god either through his revelations in sacred scripture or by studying what was thought to be his other great work of symbolization—the world; we applied ourselves, that is, to natural or to revealed religion. Nowadays, when the artist deliberately disappears, he may wish it to be thought that his work "just came about" naturally; grew the way crystals collect to create a flake of snow, perhaps, or more slowly, as deltas silt, or suddenly, the way islands rise up calamitously out of the sea; or, more ideally, in the manner in which a mollusk exudes a chamber about itself, quietly from within, brooding as the old gods did upon a basin of dark cloud and wind perhaps, or with a cluck now and then like a errant clock, intuitively shaping a shell. In this case, when the artist hides, it is in order to represent skill as instinct, intellect as reflex, choice as necessity, labor as slumberous ease.

Valéry writes:

> Perhaps what we call *perfection* in art (which all do not strive for and some disdain) is only a sense of desiring or finding in a human work the sureness of execution, the inner necessity, the indissoluble bond between form and material that are revealed to us by the humblest of shells.[6]

---

6. Paul Valéry, "Man and the Seashell," translated by Ralph Manheim for Vol. XIII, *Aesthetics,* of *The Collected Works in English* (New York: Pantheon, 1962), p. 27.

For Joyce, of course, this writing from which its designer—the deity—disappears seems authorless because there is no book to weigh in one's hands, no print, no page, no poet's voice: it is *performed;* the theater buries the text inside the bodies of its actors where their organs are. But we are also aware of the similarly scenic art of Henry James, of his effaced narrators and substitute selves, of various Ishmaels and many Marlowes, or of those poems which appear on parchmented pages as though scratched there by creatures long extinct.

> Calm covers the peaks.
> Among the treetops
> a breath hangs like a leaf.
> In the deep woods
> birdsong sleeps.
> At the foot of hills
> slopes find their peace.
> Be patient. Wait.
> Soon, you too, will cease.[7]

Richardson slips onto the title page of *Clarissa Harlowe* disguised as S. Richardson, the simple printer who has collected and edited the letters which comprise her unhappy history; Defoe suggests that Moll Flanders is the pseudonym of a well-known lady who tells her somewhat unwholesome story in his book; *Gulliver's Travels* is introduced by one Richard Sympson, an "ancient and intimate friend" of the author, and the man into whose economizing hands these papers have fallen (he tells us he's cut out dull stretches of seafaring stuff); while *The History of Henry Esmond* is brought before us by that late Virginia gentleman's daughter, Rachel Esmond Warrington, now, alas, a widow. These novels have very ostensible authors, to be sure, but they are artificial ones, surrogate pens or "dildos." Still, no one will imagine that Defoe or Swift or Thackeray felt that by placing these fictions in front of himself he was risking anonymity. A dildo is the discarded part of a dream.

Actually, a volume of letters, however modestly brought before the public, inordinately multiplies "authors," whose names appear, we suppose, at the end of every communication. These artful dodges (and it would be absurdly awful if they fooled anyone) strengthen the concepts of source and voice and purpose, control and occasion, which are central to the notion of a commanding creator, precisely because they call

---

7. Adapted from Goethe.

them into playful question. Thackeray pretends not to be responsible for *The History of Henry Esmond,* neither for writing it nor for bringing it to public notice, but Thackeray intends to accept all praise and monies due.

A few writers like us to believe that they are simply telling a story they have heard elsewhere; that they are therefore just "passing on," somewhat as any gossip might, some juicy bits, and cannot be held accountable for the sad and sordid facts involved; but many authors accept their responsibilities calmly enough and make no effort to conceal themselves or minimize the extent of their powers. Trollope, for instance, is a comfortable theist who appears on page after page in order to sustain and continue and comfort his creation. He is invariably concerned and polite. "We must beg to be allowed to draw a curtain over the sorrows of the archdeacon as he sat, sombre and sad at heart, in the study of his parsonage at Plumstead Episcopi." Furthermore, he will try to talk the reader out of what might be, perhaps, a too hasty judgment of character and motive. "He was avaricious, my readers will say. No—it was for no love of lucre that he wished to be bishop of Barchester."

The appearance of the author by our fireside; his chatty confidential tone; his certainty that he knows what we think and how we feel; his slightly admonitory manner; the frequent comparisons he draws between our condition and that of his characters; the comfortable clichés he draws around us like a shawl: these devices more readily make his world and his people real; whereas deists like Flaubert, like Henry James, like Joyce, who are satisfied to kick their creations out of the house when they've come of age; who wind their works up and then let them run as they may, and who cannot be recalled to rejoin or revise or reconsider anything by any plea or spell of magic or sacrifice or prayer; who leave it up to us to calculate and judge: their world is far less friendly, far less homey, far less "real." When Trollope comments: "Our archdeacon was worldly—who among us is not so?" he deftly implicates us in his activities.[8] We are all together in this, he suggests; I am speaking of the world each of us lives and loves and suffers in—no other, he implies; whereas the brilliant opening of *The Fifth Queen* is so immediately vivid and pictorial we must be somewhere outside it, viewing it as we might a painting or a movie screen. Trollope's relaxed and slippered style is just as skillful in its way as Ford's, but Ford's world is unmediated and set adrift; we shall never find a path through its cold and passionate landscapes on which our feet can be safely set; we shall only be able to observe these

8. These quotations are, of course, from the opening chapter of *Barchester Towers.*

historical figures connive and betray and ruin, and the light fall unsteadily on walls wet with the cold sweat of another age.

Pantheism is not out of the question as a possibility either. *The Notebooks of Malte Laurids Brigge* invent "another self" whose very name is a rhythmic echo of Rainer Maria Rilke; yet this other self, its almost unendurably beautiful and squalid encounters, these records of lonely reading and empty rooms and lovely yet lost objects, this static parade of exquisite perceptions that constitute the frozen friezelike flow of the book, are so infused with the poet's presence, the poet's particular sensibilities, that Malte, his surrogate, cannot avoid surrendering his self to his author's *style,* even when the outcome of his life appears to be different from his creator's. We might permit Malte to possess the thought that *"Denn Verse sind nicht, wie die Leute meinen, Gefühle (die hat man früh genug),—es sind Erfahrungen,"* but the movement of the mind (from cities, people, and things to animals, birds, and blooms), the music of the words (*"Um eines Verses willen muss man viele Städte sehen, Menschen und Dinge, man muss die Tiere kennen, man muss fühlen, wie die Vögel fliegen, und die Gebärde wissen, mit welcher die kleinen Blumen sich auftun am Morgen"*[9]), the romantic innocence of the idea, are unmistakably Rilkean. As we read along, Trollope's manner discreetly retires from sight and Mrs. Proudie and Mr. Slope are shortly there before us as plainly as two dogs in the yard. Malte feels, to be sure, yet what Malte feels can only have been informed and inhabited and carried to him by his ceaselessly zealous Creator.

When authorship is denied, it is often in order to extol certain sources or origins instead. It is easier for poets to pretend that they are merely an ear trumpet for the muse; that they have been so smitten with inspiration they scarcely recognize their own rhymes; because the creative pain of the poet can sometimes be measured in moments, especially if she scribbles; but the novelist cannot persuasively invent a spirit whose relief requires several years of sluiced transcendence, as if somewhere a spigot had been left on. Our author, in this unlikely case, is simply a conduit, or a place where the collective unconscious has risen up to refresh us like a bubbler in the park.

The *Geist* has been known to gather up unwary authors somewhat as

---

9. "For poems are not, as people think, simply emotions (one has emotions early enough)—they are experiences. For the sake of a single poem, you must see many cities, many people and Things, you must understand animals, must feel how birds fly, and know the gesture which small flowers make when they open in the morning." From Book I, Section 14: "I think I ought to begin to do some work . . ." This is Stephen Mitchell's translation (New York: Random House, 1983).

Zeus used to do with fleeing maidens, and plump them with proper thoughts and attitudes. If writers were not the instruments of history, as princes and politicians often were, they were at least a showcase, a display of the spirit, like a museum's costumed effigies, if not one of its principal actors. Historical forces of this sort are as crudely imaginary as deities have always been, although probably not nearly as harmful since they cannot capture the imagination of millions the way divinities do, especially the dime-store kind. But of course the *Geist* can go behind a curtain and come back out as the *Volk* or the *Reich* instead of the *Zeit*. Taine's version of this recipe would certainly have been familiar to Barthes, whose notion combines the concept of the author as conduit with that of the author as focal point: that hot spot where many causal rays have been concentrated.

Taine wished to understand his subjects (whether Spenser, Lyly, or Milton), in the first place by recreating the so-called external image of the man; by setting him out in the kind of clear hindsight which is the common sense and direction of history; and then to penetrate that picture to the moral condition which lay behind those features and animated them. Finally, he sought in race, epoch, and environment the conditions which came together to create the local climate of his case. He fashions, in other words, a chain of authors: the public figure, the inner man, the milieu. It is the right pull upon that chain which brings the gush.

There is clearly considerable satisfaction to be had in the removal of the poet from his or her position in the center of public adulation. Taine maliciously writes about

> A modern poet, a man like De Musset, Victor Hugo, Lamartine, or Heine, graduated from college and travelled, wearing a dress-coat and gloves, favored by ladies, bowing fifty times and uttering a dozen witticisms in an evening, reading daily newspapers, generally occupying an apartment on the second story, not over-cheerful on account of his nerves, and especially because, in this dense democracy in which we stifle each other, the discredit of official rank exaggerates his pretensions by raising his importance, and, owing to the delicacy of his personal sensations, leading him to regard himself as a Deity.[10]

Indeed, it is no longer the painter or the poet whom the public looks for, talking or scribbling away in some café's most prominent corner, but

---

10. Hippolyte Adolphe Taine, *History of English Literature,* trans. by Henry Van Laun, 3 vols. (New York: Colonial Press, 1900), Vol. I, p. 2.

(after Cocteau, who taught everyone the trade) a Sartre or a Barthes whom we hope to catch a glimpse of—a Lacan or Foucault, or some other impresario of ideas.

Parlor games, in which a poem is composed one line at a time by ine-briated guests, cancel authorship by allowing too many cooks to stir the broth. Occasionally, for sport and in despair, fiction writers will alter-nate the writing of a novel's chapters, and equally rarely, talents like Ford's and Conrad's will collaborate with a modest sort of success. In most cases, the schoolboy botches which result are so far from creating "a sense of a world" that no one would think to wonder about that world's authorship anyway.

The *renga,* a chain poem which made its first appearance in Japan in the eighth century, is a more serious collaboration; it is more serious simply because the participants generally are. When contemporary poets turn to it, their feelings are not dissimilar to Barthes':

> In contrast with the conception of a literary work as the imitation of antique models, the modern age has exalted the values of originality and novelty: the excellence of a text does not depend on its resemblance to those of the past, but on its unique character. Beginning with romanticism, tradition no longer signifies continuity by repetition and by variations within repetition; continuity takes the form of a leap, and tradition becomes a synonym for history: a succession of changes and breaks. The romantic fallacy: the literary work as an odd number, the reflection of the exceptional ego. I be-lieve that, today, this idea has reached its end.[11]

When, however, the *renga* turns out to be a chain forged in four different languages, we can justifiably suspect that oddness, and difference, will be its most striking distinction, and that the four authors will neither hide themselves behind one another nor disappear into the collective anonym-ity of the text, but will sign their names to the poem, and write of the feelings they had while composing it in reports which remind one of the ecstatic early accounts of group sex.[12]

It is not that "authorless" work in any of the senses I have so far sug-

---

11. Octavio Paz, from his introduction to *Renga: A Chain of Poems,* by Octavio Paz, Jacques Roubaud, Edoardo Sanguineti, and Charles Tomlinson (New York: George Braziller, 1971).
12. Ibid. Paz speaks first of a "feeling of abandonment," then a "sensation of oppression," followed by a "feeling of shame," a "feeling of voyeurism," a "feeling of returning." It is all very operatic. They are only writing a poem, after all, these poets; but they must pretend they are having a religious experience. The fiction is that the poem is all-

gested can never be excellent, or that novels with a great degree of authorial visibility must always be romantic, bourgeois, and decadent, because fine work of both kinds exists; rather, it should be recognized that the elevation or removal of the author is a social and political and psychological gesture, and not an esthetic one. We can characterize art as anonymous or not, but this characterization will tell us nothing, in advance of our direct experience of the building, the canvas, the score, or the text, about its artistic *quality*. Furthermore, this "anonymity," as we've seen, may mean many things, but one thing which it cannot mean is that *no one did it*.

Unless one imagines a computer which has been fed every rule of language, the principles of every literary genre, the stylistic tics of all the masters and their schools, and so on. Then poem and story might emerge from this machine, to the astonishment, boredom, or ruin of readers, like race or market results; and it could say—if asked as Polyphemus was— that no man did it.

So art can seem authorless to me because *I don't know who did it;* or because *I can't tell who did it;* because *I don't care who did it;* or because *it simply doesn't matter who did it;* or because *it just happened and nobody did it*. That is: one is the piece of sea wrack I pick up from the beach; another is like "ding dong bell, pussy's down the well"; still another resembles your average TV serial segment; and then there is that tune I know from somewhere, but can't remember, and can't guess; and that enigmatic couplet carved on an ancient rock whose author has vanished forever into the hard lilt of its cruel vowels.

It may at first seem that the effacement of the author was an act of modesty, and the familiar fatherly storyteller's style of Trollope, and other writers like him, was authoritarian and manipulative, in as much as they gave nothing away to the reader, and took on the point of view of a tower; but the opposite is clearly the case. Trollope knows everything necessary to tell the tale, to be sure, and presents himself comfortably in that cloth; but Flaubert is not telling a tale, he is constructing a world; he is putting it together atom by atom, word by word. Trollope is merely inserting his characters into the well-known world of his readers, readers who take their daily life enough for granted that long ago they stopped looking at it; they scarcely any longer even live it, but use all their inner

---

important, when only the fact that they are writing it together really is.

Anonymity can be chosen by the poet because it is a humbling or self-mortifying condition. One wishes to give up the selfish self and become a selfless self. Selflessness is the highest form of selfishness there is because of the demands "it" makes upon others.

tubes to float on top; so that when Trollope looks and lives, his readers are surprised at what they see and feel. Flaubert, however, cannot count on the comfortable collusion of his readers to solidify his world through their inattention and neglect; it is not the reader's funny bone he wishes to tickle, but the text he wishes to shape so securely a reader will not be necessary. Flaubert wants to expose his "readers" to their world of papered-over problems and foully bloated hopes by unupholstering their souls, lowering their ceilings to the true level of their aspirations; he wants to demonstrate to them that they are only devouring the world and making shit out of their lives; he can hardly count on their help; their "help" would subvert his enterprise. Flaubert cannot ask for, cannot count on, readers in the old sense, then, for each is only too likely to be another *hypocrite lecteur,* however much each also is *mon semblable, mon frère.* Thus the author becomes a god, instead of someone's garrulous uncle, because the author now disdains those lower and local relations, and has left home sweet home in disgust. *Madame Bovary* is not a chair for a fat burgher's Sunday snooze; it *is* the fat burgher himself, breaded and greasy and mostly buns. His home is a White Castle.

When the author detaches himself from the text, he detaches the reader at the same time, then, and it is this unpleasant consequence which Barthes is responding to. Trollope is telling his story to someone, and even when, as in the case of the epistolary novel, the messages are not addressed to the reader directly, they are addressed to someone; they remain communications; and the three-term relation of writer-letter-recipient is maintained. But if no one has written or posted the word, then no one is addressed by the word. The letter is no longer a letter. A does not equal A. What would the sign BUY BILGE'S BEER mean or be, if it were carefully posted at one of the poles?

The author becomes a god at the moment he no longer believes in gods, and just because the gods are dead; yet not because, as Taine implies, he suddenly sees a vacancy (although socially that might very well describe his motives), but because a world without god must be a world without true believers too. Yet this writerless, readerless world must be made by someone, a deity of the undivine kind, a god in lower case.

The moment god goes, the text becomes sacred (unalterable, revered, studied, paraphrased, guarded, handed on). Consider the deist's contention. If god is on permanent vacation elsewhere, then this world is all there is; it is the entire text; only from it can truths be learned; and if this world is to run, and run successfully, it must run on by itself, on its own four wheels; while, finally, if god gave us a message when he made this world, he did not wait around for our understanding or reply, both of which become, if not irrelevant to us, certainly irrelevant to him (since he is out of hearing), as well as to the world itself (which is blind and dumb and deaf and thoroughly uncaring). It is not clear that it is a text in the traditional sense. Suppose that idling down an alley as is my wont, I pick up a scrap of paper which has blown from some pile of trash. Examining it, I read:

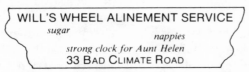

WILL'S WHEEL ALINEMENT SERVICE
sugar
nappies
strong clock for Aunt Helen
33 BAD CLIMATE ROAD

Like the sign that said 𝔅𝔲𝔶 𝔅𝔦𝔩𝔤𝔢'𝔰 𝔅𝔢𝔢𝔯, these words have wandered away, even from one another. A reminder without mind, purpose, or point, like works of modern art, they merely appear. Made of words, they are not now a message. What is there here to take to heart, to puzzle over, to believe?

The basic folly of Bouvard and Pécuchet (those two aforetime Beckettean clowns) is that, in a world like WILL'S WHEEL ALINEMENT SERVICE, they do, nevertheless, believe things; they believe them right into the ground; they sincere systems to death; they accept explanations like a crematorium its corpses. In *Finnegans Wake* a hen scratches a meaningless message out of a midden. Both world and work are simply *here*. No one asked for either. John Barth's Todd Andrews has enormous difficulties making up his mind what is what or which or whether.[13] The world we're in is one of authorless accident, comical suffering and tragic confusion; it is the world of WILL'S WHEEL ALINEMENT SERVICE, while the *Wake* is entirely internal, its "nothing" signifying sound and fury. The *Wake* is a replacement for the world. Unlike the world, it is over-made of meanings. Like the world, it does not mean.

If the author goes, taking the reader with him, into some justifiable oblivion, he does not omit to leave his signature behind, just the same. Indeed, he not only signs every sheet, he signs every word. Erased, Flaubert's careful concern cries out, "Me me me." Removing himself, Henry James in his late manner *maître d*'s everything. The *Wake* calaminates, just before it doesn't conclude: "mememormee! Till thousendsthee." Here is a further example of pure signature prose:

---

13. In *The Floating Opera* (New York: Doubleday, 1956). Barth is not to be seen. Andrews is writing his own story, but he immediately points out how limited his powers are: he cannot imagine, he is stuck with the truth. "I look like what I think Gregory Peck, the movie actor, will look like when he's fifty-four . . . (The comparison to Mr. Peck isn't intended as self-praise, only as description. Were I God, creating the face of either Todd Andrews or Gregory Peck, I'd change it just a trifle here and there.)" When a fictional figure speaks to the reader the way Trollope spoke to him, and as Todd Andrews not infrequently does, he intends the reader to become a fiction. How else will they hold a conversation?

> . . . I felt acutely unhappy about my dutiful little student as
> during one hundred and fifty minutes my gaze kept reverting
> to her, so childishly slight in close-fitting gray, and kept ob-
> serving that carefully waved dark hair, that small, small-
> flowered hat with a little hyaline veil as worn that season and
> under it her small face broken into a cubist pattern by scars
> due to a skin disease, pathetically masked by a sunlamp tan
> that hardened her features, whose charm was further impaired
> by her having painted everything that could be painted, so
> that the pale gums of her teeth between cherry-red chapped
> lips and the diluted blue ink of her eyes under darkened lids
> were the only visible openings into her beauty.

The "I" of this brief instructional tale[14] is not that of the great Vladimir,
Napoleon of Prose, but the style is certainly his. We are meant to be daz-
zled, humbled, tossed into awe as though it were a ditch alongside the
road.

The "I" is not Nabokov—no—yet this "I" teaches literature (French,
not Russian) at a girls' college (not a women's college, not Cornell) in an
Ithaca, New York, climate (no mistaking that upper New York snow and
ice, icicles carefully described), so that we are led roundabout to wonder
if. Again, this sort of teasing is deliberate.

Whether the scholar sees the genial Trollope seated comfortably in
the text, or the irascible Flaubert skulking angrily behind his, critics continue to "tyrannically center," as Barthes puts it, "the image of literature
on . . . the author, his person, his life, his tastes, his passions . . ."[15]
but they have reached their quarry by different routes: content in the
first case, style in the second. Of course, Trollope's tone tells a tale as
well as Nabokov's does, but Nabokov's arrogance is formal, relational,
and his control is not that of a fatherly Czar but that of the secret police.
The performative "I declare," "I sing," "I write," does not, in fact, cut
the text off at the point of the pen, as Barthes seems to think. Nabokov's
passage *is* a performance . . . and a good one. In this sense, Trollope's
touch could only dull the master's quill.

The problem is not, I think, whether the author is present in the work
in one way or another, or whether the text will ever interest us in her,
her circle, her temper and times; but whether the text can take care of

---

14. Vladimir Nabokov, "The Vane Sisters," in *Tyrants Destroyed and Other Stories* (New
York: McGraw Hill, 1975). The balance of "between . . . lips" and "under . . . lids"
is particularly artful, as is the repeated use of 'small,' and the music of passages like "the
diluted blue ink of her eyes . . ."
15. "The Death of the Author," in *Image, Music, Text*, p. 143.

itself, can stand on its own, or whether it needs whatever outside help it can get; whether it leads us out and away from itself or regularly returns us to its touch the way we return to a lovely stretch of skin. Certainly some readers are anxious to be distracted, and arrive in a work like a nervous traveler at a depot. There are four winds, and four cardinal points of the compass; there are seven precious metals, seven days of the week, and ten wonders of the world; but there are six regularly scheduled trains out of the text:

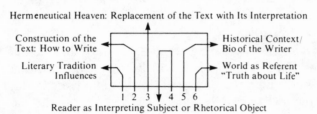

Hermeneutical Heaven: Replacement of the Text with Its Interpretation

Construction of the Text: How to Write

Historical Context/ Bio of the Writer

Literary Tradition Influences

World as Referent "Truth about Life"

1 2 3   4 5 6

Reader as Interpreting Subject or Rhetorical Object

When Nabokov halts his "I" on its walk in order to render an icicle in full formation, there is no question that the world, with its notions about the proper procedures for freezing and thawing, is partly directing his pen. Is it, then, the artful author of this passage?

> . . . I had stopped to watch a family of brilliant icicles drip-dripping from the eaves of a frame house. So clear-cut were their pointed shadows on the white boards behind them that I was sure the shadows of the falling drops should be visible too. But they were not. The roof jutted out too far, perhaps, or the angle of vision was faulty, or, again, I did not chance to be watching the right icicle when the right drop fell. There was a rhythm, an alternation in the dripping that I found as teasing as a coin trick.

And are the laws of light and shadow determining this?

> And as I looked up at the eaves of the adjacent garage with its full display of transparent stalactites backed by their blue silhouettes, I was rewarded at last, upon choosing one, by the sight of what might be described as the dot of an exclamation mark leaving its ordinary position to glide down very fast— a jot faster than the thaw-drop it raced.

And is the world of melting snow and forming ice our readerly destination? Do we want to stand in the snow, too, with this "I" which is soon then to be ourselves? But this "I" cannot be ourselves, for its observations are both beyond us and beyond the world.

> This twinned twinkle was delightful but not completely satis-
> fying; or rather it only sharpened my appetite for other tid-
> bits of light and shade, and I walked on in a state of raw
> awareness that seemed to transform the whole of my being
> into one big eyeball rolling in the world's socket.[16]

Physical phenomena clearly have a finger if not a hand in the composition of these passages, but the choice of event, selection of details,
arrangement of elements, turns of phrase and pace of words, all the
higher functions of relevance and association, imagery and implication:
these are controlled by Nabokov and increasingly by the character of
the little device he is creating; that is, a short story about two sisters,
Cynthia and Sybil Vane (Sybil will be a suicide, Cynthia a victim of
heart disease), and Cynthia's belief in haunting shades and interfering
spirits. As the text grows, its demands grow; but the text can make these
demands only in terms of certain principles of composition which the
author accepts: coherence, for instance, fulfillment of expectation, sufficient reason, and so on.

Imagine, for a moment, that our text were a chair. We might say our
six kinds of thing about it, and each remark might be relevant to some
interest or other we might have; but what is important to notice, here,
is what gets left out, goes unsaid.

(1) This chair has clearly been built in accordance with patterns first
displayed in Clarence Chipfall's design book (1837). Certainly not
early, probably not late, I should say it was a mid-Chipfall chair. Fes-
tooning the legs with shredded velvet, however, suggests an Ottoman
influence, probably added later.

(2) If you tip the chair over you can see that it is fashioned of inter-
locking pieces of cherry and lime wood, grooved so as to pass the seater's
energy along a transfiguring path into the large fat oak legs.

(3) The stern right-angularity of this steel-stiffened chair signifies the
puritanical ideal in one of its revengeful modes. This is an electric chair,
if you like, before electricity.

(4) Anyone who sits in this chair will be reminded of two things principally: their onerous duties and their extraordinary powers, for its
harshness is regal, its squareness that of the pew in a country church.

(5) Chipfall's mother had carried little Chipper in a wooden tube
upon her back until well past twelve, whereupon he erupted from the
tube with a terrible cry; that cry is probably the pain behind the painful
sidearms this chair presses against us.

---

16. "The Vane Sisters," in *Tyrants Destroyed and Other Stories*. These three passages are
from pages 119, 120.

(6) We would expect chairs of this sort to come from the kind of hung-up and repressed Capitalist lackey which Chipfall represented so perfectly.

Although there are many references, here, to how this chair must feel when sat in, they are used only as evidence for other elements and aspects, and whether the chair is handsome, or not; whether it is lovely to look at, to touch, to loll in, to place in positions of interest in a room: these qualities are ignored. Yet in fiction, quality ought to author everything.

Actually, Roland Barthes, while appearing to free the text from such externals, is going to tie it rather firmly to two of them: the literary tradition and social usage on the one hand, and the reader's caprices on the other. He sees the writer as a kind of whirling drain, sucking texts into its ambiguous body and then concentrating their fall upon the page. The text, Barthes argues, is

> a multidimensional space in which a variety of writings, none of them original, blend and clash. The text is a tissue of quotations drawn from innumerable centres of culture. Similar to Bouvard and Pécuchet, those eternal copyists, at once sublime and comic and whose profound ridiculousness indicates precisely the truth of writing, the writer can only imitate a gesture that is always anterior, never original. His only power is to mix writings, to counter the ones with the others, in such a way as never to rest on any one of them.[17]

Let us shape a situation which will really fit Barthes' conditions. The lanky young man who bags our groceries has just dropped the flour on top of the broccoli. He hoists the sack into the cart, and says, with a vacant smile he points vaguely in our direction:

HAVE A NICE DAY

---

17. "The Death of the Author," in *Image, Music, Text,* p. 146. These views are the consequence of Barthes' work on *S/Z,* and his disclosure of all the "codes" which come together in "Sarrasine," the Balzac short story which he has taken as his specimen text, and quotes again in his essay on the death of the author.

Our young man is scarcely the author of this unmeant hope we have just now been commanded to realize. The English language provides its grammar and vocabulary; our present sales and marketing customs furnish the expression itself; the manager of the store supplies the impulse and determines its timing (so that the bagger does not utter his platitudes· and *then* bruise the broccoli). The carry-out boy (whose jacket says, "I'm Fred," although this is a bit misleading since he's borrowed the coat from a friend, having forgotten, in his habitual a.m. haste, to wear his own) is a willing automaton. Still, we can see his lips move inside that smile like a little wrinkle in a wrinkle, and we hear the words issue from him. Suppose they were written on his jacket? that jacket whose name is Fred. In that case, there wouldn't even be a cartoon balloon around the words, with a string depending from it toward his mouth. The expression would resemble our odd scrap on which WILL'S WHEEL ALINEMENT SERVICE was found—'alignment' spelled, we would have to observe, in a typically lower-class way, obedient to the social code. As Barthes argues, writing removes the writer from the words.

Our author thinks, "Orlando—Orlando was," and then writes 'He' (to stand for Orlando, for there could be no doubt about his sex, though the fashion of the time did something to disguise it); writes that Orlando was in the act of slicing—swinging—cutting—slicing—using words which are transcribed by her secretary's typing machine (losing the effect of that lovely swirling hand, so especially graceful at crossing tees), and subsequently mailed to an editor who will peevishly mark it up (wondering if our author oughtn't to write 'blackamoor' instead of simply 'moor' and a whole lot else in the same vein), only to pass the ms on to a printer who, in due course, will produce new and original errors in the galleys. When the galleys are finally corrected, everyone within reach of both a pencil and the words will have had a hand in them. During this process it even might look for a time as if Orlando were going to be replaced by Rudolph at a pretty copy editor's suggestion, but, to the relief of literature, at the last moment a *stet* is put beside his name, allowing Orlando to remain. So now he can be seen (for there can be no doubt about her sex) at the top of the book's first page, slicing at the head of a moor which is swinging from the rafters.

Office memos, guidelines, brochures, official handouts, architectural programs, presidential speeches, screen plays, are oftener in worse case because they are customarily constructed on assembly lines, by gangs and other committees, by itinerant troupes of clerical assistants. The Surgeon General warns us that smoking is hazardous to our health. Does *he?* Does *he* indeed?

Every step I have described has taken us away from the vocal source (if there was one, for perhaps she never said aloud or to herself, "Orlando," since it is a name people are often embarrassed to utter), and removed its original maker from significant existence the way Will's scrap of paper, which we fetched from the wind and took to the pole, was removed; yet this is hardly surprising because no one *authors* their speech, they simply speak it. It is necessary to say we author what we write precisely because what we write is disconnected from any mouth we might actually observe rounding itself for the 'Os' required to produce 'Or lan dO'; so that the question imperatively arises: who, indeed, has made these marks? whose is the responsible pen?

"Suddenly a burst of applause which shook the house greeted the prima donna's entrance," Balzac writes,[18] after carefully collecting the correct clichés, for applause always bursts; when it does so it always shakes the house; it invariably greets an entrance, which, of course, is what actors and actresses *make*. No wonder Barthes uses "Sarrasine" as an example of the dead hand of the author, for it would be hard to compose a more dismally anonymous sentence, except that Balzac has had practice, and this one is succeeded and preceded by hundreds of others its equal. "The Marquis went out at five," Paul Valéry's *bête noire* (it was certainly not his *bête bleue*), is, by comparison, inimitable. Balzac creates strangeness out of phrases which his readers will be *completely used to and entirely comfortable with*. As his readers sail along through the story, they will not have to think or realize or recreate or come to grips with anything. Nothing can trouble this salvelike surface. "Sarrasine" is a story whose merit is to seem not to be there, and one can imagine Balzac removing originality from it like unwanted hair.[19]

Virginia Woolf no doubt changed many things while she wrote, adding images, crossing out details, removing words, transposing paragraphs, perhaps pages, reconceiving the entire enterprise, falling into foul moods, later climbing out of them, altering herself when she mooned over Vita Sackville-West and remembered Knole, somewhat as her hero progresses from one sex to another. Was Joyce the selfsame man who began *Finnegans Wake* when, fifteen years later, he woke from it? Certainly Malcolm Lowry's bout with *Under the Volcano* (begun when he was a much younger and certainly less well informed writer than Joyce

---

18. "(216) ★ ACT.: Theater: 6: entrance of the star," in *S/Z*, translated by Richard Miller (New York: Hill and Wang), 1974, p. 111.
19. Every attempt at something striking, such as the features of a beautiful woman—"each pore has a special brilliance"—is catastrophic. Ibid., p. 34.

was when he began the *Wake*) involved more than one personality and bears witness to different levels of skill and conception. *Malte Laurids Brigge* is many things, and one of them was to be a course of therapy for a deeply troubled Rilke so that he would not become "his other self." It is unlikely that one inflexible self wrote *Orlando,* nor did it spring into being all at once as it does when we open its covers now. We know how all the other Orlandos influenced her; how she researched the Great Frost before she composed that amazing description of it; how faithfully she frequented the British Museum, and how much she loved memoirs, biography, and other historical texts.

A poet's life, like Chatterton's, may be no longer than a midge's, and yet many poems may be appended to his name, because poems can occasionally be blurted; but works of prose, as I've pointed out, involve time in an essential way, and can have a single author only in the traditional metaphysical sense that they possess (as even the saddest of ordinary mortals does) an enduring, central, stubbornly unchanging self, that "me" that is the permanent object of the "I," perhaps within the child as a state of lucent potentiality, and translucent to the point of invisibility when past its prime, but an unshakable unity nevertheless.

Even quite integrated normal persons, as we know, have many capabilities and moods and temperaments, so that simple "evenness" is not the answer, although it is commonly felt that a unified work of literature should seem to have a single author (unless, like the style of much of "Sarrasine," the work is so undistinctive, bland, and featureless—so anonymous, so nerdsome—as to suggest a corporate, collective self); so that what any actual author must do, divided as she often is into whore and housewife and shrew and mum and cook and clotheshorse and girl scout, nanny and nursemaid, choirgirl and choregirl and list maker, cheerleader and hash slinger and Model C, Gentle Annie and Madame La Morte and La Belle Dame Sans Merci, into left breast—ummm!—then right, and eardrum off which the brags of men bounce with a siss-boom, boomsiss we all enjoy, and eye in whose loving gaze great men grow up from little lads and finks and fat louts into troubadours and totem designers and business thieves and all that . . . while contriving to preserve as many faces as the moon . . . to vary and interest and entice . . . and all that . . . is to construct the ideal abstract author of her text, and then try to accommodate, corset if necessary—constrict—her multifarious nature to that less variable but often more reliable and attractive, though entirely artificial, being: the real fiction of the fiction. From the poem the reader projects the poet, too—not a person but the poet of the poem.

Hume has warned us that if we wish to infer a creator solely from the evidence of a creation, we cannot attribute to it any other character, qualities, or power than would be strictly necessary to produce the thing, the song, or world in question. Nor can we forget (when we are busy imagining the author of *Waverley* or *Lady Chatterley's Lover* or *The World as Will and Representation* or *The Life of Reason*) the silly, incompetent, or wicked things the work accomplishes as well—the insane mix of planning and chance, absurdity and design, incompetence and skill, which is the rule in most cases—just because we wish to bring "good ole glory" to a name, for the name will no longer designate the necessary author or the less necessary personality behind the art, but still another kind of slippery fiction.

The intention of the author is only occasionally relevant, but if we believe at all in the Unconscious, or in the impossibility of literally nothing escaping the author's clear awareness and control, then the artificial author (the author which the text creates, not the author who creates the text) will be importantly different from the one of flesh and blood, envy and animosity, who holds the pen, and whose picture enlivens the gray pages of history. Strictly speaking, Scott is both more and less than *the* author of *Waverley*.[20]

In so far as an expression such as "the author of *Waverley*" is a definite description of Scott and is, like his various names and nicknames, substitutable for him in any sentence, then it is possible to write: "The author of *Waverley* was born last night during a rainstorm." This suggests considerable foreknowledge, or it suggests, as it did to Leibniz, that one's future is indeed a seed inside the self. But the death of Scott did not coincide with the death of the author of *Waverley*. The author of *Waverley* is still alive.

In certain cases, further complications arise. When an author devotes a great portion of a writing life to one work, as Dante did, or Spenser did, or Proust, then the likelihood that the work itself will begin to overwhelm and almost entirely occupy the arena of ordinary life grows great, because the writer will surely have imagined marriages more interesting than her own, deaths more dismaying than that of Uncle Charley, or invented characters with more quality than her children, who simply sniffle, skin knees, and fail in school; she will not carry on her fictional affairs like boring conversations; she will have fallen in love with a rake of her

---

20. For example, consult the little parable "Borges and I," in *Labyrinths*, edited by Donald A. Yates and James E. Irby (New York: New Directions, 1964), pp. 246–247. Borges writes: "I live, let myself go on living, so that Borges may contrive his literature, and this literature justifies me."

own devising. Proust's book became a second cork-lined room around him; Flaubert's letters reflect the fact that his writing desk is both board and bed; the nighttime life of the *Wake* compensates for a failing sight. That is, works not only imply an artificial author, they profoundly alter, sometimes, the nature of the historical one. God, himself, I suspect, has been made worse by the world.

That characters get out of control, that the uncompleted text takes over its completion, was a commonplace long before E. M. Forster complained of it,[21] or Flann O'Brien made it a compositional directive.[22] And Vladimir Nabokov's little story about the Vane sisters doubles the dialectical interference of text with intention, intention with text. Cynthia's death provokes in the narrator the expectation of her ghostly appearance. His sleep is soon troubled by a dream about her, but this is hardly the apparition he hopes for and fears. Though the narrator puzzles himself about it, the dream yields him nothing. He and the story conclude:

> I could isolate, consciously, little. Everything seemed blurred, yellow-clouded, yielding nothing tangible. Her inept acrostics, maudlin evasions, theopathies—every recollection formed ripples of mysterious meaning. Everything seemed yellowly blurred, illusive, lost.[23]

Nabokov, however, has not concluded *his* fun, for the first letters of the words which make up that final paragraph provide a message: 'IciclEsbycyntHiameterfrommesybil'; that is: "Icicles by Cynthia, meter from me, Sybil."

If the author had not waited until the twentieth century to pass on, but had gone off more quickly, rather like fish, Galileo wouldn't have had to publish his work anonymously and in another country far from his own place of residence; neither would all those amiable works of erotica have had to hide their heads—they could have ridden out happily headless, written simply by a raunchy *Weltgeist;* Charlotte Brontë wouldn't have had to give birth to Currer Bell or die as C. B. Nicholls while trying to recover from her pregnancy; neither should we have seen originate a distinct species of posthumous writing, a genre practiced to perfection by Kafka, and one to which some work of Descartes, and the

---

21. In *Aspects of the Novel* (New York: Harcourt Brace, 1927), p. 102.
22. In *At Swim-Two-Birds* (London: 1939). O'Brien is a text weaver, his novel is a "book web," and he even uses a pseudonym, yet few novels belong more completely to their maker.
23. "The Vane Sisters," in *Tyrants Destroyed and Other Stories,* p. 238.

Dialogues of Hume, belong. The pseudonyminal pranks of Saki, Kierke-gaard, and Brian Ó Nualláin (a.k.a Brian O'Nolan, Myles na gCopaleen, John James Doe, George Knowall, Brother Barnabas, the Great Count O'Blather, and Flann O'Brien) would not have been necessary.

The author of *At Swim-Two-Birds* may have been born during a rain-storm, but Flann O'Brien, which is the name of the author of *At Swim-Two-Birds,* was not. Many and sharp are the philosophical rocks in this apparently calm cool pool.

If Roland Barthes had been interested in radically simplifying the Final Solution to the Author Question (and I've tried to indicate and describe, here, some of the members of this rather heteronomous race) by removing those authors who come to claim every fresh text like red ants to a wound, he could have adopted the "single author" theory first, either as it is alluded to by Borges or proposed by Gertrude Stein or im-plied by Hegel. Then, with this plurality of persons—real, inhuman, arti-ficial, and imaginary—reduced to manageable proportions, a single stroke across the top of the word would have been enough. An ~~author~~ can't author anything.

Stein distinguishes (to consider her version for only a moment)[24] be-tween what she calls human nature, on the one hand (a physical exis-tence which establishes for the writer a notable identity in time and a visitable locale in space; the person whose likeness is taken up to put on postage stamps, who cashes the checks, and whose character can be counterfeited if one gets hold of the appropriate documents and facts; the "I" of "I am I because my little dog knows me," the border guard's identity), and the human mind, on the other (a universal level of cre-ativity and thought which moves evenly between Kant-like entities, be-tween *Dings* and *Sichs;* that elevation we refer to when we speak of the way a work may transcend its Oxford, Mississippi, milieu, for instance, its Colombian quaintness, the author's alcoholism or mushy obsession with mom, to achieve a readily understandable meaning and an imme-diately shareable emotion; the "I" of "I am not I any longer when I see," because I have allowed myself to become the object).

Every author has an identity, but masterpieces are written by the hu-man mind, not by human nature, which only lends them their common smell and color, their day-to-day dust. The implication is that readers differ as dogs do, though all have a nose and a tail. Readers dislike works which seem superior to them, indifferent to them, proud. It is

24. Gertrude Stein, *The Geographical History of America,* with an introduction by W. H. Gass (New York: Vintage, 1973). This book develops, perhaps at unnecessary length, ideas contained in her somewhat earlier essay, "What Are Masterpieces, and Why Are There So Few of Them?"

sometimes pedagogically profitable to pretend that *Mansfield Park,* for instance, was written by Thomas Mann, just to see what such an assumption does to our ordinary expectations, and normal ways of reading. A masterpiece is often read (without any classroom coaxing) as if it were by James Michener or Harold Robbins (it is the principal way Proust suffers from his society-swallowing and gossipacious fans); but the works of the human mind are really addressed to other human minds. The ineffable persona which a poem implies will be "the human mind" if the poem achieves greatness in someone's otherwise empty head, may flatter its eager reader into a feeling of self-transcendence, but that will be as temporary as any flatulence; meanwhile, the fatuous little *New Yorker* story that has caused an additional foot to fall along the avenues, will fasten its agreeable reader to a nice white rock in Westchester or to a club in O'Hara country, and leave him to be consumed by what consumes him: hungry trademarks and vicious localisms and greedy proper names. It will stimulate his determinate and causal—his purely chemical—self. The anonymity which the superb poem or fiction presumably possesses, according to some theories, may consequently depend on a kind of spiritual consanguinity.

The ordinary author, then, may indeed be no more than a blender of texts, and hence may have no "life" left when times change, fads fail; but Roland Barthes is not hailing the death of these authors—inevitable anyway—but the death of the *real* ones, so that their texts may survive in the hearts of their readers. Why must they be orphaned, if not to find new homes? The death of god, the death of the author—aren't we really calling for the death of the father?

Because we borrow, beg, buy, steal, or copy texts; because texts enter our eyes but remain in the blood; because we are, as authors, plagiarists and paraphrasers and brain pickers and mockingbirds; because of these and other like habits we are, in effect, translating texts from one time to another and one context to another and one language to another. If, instead of repeating, "Have a nice day," we suggested to strangers that they "lead a good life," we have simply rearranged a slightly different little cluster of clichés. But all that any author works with, in the beginning, is given her by one corrupted magus after another: the language, the life she leads, the literary tradition, schools she attends, the books she reads, the studies she has undertaken; so she cannot lay claim to some syntax or vocabulary, climate of ideas or custom of entertaining, as hers, and hers alone, and therefore as special as she is. Neither is that inadequacy she is supposed to feel at the close of her office hours the feeling of a freak. Of course a great deal of what we all do and think and feel and write is no more uniquely had or imagined than the balloon I drew to represent the voice cloud of the bagger; the stream of life is rarely more than a pisser's trickle; and literally millions of sentences are penned or typed or spoken every day which have only one source—a spigot or a signboard, and not an author;[25] they have never been near a self which is so certain of its spirit and so insistent on its presence that it puts itself in its syllables like Mr. Gorgeous in his shimmering gown. "When all that was was fair," Joyce writes, describing Paradise, and in that simple rearrangement of the given and the inevitable and the previous, he triumphs, making something new, in Pound's sense, and in that way *breaking through the circle of society*. With one's pittance, one can make another pittance or a palace.

The Goethe poem, which I quoted earlier with deceitful intent, is scarcely his any more (nor would he claim it).[26] None of the formalities match. The idea may still be there like an ancient tree in a neglected park. But that's what we do: for good or ill we incessantly transmute. What I am emptying my bladder of, behind that tree in that neglected park, was once a nice hot cup of green tea.

Balzac never betrays the bourgeois, never breaks through the circle of society, because he employs forms which they understand and use themselves (for instance, the ladderlike structure of life in school—first grade, second grade, third grade, and so on; the ladderlike structure of life in the family—birth, bawl, crawl, walk, talk, read, write, disobey; the ladderlike structure of life in the church—birth, baptism, confirmation . . . in business, in society, the same sort of ladder; each rung of which points the way and evaluates all progress, not just from cradle to grave, but from birth to bequest); Balzac relishes their stereotypes and pat phrases and vulgar elegancies; his taste is that of the turtle which has found itself in a robust soup; he, too, would flatter the reader, the public, the world which receives him until it receives him well and warmly; and Roland Barthes, for all his fripperies like lace on a sleeve, for all his textual pleasures, which imply a more courtly era, is no better, accepting a pseudoradical role as if it were the last one left in the basket.

---

25. "(439) *This was woman herself, with her sudden fears, her irrational whims, her instinctive worries, her impetuous boldness, her fussings, and her delicious sensibility.* ★ SEM. Femininity. The source of the sentence cannot be discerned. Who is speaking? Is it Sarrasine? the narrator? the author? Balzac-the-author? Balzac-the-man? romanticism? bourgeoise? universal wisdom? The intersecting of all these origins creates the writing." *S/Z*, pp. 172–173. In "The Death of the Author" (p. 142), this condition is suggested as the norm for *all* writing.

26. "*Über allen Gipfeln/ist Ruh/in allen Wipfeln/spürest du/kaum einen Hauch. Die Vöglein schweigen im Walde. Warte nur: balde/ruhest du auch.*"

Balzac's revelations, however critical and "daring" and suggestive, pet the bourgeois to the purr point because they are revelations which remain in their world and in their language like dummies in a window. Though more perceptive than most, more sensitive, even more moral and upright (let us grant), and undoubtedly a genius, Balzac is more moral the way more money is more money; his is the ultimate hosanna of utility; however hard his eye, his look will land light.

"Sarrasine" is corrupt in both its art and its attitudes, and this is the one thing Roland Barthes' extensive commentary neglects to point out. Rodin's statue of a nude and arrogant Balzac is a bother to us, but not Balzac, whose arrogance is the arrogance of the best men of business, and who deserves to be wearing at least a hat. That is why we need authors: they re-fuse. Readers, on the other hand . . . readers . . . readers simply comprise the public.